A DINÉ HISTORY OF
NAVAJOLAND

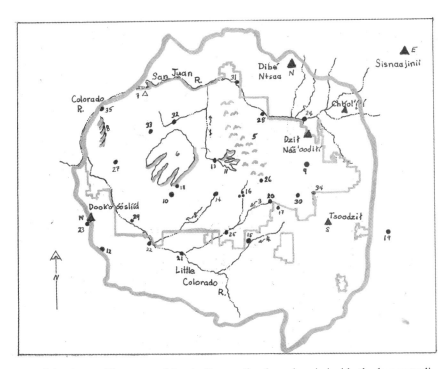

Navajoland map. The present Navajo Reservation boundary is inside the larger tradi-tional Navajo homeland. Triangles show the Six Sacred Mountains. Other places are: 1 Chinle Wash; 2 Pueblo Colorado Wash Valley; 3 Rio Puerco West; 4 Zuni River; 5 Chuska Mountains; 6 Black Mesa; 7 Navajo Mountain; 8 Echo Cliffs; 9 Chaco Can-yon; 10 Tallahogan; 11 Canyon de Chelly; 12 Mormon Lake; 13 Chinle; 14 Ganado; 15 Zuni Pueblo; 16 Fort Defiance / Saint Michaels / Window Rock; 17 Fort Wingate; 18 Keams Canyon; 19 Albuquerque; 20 Gallup; 21 Holbrook; 22 Winslow; 23 Flag-staff; 24 Farmington; 25 Chambers; 26 Tohatchi; 27 Tuba City; 28 Shiprock; 29 Leupp; 30 Crownpoint; 31 Aneth; 32 Kayenta; 33 Shonto; 34 Borrego Pass; 35 Page. Credit: Map by Garrett Francis.

A DINÉ HISTORY OF NAVAJOLAND

KLARA KELLEY AND
HARRIS FRANCIS

THE UNIVERSITY OF
ARIZONA PRESS

TUCSON

The University of Arizona Press
www.uapress.arizona.edu

ISBN-13: 978-0-8165-3874-4 (paper)

Cover design by Leigh McDonald
Cover art by Ryan James, Warpony Designs

Library of Congress Cataloging-in-Publication Data are available at the Library of Congress.

Printed in the United States of America
♾ This paper meets the requirements of ANSI/NISO Z39.48-1992 (Permanence of Paper).

CONTENTS

ACKNOWLEDGMENTS

T HE CHAPTERS of this book were developed over most of our working lives, so we have many people to thank for helping us along the way. We have never had a chance to thank most of them in print before now. Our foremost thanks go to Diné hataałiis and elders for teaching us about Diné traditions and history by word and example over the decades. We honor them here, including those no longer with us: Nevy Jensen, Frank Isaac, Joe Dennison, Norris Nez, Clyde Chee, Taylor Dixon, Hoskie Tom Becenti, Clark P. Smith, Alfred Yazzie, Jake Chee, Thomas Morris, John Holiday, Steven Begay, Navy James, Sam Slivers, James and Carolyn Bluehouse, Ernest Bitsie, Ronald Largo, Timothy Begay, Clara John, Anderson Hoskie, Richard Anderson, Robert Begay, Henry Lane, Dan Taylor, Teddy Draper Sr., Mabel and Hazbaa' Morgan, Harry Walters, Harry Goldtooth, Henry Barber, Arnold Clifford, and Duane "Chili" Yazzie.

To the Diné and others who gave us the stories on which this book is based, both those named in the text and many more who chose not to be named here, Ahéhee'.

We thank Harris's family, the Tom Claw family, and David Kelley.

Thanks also to our many colleagues over the years for research opportunities, encouragement, help with sources and technicalities (especially archaeological), and reviewing all or parts of this book, first and foremost, David M. Brugge. Thanks to the staffs of the Navajo Nation Historic Preservation

Department, the Navajo Nation Archaeology Department, all the CRM consulting firms, and all the other programs and enterprises that have enabled us to consult people all over Navajoland about history and culture. Thanks also to J. Lee Correll, Clarenda Begay, and Manuelito Wheeler of the Navajo Nation Museum; Father John Lanzrath of Saint Michaels Franciscan Mission; Kathy Tabaha of Hubbell Trading Post National Historic Site; Wilson Hunter of Canyon de Chelly National Monument; Irvin Nelson and Lynda Curtis of the Navajo Nation Library; Roman Bitsuie of Navajo-Hopi Land Commission; Lori Goodman, Adella Begay, Anna Frazier, and Earl Tulley of Dine CARE; and colleagues Richard Begay, Alexa Roberts, Rena Martin, John Stein, Taft Blackhorse, June-el Piper, Jennifer Denetdale, Charlotte Frisbie, Lillian Makeda, Margaret Hiza Redsteer, Eric Henderson, Dennis Gilpin, Ron Towner, Jim Copeland, Sarah Herr, Cherie Scheick, Dave Snow, Miranda Warburton, Kelley Hayes-Gilpin, Dave Wilcox, Reed Tso, Scott Russell, and Anna Rondon.

Finally, we thank the hardworking editorial staff of the University of Arizona Press and the reviewers of our manuscript for helpful suggestions. Special thanks are due to Kristen Buckles for seeing merit in the rough early version of this book.

A DINÉ HISTORY OF NAVAJOLAND

INTRODUCTION

The Diné, the Land, Oral History, and Sovereignty

T HE DINÉ (the People) are also known as the Navajo. This book tells about pieces of Diné history, from long before Columbus to recent times. We foreground Diné oral history as much as possible, with archaeology and documentation in the background. The theme of this book is that by telling how we came to be who and where we are, oral tradition makes a bond between the land and the people. The bond strengthens sovereignty even as sovereignty protects that bond. Diné express the bond by saying, "We don't own the land; the land owns us." Traditional oral history is a living history. Like the batter of the Kinaaldá alkąąd (a girl's coming-of-age ceremonial corn cake), oral history holds the other ingredients together. It nourishes people with lessons about living today. We hope this work contributes to the ongoing Diné struggle for sovereignty by reinforcing in readers a sense of Diné personal and cultural power.

We have put these stories together during more than 30 years of work on historic preservation projects in all of Navajoland's 110 chapters (Diné communities and units of local governance). In seeking those who know the most about Diné oral histories, we asked chapter officials and other residents for referrals (as also required by the Navajo Nation Historic Preservation Department's research permits). We wrote most of the original versions of these chapters at different times to be published or otherwise used separately. Here we have updated, reframed, and interrelated the original versions. This book was created to give something back to the People.

DINÉ ORAL HISTORY

"Oral tradition," "oral history," and "traditional history" as used here all mean stories that older generations tell to younger. Diné oral history (jiní, "as it is told") tells the histories of Diné ceremonies, clans (matrilineal kin groups), families, and communities. As Diné scholar Harry Walters (1991) has pointed out, the histories of Diné ceremonies are set in times before domesticated animals, wheeled vehicles, fabricated metals, guns, and non–First Nations people appeared in present Navajoland—the time that historians and anthropologists call "precolumbian." The histories of clans span the times before and after contact with Europeans. The histories of families and communities cover the past 200 years or so as they emerge from the life histories of individuals and other family stories. Since the 1880s, Diné hataałii (religious leaders: chanters, singers, ceremonialists) and other elders have given much oral tradition for published and unpublished transcriptions and English translations.

Oral history, of course, is stored in people's memories and passed down by telling and hearing. Even today, traditionalists rely on oral transmission rather than the versions written down. The histories of Diné ceremonies are in the care of the chanters, who tell them in connection with ceremonies. Those ceremonies are performances that extend over one to nine nights to heal one or more people of illness or misfortune or to restore harmony to a family or community. When asked by a sponsoring family, a chanter and helpers administer herbal and other medicines along with prayers, songs, sandpaintings, offerings, danced performances, and other ceremonial acts, all chosen from a repertoire of things that the chanter has learned from long study with an older chanter. The student chanter also learns one or more long narratives that trace the events by which the various things in the repertoire have come together. The chanter recounts excerpts from these narratives during the ceremony. These versions are for the public. Chanters leave out esoteric details that only chanters should know.

Every telling is a unique combination of oral tradition and the interpretation of the teller. Some ceremonial histories have been recorded in several versions given by different chanters in different times and places. Yet the different versions usually are much alike, because the student must learn the story itself

FIGURE 1 Chanter in a ceremonial hogan, where people tell and hear traditional, empowering stories between ceremonial events. Decades before this photo, chanters started letting non-Diné record them on paper, film, and wax. Credit: Photographed by Milton Snow, courtesy of the Navajo Nation Museum, Window Rock, Arizona, neg. no. NH1-25.

exactly as told (though the student does not necessarily have to learn the teller's interpretations so exactly). Exactitude is crucial, because the story governs the order of songs and prayers in an actual performance. Thus sacred traditions remain stable over time. The popular versions told publicly at ceremonies also used to be told by elders to the family at home on winter nights and to youngsters during visits to places in the stories.

Diné clans are named "exogamous matrilineal descent groups." One belongs to the clan of one's mother (matrilineal descent). In a more distant way, one is born for the clan of one's father and loosely associated with the clans of one's maternal and paternal grandfathers. Marriage into one's own clan is incestuous and strictly forbidden. One should avoid marrying into one's other three clans as well (exogamy). There are more than 60 clans, each with its own unique history (Young and Morgan 1987:351). Some clan histories are also linked to the history of the Blessingway ceremony, which is the most fundamental of all Diné ceremonies. These and other clan histories are taught by elder clan members to younger ones. The stories are not sacred and vary among clan members of different places, as each local branch of a clan adds its own historical details. Individual, family, and community histories are based on personal experiences, which differ among people and families. These stories can be told anytime, anywhere. Unlike the ceremonial histories, they are particular to local communities and people, and they are probably not as stable through time. Elders teach these stories both at home and on visits to places in the stories. The ceremonial, clan, and individual-family-community histories correspond to the following major time periods (all dates in this work are AD unless stated otherwise): beginnings and ceremonial histories, precolumbian times, especially before 1300; clan histories, late precolumbian and early postcontact times, about 1300–1800; and individual-family-community histories, more recent times, about 1800–present. These dates for Diné oral histories are based on scholarly dates for archaeological and historical sites and for events mentioned in the Diné oral traditions.

The ceremonial histories and those of many clans are the kinds of stories that used to be called myths when that word meant an empowering story widely known and respected by a group of people who interpreted it for lessons in living. These stories are empowering because they tell about physical and cultural survival, about a people finding a new relationship to the world around them, often through a victory, however short or partial. Empowering stories are not limited to the remote past, as this Introduction will show. We believe that empowering stories arise from the larger fund of stories within the group as networks of people and their leaders come to favor them. Outsiders may disparage the empowering stories of a group not their own, and group members themselves may disparage some interpretations. This kind of disparagement has led to today's understanding of the word *myth* as something untrue. Therefore, we substitute the term *empowering story*, the truth or falsity of which lies in the interpretation.

Many scholars do not think that oral tradition contains historical truth, especially about the remote past. Chapter 1 addresses those scholars who argue that Diné were not even present in the Southwest until 1500, and chapter 4 presents facets of Diné relations with Navajoland's precolumbians. Traditionalists themselves consider jiní to be the most stable holder of knowledge, but interpreting the stories to get at the lived history through which the stories have passed is no easy task. The stories have developed over hundreds of years or more, passed by word of mouth through generations of people whose ways of life have changed dramatically. The ceremonial stories, especially, and many clan stories change little over time in their actors, events, and places. But the People no doubt have changed their interpretations of the stories as their ways of life have changed, as peoples the world over do.

We think that the ceremonial and clan stories also still have traces of earlier meanings that people may no longer recognize. Here and there in this book we suggest these earlier meanings. Our interpretations recognize that people unintentionally make stories more memorable by compressing events and personages that seem alike and even time itself (Foley 1988, 1995; Havelock 1986; Rubin 1995; Vansina 1985). The historical dimension is one of many along which one can interpret Diné oral tradition (Benally 2006:18). Overall, this book, by foregrounding Diné oral tradition, critiques scholars' stories based on archaeology and documents. But we also use reinterpreted documentation and archaeology to make backstories for Diné oral tradition. How we put oral tradition together with the archaeology and documents is a work in progress, a unique combination of traditional material and interpretation done with some guidance from chanters and other elders. We offer our interpretations of Diné history hoping that others, especially Diné, old and young (hopefully talking together), will come up with more and better ideas. We also hope these studies will show the time depth, diversity, richness, and, yes, historical truth in Diné traditional histories.

ORAL HISTORY AND SOVEREIGNTY

Diné scholars today say that oral history and interpretations of it form a foundation of Diné identity and sovereignty (Austin 2009; Davis 2017; Lee 2017). Since earliest Spanish colonial times, Diné, like other First Nations peoples, have struggled against the colonizers to maintain their own ways of life and self-determination—sovereignty. Since the mid-twentieth century, scholars have formalized that struggle as a topic for academic study. Perhaps the mass schooling of First Nations children after World War II led some to seek advanced education as a way to advance the struggle. And every day came news of the struggle: the civil rights movement, the Vietnam War, and Red Power.

Among the earliest and most influential scholars of the struggle is the First Nations writer Gerald Vizenor, who also gave us a term for it: "survivance." Using a French legal term for reversion of an estate, Vizenor (2009:24, 102–103) has punningly redefined it as a compound of "survival" and "resistance." Vizenor considers theories of survivance "elusive and imprecise," but the practices of survivance "are obvious and unmistakable in native stories," both imaginative ones created by individual "storiers" and oral history. Stories can be sources of survivance by instilling in hearers and readers a sense of "native" presence, responsibility, and resistance. They also counter stereotypes of "Natives" as people with no history of their own or as helpless victims, stereotypes found in colonizers' empowering stories, such as Manifest Destiny. The survivance stories use irony, among other devices, to critique colonizer stories.

Perhaps the most massive and ironic critique comes from Indigenous historian Roxanne Dunbar-Ortiz (2014). Stating that "settler colonialism"—the form of colonialism that afflicted the Indigenous peoples of North America—"is a genocidal policy" (6), she then uses the colonizers' own archaeology and documents to discredit their Manifest Destiny fiction and bring forward Native peoples' own histories. Those who survived the genocide now have what Indigenous scholar Audra Simpson (2014:12ff.) calls "nested sovereignty," which she analyzes through a dramatic assertion of Indigenous sovereignty rooted in traditional history, the "refusal" of Canadian or U.S. citizenship, and thus the rejection of colonizer political meddling by Kahnawà:ke Mohawk and other members of the Haudenosaunee (Iroquois) Confederacy.

Today, according to activist-scholar Kim TallBear, new challenges to tribal survivance and sovereignty come from genetic scientists "showing us 'how we are all related,' how we got to where we are today" (2013:151). Through Indigenous peoples' statements and those of the scientists, critically scrutinized, TallBear shows how the scientists' agendas may subvert Indigenous "assertions of identity and peoplehood [that] turn on complicated intergovernmental policy decisions, laws, collectively held histories, practices, and landscapes" (2013:152). Dunbar-Ortiz, TallBear, and Simpson denounce colonizer states dictating rules by which the state recognizes an Indigenous group as a sovereign polity and meddling with the group's rules about who can "belong."

Instead of dismissing Indigenous oral traditions, some colonizers (and even some Indigenous people) have exploited Indigenous oral traditions by reframing them in alien contexts for personal, professional, or political gain. The Indigenous defense usually has been refusal to give information to researchers, though some have done so in order to preserve traditions for future generations of their own people. Along with the works cited here by TallBear, Simpson, and Jennifer Denetdale are many recent works (e.g., Younging 2018) with guidelines for nonexploitative approaches to research with Indigenous peoples.

Many Diné scholars have contributed to the literature on survivance by writing about "cultural survival," "cultural sovereignty," and "sovereignty." They reject the idea of sovereignty as defined by federal Indian law because it is based on colonizer legal traditions; because it is restricted to political sovereignty (governance); and because it is limited by the larger power of the United States as a nation-state that designates First Nations peoples as "dependent sovereign nations" (see Wilkins 2003 [1999]:15ff. for a discussion of sovereignty). In the Navajo language, nááts'íílid, "rainbow," signifies sovereignty (nááts'íílid nihináázt'i'í, "rainbow around us") by referring to the rainbow image around the outside of many ceremonial sandpaintings, with powerful icons of the deities, the land, and everything else within. Diné also invoke sovereignty with a saying they have heard since childhood, "T'áá hó ájít'į" (Do it yourself). Diné legal scholar Raymond Austin (2009:32) describes sovereignty as "the guardian and protector of Navajo lands and resources, Navajo people and their society, and all that is Navajo—including government, laws, culture, language, and spiritual beliefs" (see also Denetdale 2017; Lee 2017:10–11). Full sovereignty, encompassing both political ("do it yourself") and cultural ("do it the Diné way"), is self-determination in its widest sense. Diné scholars study the struggle for sovereignty in ways that also contribute to the struggle. These scholars typically do not frame their analyses with existing theories about sovereignty; instead, they use traditional knowledge as a framework for critiquing colonizer narratives.

For example, John Redhouse has studied colonizer documents from a position as an ironic Diné outside the colonizer cultural frameworks. He exposes the behind-the-scenes chicanery involved in federal-corporate appropriation of Diné land and resources on Black Mesa (1985a, 1986) and in the eastern Navajo Checkerboard (1984, 1985b). Besides irony, Diné oral traditions about sacredness, use, and occupancy of the lands form the foundation of his critiques.

To Larry Emerson (2014) and Denetdale (2014), oral tradition is crucial to the struggle for sovereignty because embedded in it are Diné traditional thought and practice. In her work to "reclaim Diné history," Denetdale (2007) interviewed her relatives to make a detailed history of her family, within which she has also assessed and incorporated colonizer documentation. The story that emerges starts with her great-grandmother Juanita, whose husband led the final

Diné resistance to conquest and was recognized by U.S. authorities as the paramount leader Manuelito. Denetdale's use of Indigenous oral history to frame information from other sources is the approach to writing Indigenous history that we follow in this book.

Former Navajo Nation Chief Justice Raymond Austin (2009) recognizes the traditional creation and journey narratives (our "ceremonial histories") as the sources in which the most basic Diné legal principles are embedded, while family and community customary practices are the basis of Diné common law. Austin compares the fundamental and common law of the People with laws that federal and state governments have applied to the People, thereby identifying particular mainstream legal practices that undermine Diné ways of life and sovereignty. Through such analyses embedded in Diné oral tradition, Justice Austin and his colleagues have developed the Diné legal system into a strong force for sovereignty.

AnCita Benally (2006) chronicles changes in Diné leadership, governance, and sovereignty ("autonomy, self-reliance"). She finds a deep tradition of leadership whereby families educated promising youngsters through ceremonies and social relations to become leaders who served selflessly for life. Local groups chose their leaders by consensus, and their leaders governed together through networks, notwithstanding the colonizer stereotype of Diné having no central leadership. Leadership and sovereignty have suffered under colonial rule, but "the core of the people's ways" has survived (2006:138–139).

Andrew Curley (2014) critiques colonizer documentation for making conquered people "legible," that is, defining them in terms of colonizer political-legal categories the better to manipulate and control them. He shows how Diné, through such means as refusal, have often resisted becoming "legible." But he also notes that oral accounts, in the process of becoming empowering stories, may legitimize colonizer-induced practices by identifying them with traditional practices. In this and other ways, the drive of empowering stories to enhance sovereignty may compromise their factual accuracy.

Luckily, oral tradition typically offers different versions of particular stories, including versions found in other groups, even colonizers, that can reveal such changes, as Lloyd Lee shows. Lee (2006, 2013, 2014, 2017) focuses on diversity among Diné today about various contemporary issues (identity, masculinity, sovereignty) and how those issues relate to ideals found in traditional history. His work stresses the importance of diversity among the People in their various versions of oral traditions, none of which alone can be considered authoritative.

Through such diversity, traditional knowledge remains complex and thereby more effective in the struggle for sovereignty. Lee has also critiqued the federally mandated blood quantum criterion for tribal membership.

Kerry Thompson (2009; Thompson and Towner 2017) uses Diné oral tradition to analyze information recovered from archaeological sites. The resulting analyses counter scholarly archaeologists' narratives about how Diné have absorbed the "cultural traits" of other groups. This more or less passive process of acculturation attributed to the People evokes the colonizer stereotype of First Nations people as absent or only half-present, since they lack a distinctive culture until they become acculturated to Puebloan-type farming, which is sedentary, like that of the colonizers. Thompson's (2009) study of archaeologically recorded hogans shows that despite the dramatic changes in southwestern history under the colonizers since the 1600s, Diné hogans have kept certain construction details required by the Blessingway. This persistence shows that Diné have steadfastly continued important traditional ways as they adapted to the changes around them.

In our view, when elders tell traditional histories and then take youngsters to the places in the stories, a bond forms. As the elders say, the land gets to "know" the youngsters. These bonds collectively are the bedrock of Diné traditional life. Struggles for sovereignty—for the People's capacity to maintain important traditions amid changes that they choose to make—are, at heart, struggles to protect this bond. The chapters of this book tell about the Diné bonds with the land and struggles for sovereignty in various times and places during the span of Diné history. Diné history is geography, so we have preserved geographical details along with the diversity and local particularity of histories that exist in pieces spread widely among the People. Except for the emergence story, there is no master narrative among the elders, although certain widely known empowering stories can be strung together chronologically to form such a master narrative.

Yet a master narrative can help one to understand how the particular local pieces relate to each other and to the ongoing, centuries-old Diné struggles for the land and sovereignty. Many published works offer such master narratives (see, e.g., Bailey and Bailey 1999; Iverson and Roessel 2002; Kelley and Whiteley 1989). Most such works, though, keep Diné traditional history in the background. The rest of this introduction therefore sketches an alternative larger narrative, with Diné empowering stories in the foreground, arranged chronologically. These stories stress the bond between the People and the land

and how the People have struggled to maintain it. Some interpretations of these stories emphasize victimry, thereby disempowering the stories; the interpretations provided here emphasize survivance.

But behind and between these stories lie smaller stories about particular events, people, and places that tell each Diné more specifically "how we came to be who and where we are." The chapters that follow tell a few of these stories, supplemented with perspectives from colonizer documents and archaeology. Unlike the empowering stories, these stories have many complicating details that the larger stories gloss over, and they do not necessarily end in victories. An afterword addresses what the chapters taken together tell about the book's theme, the relationship between oral history and sovereignty, the People, and the land.

EMPOWERING STORIES OF THE LAND, THE PEOPLE, AND SOVEREIGNTY

BEGINNINGS, CEREMONIAL ORIGINS, AND EARLY CLANS TO CA. 1300

The oral histories of this time are the foundation of traditional land-based Diné life. The traditional history of human life in present Navajoland is in part the history of the Blessingway ceremony (see Wyman 1970a for the Blessing Way histories; for other ceremonial stories of this time, see Benally et al. 1982; Fishler 1953; Haile 1981; Klah 1942; Matthews 1994; O'Bryan 1993). The story tells how the land originated, how Diné ancestors came to it and learned the culture to live there. This history began when First Man, First Woman, and other Diyin Dine'é (Holy People, immortals), driven by discord and a flood, emerged from worlds below. At Hajíínáí, the Emergence Place, they created prototypes of the traditional Diné sweathouse and hogan. Then they placed landscape features on the earth's surface, set the celestial bodies in motion, and established the core of what would become the Navajo Blessingway ceremonies. First among the landscape features placed were the six sacred mountains: Sis Naajinii (Blanca Peak, Colorado), Tsoo Dził (Mount Taylor, New Mexico), Dook'o'óoslííd (San Francisco Peaks, Arizona), and Dibé Ntsaa (La Plata Mountains, Colorado) in the four (intercardinal) directions, plus Ch'óol'į'í (Gobernador Knob, New Mexico) and Dził Ná'ooditii (Huerfano Mesa, New Mexico) in the center.

FIGURE 2 Petroglyphs near Huerfano Mesa. The shield represents Monster Slayer, and the hair bun (the hourglass shape left of the shield) represents Born for Water. Corn is central in the Blessingway ceremony taught by their mother, Changing Woman. Credit: Klara Kelley photo.

Then the Holy People, humans, animals, and plants spread over the earth. Next came a time of turmoil, when monsters massacred the Anaasází, who had built the big precolumbian archaeological sites in present Navajoland. The time of the monsters and turmoil ended when the beloved Holy Person, Changing Woman, appeared on the earth. When she came of age, the Holy People had the first Kinaaldá ceremony for her. She mated with the Sun and gave birth to two sons, Naayéé' Neizghání (Monster Slayer) and Tó Bá Jishchíní (Born for Water), who grew up to kill or tame the monsters. The home of Changing Woman and her sons during this time was Huerfano Mesa.

After the slaying of the monsters, the Anaasází were also gone (along with most, if not all, other humans). Changing Woman moved to a home off the Pacific coast, where, to relieve her loneliness, she created humans. These people, four or six paired men and women, sometimes called the Water People or Western Water Clans, went eastward to resettle the land amid the six sacred mountains. Different versions of the Water People's migration story describe different routes northeastward from around the San Francisco Peaks. As they traveled, groups of people joined them and formed kinlike links with various pairs of the Water People. The original pairs and the other groups also took names, which designate today's Diné clans. Along the route, some of these groups settled and farmed for a while, including at sites that archaeologists date to the 1100s and 1200s.

As the events of the Blessingway history unfolded, other kinds of Diné ceremonies were also coming together. The traditional histories of these ceremonies tell of the travels of youngsters (ceremonial initiates) around Navajoland and beyond. Each initiate would trespass on the domains of certain Holy People, who would then give the initiate the means to correct the blunders. These gifts together became the "repertoires" from which a chanter can choose elements for a particular performance. Many events in these histories happened at the large precolumbian Anaasází sites of Chaco Canyon, Aztec, and Mesa Verde in the San Juan River basin of eastern Navajoland and farther west in Canyon de Chelly and Antelope Mesa, east of today's Hopi villages. Chapters 1–4 show how ceremonial and clan histories establish an ancestral Diné presence on the land and provide verbal maps to teach youngsters.

GROWTH OF THE CLAN SYSTEM, 1300–1800

Along with the Water People and those who linked to them, more clans grew up in different places amid the sacred mountains. Gradually, ancestors of most of today's 60-plus Diné clans came together in the upper San Juan River drainage. In the late 1800s, chanter Hataałii Nééz (Tall Chanter) told the Fort Wingate army surgeon and anthropologist Washington Matthews (1994) the stories of most of these clans as they came to the San Juan between Anaasází times and the 1700s. Meanwhile, in the early 1700s, clans were also forming in the hinterlands of Antelope Mesa as villagers fled attacks by Hopis from farther west and joined Diné in southern Black Mesa and Canyon de Chelly (see chapters 4 and 5). The story exists in fragments told by Navajos (Nát'oh Dine'é Táchii'nii Clan People 1981; O'Hara 2004; Van Valkenburgh 1999:11), Western Apaches (Goodwin 1942:608, 620), and Hopis (Courlander 1971:175,184, 1982:55–60; Yava 1978:88–97). Another Diné story tells how warfare with the Spanish also eventually drove the People from the upper San Juan westward to Canyon de Chelly (Van Valkenburgh 1940b). Chapter 5 tells about these troubled times through oral tradition about places of conflict. Most clans have long had members living in various parts of Navajoland, and each local group within a clan may have its own traditions about its history (see chapter 4).

Meanwhile, two children, descendants of the Water People, were mysteriously transported from the southern San Juan basin to the home of Changing Woman at the western ocean. There she taught them the Blessingway ceremony as it had come to be among the Holy People in earlier times. Then the children reappeared at home and taught others, who have passed the ceremony down through generations (Klah 1942:122–124; Mitchell 2003:186–188; O'Bryan 1993:175–179; Wyman 1970:293, 459–460). One way or another, Blessingway is the basis for Diné self-identity today. Chapter 4 explores what ceremonial and clan oral traditions reveal about unfolding Diné self-identity over the generations.

LATER POSTCOLUMBIAN TIMES, 1800–PRESENT

Where the stable, widely known histories of ceremonies and of many clans end, histories of families, individuals, and communities begin (see chapters 5–11). Empowering stories after 1800 include the Long Walk of 1863–68, the stock reduction of the 1930s, the origins of modern Navajo government, the heroism of the Navajo Code Talkers in World War II, the miseries of boarding school in the 1920s through the 1950s, the sacrifices of Diné uranium miners from the 1940s through the 1980s, and Diné relocation from Black Mesa from the 1950s to the present. These are the stories most often invoked in local popular media and public presentations. As educators who recorded eastern Navajo stories of the Long Walk have said about that empowering story, "Details of incidents have become blurred or merged with other events. But what has not faded is the significance of that historical period to the Diné whose lives reflect its legacy" (Diné of the Eastern Region 1991:1).

According to Diné oral history (Benally 2006; Benally et al. 1982; Bingham and Bingham 1994; Denetdale 2007; Diné of the Eastern Region 1991; Etsedi 1937; Luckert 1977; Mitchell 2001; Roessel and Johnson 1973), before the Long Walk was a time of raiding and warfare, when Navajos, other tribes, and Spanish or Mexican settlers all fought each other amid the landscapes of chapter 5 and elsewhere. People took captives from each other to sell as slaves. Ambitious young Diné raided the Spanish, Mexicans, and Puebloans for livestock. (Documents tell the same story, from the mid-1600s to the 1860s, under Spanish, Mexican, and finally U.S. colonial rule, though the finger of blame wags in different directions depending on the teller [Correll 1976, 1979; McNitt 1972; Thompson 1976].) Finally, in the Diné tellings, the U.S. Army under Bi'éé'

Łichíí' (Red Shirt, or Kit Carson) waged all-out war against the People. In the fall of 1863, the troops scoured all but far western Navajoland, burning crops and killing people and their livestock. Families from all over Navajoland fled to sparsely settled, outlying, and inaccessible lands in all four directions. The army put out the word that people would be fed and protected from marauding Utes and Hispanics (whom the army had given free rein in the first place). Many families straggled into the army headquarters at Fort Defiance, Fort Lyon (present Fort Wingate), and old Fort Wingate (near present Grants, New Mexico). Some tellers suggest that this was a trick: U.S. soldiers attacked some who were coming in to surrender. Descendants of these people say that their ancestors were hoping for temporary refuge only, but the army had other plans.

The soldiers marched large groups of the People on the Long Walk eastward to Albuquerque and then on to Hwéelde (Bosque Redondo, Fort Sumner) in eastern New Mexico. Wagon trains accompanied the groups, and some elders and children are said to have ridden in the wagons. One person recalled that his grandfather took his large herd to Fort Sumner (Mitchell 1978:22). But most tellers emphasize the brutality of the troops toward their captives, how they killed those who could not keep up. Elders have also recalled forebears who escaped capture by moving from one hiding place to another and others who escaped from Fort Sumner and found their way home. Many encountered either threatening or helpful snakes, wolves, bears, and owls. People hid in the canyons of the upper San Juan River and Chacra Mesa on the east, in the rough country of the Western Apaches to the south, on Black Mesa and in the Grand Canyon to the west, in the canyons and mountains north of the San Juan and Colorado Rivers, and elsewhere. More people from the west than from the east seem to have ancestors who never went to Fort Sumner. The holdouts held ceremonies at the home of the War Gods on top of Navajo Mountain and elsewhere to bring their kinfolk home.

Meanwhile, at Fort Sumner, Comanches and other tribes attacked, and Navajos sometimes left Fort Sumner on counterraids or to escape for home. People survived on skimpy government rations and ate the sheep they had brought with them; they even ate crows, coyotes, skunks, and dead animals. Everybody remembers that people got sick at Forts Defiance and Wingate, as well as at Fort Sumner, because they did not know how to cook the rations they were given, especially white flour and coffee beans. People danced and sang about their experiences and held ceremonies under cover to keep hopeful. At the end of four years, there was a rumor that the army would let the people go home. To divine the truth, after a secret Enemyway ceremony, people surrounded a coyote and put a bead in her mouth, then watched to see which way she would turn. Imagine their relief and joy when she went west!

Documents attest that the government intended Fort Sumner to be the permanent Navajo Reservation. But four years of drought and withered crops showed that the People could not feed themselves there. So in 1868 the U.S. government negotiated a treaty with the captive Diné headmen that set aside a reservation in the middle of their homeland. This reservation of about 65 by 80 miles included the Chuska Valley, Chuska Mountains, Defiance Plateau, and Canyon de Chelly / Chinle Valley. It left out most of the country where the People had ranged, including all six sacred mountains and their well-watered uplands (Navajo Tribe 1967), but it was still a victory of sorts. Twelve headmen and 17 members of a "council" signed the treaty, most of them seemingly from eastern and central Navajoland. (Tótsohnii Hastiin [Ganado Mucho], Barboncito, and Hombro [Biwosii] may have been the only headmen whose entire range

FIGURE 3 Diné leaders and followers during captivity at Fort Sumner for treaty making with the U.S. government, 1868. Credit: National Museum of the American Indian, Smithsonian Institution, catalog no. P20819.

was west of the Chuskas.) Leaders of the holdouts who never went to Fort Sumner were not there to sign.

Then the People walked home. Perhaps 8,000 or 9,000 had gone, and 7,000 or so returned (for the different numbers, see Kelley and Whiteley 1989:207; Redhouse 1986; Thompson 1978). They were supposed to stay inside the treaty reservation but instead simply returned to wherever they had lived before, joining kinfolk who had stayed behind. Later additions to the reservation have never taken in the whole homeland of the time before the Long Walk (Correll and Dehiya 1978; see chapters 6, 7, and 10).

The People then found themselves enmeshed in the intricacies of U.S. colonial administration (Washindoon). The enmeshing began around the administrative center of Fort Defiance and on the southern edges of Navajoland, where rancher settlers and the new transcontinental railroad were encroaching. Suddenly, government documents multiplied to show this process from the administrative viewpoint, which since then has threatened to divert students of history from the People's own oral histories, many of which have also been lost along with the land. Nevertheless, as chapters 6 and 7 show, the documents, considered ironically, tell much about the People's struggle to keep their land and way of life outside the reservation. No empowering story has formed about this dark time.

Before the Long Walk, the People had ranged far and wide to hunt and gather, farming here and there, herding the sheep and goats that fed them with meat and milk. When they returned with the surviving flocks and more that the government issued, they restored their herds. By the early 1900s, livestock numbers surpassed what they had been before the Long Walk (Kelley and Whiteley 1989:208). Having lost their best hunting, gathering, and grazing lands, the People kept their economy going by producing meat and crops for themselves while trading wool and weaving for mass-produced food and other goods at trading posts, which first appeared mostly along the railroad and then spread all over Navajoland in the next few decades. These posts were the seeds from which most of today's Navajo communities grew. They attracted missions, schools, and government facilities. They were the first meeting places of chapters, today's units of local governance. And, for good or ill or both, they channeled U.S. colonizer culture into the Diné world. Chapter 8 shows that some early traders were themselves Diné, and many of them used trading to enhance their own family-based stockraising. Chapter 9 unrolls the workings of a typical trading post from the heyday of the trading post system to the present, showing how the People adapted trading post goods to their traditional herding way of life even as this trade enmeshed them and their lands in national and worldwide capitalist markets to the detriment of their bond with their family lands and sovereignty. The People eventually abandoned the trading posts, only to become more deeply entangled in the world economy. Like the stories after the Long Walk, the trading posts have not given rise to an empowering story. Even the weavers, whose products were the backbone of the early trading post system (M'Closkey 2002), have not given rise to such a story, though the textiles themselves are legendary, and life histories of weavers have been recorded (e.g., Winter 2011).

In 1930 Washindoon put a stop to the livestock increase when it imposed the stock reduction program (see chapter 11). Supposedly, overgrazing was destroying the land by erosion, and the resulting silt in the Colorado River would clog the new Boulder (Hoover) hydroelectric dam, as late 1930s Tribal Council vice president Howard Gorman recalled (Roessel and Johnson 1974:73). (In hindsight, the long-term drying trend that we now recognize as an effect

FIGURE 4 Sheep dipping at Round Rock, 1941, with a federal range rider in the background to identify families with herds exceeding their permits. Credit: Photographed by Milton Snow, courtesy of the Navajo Nation Museum, Window Rock, Arizona, neg. no. NN11-16.

of global warming and climate change was at least partly to blame.) Many elders have recalled their experiences with stock reduction in life histories and shorter pieces (Bennett 1964:243–255; Curley 2014:144; Holiday and McPherson 2005:116–122; Mitchell 2001:210–212; Nez and Avila 2012:71–76; Roessel and Johnson 1974; Young and Morgan 1954:60–74, 132–147; see also Ward 1951). Government workers drove the animals to the railroad for sale, but also, both far from and close to the railroad, they shot those too weak to go the distance or even massacred them and left the remains to rot (Bennett 1964:249–250; Nez and Avila 2012:74ff.).

Washindoon issued each family a grazing permit (dibé binaaltsoos) that specified the maximum number of animals allowed, half or less of what most had owned. Some resisters were jailed. Documents show that by 1940 the number of Navajo sheep had been reduced by almost half, from over 1,000,000 before reduction (Young 1961:167). In chapter 11 elders tell how stock reduction and its legacy, the weakening of bonds to the land, are involved with climate change. Unlike most empowering stories, the victory in this one, if there is one, is the persistence of many families in raising some livestock and keeping their land and culture.

Besides the present regulated grazing, stock reduction also ushered in many other fixtures of modern Diné life. One was the Navajo Tribal Council in its present form (Navajo Nation Council since 1969). In the decades after the Long Walk, Washindoon added lands to the treaty reservation and agency jurisdictions to administer them. Formal involvement of the People in government was limited to small groups of local leaders who advised each agency (Austin 2009; Benally 2006; Wilkins 2003 [1999]; Young 1978). In 1923 oil companies wanted to put wells around Shiprock, and Washindoon ruled that they would need consent from the entire Navajo people. Each agency superintendent sent out word for people to come to the agency headquarters to vote. The result was a council of six delegates and six alternates, who signed leases and consulted with Washindoon (Young 1978:59–60). In 1933 Washindoon got the council to consent to the stock reduction program, destroying with a stroke of the pen the People's respect for the council (Henderson 1985:118–119). So in 1936 Washindoon got the council to dissolve itself and organize the election of its replacement. That 74-member body is the basis of the present council, later increased to 88 (Young 1978) and then in 2010 reduced to the present 24.

Meanwhile, local governance developed through the chapter system (Benally 2006; Bingham and Bingham 1987; Rodgers et al. 2004; Wilkins 2003 [1999];

FIGURE 5 Navajo Tribal Council chambers, 1943, designed and built by the U.S. government to house the council it was trying to reorganize. Credit: Photographed by Milton Snow, courtesy of Navajo Nation Museum, Window Rock, Arizona, neg. no. NE19-2.

Williams 1970; Young 1961:335–339, 371–428, 1978:66–68; Yurth 2017). Chapters started a few years before stock reduction, at the end of what now seems the "classic" period of traditional life. The BIA encouraged its agents to start local self-help organizations, and in 1927 Superintendent John Hunter of the Leupp Agency did so by urging the People to meet with him regularly when and where they chose. The idea took hold throughout Navajoland, and soon there were about 100 such organizations, a number that has varied little since (today there are 110). The chapters formalized earlier ways of local governance, when families would meet as needed to make decisions or settle disputes, having a local respected elder/leader to mediate, and making decisions by consensus. People met at public places such as wells and trading posts until agency superintendents offered them money for materials with which to build meeting houses.

Government officials were quick to use the chapters to push stock reduction and other innovations such as day schools. The People themselves were just as quick to use the chapters to voice their demands (Iverson and Roessel, eds. 2002:49ff.; see also chapter 7). As chapters became hotbeds of opposition to stock reduction, Washindoon tried to squelch them. In 1935 the People also voted against adopting the Indian Reorganization Act, which set forth Washindoon's requirements for tribal governance, and later elected a tribal chairman, former Diné trader Jacob Morgan, who had campaigned against the act.

But the chapters were here to stay. After World War II and the 1950s oil-and-gas boom on the reservation, the growing Navajo tribal government strengthened its ties to and control of the chapters, spending oil royalties on new chapter houses and various chapter programs. Since then, chapters have steadily gained control of government resources (Benally 2006; Lee 2017:105, 135; Powell 2015). Thus has Diné political sovereignty advanced, the price being dependence on resource extraction by and for outsiders.

Another result of stock reduction was that more people sought wage work to sustain themselves. Chapter 10 tells the stories of a neglected group of early Diné workers, underground coal miners around Gallup, New Mexico. In this case, wage work became necessary even before stock reduction, as mining companies took grazing land from Diné families. In general, jobs were scarce until World War II, when many men took railroad jobs emptied by the draft, and 3,500 (out of an undercounted population of 50,000) enlisted in the military (Kelley and Whiteley 1989:207; Lapahie 1997), even though the states denied them voting rights until after the war. Before Washindoon even recognized First Nations citizenship, Diné had served as scouts for the U.S. Army during the Apache wars of the 1880s (Collman 1975), then in World War I, when many apparently were drafted from boarding schools. Stories of Navajo women in war are little known.

The best-known stories from World War II are those of the Navajo Code Talkers, whose memoirs have been published in recent years (Greenberg and Greenberg 1984; Holiday and McPherson 2013; Johnson 1977; Lapahie 1997; Nez and Avila 2012; Tohe 2012; see also McClain 2001). They were a special group of Marine Corps radiomen who created a code based on the Navajo language, including ceremonial terms, to transmit messages in the Pacific theater. The Japanese were never able to break the code, even though they forced Diné captives to translate intercepted messages, because the Navajo language itself was encrypted and the captives did not know the code. The code included several hundred technical military terms and the Diné term assigned to each, often a ceremonial term or name of a creature with some kind of resemblance to the English item. Knowledge of Diné ceremonies helped the men remember these terms.

The U.S. military had made limited use of First Nations Code Talkers in World War I and now started a more ambitious plan. A group of 29 Diné created

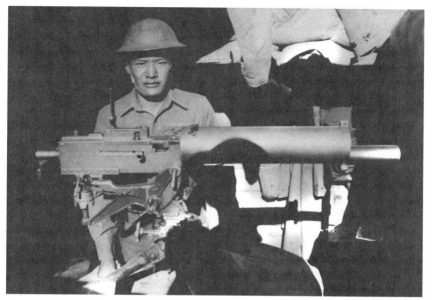

FIGURE 6 A Diné soldier in basic training, San Diego, 1942. Credit: Copied by Milton Snow, courtesy of Navajo Nation Museum, Window Rock, Arizona, neg. no. NO7-140.

the code, and another 400 or so joined later (Tohe 2012). Code talkers say they joined to defend their land and to help their families with a paycheck; some even joined because the uniforms looked sharp. They were teenage boys who had grown up with the typical hard Diné living conditions but had also gone to boarding school.

Those who survived returned home, where many had Enemyway ceremonies to cleanse themselves of the effects of enemies (now called post-traumatic stress disorder) and to put them back on the Blessingway pollen path of healthful Diné living. The Enemyway ceremony requires a "scalp" from the enemy— something personal, like hair or a scrap of clothing. Some Diné soldiers sent such items home for their own future ceremonies, items that chanters also bought for repeated use. The army told the Code Talkers not to talk about the codes, which kept them from dealing with their traumas. They received little public recognition because the code was still classified as a military secret until 1968. In 1982 the last day of the war in the Pacific became national Navajo Code Talkers Day. Only in 2001 were they recognized with the Congressional Medal of Honor. Later in life, many wounded Code Talkers, including some with Purple Hearts, had to sue the U.S. government to get disability benefits.

Many Code Talkers have said that they found inspiration to keep on later in life from protecting their Diné homeland and people. They are proud of the power of the Navajo language, with the names of plants and animals used in the code, to protect the actual land of those plants and animals and to bring about victory in the Pacific. The Code Talkers probably saved thousands of lives, but some considered the bombing of Hiroshima and Nagasaki the same kind of inhumanity that an earlier U.S. military had visited on their own forebears before and during Fort Sumner. In this empowering story, the Code Talkers made their service part of the Diné struggle for sovereignty.

Stock reduction also boosted school attendance and gave rise to the widespread experience of boarding school miseries. Schools had been in Navajoland since the return from the Long Walk, as the treaty required. The first boarding school was at Fort Defiance (by 1883; an earlier school was there in 1869). Between the 1880s and the 1920s, as U.S. presidents added land to the reservation, Washindoon also established more administrative centers (agency headquarters) with boarding schools and other schools elsewhere. Washindoon added more schools, both boarding and day, in the 1930s and 1950s (Frisbie

FIGURE 7 Boarding school dishwashing, Chinle, 1946. Credit: Photographed by Milton Snow, courtesy of Navajo Nation Museum, Window Rock, Arizona, neg. no. NE14–68.

1996; Van Valkenburgh 1999). Government agents and school people went into the countryside to round up children for the schools, with or without their parents' consent. Most children, though, were able to hide or otherwise avoid school until the 1950s, when Washindoon launched a huge school construction program and the Navajo Tribal Council made school enrollment a top priority. By that time, owing to stock reduction, parents no longer needed all their children for herding, welcomed the food and clothing that the schools offered, and recognized that, without livestock, their children must have skills to get wage-paying jobs (Iverson and Roessel 2002:190–197; Young 1961:7ff.).

Many Diné have told of their boarding school experiences from the early 1900s on (Benedek 1995:101ff.; Bennett 1974:209ff.; Holiday and McPherson 2015:43–44; Iverson and Roessel, eds. 2002:80–89; *Leading the Way* 2002–2017; McPherson et al. 2012:94ff.; Nez and Avila 2012:41–62, 84–85; Stewart 1980; Tohe 2012; Twenty-Two Navajo Men and Women 1977). Collectively they tell of regimentation, punishment, alienation, and even, in the early days, extreme hunger, cold, and epidemics. During the summers, the schools sent many students to do manual labor for farms and other businesses outside the reservation (the "outing system"). Some students did not see their families for years.

Punishments were frequent and harsh. Runaways were shut in dungeonlike basements. Staff who caught students speaking Navajo forced them to chew soap, beat them with belts, or made boys wear skirts and girls wear pants. Even the future Code Talkers were punished for this offense. Forbidding the Diné language persisted in some schools even to about 1960, never mind the government-funded bilingual textbooks used since 1940. By the 1940s, some high-school students were attending border-town public schools and bunking at nearby boarding schools like Fort Wingate (Nez and Avila 2012:84–85). Beginning in the 1950s, public schools appeared on the reservation (Young 1961:19ff.). But the boarding schools did not succeed completely in pulling the People away from the land or replacing their traditional culture and language with those of the colonizers. Now most students go to public schools, where the latest episode of this story is the grinding struggle for meaningful language and culture teaching.

Stock reduction and World War II also gave rise to uranium mining, which has poisoned Diné uranium workers, their families, and the land. Many such workers and their families tell about struggling with illnesses that uranium work has caused and for disability compensation (Brugge et al. 2006; Eichstaedt 1994:172–192; Holiday and McPherson 2005:103–112; McPherson 2012:158–178;

FIGURE 8 Diné uranium miners in the Chuska Mountains, ca. 1950. Credit: Photographed by Milton Snow, courtesy of Navajo Nation Museum, Window Rock, Arizona, neg. no. NG6-5.

Moon 1993:181; Pasternak 2010; Navajo Uranium Miner Oral History and Photography Project 1997). Uranium mining in Navajoland began during World War II in Monument Valley and the northern Chuska range at vanadium deposits located 20 years earlier by traders and Diné and worked by Diné. The World War II mining was top secret—to supply fuel to scientists at Los Alamos and White Sands, New Mexico, who were developing the atomic bombs that later wiped out Hiroshima and Nagasaki. After World War II, mining in Navajoland and neighboring Utah and Colorado reached a frenzy to supply the United States in the nuclear arms race with the Soviet Union (Brugge et al. 2006; Eichstaedt 1994; Pasternak 2010; Voyles 2015).

Until about 1970 in most of Navajoland and the late 1980s in eastern Navajoland, about 2,500 Navajos worked in the mines (Brugge et al. 2006:42). Some were entrepreneurs with mining permits, but most were laborers. As these workers and their families have recalled, working and living conditions exposed them all to high doses of radioactivity with few protections. They recall that companies did not provide adequate ventilation or other protective

measures or even warn them that they were at risk for lung cancer. The workers learned later that Washindoon had known that uranium miners had been at
great risk of lung cancer since the late 1940s but did not make the companies
warn workers or provide protection until the late 1960s. By that time, many
were suffering from lung cancer and other serious respiratory illnesses. To get
reparations from Washindoon for looking the other way, workers organized
and got support from the Navajo Tribal Council and unions. The result was
the Radiation Exposure Compensation Act (RECA) in 1990 (with later amendments), a partial victory, though the land and way of life have been sacrificed.
The struggle continues to expand compensation and to restore the land and
water. The families point out that they, like military veterans, sacrificed their
health and even their lives for World War II and the Cold War. Like RECA,
the Navajo Nation government's 2005 ban on uranium mining on and near
Navajoland is a victory of sorts.

Meanwhile, beginning around 1950, with too little livestock and too few jobs
to support the People, Washindoon started a program ("cultural genocide" to
critics) to get them to leave Navajoland and "relocate" in distant cities or on the
"excess land" of other tribes on the lower Colorado River (Redhouse 1986:18ff.;
Young 1961:232–238; see also Hodge 1969:53–65; McPherson et al. 2012; Nez
and Avila 2011; Tohe 2012). Alongside Washindoon's relocation efforts came
development of Navajo Nation energy and water resources, which triggered a
different kind of relocation: the relocation of Diné from Black Mesa, a story
that actually goes back to stock reduction and even earlier, to a reservation
established in 1882, as told in chapters 6 and 7.

In the 1950s, encouraged by the U.S. government, oil and then coal companies targeted northern Black Mesa for fossil fuel extraction. They set in motion
a complex drama involving the Hopi and Navajo tribal governments to establish
coal-fired electrical generating plants, coal strip mines, and water rights on the
Colorado River, as told in chapters 7 and 11. The whole complex was dedicated
to supply water and power to the booming cities of southern Arizona, Nevada,
and California. Diné were relocated from the coal mine leases, but their numbers paled before the thousands relocated from the 1882 reservation beginning
in the 1980s. Those relocations were the outcome of a Hopi lawsuit against
the Navajo Tribe for jurisdiction of the 1882 reservation, which resulted in the
division of the reservation into exclusive Navajo and exclusive Hopi halves.
Between 2,500 and 4,000 Diné families and about a dozen Hopi families found

FIGURE 9 Making the fence on the Navajo-Hopi partition line, Black Mesa, 1985. Credit: Klara Kelley photo.

themselves on the wrong side of the land and had to move. Many relocatees and their advocates consider this outcome an indirect result of corporate manipulation (Brugge 1994; Redhouse 1985a, 1986).

Most Diné families decided not to resist relocation. They moved into other parts of their range on the Navajo half, or to lands farther away where they had relatives, or to ranch lands (the "New Lands") that the Navajo Nation bought with dedicated federal funds (see chapter 7), or to border towns. Washindoon paid for new housing and other relocation costs. Relocatees have testified to corner-cutting on the housing construction and other inducements to move (Benedek 1993:295–304). Some who moved to border towns lost their houses in payment of debts to auto dealers and others. Far worse, though, has been demoralization and untimely death from losing traditional lands and the bonds to it through stockraising and farming surrounded by relatives.

Others have stayed on the land, where the sovereignty struggle is hard but better than relocation (Benally 2011; Benedek 1993; Bingham and Bingham 1994; Kammer 1980). Federal and Hopi rangers harassed them, impounded their livestock, even jailed them (grandmas too). Finally, the Navajo and Hopi governments agreed that each family could lease a three-acre homesite (too small for livestock) on Hopi land to legalize their presence for 75 years. Many signed,

FIGURE 10 Roadside sellers north of Gallup, 1985. Credit: Klara Kelley photo.

but others found the terms too restrictive. The mostly elderly resisters now found themselves in an empty land where the Hopis had bulldozed the home-sites of their relocated relatives and where their children could never have their own homes. Still they remain. Katherine Smith, who famously ran a fencing crew off at gunpoint, stayed on her land to the end of her long life, when she said, "I won this battle" (Allen 2017).

Finally, here is an empowering story in the making. In the decades since stock reduction, the People have supported themselves mainly with wage work. But there is never enough, and public assistance since the 1960s does not go much farther. Many Diné have taken up "selling"—providing services like babysitting, house cleaning, auto repair, and construction work or vending handicrafts and food at flea markets, in offices and laundromats, and along the roadside, all for cash off the books. Probably the most commonly sold products are foods (see Frisbie 2018 for an oral history of Navajo foods and diet). The stories of many sellers and how they got that way after stock reduction have been collected by Michael Francisconi (1998:222–225). Here is one:

> I was born in Canyon de Chelly in 1924. . . . We were poor because we had a
> small herd, we raised all our crops however, most important was corn. We traded

corn to other Navajos and ate corn for every meal. . . . When I was growing up the women folk did everything necessary to take care of the corn. We planted, weeded, and harvested the corn. We young girls prepared the corn, and the older girls and women cooked it. Every morning before breakfast I ground the corn meal for the day. Everyday even in the winter I ground the corn outside no matter how cold or how wet. . . .

We had few "livestocks," but our richer relatives gave us "sheeps," goats and horses to herd for them and we could share the natural increase. The men and boys would follow the cattle. . . . During the winter our relatives took the "sheeps" and goats to winter camp and gave us supplies to last the winter. . . .

Everything changed when I was fifteen years old. The tribal police found out I was not in school. . . . They sent me to the boarding school in Chinle and when I ran away they sent me to the boarding school in Phoenix. . . .

When I returned my parents went to the home of a young man in Chinle and proposed marriage for me. They told him I was a hard worker and would work hard for him. While I was in school there was a stock reduction and my relatives could no longer afford me. After the marriage I moved to live with my husband in Chinle. The government found him many jobs but always off the Reservation. He worked on the railroad in North Dakota and Montana. After the War he worked construction in California. He was a good provider and always took care of us. He came home to visit every chance he could and we had seven children together. When my youngest started school I began my career as a housekeeper. I cleaned people's homes in Chinle and always had as much work as I needed. I still clean people's homes in Tsaile. All my life I never went on relief.

. . . After stock reduction there were too few jobs for Navajos and most were outside the sacred mountains. Most people had to go on public assistance. This turned Navajos into beggars, who go to the welfare worker to ask for assistance. The welfare controls people's lives, telling people what they must spend their money on and makes sure everyone reports what they do to the welfare worker. Poverty has become a way of life for most Navajos and most people never expect anything different. (© 1998 from *Kinship, Capitalism, and Change: The Informal Economy of the Navajo, 1868–1995*, by Michael Francisconi. Reproduced by permission of Taylor and Francis Group, LLC, a division of Informa plc.)

Those who have engaged with various forms of public assistance, often alternating with selling, also have stories and history lessons for us.

The chapters of this book explore many aspects of Diné history. Here is the thread that connects them to our theme. Chapters 1–4 show that Diné ancestors have been in Navajoland since remote precolumbian times, and the stories that have come down from them instill a bond of great time depth to places and landscapes. Chapter 1 asserts that those precolumbian ancestors include hunter-gatherer-farmers who lived among the village-dwelling Anaasází. Chapters 2 and 3 introduce stories that bond people to landscapes through shared ceremonial and travel experiences. Chapter 3 is crucial to our theme by showing how elders travel with youngsters along storied routes to instill a bond with the land. Chapter 4 shows that many Diné recognize among their precolumbian forebears not only the hunter-gatherer-farmers but also the Anaasází themselves, directly or through their Puebloan descendants. The chapter then explores how these people came together in Navajoland through ethnogenesis to form the modern Diné as a self-conscious sovereign people with shared oral traditions that bond them to the land. In chapter 5, in landscapes of stories that still resonate with Diné today, the People struggle to defend their land and sovereignty against colonizers who ultimately compromise Diné political sovereignty but do not relinquish their hold on the land. Soon, though, colonizers disrupt the People's bond with the land through settler encroachment (chapter 6), relocation (chapter 7), loss of land-based self-sufficiency through entanglements with the trading post system (chapters 8 and 9), and energy-resource extraction (chapters 10 and 11). These chapters also show how the People nevertheless have kept some traditional bonds with the land. In chapter 11 elders blame the effects of climate change on the disruption of those bonds and the caretaker ethic that expresses them. An afterword looks again at sovereignty through the foregoing Diné historical experiences. To young Diné readers, the goal of this book is to help you know your past for your future.

1

AN ARGUMENT WITH ARCHAEOLOGISTS

A T A meeting of Diné cultural resource managers on March 7, 2018, several participants said,

When we would go to meetings with other tribes to discuss [with federal agencies] issues about Anaasází sites in Navajoland, someone would always say, "What are *you* doing here? *Your* people didn't come here until 1500. You have no say in this."

I'm proud to say that my Cheii was Kiyaa'áanii, from Kin Yaa'á, right in the middle of Chaco country, and I have Chacoan DNA.

The archaeologists tell us, "Your oral traditions are just made-up stories. *We're* the ones who know about the past."

In this chapter and the next three, we refute the archaeologists' "late arrival" stereotype of Diné origins first by critiquing the scientific foundations of that story and then with Diné traditional histories that tell of the Diné ancestral presence from precolumbian times. These stories of the ancestral presence validate and strengthen the bond of the People with the land, which is a foundation of sovereignty.

Many archaeologists and other anthropologists think that the Navajos and Apaches (both being Southern Athabaskans) migrated from the Far North into the U.S. Southwest around 1500, not long before the Spanish (Seymour 2012:2ff.; Wilcox 1981). In the past 20 years or so, more non-Indigenous archaeologists see the history in Diné ceremonial oral traditions (Lekson 2009:246; Snow 2006; Thompson and Towner 2017; Weiner 2018; Wilshusen 2010). Yet both Diné and others are still encountering the old scholarly tradition and "we know better" attitude in schools, in books and articles on the Southwest, and in struggles for land, water, and cultural resource rights (Marek-Martinez 2016; Navajo Nation Human Rights Commission 2012:67).

The old scholarly tradition is based mainly on language studies and on the supposed lack of any Navajo archaeological sites that date before 1500—sites with "material culture" (forked stick hogans, sweathouses, pottery) that archaeologists recognize as Southern Athabaskan. But archaeologists have been selective about the dates they use, the dating methods themselves have problems, and archaeologists are choosy about what they try to date with these methods. Finally, when those methods give them early dates, they are likely either to throw out those dates or to decide that they are too early to be Southern Athabaskan.

LINGUISTIC UNCERTAINTIES

The old scholarly story of Southern Athabaskan "origins" is based on a method of dating languages called "glottochronology." This method estimates very roughly the times when a group of people who spoke a common language ("speech community") started drifting apart and speaking separate versions ("dialects") of the original language. The studies suggest that the Athabaskan language family, which includes Navajo and Apache languages, spread into the Southwest sometime between 600 and 1500. Linguists consider these dates very approximate at best (Baldwin 1997:46, citing Hymes 1957; Campbell 1997:104, 112, 210; Rice 2012; Young 1983:393). Archaeologists who rely on the end-date of this time period to date the Athabaskan "arrival" have also distorted the linguistic studies, for whatever they are worth.

Furthermore, migration by a speech community is not the only way that a language can spread. A language can also spread among people who have lived in a place long before they adopted that language. Languages can also spread because of changing relationships among people of different speech communities, where one adopts the language of another without necessarily moving (Nichols 1997). Neighboring peoples who trade learn the basics of each other's languages.

DINÉ WOOD-USE CUSTOMS AND UNCERTAIN DATES

The earliest sites that archaeologists recognize as Navajo are in the upper San Juan River basin of northwestern New Mexico, which archaeologists call "Dinetah." According to archaeologist Richard Wilshusen (2010:203ff.), these "earliest Athapaskan" sites have remains of dwellings that archaeologists interpret as forked-stick hogans, as well as Navajo-type plain gray pottery, ground- and chipped-stone artifacts, hearths, sweathouses, and other features, along with evidence of corn, wild plants, rabbits and rodents, deer, and other big game (not all these remains appear on any one site). The dates come from wood used in structures (by tree-ring or radiocarbon dating); hearths, plant, and animal remains (by radiocarbon dating); and pottery (by comparison with pottery from other dated sites or by thermoluminescence dating).[1] Archaeologists argue over how to interpret the dates from the various methods and therefore how early the "Athabaskans entered the Southwest" (Towner 1996). The standard practice is to disregard pre-1500s dates.

FIGURE 11 Forked-stick hogan with silversmith and forge, 1890s. Forked-stick hogans of the late 1400s to 1500s were smaller and less robust and perhaps lacked the heavy earth covering. Credit: National Anthropological Archives, Smithsonian Institution, gn_02427.

Wilshusen notes that it is hard to distinguish early Navajo sites from those of other early Southern Athabaskans, Utes, or even "early Basketmaker" precolumbians. One reason is that the remains of dwellings on sites that archaeologists consider early Navajo are "small and shallow, dished-out circular features with a scattering of charred structural timbers [that] are very similar to what might remain of an early Apache wickiup or brush structure" (as well as to brush structures of other groups, including precolumbians) (Wilshusen 2010:205). Only remains dated after 1650–1700 have clear "evidence of the characteristic forked-stick superstructure" (205). Wilshusen thinks that the early (1450–1650) sites belong to the earliest Athabaskans in the Southwest, before the Navajos became distinct from other Athabaskans, and that the 1650s–1750s sites show the Navajos developing a separate identity with their own special house form (forked-stick hogan), painted pottery (Gobernador Polychrome), heavy dependence on farming, and specialization in deer hunting, as well as ceremonies and other aspects of traditional Navajo culture. To his credit, Wilshusen finds that the Navajo oral tradition of the clans coming together in Dinetah (see the introduction), or "ethnogenesis," describes the period from 1450 to the 1700s

FIGURE 12 Sweathouse in use ca. 1940. At the Emergence Place, the Holy People gathered in a sweathouse to design the forked-stick hogan, enlarged to encompass traditional Navajoland. Credit: Photographed by Milton Snow, courtesy of Navajo Nation Museum, Window Rock, Arizona, neg. no. NE6-3.

FIGURE 13 Diné potter Kinipai and traditional pottery, Buck's Store, near Whitehorse Lake, New Mexico, 1933–34. These unpainted, pointed-bottom pots look much like those of the 1700s and 1800s. Credit: National Anthropological Archives, Smithsonian Institution, J. P. Harrington Papers, neg. 55,619.

(see chapter 4 on ethnogenesis), and he recognizes that early ancestral Navajo sites may lack the signature forked-stick hogans and pottery. But he follows archaeological convention in ignoring sites that date much before 1500.

Nevertheless, archaeological excavations in the mid-1980s at several sites in northwestern New Mexico with Navajo pottery yielded dates as early as the 1300s, though archaeologist Gary Brown (1996:56) believes that these sites were used around 1500 but not necessarily earlier. Also of note are a hogan with tree-ring dates suggesting construction around 1400 (Ford 1979; Kelley and Francis 1998a) and a campsite with an early Navajo pottery jar (Dinetah Gray ware) and dates from a hearth between 1200 and 1400 (Brown 1996:65). Interpretations of both tree-ring and radiocarbon dates of wood from Navajo structures (e.g., Brown 1996:56) tend to ignore the Navajo wood-use customs that anthropologist David Brugge and his colleagues learned from elders during research for the Navajo Land Claim before the Indian Claims Commission in the 1950s and 1960s (Navajo Tribe 1967:762–765).[2] To archaeologists, unexpectedly early tree-ring dates show that Navajos used long-dead wood in construction. But Diné have rarely used dead wood for dwellings except for timbers from earlier family structures, because unfamiliar dead wood might have been "claimed" (struck) by lightning or wind. Therefore, an "anomalously early" tree-ring date from a hogan is likely to come from an heirloom timber salvaged from another family homesite nearby.[3]

The discoveries since the mid-1980s (and also reassessments of "anomalous" early dates from other sites) also narrow the gap between the "earliest Navajo" pottery and the Navajo-like pottery on sites of the Gallina people of the 1100s through 1300s in eastern Dinetah. The Gallina sites consist of clusters of pithouses and small surface rooms; a few sites have towers. The pointed-bottom pots of these sites "are not a characteristically Anasazi trait" and suggest contact with Great Plains or Mississippi Valley groups (Cordell 1997:142). Archaeologists once thought that Navajo ancestors had left these Gallina sites because of their Navajo-like pottery (Cordell 1984:357; Wilcox 1981:215). Archaeologist Donna Glowacki (2015:214–215) has suggested that Anasazi migrants from Mesa Verde moved among the Gallina people in the late 1200s. Her suggestion harmonizes with Diné oral tradition, which says that the first clan forebears to come into Dinetah were the Tsénjinkiní (Cliffdwellers) clan, created not far north of Mesa Verde at the Emergence Place around the year 1170—seven times an old man's lifespan (102 or 104 years) before the late 1880s telling (Matthews 1994:137–138; Young and Morgan 1987:684).

EARLY DINÉ HUNTING-GATHERING AND "ABSENT" ARCHAEOLOGICAL EVIDENCE

Regardless of how one interprets the dates of these items and their relations to the Diné, why assume that ancestors of today's Diné had pottery or house forms like more recent types? Why assume that all Diné ancestors had the same type of house form and pottery? Pushing back the date of the earliest Navajo-like ceramics and house forms by a century or so does not mean that the people who made them had just "arrived." Morris Opler (1983:381–382), Linda Cordell (1984:58), and Gary Brown (1996:64–69) have suggested that recognizable Southern Athabaskan remains (such as Navajo forked-stick hogans) are adapted to local conditions and therefore, as Wilshusen says, may not be the earliest traces of Southern Athabaskans. Those are more likely to be the sparse and generic leavings of hunter-gatherers, as the earliest Southern Athabaskans are thought to have been.

If migrating people could be counted on to leave a trail with an unchanging type of house or pottery, then archaeologists would have found the Southern

Athabaskan migration route somewhere in the archaeological record of the western United States. Absence of evidence may not be evidence of absence, but after almost half a century of looking for evidence of migration, they have not found anything they can agree on (Cordell 1984:358; Seymour, ed. 2012). One reason that archaeological remains do not mark out an obvious trail of migration may be that observed examples of an entire community migrating into the territory of another are rare. Archaeologist Linda Cordell (1984:333–334) has admitted, "More commonly, individuals and family groups follow separate migration paths, integrating themselves into ongoing communities where they have kinship or friendship ties."

Using work of earlier anthropologists based partly on interviews with Apache elders, archaeologist Deni Seymour (2012:401) has suggested that "bands" of Athabaskans (small groups of a few families) might have moved in and out of territories overlapping those of neighboring groups that were not necessarily related by language or culture. They might have taken on "the attributes of surrounding groups as they intermarried and adopted new technologies while settling into a new area." As local groups ranged over large zones that overlapped those of other groups, people also moved back and forth between groups, and groups sometimes joined together, only to divide later. Intermarriage and other relationships would have made moves easier. Land-use zones and their users were constantly changing. In this way, groups of Athabaskan speakers could have spread, picking up members from neighboring non-Athabaskan groups and sharing various cultural practices.

The conventional archaeological story about the precolumbian Southwest also says that before the Southern Athabaskans, the Navajo homeland on the Colorado Plateau was the home of the prehistoric "Anasazis" (see chapter 4 for a discussion of various usages and spellings of this term). Archaeologists long thought that these precolumbians abandoned most of the central Colorado Plateau around 1300, drought and erosion being the most popular recent explanations. Many archaeologists proposed a Southern Athabaskan invasion as the cause until the 1950s, when they got hold of the glottochronological dates for Athabaskan language separations.

Today, archaeologists suggest that precolumbians from Navajoland (whom they now call "ancestral Puebloans" rather than "Anasazi") regrouped in various places, including southern Black Mesa, the Rio Grande watershed, southern Arizona, and the New Mexico edge of the Great Plains (Cordell and McBrinn 2012:247; Glowacki 2015; Lekson 2009; see chapter 2). Archaeological evidence in these places suggests that the population grew suddenly after the late 1200s. The people already living there absorbed the immigrants and become the various First Nations (Puebloan) villagers whom the Spaniards encountered. Some archaeologists have suggested that some people did stay in the traditional Navajo homeland after 1300, living a much simpler life than those who left the big archaeological sites of Chaco, Aztec, and elsewhere (Cordell 1984:304–361; Glowacki 2015:211–213, but see also 217). Large villages then appeared in parts of the Southwest that earlier were only thinly settled (Cordell 1984:328). Cordell added that families probably moved away independently. Therefore, she said, one cannot connect post-1300 large villages of the Rio Grande or western Pueblos with particular parts of the central Colorado Plateau before 1300 (Cordell 1984:333–334; Cordell and McBrinn 2012:277).

Today, most archaeologists give the impression that the abandonment of present Navajoland around 1300 was complete. They focus on fairly large archaeological sites of settled farmers and how these villagers interacted (Cordell and McBrinn 2012:247). An example is the influential Coalescent Communities / Southwest Social Networks database developed by the University of Arizona and other research programs, which has given rise to studies of the population shifts and social transformations that took place between 1200 and 1500. The database consists of information from archaeological sites with at least 12 rooms (Archaeology Southwest 2017). It does not include the small campsites left by mobile hunter-gatherer-farmers like the Southern Athabaskans and therefore cannot address questions about their presence.

David Brugge (1989:1) suggested that after 1300 Southern Athabaskans then moved into the depopulated traditional Diné homeland:

> [The Southern Athabaskans] must have arrived in the regions abandoned by the Anasazi and their neighbors within a century of the [1300] withdrawal of the prehistoric agriculturalists or their occupation would have been prevented by others getting there first. . . .
>
> I do not mean to imply that one people cannot displace another, but I believe that except in the face of catastrophic events such as ecological disasters, arrival of deadly pathogens or intrusion of technologically more complex societies, replacement is rare and ethnic continuity the norm.

Later, Brugge (2012) suggested that Athabaskan-speaking people moved into the area around 1300 and intermarried with those the Anasazis had left behind.

FIGURE 14 Windbreaks on 1980s ceremonial site near Teesto, Arizona. Diné have used windbreaks for shelter since before the classic forked-stick hogans like that in figure 11. Credit: Klara Kelley photo.

The traditional Diné homeland is full of hunter-gatherer campsites that date from early precolumbian times to postcolumbian times. They include hunter-gatherer camps around the Continental Divide in the southern part of the homeland dating from the 1400s to the 1600s. These camps are considered to be Southern Athabaskan by the archaeologists who analyzed the materials recovered (Hayden et al. 1998; Oakes and Zamora 1999; Seymour, ed. 2012). Many other campsites, similar but undated, have been recorded throughout the traditional Diné homeland. These sites have evidence of hearths and chipped-stone artifacts and perhaps traces of windbreaks, all of which are common to many ethnic groups. They remain unexcavated and undated because archaeologists think they contain little information. A few archaeologists, however, suggest that some of these campsites could have been left by the hunter-gatherer ancestors of Navajos and Western Apaches in "Anasazi" times (Snow 2006; Warburton and Begay 2005; see also Oakes 1996; Seymour, ed. 2012:chapters 5 and 17). Archaeologists are therefore mistaken to assume that a time period without evidence of forked-stick hogans is a time period without Diné ancestors, whether Southern Athabaskan or something else.

DINÉ ORAL TRADITION

Regardless of what archaeologists think, Diné ceremonial histories are full of landscapes, both remote and accessible, all over the central Colorado Plateau. They describe a time without domesticated animals and non–First Nations people, when the great ruins that date before 1300 were still in use. As Brugge has said, "Taken literally, the sacred traditions would indicate that the Navajos' ancestors were living in close association with the Anasazi, that their homes and camps were intermingled with the settlements of the village dwellers, and that their wanderings took them throughout the country among the various Anasazi centers, . . . Mesa Verde and Mancos Canyon, Canyon de Chelly, the Hopi Mesas, Aztec Ruins, and Chaco Canyon in particular" (1992:33). Though the stories seem to say that Diné were in the area perhaps as early as 1000, Brugge thought the stories more likely "describe the history of peoples whose ancestors were not Navajo, but who were incorporated into the Navajo Tribe" (1992: 33). Some were Puebloan refugees who fled the Spaniards in the 1690s and perhaps occasional fugitives earlier. Others may have been people who had been living in traditional Navajoland since before the Anasazis, a few of whom were left after the Anasazis, still pursuing the "Archaic [hunter-gatherer] lifeway [and] were absorbed by the Navajo as they entered the region" (Brugge 1992:33; see also Brugge 2012).

We suggest that more Diné ancestors might have been some of the farmer-hunter-gatherers in the small extended family sites scattered in the backcountry around the big pre-1300 Anasazi "great houses." Then came the 1300s and early 1400s, when most people moved into new, big "coalescent communities" in the Rio Grande basin and southern Arizona, while a few stayed to live in the simplified way of hunter-gatherer-farmers. From the 1400s on, we suggest, the depopulated areas supported a thin scatter of families whose simple life left archaeological traces easily dismissed as "bad dates," "old wood," or not worth the cost of dating—in a nutshell, ancestral Navajo (and Apache) sites. Some of these families may have been newcomers, others descendants of earlier residents, including descendants of Chacoans, Mesa Verdeans, and the like.

We wonder if Southern Athabaskan speakers, both before and after 1300, could have been among the traders who linked the Great Plains with the Pacific and the Gulf of California, as Diné ceremonial stories hint. In these stories, sketched in chapter 2, turquoise, obsidian, marine shell, and buffalo crossed the central Colorado Plateau and beyond on routes that match "traditional" (precolumbian) long-distance trade routes (Ford 1983:719). We suggest that Southern Athabaskan might have been a common language for such trade. Then, after 1300, this language for trade became the language of the scattered bands in the depopulated parts of the central Colorado Plateau. Southern Athabaskan would have split later into Navajo and other Apache languages as a result of colonial intrusion, territorial encroachment, and divide-and-rule practices.

Most of the People today still seem to accept what their elders have said, that their ancestors were in Navajoland far back in precolumbian times. As chapter 4 tells, many Diné today acknowledge at least limited connections with the Anaasází. The Diné stories that Brugge describes above tell about the origins of ceremonies and about precolumbian life as Navajo ancestors witnessed it. These stories were recorded between the 1880s and the present (most were recorded between the 1920s and early 1950s) in English and sometimes also in Navajo. They represent at least 44 tellers, 66 narratives, and 21 ceremonial repertoires. The list is too long to include here; sources cited to support each statement below are only examples.

These stories tell that the Diné originated at Haajíínái (Emergence Place), not far north of their present homeland in the central Colorado Plateau (Fishler 1953:87; Matthews 1994:219n43). Diné and Kiis'áanii (villagers, including precolumbian Anaasází) originated together (Stephen 1930:102). The criteria that distinguish Diné from Kiis'áanii in the stories are house form, settlement pattern, and perhaps preferred environment; skillful farming; and hairstyle. The two groups traded and intermarried. Language is barely mentioned (Goddard 1933:24, 133; Matthews 1994:77–78). Diné and Kiis'áanii in these stories embody a cooperative opposition between "hunters" and "farmers." This opposition is found in origin stories widespread in the Western Hemisphere (Brotherston 1992:140).

Events occurred when people still lived at dozens of Anaasází archaeological sites. The Diné lived outside the large ceremonial centers and interacted with their inhabitants at Chaco Canyon, Mesa Verde (Mancos Canyon), Canyon de Chelly, Tsegi Canyon, and Awatobi, centers dating between the 800s and 1200s south of the Little Colorado River, and elsewhere in the traditional Diné homeland. At Chaco, the Great Gambler appeared and enslaved the people to build the monumental buildings there until a Diné-like challenger from the backcountry defeated him (Fishler 1953; Goddard 1933; Haile 1978; Matthews 1994; O'Bryan 1993; Wheelwright 1958).

As told in the introduction, the people of the traditional Diné homeland, both Diné and Kiis'áanii, or Anaasází, were beset by powerful monsters (malevolent gods), by natural disasters, and by epidemics, which killed off the people (Haile 1981; Matthews 1994). Some say no one survived. Other stories suggest that small groups survived and stayed in the traditional Diné homeland (Matthews 1994:145). When the Water People from the West Coast and others moved in later, they settled alongside occupants of the precolumbian buildings at Betatakin and Kin Yaa'á. Small bands of isolated wanderers joined a growing network of other bands to form a society of intermarrying clans (Fishler 1953:89; Haile 1981; Klah 1942:107–108, 114–122; Matthews 1994:135–159). According to chanter Hataałii Nééz, members of these different groups ended up in Dinetah, where some of the earliest spoke a language unlike Navajo but then shared their language with later arrivals to make a common language much like Navajo of the late 1800s (Matthews 1994:143).

Still later, some Kiis'áanii from the edges of the traditional Diné homeland moved back among the growing population of the area. They joined existing Diné clans or were recognized as clans in their own right (Brugge 1994:8–9; Matthews 1994:63, 145–159; Mitchell 1978:168–191; Preston 1954; Van Valkenburgh 1941:80; see also Benedict 1981 [1931]:1; Courlander 1971:70–71, 177–184; Yava 1978:36). During this time of clans coming together, as the introduction tells, Changing Woman taught the Diné the Blessingway ceremonies, which are the root of Navajo ceremonialism as we now know it. One purpose was to keep peace among the people (Mitchell 1978:185–186; Wyman 1970; see also chapter 4).

Early in the 1900s, archaeologist Jessie [Jesse] Walter Fewkes (1919:262–281) laid out how various clans could have brought certain ceremonial iconography (images) and practices from various archaeological districts to Hopi. We suggest that one can generalize this process to all southwestern First Nations clans. The histories of different clans start in different regions among different speech communities. Groups of people break away and move through a series of places. As they move, they change language, pick up people from clans of their hosts, and move on. The result today is that members of a particular clan and others linked to it are spread among various Puebloan, Navajo, Apache, and other communities.

Diné oral history and its implications are at least somewhat compatible with archaeological findings, if one admits the uncertainties of the archaeological findings. More important, one must also avoid assuming that language, "material culture," and ancestry have all existed among the same group of people from time immemorial. Diné scholars Harry Walters (1991) and Clyde Benally (1982) have combined information from anthropology and Navajo oral history in ways similar to what we propose here.

Probably all postcontact southwestern First Nations groups, including Navajos and Apaches, are descendants of precolumbian hunter-gatherer-farmers and village-dwelling Anaasází in Navajoland, as well as emigrants from the Rocky Mountains, Great Basin, and Great Plains (see chapters 2 and 4). No one modern ethnic group can reasonably claim to be exclusive descendants of the precolumbians. Diné who acknowledge connections with those precolumbians called Anaasází limit the connections to specific Diné clans, specific aspects of Diné ceremonialism, or specific precolumbian archaeological sites. Yet as the next three chapters will show, specific clans, ceremonies, and sites are parts of an integrated oral heritage that all Diné share that roots the people in the land from the deep past and creates consciousness of shared sovereignty.

A Diné story (Wheelwright 1951:8–16) dramatizes the intricate development of the shared heritage. Around the Anaasází ceremonial center now called Aztec Ruins, drought hit and people moved away. They left behind a young man. A Holy Person in the form of a bear rescued and raised him, but she also tried to devour him. He ran away and became a Ute. One of his Ute sons was likewise abandoned and raised by an owl. The son escaped and followed his forebears' trail of abandoned dwellings, pots, and fire-pokers, which pointed back to precolumbian Mesa Verde. A younger son was also adopted by Utes. Another was captured by the Hopis and recovered by Diné, whose language tells the story.

2

ABALONE SHELL BUFFALO PEOPLE
AND ANCIENT TRAILS

T HE JOURNEY narratives of Diné ceremonial histories are among the stories that make the deep bond between the People and the land. These stories place many precolumbian archaeological sites on mappable travel routes across present Navajoland, creating sacred landscapes that more recent Diné have learned about through travels with elders (see chapter 3). According to the stories, Diné forebears were in the present Diné homeland in precolumbian times and knew those routes. The Diné ceremonial histories focus on the moves of Holy People whose power is embedded in certain items. Archaeologists, in contrast, focus on how humans moved these items, especially through trade. This chapter puts these two complementary kinds of stories together, thereby providing more details about the diverse origins in space and time of many ceremonial elements and stories that today bond those Diné who experience those ceremonies to the landscape of remote precolumbian forebears.

Back in those times, the Colorado River and its tributaries drained a huge zone of shifting boundaries between southwestern farmers and hunter-gatherers of the Great Basin, Rockies, and western Great Plains. Within this zone, in Navajoland, the Chinle Wash heads in the forested Chuska Mountains and Canyon de Chelly to the east and in the high grasslands farther southwest. Flowing only when rain falls or snow melts, the wash drains north through the dry, open Chinle Valley into the San Juan River above its junction with the Colorado. South over the Chinle watershed divide, another sometimes-flowing stream, the Pueblo Colorado Wash, drains from the forested Defiance Plateau southwest through open, thinly vegetated country toward the Little Colorado River. In the past, during some centuries, these washes had permanent flows in their upper parts.

Across these and other watersheds farther east, according to Diné ceremonial histories, ancestral Diné hunters moved to trade deer and antelope skins with precolumbian farmers at big ceremonial centers like Tsé Bíyah Aní'áhí (Chaco), Kinteel (Aztec), and Táálahooghan (Antelope Mesa, Awatobi). Other Diné ceremonial histories tell of travelers across the region, beings who carried, were named for, or took the form of buffalo, antelope, deer, bighorn sheep, turquoise, marine shell, jet, corn, weaving, pottery, plant medicines, feathers (and possibly macaws), obsidian, or salt. They stopped at many places, including large precolumbian buildings.

These stories suggest that the Chinle and Pueblo Colorado drainages were part of a precolumbian long-distance trade zone. Archaeological evidence suggests that people converged on this larger zone for 2,500 years before Spanish contact (Hughes and Bennyhoff 1986). Together, the stories and the archaeology suggest that these First Nations peoples brought marine shell from the Southwest and big game from the North. This trade gave rise to trade loops in other goods, such as crops (perhaps encouraging the hunters and farmers each to specialize for trading) and later turquoise, pottery, weaving, and plant medicines, even copper bells and macaws. For a short time (900s–1200s), Chaco pulled the trade eastward into the San Juan basin of present New Mexico by circulating turquoise through the zone. This idea fits the reemerging archaeological notion that southwestern precolumbians took part in vast geographical networks (Hegmon 2000; Lekson 2009).

We have worked on several cultural resource management (CRM) projects in the Chinle and Pueblo Colorado watersheds and surrounding uplands, hereafter called mid-Navajoland. The CRM projects have allowed us to follow our own independent research into Diné oral tradition and the connections between stories and archaeology or documentation. We have compiled all place-names mentioned in most documented Diné ceremonial and clan histories, most of which were recorded between the 1880s and about 1950. We have consulted Diné chanters and other elders to find these places on the ground, to confirm links between stories and places, and, with luck, to tell us more stories. We have built upon the fieldwork of others who have studied Diné place-names and sacred places. Others, mainly CRM workers, have compiled the archaeological and documentary information.

ORAL TRADITION

In the origin story of the Diné Flintway ceremony, a young man and his family fled from Thunder, whose home was in Dibé Ntsaa, the sacred mountain of the north (Haile 1943:179–217). Thunder embodies the power of storms and war and the harm these forces can inflict. In Diné (and Puebloan) ceremonies, Thunder's power is sometimes represented by the war club (Frisbie 1971). The family was looking for the Buffalo People, whose power is embodied in (among other things) the Diné ceremonial shield (Reichard 1977a:630), which defends one against Thunder. From the San Juan River valley, the family fled west through Marsh Pass and around Black Mesa, then on west and south to the San Francisco Peaks and lakes farther south. There they found the Buffalo People, led by

FIGURE 15 Precolumbian ceremonial site in foreground overlooks the buffalo/bead corridor of Diné ceremonial histories. The corridor is the wide-open area in the middle ground near Pinon, Arizona. A trail shrine (not visible) is in the low hills in the corridor on the right. Credit: Klara Kelley photo, in Kelley and Francis (2003).

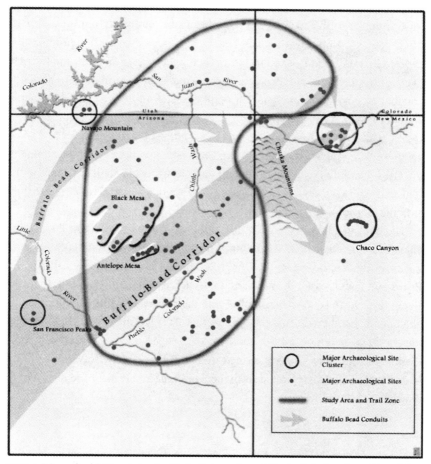

MAP 1 Map of mid-Navajoland with both branches of the buffalo/bead corridor. Other routes delineated by Diné ceremonial histories form a network that connects most of the dots, which represent big precolumbian ceremonial sites (great houses). Credit: Map by James W. Martin, in original article.

Abalone Shell Buffalo Person. The young man followed them straight northeast across Black Mesa, the middle Chinle valley, the northern Chuska Mountains, the San Juan River near present-day Farmington, and on to the Chama River and the Great Plains.

At least 25 Diné ceremonial stories describe mappable routes of beings who carry or embody various trade items.[1] These routes form two broad corridors, each connected by detours and loops. The two broad corridors correspond to the two Flintway routes described above: one from the northeast, toward the west, then south, and the other from southwest to northeast. Different routes within each broad corridor carried whatever buffalo products the Buffalo People embody, shell beads, or medicinal plants. Detours and loops in the Chinle valley carried the same items and also deer products. An antelope corridor ran from north to south through the length of the Chinle and Pueblo Colorado Valleys. Other loops carried turquoise and items exchanged for it from Chaco north across the San Juan River and west across Black Mesa, then south to Antelope Mesa (Awatobi) and east again.[2] Chaco itself was home to the Great Gambler, who controlled all the turquoise and shell and thereby the rain and who was sent back to Mexico by a young man who defeated him (Matthews 1994).

The two corridors also correspond to the pathways of the Water People, the clan forebears created by Changing Woman after the monster slaying. Coming from the Pacific coast, the Water People divided near the San Francisco Peaks and then crossed the land amid the sacred mountains through both corridors (Fishler 1953; Wyman 1970b). With their canes of white shell, turquoise, abalone, or jet, they created the springs that later fed important Diné farming places. Plant people used the southern corridor (Kelley and Francis 2000a, 2001c), and the Tobacco People, ancestors of a branch of the Navajo Táchii'nii (Red Forehead) clan, migrated from the San Francisco Peaks zone northeast to Antelope Mesa.

DOCUMENTATION AND ARCHAEOLOGY

Documented postcolumbian trails approximate long parts of the buffalo/bead and other ceremonial routes. Approximating part of the north buffalo/bead corridor is the 1829 Armijo Cutoff for the Old Spanish Trail (Hafen 1947). Parts of other routes in southern mid-Navajoland follow the ancient Palatkwapi Trail, described by the Spanish in 1582 (Bartlett 1942; Byrkit 1988; Colton 1964: trail 3). The north–south antelope corridor approximates a route shown on the 1778 Spanish colonial map by Bernardo Miera y Pacheco (1970). The Mexican colonial Vizcarra military expedition of 1823 followed the southern part of one of the routes for turquoise and miscellaneous items (Brugge 1964). Of course, one would not expect these more recent trails to correspond perfectly to those of precolumbian times, for the settlement patterns and transportation technology had changed (see chapter 3).

The routes in the 25 Diné stories mapped here also coincide with the locations of precolumbian archaeological sites with big ceremonial architecture (what archaeologists call great houses, great kivas, and compounds). Using several sources, we have made a list of such sites and site clusters with dates between 900 and 1300 (Adler and Johnson 1996; Fowler and Stein 1991, 2001 [1992]; Gilpin 1989, n.d.; Stein 1995). Mid-Navajoland encompasses most such sites west of the Chacoan heartland (the San Juan River valley and New Mexico's San Juan basin). Big site clusters just outside mid-Navajoland are at the San Juan River near present Farmington on the northeast, the San Francisco Peaks on the southwest, and Navajo Mountain on the northwest, with Chaco farther outside to the east. All these clusters are in or near where the travel corridors extend outside mid-Navajoland.

In the area from the Chuska Mountains west across Black Mesa and from the San Juan River south to the Rio Puerco of the West are 61 such sites and clusters. Of these 61, 16 are not along the trails, most being on the far northern and southeastern edges of mid-Navajoland. Of the 45 remaining, 32 (73 percent) are near landmarks that the Diné stories name to trace the routes. Many places that the stories name are the structures themselves.[3] The three turquoise and miscellaneous-item stories taken together name the most precolumbian sites. Most of the stories also name other large architectural sites and corresponding landmarks outside mid-Navajoland. The routes tend to begin and end at the big site clusters of the San Juan River, San Francisco Peaks, and Chaco.

Some of these big buildings have constructed corridors that archaeologists call "roads" leading into them (Marshall 1997; Roney 2001). We suggest that these corridors might have served to guide immortal and human travelers from the unconstructed travel routes to the big structures, which we think were involved in trade for ceremonial items. Because most of these sites have not been excavated, we do not know whether they have evidence of those trade items. However, the routes that pass these sites extend to and from precolumbian archaeological zones where lots of the trade items have been found. Published information on locations of sites with lots of shell, turquoise, big game, and other items is piecemeal. Luanne Hudson (1978) has put together information on excavated archaeological sites of 900–1500 with turquoise, shell, bells, and macaws, while more recent lists for shell (Bradley 1996), copper bells (Vargas 1995), and turquoise ornaments (Mathien 1997) are more limited geographically but include more up-to-date and detailed information. These works and others also identify the possible original sources of the items.

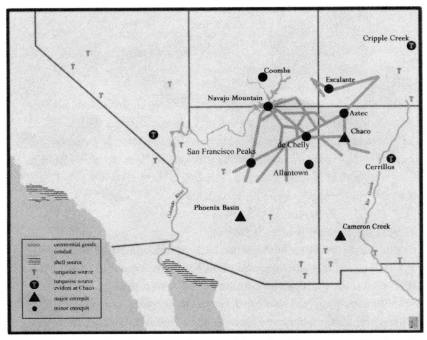

MAP 2 Map of precolumbian routes of ceremonial goods and source areas for turquoise and shell, and major and minor trading centers (entrepôts). Credit: Map by James W. Martin, in original article.

We listed the sites with the 10 largest amounts of each item, according to the four reports. The sites on this list form clusters that might have been big and smaller entrepôts (places for gathering or distributing trade goods). Big game, a major presence in this book, is unfortunately absent from the reports.

The time between 900 and 1200 was the heyday of Chaco and its ceremonial successor, Aztec (Stein and Fowler 1996). During that time, the big entrepôts for various items were Chaco (Gulf of California shell and turquoise from various sources), the Mimbres area (Gulf of California shell and macaws [Munro 2011; Watson et al. 2015]), and the Phoenix basin (copper bells; also the main production area for Gulf of California shell ornaments). After about 1200, as population started to shift south and east, so did the entrepôts. The big ones became Paquimé (Casas Grandes) in northern Mexico (Gulf of California shell, bells from the Tarascan area of Mexico, and macaws from Casas Grandes itself), the upper Salt River / Mimbres region (Gulf and Pacific coast shell), and Pecos Pueblo in north-central New Mexico after 1400–1450 (Pacific coast shell).

Smaller entrepôts could have gotten these items from their original sources in nature and fed them to Chaco through the route network described here. Of special interest is the San Francisco Peaks cluster. Taken together, the sites in this cluster, including guardianlike citadels, might form a major entrepôt that lasted until 1400 (O'Hara 2012; Pilles 1987, 1996). It is where Diné oral tradition says that the Water People from the Pacific coast, bearing marine shell and precious stones, met the Arrow People (Fishler 1953:91–102; Klah 1942:114–122; Luckert 1977:58–60; Wyman 1970:453). The Water People fought the Arrow People, whom they found in an enclosure hung with weapons, then entered their promised homeland and started to make clan links with groups already there. These relationships hint at trading partnerships. Specifics on the entrepôts for each item are as follows.

TABLE 1 Chart of source areas and centers for exchange of exotic items.

ITEM	SOURCE / PRODUCTION AREA	MINOR EXCHANGE CENTER	MAJOR EXCHANGE CENTER
	900s–1200s		
Shell	Gulf of California / Phoenix basin	Coombs, Utah	Chaco
		Winona / Ridge Ruin	Cameron Creek / Swartz (Mimbres)
		Mummy Cave (CdeC)	
	Gulf of California / Pacific?	Lost City, Nevada	
	Gulf of California (*Spondylus*)		**Allantown**
Turquoise	Cerillos/Chaco	**Escalante**	Chaco
	Zuni Mountains? / Andrews	Salmon/Aztec	
	Cripple Creek		
	Southern Nevada / Kingman	Coombs	
	Chino Valley / NA10748-52	RB 568 (Navajo Mountain)	
		Winona / Ridge Ruin	
		San Francisco Peaks sites	

TABLE 1 *continued*

900s–1200s			
ITEM	SOURCE / PRODUCTION AREA	MINOR EXCHANGE CENTER	MAJOR EXCHANGE CENTER
Bells	West coast of Mexico	Chaco	Gatlin (Phoenix)
		Winona/Wupatki	
Macaws	Southern Mexico	Wupatki	Mimbres/Chaco
1200s–1400s			
ITEM	SOURCE / PRODUCTION SITE	MINOR EXCHANGE CENTER	MAJOR EXCHANGE CENTER
Shell	Gulf of California / Phoenix basin	Chavez Pass	Casas Grandes / Chihuahua
		Kinnikinnick?	Gila Pueblo (Globe, Arizona)
		Awatobi?	Grasshopper (Mimbres)
	Santa Barbara	Chavez Pass	Higgins (Mimbres)
		Kinnikinnick?	Pecos (1400s)
		Awatobi?	
Turquoise	Cerillos/Guadalupe	Aztec?	Aztec?
	Silver City / W. Baker	Babocomari?	Pecos? (1400s)
		Awatobi?	Lower Rio Grande
Bells	Tarascan Mexico	Gila Pueblo	Casas Grandes
Macaws	Casas Grandes	Point of Pines (Mimbres)	Casas Grandes

Source: Adapted from a chart by Klara Kelley in Kelley and Francis (2003:37).

Note: Sites in **bold** are in central Navajoland.

SHELL

Gulf of California shell (*Glycymeris*) and Pacific shell (abalone [*Haliotis*] and *Olivella*) could have come into the route network of mid-Navajoland through the San Francisco Peaks entrepôt sites or through another possible entrepôt in southern Nevada (Gumerman and Dean 1989:118). Mummy Cave in mid-Navajoland at Canyon de Chelly might have been another, smaller entrepôt. One would expect an entrepôt here in the zone where turquoise, antelope, and deer circuits join the north and south trade corridors. Canyon de Chelly is so central that one wonders why sites there lack more of the long-distance trade items. Another big entrepôt is Allantown, which lies southeast of the route network and seems to have been an entrepôt that mysteriously specialized in *Spondylus*, or red-shell "coral."[4] The white shell (*Olivella*, *Glycymeris*) and abalone are two of the four sacred ntł'iz (hard substances) that made up the canes of the Water People. (For the other two, see the sections on turquoise and jet below.)

BIG GAME

The original source of buffalo would have been the Great Plains, whose range varied to the west and south. Between 900 and 1300, for example, buffalo may have ranged into northern Utah (Haines 1995:32–33). After the 1200s, the buffalo range shifted far southward onto the southern plains of present-day Texas (Anderson 1999:17). Bighorn sheep nearest mid-Navajoland, before their near extinction in the late 1800s and early 1900s, lived in the San Juan / Colorado River canyons alongside the northern route corridor and in the Rocky Mountains to the northeast, as well as east along the Continental Divide in New Mexico and through much of Arizona to the west and south (Manville 1980). The loop formed by the northern and southern buffalo/bead corridors through the entrepôt of the San Francisco Peaks could have connected with buffalo and bighorn source areas. The turquoise loop north of the San Juan River valley and perhaps Chaco itself could have also connected buffalo and bighorn source areas. At the Domínguez-Escalante site, a minor entrepôt for turquoise near present Dolores, Colorado, exchange with bighorn hunters in the nearby Rockies would have been possible (see also turquoise below). Hunters might have brought the turquoise to the site.

Archaeological evidence of big game, especially species other than deer, is rarely reported. However, available information fits surprisingly well with the locations of the suggested entrepôts. Archaeological sites of 900–1200 with unusually large amounts of bighorn remains are located north of the San Juan River (Fremont and southern Utah Anasazi), namely, the minor turquoise-shell entrepôt at the Coombs Site and sites in Glen Canyon (Jennings 1978:233). These sites are accessible to the northern buffalo/bead corridor. Another concentration of bighorn remains from this period is in the Phoenix basin major shell production / entrepôt area (the Palo Verde Ruin near Peoria [Mark Hackbarth, letter to Kelley, August 23, 1999]). Bighorn bones also reportedly have been found in late deposits at Chaco itself (Thomas Windes, email to Kelley, January 3, 2001).

After 1200, southeast of Navajoland near Pie Town, New Mexico, the Newton site (1200–1325) and upper levels of Bat Cave contained many buffalo bones, probably from hunting on the Plains of San Augustine to the east (Dick 1965; Frisbie 1971:69). Between 1250 and 1350, farmers of the middle Pecos Valley on the western edge of the Great Plains became buffalo hunters and, after 1400, left sites with shell and turquoise (Hickerson 1994:224; Snow 1970:44). These sites may signal the shift in trade networks to the east and south. Along with drought and warfare, the shift in trade networks may have led people to move out of Navajoland (Lekson 2009:236n52).

Deer and antelope lived and still live in mid-Navajoland. The route network could have circulated these locally hunted animals.[5] Though archaeological evidence of specialist hunters in Navajoland is not recognized, it may exist in sites that archaeologists assume are hunting camps of the precolumbian farmers, whose sites were plentiful in the region after about AD 1. The big architectural sites throughout mid-Navajoland and beyond may have been the ceremonial meeting places of long-distance traders passing among big and small entrepôts, local deer and antelope hunters, and herbalists, potters, and farmers.[6]

PLANT MEDICINE

Chanters who told the two stories that describe the route for plant medicines did not say what kinds of plants moved along it, but the stories offer hints. The Buffalo People, who used a variant of this route, caused certain psychoactive and other plant medicines to bloom where they camped. The section of the route from the San Francisco Peaks to Awatobi and on to eastern Black Mesa and the Chinle Valley was also a migration route of the Tobacco branch of the Navajo Táchii'ni clan (Nát'oh Dine'é Táchii'ni Clan People 1981; Preston 1954), a hint that tobacco traveled along the route. The Water People carried tobacco pouches and smoked ceremonially with the groups they encountered along their route from the Pacific to the San Francisco Peaks and northeast. The Water People found that the designs on the pouches of the people encountered were like their own and therefore recognized them as k'éí (relatives). The smoking ceremony to establish kinship is another hint of trading partnerships, with tobacco not only shared ceremonially but perhaps traded. In more recent times (1800s), Diné had such partnerships with Utes and Puebloans, according to W. W. Hill (1948:388–392), though he does not mention tobacco.

The Kaibab Plateau west of Navajoland is a traditional Diné place to get tobacco (Kelley and Francs 2000b:section 9510). The San Francisco Peaks entrepôt linked the southern corridor to the Navajo Mountain and Colorado River region, including the Kaibab Plateau. When Sunset Crater erupted around 1100 (Elson and Ort 2012) and spread ash over the surrounding area, tobacco may have been one of the first plants that grew there afterward, for it grows in disturbed ground. In any event, precolumbians grew tobacco around Wupatki (Lambert 2012:115). Tobacco from volcanic craters seems to have special power to Diné chanters (Wyman 1952:88). Another psychoactive plant, datura, grows in the region around the southern buffalo/bead corridor (and elsewhere in and around Navajoland). Tobacco, datura, and other psychoactive plants were and are widespread in the western United States and Mexico, but at least for datura, the knowledge of how to use it ceremonially may have been more localized and passed along the trade sites (see Berlant et al. [2017] about datura in Mimbres). In any case, archaeological evidence of plant medicines in and near mid-Navajoland, like evidence of big game, is probably underinvestigated and underreported.

TURQUOISE

The precolumbian turquoise source areas nearest Navajoland are Cerrillos near Santa Fe; Kingman, Arizona, and nearby southern Nevada / Virgin River; the San Luis Valley and Cripple Creek in south-central Colorado; the Chino Valley west of the San Francisco Peaks; and southeastern Arizona / southwestern New Mexico (Bennett 1966:8–9; Lekson 2009:133, 138; Snow 1970; Wiegand 2001). Turquoise from Cerrillos, Cripple Creek, and southern Nevada / Virgin River appears in Chaco, where Cerrillos turquoise may be the most common (Mathien 1996). Since turquoise sources are hard to identify, Chaco turquoise is likely to include other sources also. Though southern Arizona (Hohokam) sites had little turquoise until 1150, after Chaco's heyday (Doyel 1991:233), the turquoise loop offshoot from Antelope Mesa south could have accessed turquoise from southern Arizona and sent it to Chaco, which was a production center for turquoise ornaments (Mathien 1997; Toll 1991). At Antelope Mesa, Awatobi, including "Smaller Awatobi," might be counted as another small entrepôt owing to its reportedly plentiful turquoise and shell beads (Fewkes 1898:628).

The Cerrillos turquoise may have come straight from the mines to Chaco, perhaps along the east end of the loop for turquoise and related items. In Diné stories (Haile 1978:paras. 1–3; Kluckhohn 1967), the east loop extends to Jemez, possibly by way of the Guadalupe site near Cabezon. People at Guadalupe seem to have engaged in the turquoise trade in the 900s to 1200s and were making turquoise jewelry by the 1200s (Judge 1989:236–237; Mathien 1997:1185–1190). In early Chacoan times (950–1050), similar production seems to have occurred south of Chaco at the Andrews site, which may have been established to work turquoise from the nearby Zuni Mountains, where oral tradition hints at a turquoise source now exhausted (Kelley and Francis 2000a:section 9803).

Turquoise from southern Nevada / Virgin River and perhaps the Mojave could have come into the route network from a production center / entrepôt there (Gumerman and Dean 1989:118; Hull et al. 2014) or through entrepôts at Navajo Mountain (northern corridor) or in the San Francisco Peaks vicinity (southern corridor). As a minor entrepôt, the Domínguez-Escalante site near Dolores, Colorado, might have received turquoise from Cripple Creek and the San Luis Valley, as well as from southern Nevada / Virgin River—perhaps from hunters—through the northeastern extension of the turquoise loop. From there, it might have been sent (along with bighorn and buffalo products) down to Chaco.

JET

The sources of jet nearest the route network seem to be Colorado Springs, the Henry Mountains north of Navajo Mountain in Utah, and the Virgin River of southern Nevada and Utah (Ashley 1918; Dietrich 2015). Jet therefore could have come into the route network along with turquoise from Colorado and Nevada.

MISCELLANEOUS ITEMS: POTTERY

The Navajo stories suggest that exchanges of turquoise for miscellaneous items were commonplace. Sticks, stones, and water thrown at travelers on eastern Black Mesa probably stand for ceremonial procedures like bathing, offering precious stones, and offering prayer sticks, ceremonial matters that the chanters who told the stories did not want to reveal. But these items might also stand for pottery. We note this possibility because people of the Chinle and Pueblo Colorado Wash drainages in mid-Navajoland seem not to have made pottery between 900 and 1300 (Stein and Fowler 1996:124; Toll 1991:91). Instead, as CRM archaeological reports for the Chinle Valley show, pottery made outside came in from all directions. Traders following the turquoise loop could have picked up and carried pottery from all these different zones, exchanging them at big architectural sites along the way for turquoise, skins, cloth, obsidian, and various other items that the stories hint at. Even though it is not very portable, pottery could have served as a kind of all-purpose exchange item that people near an entrepôt could make from humble local materials to trade for more exotic items coming through.

In the big site clusters that we propose as entrepôts, some of these precious trade items came from storage space and possible workshops, but most (especially shell and turquoise) came from "high-status" graves (Frisbie 1978; Reyman 1978). Therefore, one could object that the places where archaeologists have found these items do not reflect trade. According to anthropologist Jonathan Friedman (1999 [1979]), however, trade-route entrepôts in societies like those of the precolumbian Southwest were likely to have the kind of "status burials" found at southwestern archaeological sites with large quantities of exotic items. Kin groups located to capture trade gained higher status than others and exalted their ancestors. Status burials reflect this exaltation and thereby also may reflect control of long-distance trade. Certain kin groups also may have developed high status through other regional political relations, including ties with Mesoamerican elites, and then called forth the trade in rare items as status symbols (Lekson 2009:11ff., 125–130, 139).

IMPLICATIONS

We suggest that trade between hunters and farmers in the precolumbian Southwest, including its northern edge around the San Juan and Colorado Rivers, could have worked much as described by the first Spanish contacts in the 1500s (Castaneda 1990:56–57, 60; Hammond and Rey 1953:400; Snow 1970; Wilcox 1986:137–138). The frontier between hunters and farmers that the Spanish saw was along the Rio Grande, the hunters being bands of Plains

Apaches, related by language to modern Navajos. Plains Apache families settled around Pecos, Taos, and other big Puebloan centers during the winter, where they traded the meat and hides from the buffalo that they had hunted earlier in the year on the plains to the east. In exchange they got corn, weaving, pottery, and turquoise.

In the 1500s and 1600s, Apaches (a name that the Spanish also used for Navajos) were also found settled around Antelope Mesa and the Hopi Mesas (Brugge 1983:490–491; Hammond and Rey 1966:189; Montgomery et al. 1949:9; Snow 1970). The Apaches moved constantly and were great traders who specialized in hunting to build up a tradeable surplus at all times (Anderson 1999; Castaneda 1990:60, 113; Haines 1995). Farther south were the Jumanos, whose "trade brigades" moved through strings of communities between the south Texas plains and northwestern Mexico, even to the San Francisco Peaks (Anderson 1999; Hickerson 1994).

In precolumbian times, Chaco and other entrepôt centers not only could have connected with hunters but also may have been destinations for Mesoamerican specialist long-distance traders (Frisbie 1998; J. C. Kelley 2000; Wiegand 2001; see also Lekson 2009:138).[7]

Still farther back in time, trade is evident in mid-Navajoland in the form of marine shell by 1000 BC (Gilpin 1994). Long-distance exchange of shell and big-game products might explain why some of the earliest recorded sites with corn in the Southwest are in the San Juan watershed, and many others are in the Rio Grande watershed, where an earlier wave of buffalo appeared around the same time (Cordell and McBrinn 2012:136–149; Galinat and Gunnerson 1969; Gilpin 1994; Gumerman and Dean 1989:111; Wills 1988:54, 149–50; Woodbury and Zubrow 1979). Especially noteworthy are two sites with marine shell and corn dating to 1000 BC on the route of the Buffalo People in the Flintway origin story (Gilpin 1994). After at least 2,000 years of plant domestication in the greater Southwest, full-scale farming became widespread, including the irrigation that went with shell-ornament production at Snaketown near Phoenix about 300 BC (Gumerman and Haury 1979:77–80). More productive varieties of corn appeared in the southwestern United States from Mexico around 500 BC (teosinte hybrid) and again by around 700 (Cordell and McBrinn 2012:143). Archaeological evidence of the new corn seems clustered in the middle Rio Grande drainage, as well as in the general areas of earlier new corn types, the Gila uplands in the Rio Grande watershed and the San Juan / Colorado River zone. We suggest that the buffalo/bead trade encouraged farming along the trade routes as local farmers produced surpluses to trade for big game while they waited for the shell traders to show up.

Trade between hunters and farmers who can specialize because they trade with each other (symbiosis) has been common in nonindustrial societies through the western hemisphere and even worldwide (Barth 1998; Brotherston 1994:14; Upham 2000). Many Diné ceremonial histories tell of Diné hunters visiting Chaco, Aztec, and other large Anasazi ceremonial complexes. In Diné stories, the Buffalo People and the plant medicines that spring up in their wake may be icons of this symbiosis. Other icons are Bighorn Sheep, Turkey, and Deer People with medicinal and domesticated plants in their bodies and pelts (see, e.g., Matthews 1994:160–194). These icons, which Diné stories probably share with those of many other groups, nutshell the kind of plant-animal symbiosis that led to the origins of agriculture—animals eat the plants and excrete the seeds, thereby giving them fertilizer to grow abundantly (Kuznar 2001:29–30).

Trade routes might also explain why, in the northern Southwest, what archaeologists call "early Basketmaker" (1500/1000 BC–AD 500) hunter-farmer sites seem concentrated in the zone of northern Black Mesa and along the San Juan River, Colorado River, and the tributary Chinle Wash drainage (Cordell and McBrinn 2012:139). These sites have burials and other deposits with early pottery, shell, bighorn sheep parts, and even a little turquoise. By late Basketmaker times (600s–700s), big sites with central ceremonial structures (great kivas) and dozens of pits for storing food were scattered around the region like the later big architectural sites.[8] These patterns suggest that the trade corridor network orally mapped by the Diné stories developed between 1000 BC and AD 500. The oral maps then passed down the generations of the different peoples who used the routes at one time or another. Trade seems to have been more active in mid-Navajoland than in the San Juan basin until as late as 900 (Mathien 1997:1151).

Such trade may be why hunter-farmers who left the Anasazi-like Fremont archaeological sites flourished north of the Colorado River between 1 and 1350 (Jennings 1978:155–233; Talbot 2000; Upham 2000). Fremont hunters took bison and bighorn, as well as deer and other big game. Their surviving iconography features petroglyphs and clay effigies of heavily beaded humanlike figures. Simpler clay figurines, punctated to render necklaces, have been found in Basketmaker caves south of the San Juan River on the buffalo/bead routes near Kayenta and Cove, Arizona. They date to the time of the early Fremont (Amsden 1949:135; Guernsey 1931:86; Morris 1980).

Chaco, in its heyday, seems to have drawn the earlier buffalo/bead trade corridors (northern and southern) into a network with itself at the center, perhaps by controlling and redistributing turquoise. During this time, Lost City near Las Vegas, Nevada, blossomed into a big center for trading shell bead and turquoise (Amsden 1949:30–131; Gumerman and Dean 1989:118). At the same time, the western Anasazi people (as distinguished from the Fremont) seem to have reached both their greatest numbers and their farthest northwestern location (Gumerman and Dean 1989; Jennings 1966:34–35). The Fremont and southern Utah Anasazi sites of 900–1200 with especially plentiful remains of buffalo and mountain sheep seem to cluster along shell trade corridors north of the San Juan (Hughes and Bennyhoff 1986:239; Jennings 1978:233).

From 1000 BC, for the next 2,000-plus years, trade along the corridors that crossed mid-Navajoland must have waxed and waned in response to such forces as trade along the Pacific coast and the Gulf of California; Mesoamerican trade, city building, and political upheavals; climate changes that affected supplies of shells and big game; the condition of precious mineral deposits; and regional erosion cycles that affected farming.

The blooming archaeological cultures in the southwestern United States sketched here coincide with trade shifts along the west coast of Mexico (the Gulf of California), especially the growth of Amapa between 900 and 1200 and its link to Guasave, a big coastal trade center farther north (Adams 1991:322–325; Bradley 2000; Douglas 2000; J. C. Kelley 2000; Lekson 2009). Archaeologist Joan Mathien (1997:1162) notes that Guasave turquoise jewelry is like that of Chaco from 920 to 1020. Earlier, between 400 and 900, turquoise workshops had flourished at Chalchihuites in northern Mexico near the Continental Divide. They may have been the first to open up the southwestern United States as a source of turquoise (Nelson 2000; Wiegand 2001). Chaco and later Aztec may have been the northern end of a route from northern Mexican centers straight up the Continental Divide through the also flourishing Mimbres "culture area" (J. C. Kelley 1986; Lekson 2015), which was earlier the scene of perhaps the first cultivation of corn in the southwestern United States (at Bat Cave). Many scholars think that corridor was a long-standing route of cultural and biological exchange between Mesoamerica and the southwestern United States (J. C. Kelley 2000; Smith et al. 2000:569). After 1200, western Mexican trade shifted inland to Casas Grandes on the northern Mexican Continental Divide (Bradley 2000; Vargas 1995). This shift may have helped move trade from the San Juan / Colorado Rivers east across the Continental Divide into the established routes of the Rio Grande valley.

Climate change may have been involved in this trade shift. According to various large-scale historical reconstructions of climate (Glowacki 2015; LeBlanc 1999:33–39), between 1000 and 1200 the climate of the northern hemisphere was warmer and wetter than it had been earlier (though droughts set in during the 1100s in the Chaco heartland). But by the 1200s the climate was reversing itself. Changes in ocean currents and winds must have affected marine shells and the coastal trade. (Hudson's [1978] data suggest that marine shell from the Pacific coast became more common after 1200.) Cold and drought returned to the Southwest. Times after 1400 were wetter again but seem to have stayed cold with a shorter growing season until the 1600s.

A possibility worth investigating is that pulses in climate pulled hunters toward the Southwest from the Great Basin, Rocky Mountains, and Great Plains along the far-flung extensions of the buffalo/bead routes and related networks (see Thompson 1966:97–100, 104, 150–173; Turner 1971:33–37; Upham 2000). During cold times the hunters followed the game southward, and during warm times some of them became farmers. These hunters would have included Athabaskan-speaking ancestors of Navajos and Apaches, as well as members of other language groups at different times (Sutton 2000). Biological evidence suggests that new people and earlier residents intermarried (Kaestle and Smith 2001; Lorenz and Smith 1996; Malhi 2012; Smith et al. 1999). Linguistic studies suggest that if nobody took over politically, then the language of the group most favored by a particular environmental change might have become the region's common language for a time, whether people also migrated or not (Nichols 1997:372–374, 379–380). The language that climate favored after 1300 in present Navajoland would then have been that of hunter-gatherers, including Athabaskans.

We suggest that, over the long haul, the various ancestors of Navajos and other Apaches in different times, places, and speech communities were among those affected by these processes. Climate change after 1200 undermined agriculture in the San Juan / Colorado River zone and contributed to violence and depopulation (Glowacki 2015; LeBlanc 1999:33–39, 118). The same climate shifts drove buffalo onto the southern plains of Texas (Anderson 1999:17). Perhaps the spreading buffalo caused the major hunter-farmer long-distance trade zones to shift far southward and eastward, where the Spanish found them in the 1500s. We suggest that those Navajo and Apache ancestors not already in the Southwest (see chapter 4) may have moved in during the 1200s and 1300s.

AFTERWORD

With very few exceptions, archaeologists seem to have been blind to the possibility that maps [including oral maps; see chapter 3] made within traditional societies during the historical period might reveal sites, trails, even boundaries in ancestral prehistoric societies. (Woodward and Lewis 1998:15)

Archaeologists are blind partly because they doubt oral tradition is stable enough to hold historical truth. Here, the question is how oral tradition could preserve information about an area for 700 years after its depopulation, especially when the oral tradition has come down among Diné, who many archaeologists assume were not in the southwestern United States until 500 years ago.

First, we dispute the notion that ancestral Diné were not in the Southwest earlier (see chapters 1 and 4). Second, an example of an oral tradition that endured, as we think the Diné stories did, until it was finally preserved in writing is Homer's *Iliad*. That epic of ancient Greece tells of events that happened several hundred years before the first alphabetic writing (Havelock 1986). Third, oral societies have strict procedures for transmitting their empowering stories, as discussed in the introduction (see also Rubin 1995). Fourth, certain processes help oral tradition preserve information about the past for hundreds of years. These processes involve need, mechanism, and medium. Although the region covered by the stories in this chapter became depopulated after 1300, people traveled across it and therefore needed some kind of mental map. The Diné stories contain oral maps in the form of strings of named landmarks on straight lines of travel. Whatever routes they used on the ground, travelers knew they were on the right line when they were at a particular place mentioned in the story (see chapter 3). The mechanism of transmission was ceremonialism, which has always preserved carefully and passed down the oldest Diné oral tradition, as described in the introduction and chapter 3. Furthermore, although Diné ceremonies and their stories are not the property of particular clans, most chanters seem to have lived in the landscapes covered by the stories of those ceremonies (see, e.g., Wyman 1965). Finally, as a medium, Diné ceremonial oral tradition has certain features (song or meter; rhyme; formulaic phrases, events, figures, iconography; etc.) that stabilize it during teaching and learning (Rubin 1995). The Diné stories and songs that lay out the routes discussed in this chapter are tied to ceremonies and therefore have these features in abundance. The antiquity of the Diné stories and songs about the land deepens the bond of the people to the land and their sense of shared sovereignty.

3

TRADITIONAL DINÉ MAPS

History as Geography

DINÉ CEREMONIAL histories and journey narratives, the types of traditional histories used in chapter 2, show the antiquity of Diné traditional knowledge of the land. They are also verbal maps with which Diné elders have taught youngsters. While the previous chapter suggests how the traditional stories might encode history and deepen the people's sense of their bond with the land, this chapter shows how the stories encode geography and how elders have taught youngsters by traveling with them along the storied routes. By such teaching with stories, elders instill in youngsters an attachment to land.

A DINÉ VERBAL MAP

Diné verbal maps portray linear space, such as trails, and broad geographical space, such as large zones with landforms often described as human or animal "earth figures."[1] One Diné story tells how, during the monster slaying (see the introduction), the older of the two sons of Changing Woman, Monster Slayer, chased and subdued the monster Tsé Naagháí (Traveling Rock). Around 1930, the encyclopedically knowledgeable Diné chanter Slim Curley gave a version of this story to Franciscan anthropologist Berard Haile, who put it on paper in both Navajo and English (Haile 1938:137–139). The complete translated text is as follows (brackets enclose our interpolations).

[At the end of the previous episode, Monster Slayer returned to his home on top of the sacred mountain of the center, Huerfano Mesa.] "Of walking stone it is known, that reports place it yonder, down to the west," someone said.

From here, it seems he again began his journey by means of the same sunray, which glided away with him on the summit on the farther [south] side of Cottonwood Pass [Béésh Łichíí' Bigiizh, Red Flint Gap, according to Haile's Navajo-language version], to a place called "the sun lies there" [Jóhonáá'éí Si'ání, Sitting Sun Orb; Haile uses quotation marks to show literal translations of Diné names]. To the top of "fish flows out" [Łóó' Háálíní] sunray glided with him, to the "black mountain" [Dził Dahzhinii, Black Mountain Up Above] sunray glided away with him, to the place called "dark mountain" [Dził Diłhiłii] sunray glided with him, to the top of "mountain one" [Dził Łahdilt'éí] sunray glided away with him.

"Yonder is the place where walking stone lives," was reported, and he immediately attacked it there. He struck it with the flint club, zigzag lightning quickly wrapped itself around it, fire flared up, a big fire blazed. It started on a run toward the east, but he hurried up to it by means of the sunray, and struck it with that blue flint club. A piece was chipped off, and straight lightning wrapped itself around the stone. With his right foot he stepped upon the chipped-off piece.

From there it started on a run and landed on the "flat sloping ridge" [Hahasteel]. By means of the sunray he ran up to it, and struck it with that yellow flint club which he had. Zigzag lightning wrapped itself around it, another piece was chipped off, fire flamed up, and that chip lies at ["toward" in the Diné text] Chinle [Ch'ínlį, Outflow]. Upon this he stepped with his left foot. Again it started out and landed, on the jump, at Cottonwood Pass [Béésh Łichíí' Bigiizh]. He also started out toward it, and again struck at it with the serrated flint club. Another piece was chipped from it, zigzag lightning wrapped itself around it again, another tremendous flame blazed up.

When he again stepped on (the chip) with his right foot, his strength suddenly failed him, and he breathed heavily. He began to walk about there, and he felt a tremble through his whole body. The pair of prayer sticks which lay at the doorway of First-man [at Monster Slayer's home] began to burn. "What has happened, what is the condition of things now? It is evident that the prayer stick has begun to burn! Go ahead, Born for Water [Monster Slayer's younger brother, who is supposed to rush to his older brother's aid when the sticks burn], indications are that your elder brother has been overpowered," he said to him.

Born for Water then shot the zigzag lightning arrow, which he had. Here, it seems, when Monster Slayer touched the ground in front of him with medicine, a medicine plant suddenly stood there. At once he plucked this and chewed it, then rubbed himself with it. Above him a cloud appeared, and directly rain began to fall upon him. This moisture cooled him off, the prayer stick, which had begun to burn, was again extinguished. As soon as he was cooled off, it seems, he exclaimed, "At which place, walking stone, can you outwalk me!"

At once, the sunray and the zigzag lightning bounded with him after it, and landed him again on the distant continental divide [Ahideelk'idii, Converging Ridges]. With that serrated flint club he again struck it, another piece was chipped from it, straight lightning again wrapped itself around it, another big fire blazed up. Again he stepped upon the broken piece. From there it again rushed away, and as it plunged yonder into the ocean, its rumbling (ts'ideel) noise was heard. From there he merely set out to return and arrived at Huerfano Mountain.

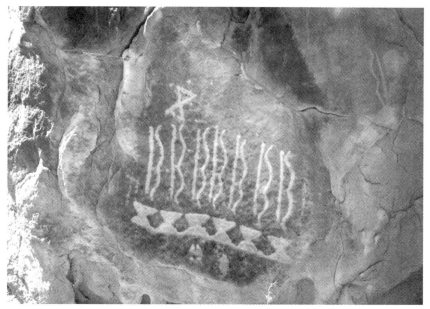

FIGURE 16 Petroglyphs in Dinetah (upper San Juan River basin) with icons of Monster Slayer, the bow, and Born for Water, the hair bun. The powerful recurved bow appeared in the U.S. Southwest in the 1200s, possibly introduced by Athabaskans (LeBlanc 1999). Credit: Klara Kelley photo.

Embedded in this story is a verbal map with at least the following details. Monster Slayer traveled by sunray (an icon for a straight line above the earth's surface) from Huerfano Mesa westward along a series of five named mountaintops. He found the Traveling Rock far in the west and struck it. It flew away eastward, with Monster Slayer running after it. It bounced off the earth in four places, all but the first of which are named. At these places Monster Slayer struck a chip from it and stepped on the chip. The second chip fell at a place farther east between the places of the second and third bounces before Monster Slayer stepped on it. At the place of the third bounce, Monster Slayer made rubbing plant medicine. After the fourth bounce, the rock fell into the eastern ocean.

This constellation of story elements forms a verbal map, that is, a portrayal of the earth's surface. Can it also help one find one's way on the ground? Yes, if one has some background information, such as that in the next section ("context"). We have already noted one wayfinding clue: the sunray represents a straight line of travel. After the section on context are two sections about the map's relationship to what is actually on the ground and whether Diné actually have used this or similar stories to find their way over the landscape. Finally, to bring out the accumulated cultural knowledge embedded in the verbal map, we explore the question of its antiquity.

CONTEXT

The context of a story with an embedded verbal map is an enormous field that includes (but is not limited to) the following information, most of which is to be found in various oral histories that surround the story: the larger story of which the story is one episode; the story's iconography (the stereotyped traits of various beings and other elements); the history of the story; who tells and learns it and for what purposes; and why a teller tells the story in a certain way at a certain time.

This story and the other monster-slaying stories are part of the history of the Naayéé'ee (Enemy Monster Way) ceremonial repertoire. Like other Diné ceremonial repertoires, it is balanced by another one that is its opposite, Blessingway, which is discussed in the introduction.[2] Traveling Rock was one of the monsters that came up with the Holy People and eventually started killing the people of the earth. So Changing Woman appeared and gave birth to the Two (brothers), who were destined to visit their father, the Sun, for initiation into warriorhood and then for vanquishing the monsters.

After the monster slaying, Changing Woman moved to a floating home that the Sun made for her off the coast of present Southern California, accompanied by the Twelve Holy People. In some versions of the story, these 12 people survived the monsters by hiding in a cave near the junction of the Colorado and Little Colorado Rivers. They emerged, went east, and then returned west, naming places on their line of travel (Haile 1981:219–220; Klah 1942:69–72, 101–106). At the Western Ocean, Changing Woman created a new breed of humans, the Water People, who traveled east, as described in chapter 2, and resettled the former monster-ravaged land. Corresponding to the episodes in this story are sets of songs, including many that invoke the directional mountains. The westward and eastward routes of Changing Woman, the Twelve Holy People, and the Water People cross or coincide with long sections of Traveling Rock's line.

The earliest recorded versions of these stories date to the 1880s, given by elderly singers who would have learned them as youngsters in the first half of that century (Matthews 1994). Like most other Diné ceremonial histories, these stories are about precolumbian times (see the introduction). They also have episodes and iconography in common with not only Puebloan and other First Nations stories of the Southwest and North America in general but also Mesoamerican stories recorded shortly after Spanish contact (Bierhorst 1985, 1990; Wilson 2016; see chapter 4). The Diné Traveling Rock story (and the larger story of which it is part) presumably has similar precolumbian origins. Like all oral stories, however, the Traveling Rock story differs somewhat among various tellers and performances. Its form and interpretations have surely changed as the lifeways of its tellers and listeners have changed. The Traveling Rock and other monster-slaying stories are not among those that underpin Blessingway ceremonies but instead are part of the Enemyway and Enemy Monsterway ceremonial repertoires. Diné link these war-related stories to the stories of the Blessingway by identifying the part of the Blessingway history during which the Enemyway events took place.

The introduction describes how Diné ceremonial repertoires are cared for by chanters, who learn detailed, confidential versions from older chanters but may tell parts of the repertoire's stories to ordinary people at ceremonies. Commonly in the past but rarely now, elders also told the more public versions to children and grandchildren on winter nights (Kelley and Francis 1994:21–22,

49). Another part of the youngsters' education was to go with an elder to the places named in the story.

The version of the Traveling Rock story quoted above, however, was not recorded in a traditional setting. Singer Slim Curley told it to Franciscan priest Berard Haile and Diné interpreter Chic Sandoval as part of a series that Haile made with Slim Curley and other singers. Most of this work seems to have been sponsored by Edward Sapir, a linguist at the University of Chicago, whose purpose was to build a body of Diné-language texts for professional linguists and cultural anthropologists to study. Probably Slim Curley had other reasons for taking part. Perhaps, like other chanters who have consented to recording, he worried that he was teaching too few younger Diné and that his stories might be lost. Haile's interest may have been purely linguistic, though he also thought that missionaries who sought converts must know the Diné language and culture (Haile 1998).

The story appears in print in both Navajo and English, but the published version does not describe its recording or editing. In his early years, after he had learned enough of the Navajo language, Haile seems to have taken written notes in Navajo, but by the time he recorded the story, Haile had a phonograph. He probably recorded the story on wax cylinders, as did many anthropologists between the late 1800s and about 1935. Such cylinders do not seem to be among Haile's collected research materials, though. Perhaps he saved them for reuse as temporary transcription aids rather than keeping them as permanent records (Haile 1998).[3]

ON THE GROUND

Like other travel routes in Diné ceremonial stories, the line of Traveling Rock is marked on the ground by both natural landmarks and cultural features (markers made or enhanced by humans). The Traveling Rock story first names a string of landmarks east to west (you can see from one landmark to the next), then a corresponding string of what are now cultural features at named places west to east. These strings define a line across the earth about 200 miles long, from the south rim of the Grand Canyon east across the canyon-incised grassy plateau of Coal Mine Mesa, around the rim of Canyon de Chelly, over the forested Chuska Mountains, and through the grasslands of the Chaco Plateau to the Continental Divide, a traverse of many days' travel by foot or horse. In telling of travel by

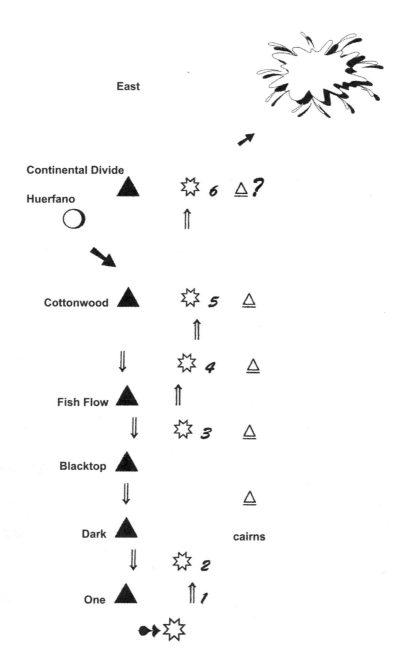

FIGURE 17 Diagram of Traveling Rock's route showing named places, rock-clubbing places, and cairns. Credit: Diagram by Klara Kelley, in original article.

sunray and flight above the earth, the story also implies that the entire line is not itself a beaten trail on the ground.

All the place-names but one (Mountain One) correspond to landmarks in Navajoland, all of which are within five miles on either side of an alignment due east and west. All but one of the landmark place-names (Sitting Sun Orb) suggest what the corresponding landmarks look like. The place-name Mountain One refers to the first of four mountains that extend around certain places of creation or in a line from them, including Changing Woman's home off the Pacific coast. Mountain One therefore implies origin places in general. Another such place is the zone in the Grand Canyon where the Twelve Holy People emerged after the monster slaying. The Grand Canyon zone is along the line of the other landmarks in the story, projected to the west. Other stories suggest a mountain on the canyon rim above this zone as a possible earth-surface location of Mountain One in the Traveling Rock story.[4] The name Sitting Sun Orb attaches to more than one place, referring to certain marks on rocks (not petroglyphs) said to represent the sun and the full moon when they rise in the same place (the equinox). The name therefore suggests "cosmography" (traditional models of the earth, sky, and underworld). A cosmographic name linked to more than one landmark identifies those landmarks with cosmography. We call such place-names "prototype place-names," another one being Mountain One. Other place-names in the Traveling Rock story, such as Dark Mountain, clearly describe the corresponding landmarks, as well as being prototype place-names.

The story, then, uses place-names to represent a geographical space (the line) by (1) naming them in sequence, (2) using names for places that match the appearance given in the name, and (3) using place-names at or near the ends of the line (Sitting Sun Orb, Mountain One) that imply the cosmographic frame— the four cardinal directions and center (zenith and nadir). These references to cosmography work much like the north-pointing arrow on Euro-tradition maps: they anchor the sequence given by the story and establish its general direction. The story itself also states the general lines of travel and locates these lines roughly in relation to the place that begins and ends this story episode, Mountain Around Which Moving Occurs (Huerfano Mesa). That place-name implies the cosmic center and attaches to a unique landmark that is also Monster Slayer's home.

The cultural features in the story are the human-enhanced traces left by Monster Slayer chipping at the rock. After Mountain One (1), their locations are, from west to east: (2) a place (unnamed) east of Mountain One, (3) a place on southern Black Mesa, (4) a place near Chinle, (5) one near Narbona Pass, and (6) one at the Continental Divide. The manifestations are Monster Slayer's footprints at places 2, 4, 5, and 6, along with a place for making medicine from plants at place 5. These are marks on rocks that humans have enhanced.

Also on the line, Diné have shown us cairns (travel shrines) at places 3, 4, and 5 and at a place that could be the more vaguely described place 2. These are conical piles of small rocks, twigs, and brush three to four feet high. The story does not clearly mention cairns but may imply them, since these piles of shattered rock appear at every place where Monster Slayer struck Traveling Rock except place 1, and another cairn is at or near place 4, where a chip from place 3 landed.

People have also shown us a Monster Slayer footprint, which is what archaeologists call a "grinding slick" (thought to be used to make medicine) in place 5, the one with the medicine and within half a mile of the cairn.[5] People have also shown us two different rocks with footprints of Holy People that could correspond to place 4. A cairn is at one of these places, and the footprint near the cairn is visible. The cairns, then, form a line from east to west that corresponds to Traveling Rock's line of travel. All the cairns are offset no more than two miles from a true east–west alignment and are spaced respectively 60,

FIGURE 18 Cairn on Traveling Rock's route where it crosses the buffalo/bead corridor of chapter 2. Still today travelers place a rock and some plants on the pile with a prayer before traveling on. Credit: Klara Kelley photo.

35, 40, and (if a cairn not yet found is on the Continental Divide) 80–90 miles apart, for a total length of at least 215 miles. Furthermore, all the cairns (and the Continental Divide) are where First Nations long-distance trails, recorded in story or memoir, cross the line.[6]

Other trails cross Traveling Rock's line, but cairns do not mark them, as far as we know from the literature, elders, or observation. The points marked by the cairns and footprints are spaced several days' travel apart. If it takes a day to cover 15–20 miles on foot, and an actual foot trail did not stray too far from the line, then the cairns are spaced two to five days apart. If it takes a day to cover 30–40 miles on horseback, then they are spaced one to three days apart. In between the cairns at the places in the Traveling Rock story are places that, according to other, related stories, once had crystals or rods of mirage stone. One is a chip off Traveling Rock in another version of that story and is about a day's walk (15–20 miles) east of the cairn near place 4. The other (not identified with Traveling Rock) is about a day's walk both east of cairn 5 and west of Chaco Canyon (Kelley and Francis 1994:68–69, 72–73). The cairns are not at springs, although springs are near—two miles away or less. Nor do petroglyphs accompany the cairns, although they may appear on or near the line elsewhere. Taken together, the landmarks, cairns, and crystal places form an east–west string of places spaced one to two days apart on foot.

DINÉ WAYFINDING AND TEACHING WITH VERBAL MAPS

We have no report of humans traveling along the line itself. The reports of human use involve trails that crisscross the line. Two such reported routes link to connect to the line between places 1 and 4. An elderly Diné couple told us that, weaving through the western part of the line, is a route called Holy People's Trail after the first beings to use it. The couple also said that Diné traveled this trail on horseback long ago but can no longer do so because of fences and other obstacles. Along the horse trail are water holes, trail shrines (cairns), and other shrines. The trail shrines that the couple mentioned include cairns at places 2 and 3 on the line itself (Kelley et al. 1991:place 196). At its northeast end, this trail connects with a trail identified by another elder called Rimrock Horse Trail, west of Chinle and place 4. The Rimrock Horse Trail links the south rim of Canyon de Chelly with the Holy People's Trail and, ultimately, the south rim of the Grand Canyon.

The horse trail that the Diné couple described was used by many different peoples. Diné used it and other trails to travel among Diné communities, to trade and attend ceremonies at Hopi, and to visit sacred places to make offerings and gather ceremonial materials. Other sources identify this trail as "Hopi" or "Indian" (Bartlett 1940:40–41; Colton 1964:93; Titiev 1937).

With a well-beaten trail, perhaps no one would have needed to use the Traveling Rock story as a map. Even on well-beaten trails, however, one might need guidance at trail junctions. Diné trading parties of the 1800s used ceremonial oral traditions during travel (Hill 1948). The typical party consisted of 25–30 men (sometimes women went too), usually from more than one place, riding horses. The leader knew about trading ritual, songs, prayers, and correct behavior. The trips lasted two to three weeks. The leader started the trip with songs and prayers, with more when the group reached the edge of the country that members knew. From there on they sang more and more, usually Blessingway songs, according to Hill. (Actually, travelers used songs from other ceremonies too, as told below.) The songs included "Hogan Songs, Mountain Songs, Songs of the Hard and Soft Goods, Talking God Songs, Corn Songs, and Journey Songs. Changing Woman and White Shell Woman Songs were considered appropriate when crossing wide valleys, Mountain Songs when traveling over rugged terrain. All types were thought to pertain to the goods which were desired and to insure successful bargaining, friendly treatment, and safe return" (Hill 1948:384). Where the party stopped to rest or camp, they offered sacred stones with songs and prayers. The return trip also involved ceremonial songs and prayers, the grand finale being a Blessingway all-night ("no sleep") ceremony when the party reached home.

Several Diné in their late eighties have given us more details about long-distance travel for trade and also for hunting and war. The late Dan Taylor of Many Farms said, "Trading expeditions would have a leader, an older man, accompanied by a young man whom he was teaching. They two would travel on horseback. They knew what was at the distant places through songs and prayers that named the sequences of places in the direction of travel. The older man taught the young man the songs and showed him the places they named. This was within the Four Mountains of Navajoland. Diné ordinarily did not go outside to trade" (original statement in Navajo, KFa, November 16, 2000). The late Jenny Paddock and her husband, the late Arnold Paddock, Harris Francis's aunt and uncle, told how elders used travel along storied routes to teach youngsters first about their own family land and then about more distant places. This practice is crucial for instilling bonds to the land in Diné youngsters. Jenny Paddock said:

> Sacred places are mentioned in the origin and ceremonial stories. Teaching started early for young people. As they grew, they learned these places by heart. The family's prayer places, springs, mountains, places that have stories, people also learned by heart by the time they reached age 10. They learned because they took part in the ceremonies at these places with their parents and grandparents. Young men were required to know these places and the stories attached to them and some of the prayers of the family's sacred places around the home.
>
> The locations of places outside the family's home area were also taught to young people at an early age. These are the major sacred places like Chuska Peak, Black Mesa, Canyon de Chelly, and so forth. When the father went to visit his family, his children went with him. On the way, the father taught his children the route and the names of the places along the way. The girls learned these routes in order to visit their father's family in the future.
>
> As for the boys, they had to learn all of these places early. When the men planned a hunt or raiding party, the boys who were old enough were invited into the sweathouse [ceremonial sweatbath before the trip], where they were taught about the rituals involved [on the trip], the places they would pass, and the springs along the way. They usually camped at the springs at night and did prayers there when leaving. These trips were all conducted in a sacred manner, starting with the sweathouse and continuing until they returned home. Prayers were said all along the way. In the hunting and war songs, places were named. This is how they found their way. The boys were taught these things.
>
> It was usually the hunting songs that mentioned the landmarks. The war songs, I don't know about. But my great-grandfather used to sing these hunting songs. These were not Blessingway songs, but usually Mountaintopway songs because these were the homes of the animals, deer, elk, sometimes antelope that were being hunted.[7]
>
> All of this was done in a sacred way. Prayers and ceremonies were done all the time. I'm sure it was the same if not more sacred when they went on a raid because that involved taking human life sometimes. When they returned [from hunting], a cleansing ceremony was done, then the Blessingway.
>
> I never heard anyone talk of going to a certain place for trading. Usually it was the men who traded among themselves. The things they got were usually for themselves and the women—guns, weapons for themselves, things like pots and

pans and cloth for the women. They usually went to the Bilagaanas or the trading post for this. I didn't hear of anyone going outside our lands to another tribe just for trading. It was usually them that came to us, like the Hopis who always came to us with their donkeys [bringing corn to trade for meat]. But I'm sure others [Diné] traded with other tribes, those who lived next to them. (Original statement in Navajo, KFa, November 24, 2000)

Arnold Paddock continued:

When a boy came of age, he was taken along and taught the locations of those landmarks and the songs that told of them. He has to know these things because one day he might have to come this way again. Even in travel one had to be in harmony with everything.

The people traveled around a lot then. One couldn't stay in one place too long as we do today. There were many things to take into consideration: water, food, enemies, and so forth. People were always on the move. Some traveled with the seasons, so everyone had to learn and know these routes and the landmarks that went with them. I've not really heard anything about we Diné traveling long distances to trade. Maybe before Fort Sumner they did this, because we weren't restricted to one area [reservation] like we are today. Most trading was done with Bilagaanas and the tribes that lived close to us.

Your grandfather [Mr. Crawler] once said that people traveling to far destinations often used the routes of the Holy People, routes like Changing Woman's trail [which coincides with Traveling Rock's line between at least places 3 and 5 and possibly also farther west]. When there were enemies around, everything that was done had to be done in a very careful manner. This included prayers, which were performed all the time, so that the Holy People were with you and protected you.

Traveling to different locations was always risky and dangerous. You never knew if the enemy was nearby waiting to attack you. Because of this, protection prayers were always done before you left. The destination was always known and discussed by all who were going on the trip. The route was discussed beforehand so the party knew where to go. With the hunting and war parties, these things were discussed in the sweathouse, and in case of attack, evasive actions were planned. They always picked a certain place to meet if they became lost or separated because of enemies. Hunting locations were named in songs that the men sang on their journey. These songs named major landmarks such as mountains, and always springs. They would usually camp near these springs and do prayers there in the Holy People's route.

These routes were well known then. The stories that go with them and the landmarks, these were taught to the children at an early age. This helped make the travel easier going north to south and east to west. But it seems no one knows these stories anymore, so these routes are forgotten. Maybe some singers and elders still know of them, but no one asks. (Original statement in Navajo, KFa, November 24, 2000)

These elders all told us that ceremonial stories, songs, and prayers performed just before and during the trip helped the party stay on the right route. Such rituals seek guidance from the Holy People whose domains the party is traveling within or toward, as well as mentioning sequences of places. These elders did not give examples of songs, prayers, or stories, but they did single out the Mountaintopway ceremonial repertoire and other songs used in hunting as rich in place-names.

Previously published versions of songs, prayers, and stories of the Blessingway, Mountaintopway, and other hunting ceremonial repertoires show that the three verbal forms differ in the kinds and variety of places they name. But published songs, even for Mountaintopway and the hunting ceremonies, mention few landmarks besides the cardinal mountains and prototype place-names implying the cardinal directions (Luckert 1975, 1978; Matthews 1907; Wyman 1970b, 1975). The lack of place-names where our consultants indicate richness suggests that the chanters have systematically withheld geographically specific songs from recording. Certain Blessingway prayers mention more landmarks, but not in lines of travel (e.g., Wyman 1970:186). Published Blessingway journey songs invoke the trail of corn pollen and cardinal mountains, but not strings of landmarks. Perhaps some chanters who led trips would use a song as a framework in which to insert the names of landmarks along the way.

By far the largest number and variety of place-names are in the published versions of ceremonial origin stories. The stories mention places, such as in the Traveling Rock example, in sequences encountered by travelers that are anchored at beginning and end to cardinal mountains or other key cosmographic locations so that travelers would know the general direction of travel. The late Blessingway singer Frank Mitchell made clear that songs do not establish sequences, only the associated stories do:

Of course it is the story that tells us the order of the songs all straight, the story of how the songs began. That's why it is simple to remember all these songs. . . . People who do not know the story have no way to remember those songs. . . . The story is like a trail. You see, a trail runs in certain ways, and if you have gone that way more than once, you know every little thing that is on that trail. That is the way you think about these songs. . . . The rows of songs on one side and the trail alongside of it: that is how you keep those two things in mind. (2003:230)

Therefore, even songs that do name places do not by themselves specify the sequence in which travelers encounter those places. Instead, each group of songs is associated with a particular story episode, and it is the story episode that names places in sequence. The story may name more places than are named in the songs (or prayers) that are associated with that story. The songs also invoke certain Holy People and name the prototype places where they live. The story is what attaches the prototype place-names in the songs to the actual places on the ground.

Returning to our example—Traveling Rock's line and the story of it as a verbal map—does the story have accompanying songs? Only one song has been published, and it is associated with a different version of the Traveling Rock story, which delineates a different line for Traveling Rock about 50 miles south of the one in our example (Wyman 1970:568–569). In any event, the song as published names no places, and any directional iconography implied (by paired black and blue figures) is north to south, not the east–west alignment in the related story version.

Up to this point, we have shown that Diné ceremonial stories include verbal maps as geographers today define maps and, furthermore, that the maps in those stories can be used for wayfinding. The Diné verbal maps work by identifying routes of travel with sequences of named landmarks and cultural features. They show the direction of travel by anchoring those sequences to icons of the cardinal directions or other places in the cosmic framework. An often-missed subtlety is that the stories also imply straight lines between landmarks to indicate an absence of trails on the ground. The story sequence forms a guideline for travelers to know which places they need to reach, in what order, and in what direction. Place-names are also guides to certain traditional resources. Not only can the stories work as maps, but in the past, Diné did use them as maps, knowing that the actual trail on the ground would wind back and forth along the guideline in the verbal map. Actual trails on the ground may shift with the changing locations of natural resources, human settlements, and means of travel. By not representing entire trails—only strings of guidepoints that any trail needs to access—the story map persists despite the vagaries of human history. Since the maps can last as long as the stories do—hundreds, even thousands of years—and to emphasize that these maps are made from cultural knowledge accumulated through time, we now address the question of permanence.

ANTIQUITY OF THE VERBAL MAP

The Diné story of Traveling Rock seems to be rooted in a world without post-columbian things. Another hint of precolumbian age is the possibility, described above, that Traveling Rock's line originally had more cairns spaced one or two days apart for foot travel. The present cairns, more widely spaced, seem better suited to those traveling on horseback. Diné tradition says that some cairns originated in the remote past with the Holy People, while others mark trail crossings where Enemyway ceremonial parties have met or were created by Enemyway chanters (Haile 1938:72–73; Van Valkenburgh 1940a). One must place a rock and plants on the pile and pray before going on. This requirement ensures safe travel—the land will know the traveler and recognize his or her purpose of being there. Ancient cairns are therefore maintained to the extent that people continue to pass by.[8]

The Traveling Rock story, the rest of the story sequence of which it is part, and just about all other histories of Diné ceremonies seem to be set in preco-lumbian times. Other stories about Monster Slayer are set at large pre-1300 sites such as Aztec ruins (Haile 1938:141–175; Wyman 1970:586–599, 1975:158–172). And the Water People, who crossed Traveling Rock's line at some of the cairns, settled at various precolumbian archaeological sites and districts that antedate 1300, including Chaco Canyon, according to one teller, which they reached by what seems to be a segment of Traveling Rock's line (Haile 1981:162–175).

There is other evidence that Traveling Rock's line may be precolumbian. Southwestern First Nations cosmologies emphasize cardinal directions and cor-responding landmarks with long-distance visibility. The only place on Trav-eling Rock's line that Diné stories portray as a central place for humans is Chaco Canyon itself. Chaco is central in the story of Great Gambler, who drew goods, people, and rain to his home there (O'Bryan 1993:50–62; Matthews

1994:82–87). But except for a recently recorded fragment of the Gambler story (Kelley and Francis 2003:262–263), which mentions the Gambler's racetrack between Chaco Canyon and Chinle, the Gambler stories do not describe all or even parts of Traveling Rock's line.

Yet archaeologist Michael Marshall (1997:62–74) has described Acoma and Zuni ceremonial routes to salt lakes or springs where people emerged from (or return to) the underworld. He considers these routes precolumbian, not used until after Chaco's heyday (900–1150) but incorporating architectural sites and "road" segments of Chacoan times. Like Traveling Rock's line, these routes are delineated by cairns and by things that flash to direct travelers (crystals?). The west end of Traveling Rock's line is a zone of both salt caves and emergence places in Navajo, Hopi, Zuni, and Western Apache traditions (see above and endnote 6). Could Traveling Rock's line form the east–west complement to the north–south line formed by the Great North Road, built in Chaco's heyday due north, toward the San Juan River (and, pointing farther north, toward a zone of emergence in southern Colorado) (Kincaid 1988; Matthews 1994:219)? Traveling Rock's line lacks any known segments with architecturally constructed roadbeds, but such constructions could lead from Traveling Rock's line (and other verbally constructed lines) to precolumbian sites with ceremonial architecture.

LAST WORDS

Traditional Diné verbal maps portray the earth's surface and can be used for wayfinding. However, as chanter Steven Begay (personal communication, February 19, 2017) has emphasized, traditional Diné maps are not for finding one's way, as in exploring. To use a traditional map on one's own would be to trespass on the domains of the Holy People—the sacred places named in the verbal map. To visit these places on one's own, one must first visit them with a ceremonialist to make the proper offerings to the Holy People of each place. That kind of knowledge makes one a steward of the place and responsible for passing stewardship on to younger generations. Furthermore, visits to such places must have a beneficial purpose, such as healing or bringing good fortune. These stories with verbal maps have served generations of Diné in learning about, bonding with, and living off the land.

We emphasize the *ethical* use of traditional maps here, because up to this point we have emphasized the wayfinding aspect of such maps, an emphasis that may encourage unethical uses. We thereby risk endangering Diné traditional ways of life. From the maps that First Nations people drew for the earliest European colonizers to today's Geographic Information System maps of present First Nations hunting-gathering areas and sacred landscapes, putting maps on record always seems to go with First Nations people losing resources and the oral tradition itself (Pearce and Louis 2008; Piper 2001:44; Rundstrom 1995:45–57; Rundstrom et al. 2003; Warhus 1997). Putting a map on record also weakens the story by making it available anytime, anywhere, and to anybody, no longer told only by knowledgeable traditionalists to initiates in traditional settings. Some Diné elders whom we have consulted over the years, invoking the sovereignty-preserving tactic of refusal, have told us flatly that nothing does as much harm as revelations to non-Diné. To reveal is to give the land away (see also Begay 2003:77).

Yet other Diné and other First Nations people have favored placing oral tradition, including maps, into the written record. This is not to be done indiscriminately but in certain circumstances where they believe that the harm done by revelations is less than the harm done by secrecy (Echo-Hawk 1993:33–52; Swidler et al. 1997). In the case of this chapter (and the earlier article [Kelley and Francis 2005b]), we have tried to minimize harm by choosing a story that was already recorded willingly by a Diné chanter, by choosing a form of record (this book and the scholarly journal before it [Kelley and Francis 2005b]) not usually consulted by the general non-Diné public, and by hiding locational details.

To avoid putting this and other information about First Nations oral tradition in the record would, we believe, speed up the dumbing-down of First Nations traditions, or the outright ignorance of them, among First Nations youth. It would also miss a chance to counter the dismissive attitude of many non–First Nations people toward the historic, natural science, philosophical, and other knowledge in First Nations oral traditions, a lack of respect still widespread among land-use and resource-management decision makers. As long as decision makers can diminish oral tradition, they can also dismiss the consultations with elders that First Nations communities more and more demand to gain the sustainable, holistic, tradition-guided management of the lands that they claim and to enhance their limited sovereignty over those lands. This is the double bind of limited sovereignty. As it is, sacred places and landscapes are routinely disturbed. However, even if the day should come when all decision makers respect First Nations oral traditions, big political changes must come before the lands are saved from disruption.

So whether or not we have done the right thing, it has been done. The late Joe Dennison, a Diné chanter who worked his heart out trying to educate decision makers to protect Diné sacred landscapes, told us, "You know what you have to do, so just do it. People will criticize you no matter what you do."

4

DINÉ-ANAASÁZÍ RELATIONS, CLANS, AND ETHNOGENESIS

I F DINÉ ancestors in Navajoland go back to precolumbian times, what kinds of relationships did they have with the precolumbian Anaasází? How did precolumbian people become the People of today? And how do the oral traditions about these relationships bond their descendants to the land? The preceding chapters show how the precolumbian histories of Diné ceremonies instill a sense of the People's long time on the land. This chapter shows that Diné clan histories do the same thing by tying each clan to a unique set of places on the land. The oral histories seamlessly link the documentless precolumbian times with postcolumbian times of endlessly proliferating colonizer documents, some of which can add to what we know about clan histories.

This chapter developed around a core of interviews with Diné living north of Black Mesa from the town of Kayenta west through the Long House Valley and Tsegi Canyon to Shonto, a region full of precolumbian archaeological sites. The present road through the once grassy Long House Valley and on to Kayenta follows a natural corridor between the lofty north face of Black Mesa and the canyon-cut red rock domes to the north. The road follows the northern buffalo/ bead corridor described in chapter 2. Before the modern road was widened around 2015, archaeologists excavated several precolumbian sites in its path. The Navajo Nation Historic Preservation Department (NNHPD), using political sovereignty to advance cultural sovereignty, also required the consultations that we made with local residents about Diné-Anaasází relations.

To plunge the reader into the complexities of Navajo-Anasazi relations, we first offer a few words on names. Hereafter, when giving Navajo oral tradition and Navajo statements about themselves, we replace "Navajo" with "Diné." The region's precolumbian inhabitants have historically been called Anasazi by archaeologists and other scholars, who adopted a Navajo name, Anaasází, following senior archaeologist A. V. Kidder in 1936, who spelled it "Anasazi." Kidder and his colleagues needed a convenient term to cover different types of precolumbian sites that they had originally thought came from different cultural traditions but had later decided came from the same cultural tradition at different times. They latched onto the word for all these sites that they had heard from Navajos who lived around the sites and worked on the archaeological excavations. Kidder translated the term as "Old People," but since then it has been commonly translated as "enemy ancestors," perhaps reflecting the scholarly stereotype of Navajo-Puebloan hostilities owing to Navajo raiding.

Many Diné object to this translation and say that "alien ancestors" more accurately suggests the real meaning—people so remote in the past that one cannot trace exact lines of descent (see Begay 2003; Walters and Rogers 2001; Young and Morgan 1987). Meanwhile, Puebloans have objected to the use of a Diné name for people whom the Puebloans consider to be their ancestors. This objection has led some scholars to substitute "ancestral Puebloan." Many Diné, however, object to the substitution, based on oral traditions that tell of ancestral Diné coexisting with the Anaasází and of certain Diné clans originating from the Anaasází. As discussed below, other Diné, especially members of clans that oral tradition says originated from the Anaasází, use the term Diné bizází (Diné ancestors) or nihizází (our ancestors) or Anoo'sází (Hidden Ancestors). The term Anaasází seems to be most common, at least when Diné talk with researchers, since only this term and not other variants just mentioned appears in the big Diné-language dictionary (Young and Morgan 1987). Whether this term was also common among Diné several generations ago is not clear, however. In their 1910 dictionary, the Franciscan Fathers used the term na'asáz, translated as "wanderers (cliff-dwellers)." Pronunciation and names also may differ regionally and may have changed through time.

Hereafter, we use all these terms, following the usage of the source being discussed. "Anasazi" (with quotation marks) is the archaeologists' usage, and Anaasází is the usage of some Diné, while other Diné use Diné bizází or Anoo'sází. The latter two terms we translate here as "ancestral Diné," a term that we also use (when speaking for ourselves) to include ancestors of Diné clans regardless of their ethnic identity. Otherwise, we use the term "precolumbians" for the people meant by all these terms.

These many and often incompatible usages have become more public owing to the federal Native American Graves Protection and Repatriation Act of 1990 (NAGPRA). That law requires federal agencies and many other institutions such as museums to identify which First Nations groups are "culturally affiliated" with lands and collections of cultural items and human remains "managed" by those institutions for possible return to the groups that claim them. Agencies and institutions also must consult representatives of those groups about "management" (research on, removal of, curation of, repatriation of) the past leavings of those groups under institutional jurisdiction.

This chapter has three parts. First, we review Diné-"Anasazi" connections in the Long House Valley / Tsegi Canyon region that earlier records of Diné traditions reveal. Second, we present the results of our local consultations. Third, we relate these findings to scholarly work on Diné culture history and especially to "how we have become who and where we are," the process of ethnogenesis. All these parts together establish the time depth and intricacy of the bonds between Diné and the land, the foundational bonds of sovereignty fixed by oral tradition as told by elders through ceremonial and clan histories.

EARLIER WORKS

TRADITIONAL DINÉ CEREMONIAL HISTORIES

As shown in chapter 3, youngsters, including would-be hataałis, traveled with elders along routes that ceremonial histories verbally map, intense experiences that bonded them to those landscapes, including the Anaasází places. For Diné in northwestern Navajoland, versions of the Blessingway history and histories of other ceremonies that include precolumbian events around the Long House Valley, Marsh Pass, and Kayenta help make these bonds. In an episode of the Windway ceremonial history, the ceremonial initiate traveled up Navajo Canyon (west of Navajo Mountain), through Marsh Pass, and on south (Wyman 1962:138–157, 162–170). Chapter 2 tells about the one recorded version of the Flintway (Lifeway) ceremonial history, in which a family traveled from the La Plata Mountains through Marsh Pass to the San Francisco Peaks, where the initiate picked up the trail of Holy People embodying both abalone shell and buffalo and followed them back (Haile 1943:166–169).

In a version of the Coyoteway history, the Corn People traveled from the western ocean to Dinnehotso, where they exhausted the game and moved west upstream to settle at Kayenta before moving on to Canyon de Chelly (Luckert and Cooke 1979:2–17). This Corn People's story is much like the Blessingway story of the Water People, who also traveled through Long House Valley, Marsh Pass, and Kayenta, according to some versions (Fishler 1953:91–102; Wyman 1970:447–459). According to one teller, Frank Goldtooth (Fishler 1953:91–102), the Water People consisted of ancestors of the following Diné clans: Mud, Near-to-Water, Bitterwater, Redhouse/Manygoats, and Blacksheep (other tellers name other clans). The people divided into two groups near the San Francisco Peaks, the more northerly travelers going first north and then east. These people settled at Ndeelk'id west of Kayenta (the name refers to the scarp of Black Mesa on the south side of Long House Valley, according to Goldtooth's son; see below). Then they split into two groups, one settling at Betatakin, a 1200s cliff dwelling in lower Tsegi Canyon, and the other settling at Kayenta. The route of the Water People and Corn People through Marsh Pass and Kayenta is part of the northern buffalo/bead corridor.

TRADITIONAL DINÉ CLAN HISTORIES

Clan histories likewise bond clan members to the landscapes of those histories. Each clan has a unique history with many different variants preserved among its members, and these variants, taken together, connect the clan to far-flung places at different times. Members of most clans are widely scattered around Navajoland today as well, so the clan histories tie clan members together in a far-reaching web that also links them to the places in the clan history. Since each Diné is affiliated with three other clans (those of father, mother's father, and father's father) and also has in-laws, the web linking each Diné to people and places is likely to extend all over Navajoland. These webs form the foundation of modern Diné consciousness as a sovereign people, with roots in the land going back to precolumbian times.

In a late 1930s census of Navajoland (Anonymous 1938) that enumerated people by their primary (mother's) clan, 60 percent of Diné belonged to clans that originated with Anaasází directly or through Puebloans, according to clan histories like those given below in this section. The census counted the people in each of the 18 grazing districts into which Washindoon had divided Navajoland to administer stock reduction and soil erosion control.

FIGURE 19 Betatakin, a 1200s cliff dwelling, as seen in 1940. Migrating Diné clans stopped here and lived for a while. Credit: Photograph by Milton Snow, courtesy of Navajo Nation Museum, Window Rock, Arizona, neg. no. NB1-5.

Districts 2 (Shonto) and 8 (Kayenta) encompass the Long House Valley / Tsegi region. Though many clans were represented in these two districts combined, most people belonged to a handful of large clans: Táchii'nii (Red Forehead), Kinłichíí'nii-Tł'ízíłání (Redhouse-Manygoats), Kiiyaa'áanii (Towering House), Tódích'íínii (Bitterwater), Áshįįhí (Salt), Tábąąhá (Edgewater), and Lók'aa' Dine'é (Reed). In the Shonto District, 79 percent of 905 people belonged to these clans, and in Kayenta, 68 percent of 1,666 did. Traditional histories of these clans, based on various sources, are as follows.[1]

RED FOREHEAD

In the 1880s Tall Chanter, recounting the histories and coming together of Diné clans, told army surgeon and anthropologist Washington Matthews (1994:145) that the Red Forehead clan originated from Anaasází who survived the monsters that the two sons of Changing Woman killed off. A Diné elder in 1993 identified a precolumbian hoganlike structure in the lower Grand Canyon as a possible trace of the Anaasází Red Forehead (Anaasází Dine'é Táchii'nii) people, who originated in the Grand Canyon, later moved to Canyon de Chelly, and became Diné (Roberts et al. 1995:27–28). In the early 1900s Kayenta trader Louisa

Wetherill recorded a story from local elder Wolfkiller about Red Forehead people who encountered inhabitants of the precolumbian cliff dwellings, Betatakin and Keet Seel, in Tsegi Canyon (Wetherill and Leake 2007:116–118; see also Comfort 1980:55–56). Some of these cliff dwellers had come from Canyon de Chelly, and others had come from Mesa Verde by way of Navajo Mountain, as drought forced them to move. Some had earlier joined the Diné, while others eventually moved on to the Hopi village of Oraibi.

This story might also trace the precolumbian spread of masked ceremonial dancing (see the section on ethnogenesis below). The archaeologist Byron Cummings (1915, quoted in McPherson [2014:150] and perhaps based on Wolfkiller's story) reported that ceremonialists of the Red Forehead clan, "the oldest Navajo clan," were "the only ones able [to readily interpret] so much prehistoric symbolism." Diné also link Red Forehead with "Anasazi" sites at Wupatki National Monument north of the San Francisco Peaks (Begay and Begay 2003:17) and the Bluebird branch of Red Forehead with "Anasazi" sites in the Chaco and Mesa Verde regions (O'Bryan 1993:115–121).

Anaasází Red Forehead people make up one of many branches of the clan. Other branches correspond to Hopi clans—Deer, Bluebird, Rabbit, Tobacco, Tansy Mustard, and Masked Deities (O'Hara 2004). As Harris Francis, who is Red Forehead of Tobacco branch, learned from his elders, members of some Hopi clans from the village of Awatobi (Tallahoghan) found refuge among the Red Forehead people nearby when Hopis from other villages attacked Awatobi in 1700 and massacred most of its inhabitants (see also Brooks 2016; Brugge 1993b, 1994a:8–9; Courlander 1971:175–184; Kelley and Francis 1998c:700; Reichard 1928:16). The Zuni branch of Red Forehead is related to Zunis (Kelley and Francis 1998c:700, 704). The Squash branch (Preston 1954:25) has the same name as a kinship group (moiety) among the Keresan Pueblos (Ortiz 1979).

According to one teller (Anderson 2018), long ago Diné traveled to trade and raid as far as the Mississippi River, Mexico, the Pacific Ocean, and Canada. They encountered Pawnees who painted their temples red, and the forebears of the Red Forehead clan, who were warriors and fearless defenders, did the same. They "were not restricted in their marriage practices. They could marry anyone," perhaps a reference to the many branches of this clan.

REDHOUSE-MANYGOATS

These two clans are widely considered the same (see also Matthews 1994:146). Redhouse people came from San Juan Pueblo (Franciscan Fathers 1910:430; see

FIGURE 20 White House, Canyon de Chelly, a clan destination and ceremonial origin place dating to 1000s to 1300s. Diné Nightway ceremonial songs (Matthews 1907:26–28) tell of Dawn Boy climbing up to White House with an offering of sacred stones and pollens. Credit: Klara Kelley photo.

also Preston 1954:24; Reichard 1928:16). They also lived among the Anaasází (Begay 2003:59, 62). They are associated with the "Anasazi" site Kin Lichee near Ganado and possibly with Wide Ruins (see chapter 5; Roberts et al. 1995:26), as well as with Wupatki "Anasazi" sites (Begay and Begay 2003:17). They are related to Western Apache clans that originated at Dance Camp (Awatobi) (Goodwin 1942:620). We wonder if some of these people spread from there into northwestern Navajoland after the Awatobi massacre.

TOWERING HOUSE

This clan is associated with the Chacoan "Anasazi" site Kin Yaa'á near Crownpoint, New Mexico (Martin 2002:55; Mitchell 1978:181, 185; Preston 1954:23–24), as well as with Wupatki "Anasazi" sites (Begay and Begay 2003:17; see also Begay 2003:59). The Masked Deities branch of Towering House came from Hopi (Kelley and Francis 1998c:705). The clan is related to Puebloans and to Western Apaches who lived with Puebloans (Preston 1954:23; see also Reichard 1928:16). The Western Apache clan of the same name originated at Dance Camp (Awatobi) (Goodwin 1942:608, 620). Anthropologist Michael O'Hara (2004) has noted that Hopis of the Tansy Mustard clan sought refuge in Canyon de Chelly and became part of the Towering House clan. Tansy Mustard people had earlier connections to Acoma and Laguna and the upper Rio Grande Tewas (Fewkes 1900:610). According to Tuba City Diné chanter Frank Nez (2008), Shonto people regard "Anasazis" of Chaco as ancestors of Towering House people and refer to the "Anasazis" as "our ancestors."

EDGEWATER

The Edgewaters are a Puebloan clan (Begay 2003:61; Preston 1954:25) related to Western Apaches, Zunis, and cliff dwellers (Franciscan Fathers 1910:431). They are said to have originated in the upper Rio Grande, possibly at the late precolumbian / early postcolumbian Pecos Pueblo or (according to David Snow, personal communication, November 22, 2015) at Tano villages to the south. Later they joined the Diné in the upper San Juan, where people from many places and communities had been coming together for a long time to form the Diné (Matthews 1994:142–143; Van Valkenburgh 1999:44). The later Zuni branch of Edgewater came from Zunis fleeing famine (Matthews 1994:142–143, 145). Clan members in northwestern Navajoland may have unrecorded stories about how their forebears came to the region.

SALT

The Salt clan is associated with Chacoan "Anasazi" sites (Haile 1981:174). This clan seems to have come from people of various "Anasazi" and Puebloan communities usually identified as captives and were thereby linked to the clans of their Diné captors, Tsénjikiní (Cliffdwellers) and Edgewater (Matthews 1994:158; Sapir 1942:93). Members are also said to be descendants of captives from a pueblo near a salt lake (Matthews 1994:158), probably meaning Zuni Salt Lake or salt lakes in the eastern Rio Grande region. Some say the Salt people originated at Acoma (Begay 2003:59). In northwestern Navajoland, there is also a branch of this clan descended from Paiutes (Shepardson and Hammond 1970:58–59) probably adopted into the clan.

BITTERWATER

This large clan is spread throughout Navajoland, yet few stories of its origins have been recorded. It is usually identified as one of the Water People. The same clan is reportedly among Zunis and Western Apaches (Forbes 1966:340).

REED

This clan is named from a Puebloan clan (Reichard 1928:16) at Hopi. Clan members ranged around Shonto and Kaibito before the Long Walk, then fled to Black Mesa to escape the Utes (Benally 2006:70). Most (80 percent) Reed clan members in Navajoland were enumerated in the Shonto and Kayenta grazing districts in the late 1930s (Anonymous 1938). For more on this clan, see "New Consultations" below.

OTHER CONNECTIONS

A popular stereotype is that Diné fear the leavings of the Anaasází—their buildings, artifacts, and burials. But actually, to Diné traditionalists, these leavings have power because they belong to the dead, just as do leavings of any deceased person, including Diné. Though one must avoid contact with these remains, certain Diné have been known to use "Anasazi" items, thereby acting out the connections with the Anaasází outlined above. Most users are chanters, who use the items ceremonially and have ceremonial ways to protect themselves. Diné have also collected grinding stones for everyday corn grinding and potsherds for pottery temper (Frisbie 1987:457n20; Kelley and Francis 1998c:709; McPherson 1992:107–109, 2014:155–158).

FIGURE 21 Diné worker restoring the walls of Pueblo Bonito in Chaco Canyon, 1938. Diné workers may have traditional protection ceremonies before working in Anaasází sites. Credit: Photographed by Milton Snow, courtesy of Navajo Nation Museum, Window Rock, Arizona, neg. no. NO16-142.

Some ceremonies require leaving an offering on an Anaasází archaeological site, especially humanlike figurines. These offerings treat children's illnesses, most of which come from a parent's incorrect exposure to things in humanlike form, including Diné or Puebloan masked dancers and their paraphernalia. The figurine is placed where the deity who controls humanlike forms can most easily find it, including at Anaasází ruins (Haile 1947; Kelly et al. 1972).

In Canyon de Chelly, at least, Diné in the past even buried some of their dead in "Anasazi" storage cists (Fall et al. 1981:191). A Kayenta elder recalled for historian Robert McPherson (1992:103) that during Kit Carson's campaign to force people to Fort Sumner, Diné used "Anasazi" ruins as refuges. The same is true of a site at Blue Gap on southern Black Mesa (Downer et al. 1988). Even as late as the 1950s, a Diné family near Shonto built their home amid the structures of an "Anasazi" site (McPherson 1992:103). We suggest that these people, who seemingly violated a strong cultural prohibition, may have considered the local Anaasází as their ancestors. Even though contact with the leavings of one's own deceased people is prohibited, many Diné historically and today have reoccupied homesites of deceased ancestors, though not a dwelling in which someone died or a homesite with a grave.

RECENT CONVERSATIONS ABOUT DINÉ AND PRECOLUMBIANS

In 1997–98 we contacted seven Diné elders and the Diné Spiritual and Cultural Society (Diné [or Navajo] Medicine Men's Association) to discuss the historical relationship between Diné forebears and Anaasází and the proper treatment of Anaasází remains when encountered in the path of construction that cannot avoid them. Consultants freely used the term Anaasází at least partly to address how archaeologists, the Navajo Nation, and the U.S. government were "managing" precolumbian sites under NAGPRA. Of the seven elders consulted, six were chanters, all but one living in the Ganado / Jeddito / Wide Ruins area of west-central Navajoland (Kelley and Francis 1998c).

About connections between Diné and Anaasází, the seven consultants agreed on the following (Kelley and Francis 1998c:702–703). The only people who really knew about the Anaasází are gone; Diné stories do not tell where the Anaasází came from; Anaasází and Diné were alike in how they lived (except for their pottery); the Anaasází were a separate people who emerged on this earth before Diné and other Indigenous groups (but see chapter 1); the Anaasází were destroyed because they painted images of Wind on pottery, and wind or a firestorm therefore destroyed them (opinions differ about whether anyone survived the forces that killed off the Anaasází and whether any modern Diné clans or other tribes can claim descent from the Anaasází); Diné have stories that tell about Anaasází times, and certain Diné ceremonial procedures originated at Anaasází sites when the Anaasází were there or use Anaasází artifacts; improper contact with Anaasází leavings can cause illness or misfortune to Diné who come in contact with them; Diné ceremonies can treat these problems (opinions differ about which ceremonies). Because of these connections between Diné and Anaasází, Diné want government agencies to consult them routinely about protecting Anaasází archaeological sites and graves both on and off Navajo Nation lands. The chanters also offered detailed guidelines for such consultations and related policies.

Since this consultation, we have heard much the same ideas when talking about Diné-Anaasází relations informally with other elders in various parts of Navajoland. Some in the western Navajo Reservation denied that Wupatki or precolumbian dwellings in northwestern Navajoland are Anaasází, associating them instead with (precolumbian) Diné Towering House, Cliffdwellers, Redhouse, and Red Forehead clans (see also Begay and Begay 2003). Some consider these Diné clans to be Anaasází descendants. Elders in Wide Ruins, Ganado area, and the southern Chuska Valley, as well as in Shonto itself during this project, have said that the Anaasází are "our ancestors" (Kelley and Francis 1998a, 2013; Martin et al. 2014). Other recent studies make similar points (Begay 2003; Begay and Begay 2003; Begay and Roberts 2003; Kelley and Francis 2013; McPherson 1992, 2014; Warburton and Begay 2005).

NEW CONSULTATIONS

The statements of people whom we consulted in 2016 are reproduced below. Most emphasize clan connections with the Anaasází either directly or through Puebloans and material continuity between precolumbians and modern Diné on the same land—through descent, using artifacts and sites, and eating a steady diet of corn grown from the same seed stock on the same land. The consultations were mainly in the Diné language, usually mixed with English. The statements below are English paraphrases of each consultation. Brackets enclose our comments and translations of certain terms and phrases.

ALBERT LAUGHTER

Mr. Laughter is a chanter. His father, also a chanter, was Hubert Laughter, the first Diné ranger in the National Park Service (Gilpin 1968:106–107), working at Navajo National Monument. Albert Laughter himself was a ranger at the monument in the 1970s and 1980s. He spoke mostly in English.

Here in Shonto we don't allow anthropological exploitation anymore. The only anthropological work allowed is for homesites and community projects that require archaeological clearance. Construction must avoid archaeological sites if possible. If they find artifacts and so forth, then they do research, maybe remove them from housing project areas. The Division of Natural Resources from Window Rock oversees this work.

About stories of Diné and the "Anasazis," as far as what the anthropologists and archaeologists say, I don't go with that. In the 1970s and 1980s I was a park ranger at Navajo National Monument. I did presentations about Navajo traditional history, about the Four Sacred Mountains and so forth.

I'm Lók'aa' Diné'é [Reed], which came from the Hopis, Kiis'áanii. We call our ancestor "nihichó" [our remote maternal great-plus-grandmothers]—they were here before the Bilagáanas. Nihichó was named Asdzáán Bidee'í, Lady Horn. She was a small lady and came here [from the Hopis] on a donkey. We are all descended from her. That's who we are.

We Diné ourselves here use the [precolumbian] ruins and petroglyphs. The ruins tell us there were people here before us, and we have used their buildings and artifacts. People living here use [precolumbian] potsherds. We have planted in the cornfield areas associated with the sites. We have taken some artifacts from there— projectile points, beads, eagle-bone whistles—these are our ceremonial items.

With that in mind, I contributed to an article titled "Our People, Our Past," published in the *National Geographic*, July 1979, about our clans. We say Anoo'sází, not Anaasází—meaning "Hidden Ancestors" because this was a hidden civilization. These people were here before the Lók'aa' Diné'é, but they are also our ancestors, but more remote. There have always been people here, others before the Anoo'sází.

They [archaeologists] dug some graves. Some say those people were short, but really they were of different heights. They had cornfields and herbs [presumably referring to results of microbotanical studies]. They had petroglyphs in the kivas that were like calendars—the sun moves this way, then that way, and would shine on the petroglyph only at a particular time. They also had petroglyphs of the stars, like Dilyéhé [Pleiades]—these are like ours. Their calendar was like our traditional calendar. Our prayers come from their ruins. I learned from my maternal grandfather, who was also Lók'aa' Diné'é [mother's mother's brother]. His prayers came from Kinníí' Na'ígai [White House Ruin, Canyon de Chelly], prayers for the dawn.

Chanters here have our own prayers and songs. What we generate in this area stays in this area. When I go elsewhere, I listen to the stories and songs there. They differ according to location.

We have [precolumbian] sites all over here, in the dunes, in places where dams are made. No one bothers them. We know how to live with them. Our songs come from them. The Yé'ii Bicheii [masked deity] comes from them. We have gotten corn from these sites and grown more corn with it. The corn here is different from corn elsewhere. We use this corn to pray with—white corn, yellow corn, corn pollen, offered and used for ceremonial footprints, as well as food. We Lók'aa' Dine'é here are known for our corn. We are part of Anoo'sází; that's how our origination is.

Art books from the 1930s show that we have the same ceremonial paraphernalia—projectile points, prayer sticks. Ours are the same as Anoo'sází. And our blackening ceremony is the same. The songs come from them.

There is a clan here, Chíshii Dine'é—a group came here fleeing a fire in their area, said they were from Dzilghą [the White Mountains]. They lived among the people on top of Black Mesa. A young lady from here was sent up there to make food for them. When she came back, she was pregnant. From her originated the Chíshii Dine'é clan [the child would have been "born for" Chishii]. Then Tsi'naajini [Blackwood Streak clan] arose here from the ruins.

In the canyon were also Ts'ílí Dine'é, people with little dogs like chihuahuas. When you're sheepherding in the canyon [Tsegi], you can still hear them barking.

Other tribes came from the Anoo'sází. The Paiutes migrated to use these canyons. Some other tribes whose people came among us have their own generating stories; these stories are not in books. My father was part Paiute—Nóóda'í—the ones that migrate, naadaahii—they traveled together in a line. They came here among the Táchii'nii clan people and were absorbed into that clan. From there the stories extend. Some of these stories go with songs, too.

I'm Lók'aa' Dine'é, born for Nóóda' Dine'é Táchii'nii, Tódích'iinii (Bitterwater) being my maternal grandfathers and Tł'ízíłání-Kinłichíí'nii (Manygoats-Redhouse) being my paternal grandfathers. My children are Tótsohnii (Bigwater). I was born and raised here. This is my mother's family land. (March 14, 2016)

JIMMY BLACK

Mr. Black has a horseback tour business taking people around the surrounding area, including up toward Navajo Mountain. He also works seasonally for the Park Service at Navajo National Monument in the interpretive department, guiding such tours for Navajo National Monument and giving cultural presentations to the tourists. Speaking mostly in English, Mr. Black provided translations of Navajo proper names.

My father, Bob Black, worked for the Park Service at Navajo National Monument. That opened up an opportunity for him to get knowledge of the Anaasází. The name Anaasází means "people of long ago," *not* "enemies." Working in the park's interpretation department, I tell visitors that these people here [Anaasází] were peaceful—there are no weapons at these archaeological sites, only weapons for hunting, such as arrowheads.

My father said that the [Anaasází] people came from the rocks and went back into the rocks. A big tornado or a big fire came—it made me think of a meteorite. In the surrounding area there's lots of wood that clearly burned long ago, but no one has come to take dendrochronology samples of them; they only take such samples from the ruins. The latest date from such a sample was something like 1268. Before that were the Basketmakers, around the year 500. We don't know if these stories are true, the ones from the archaeologists. Here at my homesite, a friend said there was a farming area. There was seepage from the cliffs. Studies show that corn originated from the Rio Grande valley [see chapter 2]. Before that, [precolumbian] people ate such things as wild berries, including juniper berries.

My father was of Kinłichíi'nii clan and said that the clan came from Hopis. The same is true of certain other clans, and through the Hopis they are related to the Anaasází. Therefore, we Navajos respect the Anaasází.

In the 1950s, the roads from Black Mesa and elsewhere were bulldozed through and exposed Anaasází archaeological sites.

Some believe that the Navajos came through here in the 1700s and 1800s. Our [Diné] stories say we came from southwestern Colorado [Emergence Place], but anthros say we came from the north. We pick up arrowheads to use ceremonially for protection—just like on the Navajo Nation seal.

Younger [Diné] people need to be taught. They think they *own* land, but it is just borrowed. It is trust land. Once it was different, but we made an agreement with the [U.S.] government so we could lead a different life [refers to the 1868 treaty], and that agreement turned our land into federal land that we have "borrowed." Our daily technology today has come from the Bilagaanas.

When I take people on tours, I tell them a story about the storage room. Here people stored food away from the village. When in need they would go out and get that food, not like now, where we just run to the store. The people here were very conservative, I am sure. They lived off the land. Now we [Diné] don't do that.

I am Bitterwater clan, people who worked their way eastward [he refers to the migration of the Water People after they were created by Changing Woman in the west]. Most people in this area are Bitterwater. My father's clan, Kinłichíí'nii, Red-house, is linked to Tsénjikinii, Cliffdwellers, and Kiiyaa'áanii, Towering House. My maternal grandfather was Yé'ii Dine'é Táchii'nii, and my paternal grandfather was Tsi'naajinii and Salt. About Yé'ii Dine'é Táchii'nii—Yé'ii refers to deities. I was told the clan came from Paiutes and Utes, but it could have come from Hopi. Mainly, our ancestors are Puebloan from the Rio Grande, like Jemez. (March 7, 2016)

HARRY GOLDTOOTH

Mr. Goldtooth was born in 1936 into the Bįįh Bitoodnii (Deer Spring) clan and born for Tł'ááshchí'í (Red Bottom). His father, Frank Goldtooth, was a chanter well known throughout Navajoland. In 1950 Frank Goldtooth recorded a long narrative of Diné traditional history, including the story of the Water People who passed through Long House Valley, described above (Fishler 1953). The Navajo culture magazine *Leading the Way* (vol. 11, nos. 9 and 10 [2013]) has published two articles in which Harry Goldtooth offers a tour of sacred places on the plateau east of the Grand Canyon. Our consultation with Mr. Goldtooth occurred on two days, first at his home in Tuba City and then on a drive between Tuba City and Kayenta. He spoke in both Diné and English; we have preserved his usage and translations of proper names in the following.

In 1955 I worked for the BIA on the engineering survey of what is now U.S. Route 160. In the Long House Valley area, bulldozers leveled the road corridor and exposed [precolumbian] sites, while surveyors inspected drainages down the northern face of Black Mesa. The whole area is full of [precolumbian] sites. . . .

[HF asked about Diné, rather than archaeological, stories about Anaasází in this area.] My father told such stories. Changing Woman had a Kinaaldá [girls' coming-of-age ceremony, part of the Blessingway] near the San Francisco Peaks, and from there the people [Water People] came to Eldon Spring northeast of Flagstaff. There they divided. One group went east through Leupp, and the other went northeast. That group went to the spring above the petroglyphs near Moenave [Tutuveni National Register site], then to the Long House Valley, where they lived for a while. My father said there was a dam there made of long rock slabs that could [impound enough water to] irrigate the whole area around Kayenta. They settled at Bitáátahkin. Then they went to the foot of the mesa west of Kayenta, where there is a big area covered with potsherds, which were theirs.

The travelers continued to Verde Mesa [Mesa Verde] and to Alamosa near Sis Naajinii, the eastern sacred mountain.

[Two days later, driving between Tuba City and Kayenta, Mr. Goldtooth told us the following. We have eliminated repetition of information from the first consultation.]

This is the way that the Tódích'íí'nii [Bitterwater] people migrated.

[At Middle Mesa] the people offered turquoise for safe travel, and people still do so today.

The people took separate routes from the San Francisco Peaks. The Tódích'íí'nii group went northeast to Tséyaató [Cortez], then to one of the Mesa Verde ruins, then Dolores, then Alamosa near Sisnaajinii. The Kiiyaa'áanii [Towering House] group went to Winslow, Snowflake, Springerville, and Acoma. At Acoma, some used hand- and toeholds to climb the mesa and from that got the name Dziłtáá'nii [Hillface People, another Diné clan]. Those at the bottom were Kiiyaa'áanii. Then they moved to the lava buttes near Rio Rancho [Albuquerque west mesa volcanoes], then to Santa Fe, Española, Taos, and on to Alamosa. At Alamosa, all planted, and that is the location of Dá'ák'eh Hóteel, the Wide Cornfield in the ceremonial songs. There the Holy People taught them songs and prayers.

At some ruins along Route 160 lived the K'aa' Dine'é, Arrow People—they had long arrowheads like ours. These were our ancestors, danihizází. They moved back to Navajo Mountain. These people all used to be called Diné binaa'zází. Bilagaanas mispronounced it as "Anasazi."

The Elephant's Feet [an outcropping landmark along Route 160 near Tonalea] were once a boy and a girl. They were digging onions on the mountain [Black Mesa to the south] when the people came through. There they were turned to stone to mark the migration route for the future.

Along this part [southwest of Cow Springs] are pottery sites left by Manygoats-Redhouse people and the related clans Deeshchíí'nii, Tł'ááshchí'í, and Tsi'naajinii. Tódích'íí'nii and Kiiyaa'áanii were from Holy People [Water People, implying that the other clans were different and linked up with individual Water People clan forebears as the Water People passed through].

From Cow Springs [northeast] are lots of sites all along the highway. People planted in this valley. Some stayed here; others went on. Some also were at Preston Mesa [north of Tuba City], where the Twin War Gods [monster-slaying sons of

FIGURE 22 Aghaa'łá near Kayenta, Arizona, a clan migration stopping place. Diné have made rain prayers here for storms to come from the Pacific, as did the precolumbian Water People. Credit: Klara Kelley photo.

Changing Woman] had a place with two pine trees where people prayed until someone recently cut down the trees.

Ndeelk'id is the name of the rim of Black Mesa overlooking the Long House Valley. . . . People of the Long House Valley were Bééshiist'ogí Diné'é, Long-Arrow People. The occupants of Betáátahkin were nihizází [our ancestors].

[In the Kayenta area,] there are sites all along Laguna Creek, also orchards in the canyons. These were not planted by modern people. The fruits are called jiłhazhí [hackberry, elderberry; another name is béégháázhí, "gnawed on," and they are like wild apricots]. The [precolumbian] Diné bizází planted them.

At Aghaa'łá [a volcanic outcrop north of Kayenta], people turned into the volcanic spires to mark the route of the travels of the people

Ruins in the Grand Canyon were where the Yé'ii Diné'é [Masked Deities clan] came from. (March 9, 2016)

HOSKIE BLACK

Mr. Black is of the Bitterwater clan born for Redhouse-Manygoats, with Reed as his mother's father's clan and Salt as his father's father's clan. He performs traditional Diné ceremonies and also Native American Church ceremonies. He spoke entirely in Diné.

> I was born here in a forked-stick hogan and raised here. We farmed in the Long House Valley. Back then there was lots of rain and lots of fields, but not today. I was one of six siblings, three of whom are now left. I went to school in Phoenix, then Chilocco [Oklahoma], for a total of six, seven, eight years. Then I joined the National Guard.
>
> The Anasazis looked like us, with long hair. They lived in nástł'ah [alcoves], which have been disturbed. I don't know if they had clans like Diné. All we have is our ceremonies, our pollen pouches, our protective arrowheads [bééshiist'ogii]. The Bilagaanas came across, then missionaries, and now we are going crazy, burning our jish [ceremonial bundles; may refer to an evangelical Christian ceremony at Lower Greasewood in 1976 when jish reportedly were burned (Frisbie 1987:185, 207, 452n27)]. There used to be many chanters, but not now. Only our ceremonies help us.
>
> The Hopis say the Anaasází are theirs. They copy designs off Anaasází pottery and then say the Anaasází pottery is theirs [maybe referring to the historical revival of Sikyatki yellowwares ca. 1900 by Nampeyo].
>
> My father was Manygoats-Redhouse and worked for the Park Service at Navajo National Monument. [HF asked about Táchii'nii people being connected to the cliff dwelling Betatakin.] My father worked on the stabilization of the ruin, so maybe it now looks more like a Manygoats-Redhouse site! (March 10, 2016)

NAME WITHHELD BY REQUEST

The consultant is a chanter who lives near Kayenta. He spoke entirely in Diné.

> Yes, the Anaasází were nihizází [our ancestors], as they say. We came from them, as they say. [HF asked about clans that might be connected to the Anaasází, like Táchii'nii.] I'm Yé'ii Dine'é Táchii'nii, and that clan came from Tséyi' near Chinle [Canyon de Chelly].

ETHNOGENESIS

We have shown that many Diné claim cultural connections with the "Anasazi," which they base on Diné ceremonial and clan histories. (Here, when giving scholarly views, we follow scholarly usage for group names, if necessary for clarity, including "Navajo" for modern Diné.) Yet as shown in chapter 1, archaeological tradition contradicts this claim, asserting instead that the Navajos, or "southern Athabaskans" (speakers of Navajo and Apache languages), migrated into what is now the U.S. Southwest around 1500, two centuries after Anasazi occupation ended in most of Navajoland. Chapter 1 shows that this notion is based on flawed assumptions and interpretations of scholarly data.

Navajo and Western Apache oral traditions identify precolumbian and postcolumbian Puebloan peoples as ancestors of certain Navajo and Western Apache clans. Members of clans connected to Puebloan-Anasazis are numerous not only in the Long House Valley / Tsegi region but also throughout Navajoland. In 1938, 60 percent of all Navajos belonged to clans with connections to Puebloans or Anaasází.[2] Owing to the connection of each Navajo to three other clans besides mother's clan, most Navajos probably have a clan link to Anaasází either directly or through more recent Puebloans. These mixed ancestries also show up in recent genetic studies: among Navajos are both genetic material found among Northern Athabaskans but not among Puebloans and genetic material found among Puebloans but not among Northern Athabaskans. The geneticists also suggest that the southward-moving Athabaskan population was small and absorbed people from other groups along the way, until in the Southwest Puebloans greatly enlarged it (Barbujani 1997; Carlyle et al. 2000; Lorenz and Smith 1996; Malhi 2012; Smith et al. 1999, 2000; Torroni et al. 1992). (In 2002 the Navajo Nation government placed a moratorium on genetic research, which it is now reconsidering [Denetclaw 2017].)

As chapters 1 and 2 show, Navajo oral traditions identify precolumbian "Anasazi" archaeological sites as sources of many ceremonial elements and practices. Navajo and Puebloan ceremonial and oral traditions, together with everyday material culture (architecture and artifacts) and the technologies used to produce them, have much in common.[3] Many scholars believe that having so much in common most likely reflects a long period of interaction (Opler 1983:373; Riley 2005:194, 242n53; Towner 2003:17–19, 212–216; see also Seymour, ed. 2012). Also, Navajos and Apaches share many culture elements with other peoples between Canada and Mexico (Carter 2009:13–23). Perhaps these widely shared cultural elements resulted from a precolumbian "interaction sphere" embracing the Great Basin, the Southwest, the western Great Plains, and northern Mesoamerica (Upham 2000). Chapter 2 is about what may have been the southern part of this interaction sphere.

Reports of the earliest Spanish ventures into the traditional Navajo homeland, 1540 and 1583, mention "Corechos" in southeastern Arizona and around Acoma and Hopi, as well as farther east around Pecos Pueblo in the Rio Grande basin. Many scholars consider the Corechos to be Southern Athabaskans (Blakeslee et al. 2003; Brugge 1983:490; Opler 1983:387; Riley 1995:90, 221; Wilcox et al. 2006:204; Wilshusen 2010:196). Thus, Navajo Athabaskan ancestors were already widespread throughout the traditional Navajo and Apache homelands when the Spanish arrived. They were too widespread to have first appeared in the region only a couple of generations earlier. And of course, Puebloan ancestors of certain Navajo clans are prominent in the Spanish documents from the very first reports, those of the 1539–41 Coronado expeditions.

So how did the ancestral Diné who were Anaasází and Puebloan and the ancestral Diné who were Athabaskan become the Diné also known as Navajos? The answer is "ethnogenesis," the process of becoming a distinct people. According to scholars today, ethnogenesis is the process by which a group develops a shared identity, culture, and history, usually during a time of dramatic environmental or political change (Anderson 1999:268n2; Liebmann and Preucel 2007; Mills 2002:85–86; see also Brooks 2002, 2016; Carter 2009). Ethnogenesis involves a merging of peoples with different histories, who then need a common way to organize both relationships among themselves and dealings with other groups. The process of making a common identity is likely to involve adjusting traditional social relations and belief systems to cover the whole emerging group. The traditions of the individual groups are reinterpreted to cover the emerging whole. The resulting merger, a network of smaller groups, may or may not last for a long time. Marriages among the smaller groups, as in a network of exogamous clans, make a strong way to hold the merger together. But ethnogenesis also can involve each smaller group trying to keep some kind of identity within the larger merger. Therefore, ethnogenesis contains contradictions and is always going on more or less dramatically, so group identities often change.

The practices of taking captives and marriages between different ethnic groups, as described by James Brooks (2002), could have been underpinnings for ethnogenesis. These practices go with conflict and trade between ethnic groups. As chapter 5 shows, trade and conflict can go on at the same time between two ethnic groups, as some communities within them raid each other, while others trade. Groups linked by marriages and captives can get into each other's resources in times of extreme need. In times of ethnogenesis, the need is extreme enough that groups coping through the earlier links of captives and marriages may end up merging permanently.

Late precolumbian and early postcolumbian times spanned several times of trouble, with ethnogenesis surely boiling up during catastrophes and simmering in between (Glowacki 2015:133–173; see also Wilshusen 2010). Diné stories reflect these times. One such time may have been the flowering of the ceremonial region centered on Chaco Canyon, 900–1150, which archaeologists consider a time of peace between times of violence (see LeBlanc 1999:120, 153; Lekson 2008). The Navajo story of the Great Gambler hints at an episode of ethnogenesis during those centuries. People came to Chaco from far and wide, there to be enslaved, until a young man toppled the Gambler, and the people moved away (Haile 1978:63–108; Matthews 1994: 82–87; O'Bryan 1993:50–62; Wheelwright 1946:98–100). Another hint is the story of the warrior brothers slaying the monsters (naayéé', "alien gods") who had cannibalized and (almost) wiped out the Anaasází (Haile 1981:189–205; Matthews 1994:116–132; Wyman 1970:550–577). Almost every one of the brothers' acts of iconoclasm (cutting down a powerful being) happened in the Chaco heartland. Then there is the Navajo story that wind, fire, and floods destroyed the Anaasází because they painted the images of these powerful beings on their pottery.[4]

These stories can't help but remind us of the archaeologists' story about how climate change forced the "Anasazi" to leave the Colorado Plateau by 1300. Earlier, a drought in the mid-1100s ended Chaco's heyday, and the late 1200s brought an even longer drought and unpredictable weather. Iconoclasm seems to go with ethnogenesis, when people try to discredit and recharacterize some of the old deities. They need to change their relationships to deities to help (or maybe prevent) the merging of groups. Though deities may be timeless, what people know and teach about them can change.

Another episode of ethnogenesis may have been in the 1300s and 1400s. During that time, as chapter 2 tells, archaeologists think that refugees from the Colorado Plateau were living among earlier residents of the Rio Grande valley and in southern Arizona, where they formed many bigger communities (Adams 1991; Carter 2009:215–279; Dean et al. 1985; Duff 2002; Glowacki 2015; Towner 2002). At the same time, the city of Paquimé (Casas Grandes) in the lower Rio Grande basin of northern Mexico may have taken Chaco's place, unifying a hinterland in the Southwest that encompassed Puebloans and ancestral Navajo-Apacheans (Lekson 2009, 2015; Riley 2005). The shift in trade networks south and east of Chaco after 1300, described in chapter 2, was part of the rise of

Casas Grandes. Communities interacting in this hinterland created similarities between masked-deity ceremonialism at Casas Grandes and Southwestern Puebloans, Apaches, and Navajos (Griffith 1983:764). Scholars say that modern Puebloan communities emerged during the upheavals of this time. They suggest that ceremonialism centered on masked deities (Katsinas) became a unifying force (Adams 1991; Duff 2002; Lekson 2009; Riley 2005).

Several Navajo stories may hint at this episode. One tells how precolumbians destroyed Chaco's successor, what is now Aztec Ruins (Wheelwright 1951; Wyman 1975:237–244), which archaeological evidence shows was ceremonially "decommissioned" and burned (Glowacki 2015:208; LeBlanc 1999:233; Lekson 2009). Afterward, two young women assembled what are now the Navajo Mountaintopway and Beautyway ceremonial repertoires. The stories peak in performances organized by the Rio Grande Pueblos. The story of the Water People migrating from the Pacific coast after the Anaasází were destroyed may refer to the migrations that started with the great drought of the late 1200s (see chapter 1). The story hints at a network of local groups (clans in the making) linked by kinlike trading partnerships, perhaps a last use of trade routes of "Anasazi" times, even as Casas Grandes was widening its influence. As mentioned in chapter 1, some scholars think that the sites of the 1400s to 1600s that archaeologists recognize as ancestral Navajo were left by Athabaskans moving into the area to fill a vacuum left by the "Anasazi." However, these sites might simply manifest an earlier ancestral Navajo presence previously masked by "Anasazi" archaeological manifestations (Brugge 1992, 2006, 2012; Snow 2006; see also Carter 2009:35–37; Glowacki 2015:203).

Another episode started in the 1600s, when Spanish colonizers started trading slaves, triggered epidemics, and seized land, resources, and possessions, especially among the Puebloans (Carter 2009; Brooks 2016; Brugge 1969; Preucel 2002; Weber 1999). Puebloans moved again to crowd into fewer, larger settlements in the upper Rio Grande basin and also farther west at Acoma, Laguna, Zuni, and Hopi. At the same time, Puebloans fell prey to Spanish slaving, epidemics, and starvation. Survivors "voluntarily" sought refuge not only in other Puebloan settlements but also among Southern Athabaskans and other "nomadic" groups. In 1680 the Puebloans united and drove the Spanish out. Many scholars consider this "Pueblo Revolt" a "nativistic" or "revitalization" movement whereby the Puebloans tried to return to their traditions, especially the shared Katsina ceremonialism. At the same time, the Puebloans may have reinterpreted these traditions to combine variations among the different

Puebloan communities (see, e.g., Carter 2009:56–58; Liebmann and Preucel 2007; Preucel 2002; Weber 1999).

Few scholars have addressed the question when modern Navajo self-identity emerged (many ignore ethnogenesis and assume that Navajo self-identity is timeless). Those few seem to agree that Navajo ethnogenesis was probably under way in the 1600s and 1700s. Moves of people are evident mainly from Navajo clan histories (Matthews 1994:135–159) and Spanish documents (see Brugge 1969; Correll 1976). These sources show Puebloans moving among ancestral Navajos. Scholars have long recognized that "Dinetah" (the upper San Juan region) was the scene of Navajos and Puebloans coming together. This region is full of Puebloan-like multiroom masonry "pueblitos" alongside Navajo forked-stick hogans. Early archaeologists thought that Puebloans built the pueblitos as they took refuge with Navajos after the Pueblo Revolt and Spanish Reconquest (1680–96). Tree-ring dating since the mid-1900s shows that the pueblitos were actually built decades later (Towner 2003), though many scholars still consider the region a place where Navajos and Puebloans came together.

The most coherent account of Navajo ethnogenesis is the story of Hataałii Nééz (Tall Chanter) that Matthews (1994) recorded in the 1880s. Tall Chanter described waves of groups from all over the Southwest coming together in this region over a long period of time, where they reidentified themselves and each other as clans. The story begins with the Mesa Verde Anasazi cliff dwellings, people from which became the Tsénjikiní (Cliffdwellers) clan, and ends with the pueblitos, thereby covering the centuries from the 1200s and 1300s to the 1700s. Since clanship is based on exogamy, members of these groups could only marry members of other groups, thereby forming a kinship web that tied them together into a single people. According to Tall Chanter, leaders got together to work out a common language and shared other practices. We suggest that as the People came together, they developed the Mothway ceremony to transform each refugee into one of the People, thus subjecting them to marriage outside their own group, which could then be recognized as a clan. This ceremony was recorded around 1930 (Haile 1978), when it was used to treat people with seizures or involved with incest, and is now little used (Levy et al. 1995). Since people from various Pueblos speak different languages, the Navajo language also would have been a practical common language.

Scholars have also identified what they think are new ceremonial forms in the late 1600s to 1700s. Brugge (1981:15–16, 19–21) suggested that Navajo ethnogenesis occurred during the 1700s, when ancestral Navajos rejected Puebloan cultural elements that came in with the refugees after the Pueblo Revolt. The result was Blessingway ceremonialism something like that of the present, including emphasis on the forked-stick hogan as the original Navajo dwelling form (both forked-stick dwellings and pottery were evident among ancestral Navajos by 1500 if not earlier; see chapter 1). Anthropologist John Farella (1984:183–184) has added that Blessingway emphasizes the revival of previous life forms. In contrast to Brugge, Diné scholar Harry Walters (1991) has suggested that Blessingway developed in precolumbian times, as evident from the fact that in the Blessingway history narratives there are no metal artifacts, wheeled vehicles, Europeans, and domesticated animals (the last appearing only at the end of the Blessingway ceremonial history). Similarly, dendrochronologist Ronald Towner (2003) has suggested that Navajo ethnogenesis was a longer and more complex process than Brugge proposed.

We have found Brugge's formulation somewhat at odds with how much Blessingway oral tradition and Navajo material culture of the 1700s have in common with Puebloan (Kelley and Francis 1994:216–220). We have suggested that if there was a "nativistic" movement among Navajo ancestors (merged Athabaskans and Puebloans) at that time, it might have been their reaction against the Spanish-influenced, apparently "Christianized" Pueblos. This reaction could show up in Blessingway's emphasis on earlier traditions common to Southern Athabaskan and Puebloan culture (going back to what archaeologists call the beginnings of agriculture in the "Archaic" period), such as ceremonialism relating to corn. Reinterpretation of earlier traditions may be evident in the precolumbian elements in Blessingway that Walters emphasizes.

If Blessingway practice and story took their modern form in the 1700s, they surely reorganized earlier ceremonial stories and practices. We wonder if such earlier stories and practices could have been an old form of Blessingway that defined a late precolumbian Southern Athabaskan identity. (The girls' coming-of-age ceremonies among Mescalero and White Mountain Apaches might offer clues when compared to Blessingway.) The Blessingway origin story tells that the events of Blessingway go back to remote precolumbian times, though ancestral Navajos did not learn the ceremony in its present form until the clans coalesced, when Changing Woman taught two children the repertoire. Chanter Steven Begay told us, "I would say Blessingway is part of a very early ancestral life way ideology, which is the basic foundation of horticulture-subsistent groups, which describes the majority of the 'tribes' of the Southwest.

A [ceremonial] mentor of mine mentions a very old 'ancestral' culture [from] which all southwestern tribes originated—Anaasází" (personal communication, January 19, 2017).

By the mid-1700s, according to archaeological evidence, Navajo ceremonialism, at least in Dinetah, also included the masked deities of the Nightway ceremony. Nightway is probably the largest and most complex of all Navajo repertoires and no doubt incorporates earlier ceremonial practices. The Nightway masked deities have much in common with Puebloan Katsinas (Brugge 1996a). More evidence of this ceremonialism is in the ceremonial histories (Wyman 1957:129–142, 1975:237–244), which feature Navajo forebears holding public performances of masked dancing and inviting people from post-1300 to 1400 Puebloan settlements. Western Apaches have similar masked deity dancers, embodiments of beings who inhabit Puebloan archaeological sites of the 1400s.

A Navajo traditional history in the Nightway ceremonial repertoire tells of two children of a young woman and a masked deity from Anaasází White House in Canyon de Chelly. The children were wounded in a rock fall and begged deities everywhere for a cure. Finally, through trickery, the two got beads from Tallahogan (Awatovi) for their father's fee to do the curing ceremony, which they learned and passed down in the Nightway repertoire (Matthews 1978:212–265). This story seems to offer a line of descent for masked deity ceremonialism from pre-1300 White House and "protohistoric" Awatobi.

The Navajos and Western Apaches thus had (and have) their own distinct versions of masked deity ceremonialism. Southern Athabaskans in the 1600s and 1700s evidently took part in pansouthwestern masked deity ceremonialism and may well have done so since the 1300s or 1400s. The central figure in the Blessingway, Changing Woman, the protector of the Navajo people, taught the Blessingway repertoire to the children of a masked deity of the southern sacred mountain, Mount Taylor, a mountain also sacred to Acoma and Laguna people (Wyman 1970:141, 220, 513). Here is a hint that a transfer of power from masked deities to Changing Woman occurred when the clans formed.

And what about sovereignty during ethnogenesis? In Tall Chanter's telling, leaders of equal status met to negotiate a common language and cultural practices (see also chapter 5 on the naachid). Leaders might have encouraged people to extend the clan system (k'éí), with its rule of kinlike cooperation and sharing (k'é), including through marriage outside the clan, and to make Blessingway the foundational ceremony, with its emphasis on peace and harmony (hózhǫ́), the three foundations of modern Diné cultural sovereignty (Austin

2009). Perhaps that is also why the People came to recognize Changing Woman as their main protector: she has counterparts among most southwestern and Great Basin groups, and unlike the masked deities who had earlier unified people, she embodies k'é, k'é í, and hózhǫ.

The upper San Juan region has received most attention as the scene of Navajo ethnogenesis and the first earthly home of Changing Woman. But something similar was also happening farther west. According to Navajo and Western Apache oral traditions about clan origins, their ancestors lived east of today's Hopi villages in and around Awatobi (Dance Camp in Western Apache, House of Chants in Navajo, names that sound similar in the two languages). These ancestors included the Hopi Tobacco clan, Jemez and Acoma immigrants to Hopi, and Southern Athabaskans scattered in the surrounding area: Towering House, Redhouse/Manygoats, Red Streak, and Red Forehead clan people (Brugge 1966a, 1985, 1994; Goodwin 1942; Kelley and Francis 1998c; O'Hara 2004; Yava 1978:88–97; see also Brooks 2016). Early Spanish visitors in the 1500s and early 1600s found Athabaskans ("Corechos") there (Espinosa 1934:112; Hammond and Rey 1966:189; Hodge et al. 1945:217; Tyler and Taylor 1958:286–287). As mentioned in the clan histories above, after people from the present Hopi mesas attacked Awatobi around 1700, the survivors took refuge among Southern Athabaskans to the north and south and married in. They contributed elements from Awatobi to the cultures that came to distinguish Navajos and Western Apaches before they grew apart geographically and in their self-identities.

Ethnogenesis in western Navajoland that followed the Awatobi massacre might have left traces in the origin histories and other parts of the repertoires of certain Navajo ceremonies (as well as other stories; see chapter 5). For example, a Frenzyway (Ajiłee) story tells how the ceremonial repertoire developed during the wandering of people looking for tansy mustard between Chaco and Awatobi (Haile 1978). This story reminds one of the migration story of the people who became the Tansy Mustard clan that Hopis told to anthropologist Jesse Walter Fewkes (1900:610–613). Similar connections seem evident between the Red Antway repertoire and late precolumbian people of the Lava Buttes region south of the Hopi Mesas, many of whom may have become part of emerging Zuni (Brugge 1993b; Wyman 1965); same for the Upward-Reachingway repertoire and the Zuni Emergence story (Cushing and Wright 1988; Haile 1981), as well as Navajo Windway and the Hopi Snake clan (Fewkes 1900:587–588; Wyman 1962).

As members of these different groups merged with the Diné, we suggest, they formed a shared ceremonial framework that absorbed their separate ceremonialisms and migration histories. Thus stories that were originally held within a clan could have become parts of ceremonial repertoires available to all. This shared framework perhaps took its form from what the ceremonies of the merging groups already had in common. It had to fit with the lives of small extended families, scattered and constantly moving, so it did not include big Puebloan-type village ceremonies that demanded a lot of closely coordinated workers or timing with celestial events known only to a handful of specialists. Later, the People came to tie the ceremonies even closer together by putting Blessingway above the other ceremonies. The people included certain Blessingway songs and prayers in the other repertoires, and they related events of various ceremonial histories to the main stalk of Blessingway events, as in the 1880s narrative recorded by Matthews (1994) and the 1928 one recorded by Aileen O'Bryan (1993).

By the late 1700s, violence had sent residents from both Dinetah and Awatobi/Tallahogan into the hinterlands. In the east, warfare with Utes, Comanches, and Spanish forced people out of the upper San Juan westward into the Chuska Valley and Canyon de Chelly. In the west, the Awatobi massacre and perhaps other fighting around Hopi had sent people to southern Black Mesa, Canyon de Chelly, and the Mogollon Rim (see chapter 5). Both Navajo clan histories and Spanish documents suggest that these hinterlands were already thinly populated by Athabaskans, probably including Towering House, Red Forehead, the Water People, and the groups they had encountered on their late precolumbian way east.

These moves of people also brought to their modern form two pillars of Navajo culture and identity: the Navajoland-wide clan networks, and the herding way of life. By the early 1700s, Navajo ancestors were raising horses, sheep, and goats (Hill 1940c). Perhaps they raised sheep and goats as much for wool to make tradeable textiles as for meat and milk. In some versions of Blessingway history, after Changing Woman taught Blessingway to earth-surface children, she placed sheep, cows, and horses on Sisnaateel (Wide Belt Mesa), the gateway from the upper San Juan into the Rio Grande basin (Klah 1942:124), or the children themselves left horse images there (O'Bryan 1993:175–181). Presumably after doing ceremonies with figurines from Wide Belt Mesa, Navajos then got stock by trading or raiding with Spanish and Puebloans, as Navajo family histories and colonial documents attest (Kelley and Francis 1994:204, 220).

This was especially the case in the east (Hill 1940c; Towner 2003). The west was farther from tradeable or raidable livestock, other than that of the Awatobi friars and the Hopis, so the Navajo ancestors there probably depended more on hunting and gathering than the easterners did. The herding way of life was a sort of compromise between the more mobile Athabaskan hunting and gathering with a little farming and the more settled Puebloan farming with a little hunting and gathering. It helped people to avoid the slave raiders and plunderers whom colonialism had unleashed and let more people subsist in the unfarmable hinterlands than could do so by hunting and gathering alone.

The geographical organization of what we now consider traditional Navajo society suits the herding way of life and may be rooted in earlier Diné hunter-gatherer-farmers (see chapter 1). Navajo life histories (Left-Handed 1967 [1938], 1980; Mitchell 2001; Mitchell 2003), other oral accounts (Navajo Land Claim Collection, Navajo statements), and the works of anthropologists (Fanale 1982; Hill 1940b) have portrayed Navajo communities as loosely defined geographical zones with residents linked by kinship and other social ties. We emphasize, though, that the social ties and the family moves tend to blur the geographical limits. Clan relations are an important factor in Navajo kinship. From personal experience and decades of Navajo community studies (including our own), we know that, historically, the People have tended to marry into neighboring families. Because of clan-based marriage restrictions, members of an extended family will have ties to most of their neighbors, who in turn have ties to most of their neighbors, and so on. These links form a clan-based web over a very large region. These webs (like earlier ties between neighboring hunter-gatherer bands and ties through captives and ethnic intermarriage) helped families get temporary access to distant range and water when their own customary use areas could not support them (Fanale 1982).

The decentralized webs and constantly moving families tended to keep geographically distinct local communities from forming. But other factors centered parts of such webs in certain places. Centers included places where people could come together to farm and also big, dependable water sources, both rather rare in Navajoland. Another kind of center was the home base of a local leader, usually an older man with ceremonial power and a lot of livestock, informally chosen by the relatives living around him. These were probably the main centralizing factors before the late 1800s (Hill 1940b).

Navajo and Western Apache identities, we suggest, may not have become clearly distinct, at least on the southern and western edges of Navajoland, until around 1800 (see Curley 2014:32). Among all the Apache groups, the Western Apache language and culture seem to have most in common with Navajo (Goodwin 1942; Young 1983). An even more recent episode of ethnogenesis may have enhanced the separation during the late 1800s reservation period, after military conquest and settler encroachment. Then Navajos and Apaches became separated geographically, confined to small parts of their ranges, or even relocated entirely.

Of course, today we see among Diné, as among other First Nations peoples, a struggle to keep their distinct ethnic identities in the face of U.S. national political economy and culture. For ethnogenesis involves not only historically distinct groups merging but also groups keeping distinct identities within the merger (see Brooks 2016 for examples; also Seymour, ed. 2012:390–394). This push against complete assimilation seems to be why Diné clan histories have survived down to the present. Same for the different stories among Diné about relationships to the people whom the archaeologists have historically called "Anasazi." The struggle for cultural sovereignty itself is part of ongoing ethnogenesis.

Finally, to wrap it all up, we come back to the question of names. A self-identified group has a name for itself. What happens to the name during ethnogenesis? Speakers of Athabaskan languages have always called themselves by variants of "Diné." Therefore, it seems that the name goes with the speech community, changing slightly among groups within the speech community as they separate. With ethnogenesis, people from other speech communities join in and change their language. The name for the speech community persists, even though it now has members with different past culture histories and languages. The name "Diné" thus hides the identities of the many peoples—Puebloans, Utes, others—who joined the Diné. But the clan histories and clan names tell us who these other peoples were. They include Puebloan descendants of the Anaasází, even the Anaasází themselves, all having come together on the same land base to which these stories bond the descendants as a self-conscious sovereign people.

What about the name "Navajo"? Diné often call themselves by this name, too, especially when using the English language. Other tribes have their own names for Navajos, including Zunis, whose name, Apachu, also covers other Apacheans. The name Navajo may have come from Rio Grande Tewas (Brugge et al. 1983; de Reuse 1983). The name was first imposed by Spanish colonial authorities, and the "Americans" took it up when they took over. When people call themselves Navajos, they are identifying themselves in relation to mainstream U.S. society and culture. Here is the part of ethnogenesis that involves holding on to your identity even as you are being absorbed into a larger group, using a name that distinguishes you from the larger group that supplied the name. With the onslaught of mainstream culture through public education and mass commercial entertainment (and even the "pan-Indianism" that counters the mainstream), people rightly worry about losing language, culture, and a sense of "who we are." But people know what must be done. Keep the language alive, yes. Just as important, keep names and the oral histories alive.

In this chapter we have discussed how the modern Diné emerged from various groups within and around Navajoland through episodes of ethnogenesis that likely go back to precolumbian times. In the most recent episode, members of these groups coming together reidentified themselves as exogamous, intermarrying clans, thereby forming the Diné clan system. This vast and intricate network spread across Navajoland and, through the mutual responsibilities of kin, allowed people to move widely to cope with environmental and political stresses. The collective histories of the clans in this network bond its members to each other and to the land.

5

WESTERN DINÉ FRONTLINE LANDSCAPES BEFORE THE LONG WALK

THE STORY of how the People came to be who and where they are continues in this chapter with colonial turmoil, warfare, and captivity. Here is a closer look at modern Diné identity forming in western Navajoland. These more recent stories, like those of precolumbian ancestral Diné, instill a deep bond with the land and specific places, in this case, the landscapes where their forebears struggled. Here we offer stories about some of those places.

MIDDLE AND LATE 1700s

In a corridor from Canyon de Chelly south toward the Rio Puerco of the West are several Diné defensive sites. Two are fortified stone buildings of several rooms, like the pueblitos of the upper San Juan far to the northeast (see chapter 4). These two buildings date to the middle to late 1700s, when Diné were leaving the San Juan under pressure from Utes and Comanches and renewed attacks by the Spanish. Archaeologists have suggested that refugees from the San Juan could have built the sites here. In the corridor are also defensive sites with simpler architecture on crags—stone walls, perhaps with a few small hogans and maybe a corral. Local Diné tell of a warrior named Jiłháál (spellings vary) and delineate the corridor by listing the sites that he used. The details suggest that there is more to this story than just immigration from the upper San Juan.

Who was Jiłháál? His name is not easily translated (Jett 2001:100). According to some, it refers to a war club. The authoritative Navajo dictionary (Young and Morgan 1987:489) translates it as "Always-Beaten-Up." Traditional history tellers say that he was a runner and a ceremonial hunt leader or a warrior; he was tall, with huge feet ("size 12"); and he carried long flint spear points. He was here "maybe 200 years ago" (around 1770), when enemies were all raiding and fighting—Zunis, Western Apaches, Utes, Comanches, Hopis. Jiłháál himself was rarely seen, but the sight of his barefoot tracks would strike fear into his enemies. Some said he was a wild man who sometimes fought Navajos. Others said he had a wife at each of his homes (one person said 12) and that he learned war chants against enemies from a Navajo chanter near Kin Dah Łichíí' (Kin Lichee near Ganado). He ran between his houses in the corridor and even as far as Hopiland. One person said that "Tsihał" (War Club) built an antelope trap in the Lava Buttes country south of Tallahogan (Awatobi), which would mean he knew hunting ceremonies. Others said that he ran down deer and that he went to the Ute country for mountain sheep, was captured, and escaped. A Canyon de Chelly chanter said that Jiłháál captured a Ute and also raided San Mateo, a Hispanic village on the northwestern footslope of Mount Taylor, established in the 1760s (Mitchell 2003:188). Some said he belonged to the Navajo Red Forehead clan and later moved "beyond the Black Mountains," probably meaning Tah Chee west of the corridor in southeastern Black Mesa (Brugge 1993b).

The places in the corridor that Jiłháál used and their stories are as follows, listed from north to south (for convenience, we use "Anasazi" rather than Anaasází below).[1]

Jiłháál Bitó (Jiłháál's Spring) and Kin Níí' Na'ígai (White House). The spring is in the bottom of Canyon de Chelly several miles above White House, an Anasazi ceremonial building ca. 1045–1300. Jiłháál is said to have lived at White House and to have been killed on the canyon rim during the time of raiding before the Long Walk.

Kin Dadiitł'iní (Nazlini Pueblito, Cribwork House). This small pueblito perches on the edge of a crag at the wooded head of Nazlini Wash, with a view northwest toward Black Mesa. It was built in the 1750s and has two stories with five masonry rooms. It was one of Jiłháál's homes.

FIGURE 23 Nazlini pueblito, built in the late 1700s on a high cliff south of Chinle. It served local Diné as a refuge from Ute, Apache, Spanish, and Mexican attacks, as well as perhaps storing goods for trading with these same groups. Credit: Klara Kelley photo.

Jáák'eh (Racetrack). When Jiłháál was staying at Nazlini, he ran from there south around a track on the plateau, down the open grassland toward Ganado and back.

Tséyaa Kin Sikaadii (House under the Rock). This Anasazi cliff dwelling is in the side of a wooded, grassy-bottomed canyon northeast of Kin Lichee. It has several rooms in two levels connected by a tower and probably dates to the 1000s to 1200s. Anasazi lived here, and certain local Diné clans came from them. The site was also occupied by Jiłháál and Jiłdool, who were also at Nazlini, Kin Dah Lichíí, and Round Top. They were hunters, and these buildings are linked to hunting ceremonies.

Kin Dah Łichíí' (Red House Above) and racetrack. Kin Dah Łichíí' was a 1050–1250 Anasazi ceremonial building a few miles northeast of Ganado. Diné lived here before they lived at Wide Reed Ruin in Ganado, including Jiłháál and Jiłdool. Jiłdool was an Anasazi chief who lived below the Kin Dah Łichíí' building and ran from there around a butte on the south side of Kin Lichee Wash.

Ganado, Lók'aa' Kinteel (Wide Reed Ruin), and Táál, áhodijool (Round Top) fortified crag. Wide Reed Ruin is located in the cottonwoods along Pueblo

Colorado Wash Valley near the Hubbell Trading Post. It was a large Anasazi ceremonial complex between 1250 and 1300, reoccupied by Navajos in the late 1700s and possibly earlier (McKenna 1987; Mount et al. 1993). The Round Top site is a fortified crag overlooking Pueblo Colorado Wash Valley and Wide Reed Ruin, with a cluster of forked-stick hogans and a corral inside a rock wall around the mesa tip. Diné lived at Wide Reed Ruin after Kin Dah Łichíí', and Jiłháál himself had a small forked-stick hogan below Round Top. Before Jiłháál was here, during Anasazi times, residents included Masido and Beibashdeeli, who had 12 wives.

Kin Náázíníi (Upstanding House) pueblito. This multiroom masonry building with a tower was built in the 1750s on a boulder amid piñon and juniper trees near Wide Ruins Wash. Six outlying hogans and a goat corral are in the rocks below. The site was one of Jiłháál's homes, built as a fortress, with slits in the walls for shooting arrows at enemies, and it was also used for smoke signaling. People lived around the site and on top of the hill when their enemies were Utes and White Mountain Apaches, who massacred people there. The site was also frequented by big-footed Chách'osh Dííl (Burly Chancre), as were sites at Lupton (Kin Binááz'eełí), at Canyon de Chelly, and at Ganado (note the resemblance to Jiłháál). He went around with Jiłháál, causing fear and slaughtering enemies. The people around Kin Náázíníi before the Long Walk were of the Ma̜'ii Deeshgizhnii (Coyote Pass / Jemez) clan, born for Kiiyaa'áanii (Towering House) and Kin Łichíí'nii (Redhouse) clans. People from here went to Fort Sumner. According to Hopi oral tradition, a colony of Jemez people was at Sikyatki between Antelope Mesa and Hopi First Mesa during the Awatobi times and was abandoned before the Awatobi massacre (Courlander 1982:39–52). Perhaps the Jemez clan people at Kin Náázíníi (Navajo descendants of women from Jemez) came from Sikyatki or Antelope Mesa.

In June 1775 Fray Silvestre Vélez de Escalante, with 17 Zunis and one Hopi interpreter, traveled along one branch of an ancient Indigenous route between Zuni and Hopi (Adams 1963:121–122, 136; Brugge 1995; Kelley and Francis 2013:278). If they used a more or less straight line route, they would have passed a few miles north of Kin Náázíníi. At Hopi, a messenger from Walpi (Hopi First Mesa) told the Escalante party that he had observed a meeting of more than 100 Navajos and that they were planning to attack the party on its way back to Zuni. The would-be attackers had spies in position to learn the date and route of return. When the Escalante party started back to Zuni, a Walpi leader sent 40 armed men "to find out whether some smokes that had been seen in the direction where we were going were of the Navajos who planned to kill us" (Adams 1963:136). This news seems to have induced the Escalante party to return by a different route, the lower, drier one through Tanner Springs, thereby again avoiding Kin Náázínii. We think that Kin Náázínii was positioned off but near the high route from Zuni—the one that the Escalante party used to get to Walpi—so that local Diné could watch just such travel without being seen. The pueblito itself has no big viewshed, but the surrounding hilltops provide views of terrain that these trails cross.

Wide Ruins (Kinteel). This enormous fortified compound, occupied from 1250 to 1300, was the farthest south of Jiłháál's homes.

Anthropologist David Brugge, who recorded most of the stories about Jiłháál, thought he was a Diné warrior of the mid-1700s. His Red Forehead clan and Black Mesa home led Brugge to suggest that Jiłháál was among the people who survived the 1700 Awatobi massacre. There Hopis from the present villages farther west attacked the inhabitants for misconduct and perhaps for letting Franciscan missionaries return to the church there, which they had abandoned during the Pueblo Revolt of 1680.[2] As told in chapter 4, survivors sought refuge among ancestral Navajos and Apaches in the surrounding country, including at Tah Chee and in Canyon de Chelly. Brugge suggested that Jiłháál might have been a descendant of both survivors of the Awatobi massacre and "emigrants from the Dinetah [upper San Juan] . . . people of mixed Apachean-Puebloan descent" (1993b:122).

Jiłháál's name and other characteristics suggest that he also embodied an icon of a terrible power over the land. He has much in common with immortal beings in traditional stories of precolumbian times: Navajo Yé'ii Tsoh (Big God) and Hopi Maasaw. Yé'ii Tsoh (and the Gray Yé'ii Tsoh) are giant, big-footed, big-eyed, wild-acting beings who roamed the barren Anasazi Great North Road between the ceremonial complexes of Chaco Canyon and Aztec on the San Juan. They wore grass- or yucca-fiber clothes and carried packbaskets (Condie and Knudson 1982:258–263; Jett and Watson 1997:Ye'ii Tsoh Haayáhí; Klah 1942:70–72; Matthews 1994:108; Reichard 1977a:391–392). Maasaw has big feet, dark legs, and a bloody head; wears rags, yucca, and yucca-fiber sandals; and carries a club full of seeds and a firebrand. He rules the underworld realm of death but also roams the earth's surface as a hunter and must give humans permission to settle unoccupied land (Malotki and Lomatuway'ma 1987). Jiłháál as icon might have resulted from the mixing of traditions among the Awatobi survivors and their Navajo-Apache neighbors, perhaps enhanced by more Navajos coming in from the San Juan. Perhaps Jiłháál was a human war leader named for a personage combining powers of both Hopi and Navajo deities. We wonder if he could have been a unifying figure in a local episode of ethnogenesis among Hopi survivors of the Awatobi massacre and neighboring Diné.

Whom were Jiłháál and the people of his corridor defending themselves against? Local Diné historians have mentioned conflicts with Utes, Comanches, Western Apaches, Zunis, and Hopis from pueblito times into the 1800s. In the late 1700s the corridor might have been where a little intertribal trading (and the inevitable raiding that went with it) shifted from the upper San Juan after the Spanish resumed warfare farther east. Perhaps the first pueblitos—those in the upper San Juan (see chapter 4; Hill 1940c; McNitt 1970:23; Towner 2003)—were partly an experiment in trading with the enemy. At the beginning of the 1700s, Diné in the upper San Juan sustained heavy attacks from Spanish military forces. Then Utes and Comanches, newly flush with guns from the French, started attacking both Diné and Spanish. Intending to use each other for protection, Diné and Spanish made a peace and started trading. Right at this time, the pueblitos appeared. If the raids were so hard on the People, it seems they would have moved away from this frontier, but instead, according to Diné clan histories (Matthews 1994:135–159), people, including Puebloans, moved in. Perhaps one incentive was to trade Spanish goods north to the western Utes, probably at least partly for French guns. Ute Mountain Ute oral tradition also attests to trade with the Diné of the pueblitos (Loebig 1996:81). The Utes who raided Diné were not necessarily the same as those who traded with them. Perhaps Diné built pueblitos to store tradeable crops, as well as to help them withstand the raids from various Ute and Comanche bands.

By the 1750s, Diné were leaving the upper San Juan for the country south and west. The gun trade was fizzling out, and Spanish mercenaries may have started raiding for slaves again (Bailey 1964; Towner 2003:185, 2008). In the 1770s the Spanish resumed military attacks on the People, allied themselves with the Comanches, and started fairs at Abiquiu and Taos where Utes and Comanches could trade their captives (Bailey 1973). One Diné oral history (Van Valkenburgh 1940b) offers an example of the depopulation process. In the late 1700s a headman named Bilį́į' Łikizhii (Spotted Warrior) built 12 watchtowers, including one at Pot Mesa, the southern gateway to Dinetah. A combined force of Utes and Spanish trapped Spotted Warrior and his people on Pot Mesa, where they might have died but for a rescue force of Diné from Canyon de Chelly. After the rescuers drove off the attackers, Spotted Warrior and his people moved across the Chuskas to Canyon de Chelly. Spanish documents refer

FIGURE 24 Diné warrior in traditional dress, 1893, Keams Canyon. Anthropologist James Mooney took the photo, probably while on a collecting trip for the Smithsonian Museum (Stephen 1936:283), so this man may be posing with war gear that Mooney had collected. Credit: National Anthropological Archives, Smithsonian Institution, gn_02412.

to two leaders named Antonio El Pinto (Spotted Warrior), one who died in 1793 and another who was active on the eastern Navajo frontier in the early 1800s (Correll 1976:90–95, 243). The oral history could refer to either.

By this time, Diné herds were growing, so families could substitute sheep and goats for crops as a dietary mainstay. The family could move the sheep and goats at will out of harm's way, unlike crops. Families were now taking their herds from the upper San Juan south to Mount Taylor and west to the Chuska Valley and beyond in order to move opportunistically among their widely scattered relatives who were already in these areas when the Spanish arrived (see the section on ethnogenesis in chapter 4), having avoided the trade boom on the upper San Juan for a more traditional way of life as hunter-gatherer-farmers. Even as Spanish and First Nations raiding parties soon penetrated farther west, these dispersed Diné families no longer would have needed the elaborate pueblitos to defend themselves. With fewer people and tradeable crops to store, all they needed were defensible heights with views of major cross-regional routes, enhanced with walls of rock cobbles that could also serve as missiles and maybe a few small shelters. Diné oral histories say that some families, especially in the Chuska Valley and around Mount Taylor, built up large herds through trading and raiding, and the men became local leaders. These men included Spotted Warrior himself (Roessel and Johnson 1973; see also Correll 1976:64–65).

But other families perhaps wanted to keep the more settled farming-trading way of life even as they moved south and west. The people who had moved into Dinetah included clans from the west, such as the Water People, so probably some of the Dinetah refugees were rejoining clan relatives whose forebears had stayed in the west. We suspect that Dinetah refugees, including Spotted Warrior's people, built the late pueblitos in Jiłháál's corridor (and late 1700s pueblitos farther east at Sanostee, Burnham, Chacra Mesa, and Lobo Mesa and around Mount Taylor). Maybe they briefly kept alive some trade with western Utes, now coming south up the Chinle Wash into Jiłháál's corridor, or maybe they only hoped to do so. But eventually, they stopped trading and needing such elaborate group storehouses/refuges as pueblitos. Their descendants kept using these buildings as refuges, at least at Kin Náázínii, but moved around more and did not build more like them.

EARLY TO MIDDLE 1800s

Local Diné historians attest that Jiłháál's corridor and its extension north from Canyon de Chelly down Chinle Wash was a raiding corridor during the 1800s.

(This same corridor was crossed by the precolumbian travel routes described in chapter 2.) Several recorded Diné oral histories tell the stories (Hubbell Trading Post, oral history interviews 21, 36, 44, 142; KFa, August 14, 1998).

The place-names from south to north are Anaa' Hajííná (Where the Enemy Came Up), north of present Chambers; Dziłghá Ádahjéé' (Where the White Mountain Apaches Ran Down, or Hilltop Descent), near Ganado; and Dziłghá Haaskai (Where the White Mountain Apaches Went Up, or Hilltop Ascent), near Chinle. The places near Ganado and Chinle are where Apaches came from the south through the corridor and massacred Diné. In 1858, according to Hopi traditional history, Diné killed Hopis at the place near Ganado. In one version, the Hopi expedition leader himself provoked the attack so that his martyrdom would establish a boundary (Nequatewa 1967:52; see also Stephen 1936:1018–1019). Local Diné accounts of what seems to be the same incident describe the massacre as an Apache attack on Diné, perhaps reflecting confusion between the name for White Mountain Apaches and the almost identical word for hilltop (Hubbell Trading Post, oral history interviews 44 and 142).

According to other Diné accounts (Roessel and Johnson 1973:58, 127, 258), in the 1800s or perhaps earlier, Mexican slave raiders took their captives from Black Mesa south through Jiłháál's corridor past present Chinle, Ganado, and Chambers. Another time, Diné killed Ute attackers on top of Dziłghá Haaskai near Chinle. The place-name Dziłghá Haaskai at Chinle may have some connection with a visit of Gila Apaches to Diné at Canyon de Chelly that Spanish colonial observers reported in November 1807 (Navajo Tribe 1967:286). Canyon de Chelly was a regular target for Utes and for colonial military and slaving forces starting in 1805, when Colonel Antonio Narbona, coming from the east rather than through Jiłháál's corridor, invaded the canyons with 300 soldiers, citizen militiamen, Puebloan auxiliaries, and Zuni guides. They killed 115 Diné, mostly warriors, and took 33 captives, mostly children, along with 350 sheep and goats. The captives were distributed to private citizens (Correll 1976:80). Ute attackers may have come up Chinle Wash, which extends north from Jiłháál's corridor.

Diné oral histories tell of many other attacks on Canyon de Chelly (Brugge and Wilson 1976:278–284; Jett 2001; Roessel and Johnson 1973; see also Kipp 1983). One expedition that did not make it to the canyon was that of Mexican army captain Blas de Hinojos with 1,000 citizen soldiers plus Puebloan auxiliaries. At Narbona Pass, Chuska Valley leader Hastiin Naabaahii (Mr. Warrior, Narbona) and his followers ambushed them (Correll 1976:134; Denetdale 2007:61). The Diné killed Hinojos and many others, while survivors retreated to Santa Fe. Among the Diné may have been Narbona's son-in-law, the teenage Ashkii Diyinii, later known as Manuelito.[3] Fourteen years later, U.S. Army colonel John M. Washington led a treaty-making force to Canyon de Chelly by way of the Chuska Valley, where, during a supposedly friendly gathering, soldiers opened fire on the Diné and killed Chief Narbona (Correll 1976:201–203).

Other raiding sites near the corridor recalled by local Diné historians are as follows:

K'aa' Łání (Arrowhead Butte). Diné fought Utes, "Kiowas" (Comanches?), or Apaches at this small butte west of Jiłháál's corridor near one branch of the trail between Hopi and Zuni (Downer et al. 1988:122).

Hojiighání (Massacre Place). Utes reportedly ambushed Navajos west of Jiłháál's corridor near Tah Chee and killed them all. Some local Diné dispute this story, but geologist Herbert Gregory recorded this place as a "Battlefield" during fieldwork from 1909 to 1913 (Downer et al. 1988:115; Gregory 1916:pocket map; Mitchell 2001:6–7). This place is near the precolumbian buffalo/bead route (described in chapter 2), which continued northeastward across the San Juan River. Residents near the river recalled that Comanches drove captives along this route from Hopi over Buffalo Pass and the Hogback, then up a canyon, Naa'łání Ch'ííyoodí (Plains Raiders Slave Drive) and eastward, presumably to the slave markets at Abiquiu or Taos (Kelley and Francis 2006b).

Naakai Haznání (Where the Mexicans Went Up). The peak of this name is on north-central Black Mesa, west of the Chinle Valley. Relatives of popular entertainer "Navajo Elvis" and other local historians told us how a party of Mexicans attacked Diné here (perhaps in what maps call "Yellow Jacket Valley"). The Diné stirred up a beehive and threw it down on the Mexicans, who fled. Local people have said that most Mexican, Ute, and Comanche raiders came up from the Chinle Valley at Rough Rock (we suspect down Warpath Canyon) into the upper Oraibi Wash (KFa, September 16, 2009; Mitchell 2001:6–7). The Ute and Comanche attackers probably went on down Oraibi Wash to raid Oraibi as well and farther west to Gray Mountain (see below). Hispanic "private campaigns" targeted people on Black Mesa in 1850 and 1860 (Brugge and Wilson 1978:281, 283).

The refuges of the 1800s were like the smaller defensive sites of the late 1700s in Jiłháál's corridor and 1800s defensive sites elsewhere in Navajoland: fortified crags, some with a few hogans. Like Kin Náázínii, missed by Fray Escalante on the Hopi–Zuni route, these sites were not right smack on cross-regional routes; instead, they were sequestered nearby, with good views of the routes. People also kept using the earlier pueblitos and fortified crags in

FIGURE 25 "Ute Raid Panel" on the walls of Canyon del Muerto near Fortress Rock. Several encounters seem evident, judging from headgear and weapons: from bottom to top, Western Apaches, Spanish, Utes, and U.S. Army soldiers. Credit: From *Canyon de Chelly* by Campbell Grant. © 1978 The Arizona Board of Regents. Reprinted by permission of the University of Arizona Press.

Jiłháál's corridor. Other sites west of the corridor and its extension down Chinle Wash include the following:

Upper Oraibi Wash pueblito. In north-central Black Mesa near Naakai Haznání are two small buildings perched on separate crags. One of these sites is a small masonry room with a good view of Oraibi Wash from which one could spot raiders coming from the southwest up Oraibi Wash or from the northeast by way of Rough Rock. The other, a site of two small, low masonry rooms, is about a mile north in a side canyon without such a view. The Navajo Land Claim archaeologists called this site a "fortified crag," while Ronald Towner (2003:188–189) has called it a pueblito. With tree-ring dates from the 1790s, it is the latest and farthest west of known pueblitos (NLC, archaeological site forms, site W-LLC-UO-DD). Local residents said that their forebears used it before the Long Walk, when certain local men started raiding, their victims retaliated, and they used this site to defend themselves. The attackers were Utes, Mexicans (with guns), and Plains people (Comanches?) (KFa, September 16, 2009). Hidden back from the Oraibi valley, this little fortification would have been a good refuge but not a good lookout place, for which the other, smaller structure is better situated.

Jééh Deez'áhí (Pitch Point, Smoke Signal Peak). On the east side of Low Mountain is an outcrop where people burned pitchy piñon trees to signal approaching Utes (Downer et al. 1988:118). It has a good view of the Polacca Wash valley and the buffalo/bead route there. The attackers probably came up the Chinle Valley, then turned southwest onto the buffalo/bead trail.

White Cone lookout and Hodoogą́ą́'í (Massacre Place). A low wall of lava cobbles along the northeast rim of White Cone Mesa in the Lava Buttes overlooks a spring and a branch of the ancient Hopi–Zuni trail. Local residents told Navajo Land Claim archaeologists that Navajo women and children took refuge here in the times before the Long Walk (NLC, archaeological site forms, site W-LLC-MJ-TTT). The wall seems too low for effective defense but could have hidden lookouts. Diné were massacred on the northwest side of the mesa, but some hid in crannies and survived (KFa, April 14, 2004).

Tsé Njigą́ą́'í, Rock Where People Were Massacred. This place is also in the Lava Buttes country, on the west side of Shonto Butte near Dilkon. One local historian said that around the time of the Long Walk, local Diné chased an Apache raiding party and massacred them all (Spurr et al. 1996:92). The site has a clear view of the Palatkwapi Trail, an ancient Indigenous route from the Verde Valley to Hopi (Byrkit 1988).

Castle Butte refuge and lookout. South of Dilkon is a towering butte with vertical cliffs all around. On top, above the only (and very steep) access, is a site with fortification walls, two hogans, four "shelters," a tank, and a sweathouse (NLC, archaeological site forms, site W-LLC-MB-K). An elderly chanter living nearby told us that Diné took refuge here during early warfare times, when the enemies were mostly "other Indians." Refugees would roll big boulders down upon the enemy (KFa, April 1, 2004). The site overlooks a spring on a neighboring butte and has a good view of the Palatkwapi Trail to the west.

Gray Mountain site clusters. In far western Navajoland at the north end of Gray Mountain are two clusters of sites, each site having several hogans, some with corrals. The hogans have tree-ring dates in the late 1700s and were repaired into the 1800s. Both clusters are in the general vicinity of where the east–west Hopi–Havasupai trail meets the Navajo salt trail north into the Grand Canyon. One cluster is along the Coconino Rim south of Desert View Tower, and the other is a few miles northeast in the Upper Basin near the head of the present Tanner Trail (NLC, archaeological site forms, sites W-LLC-C-B, C, E, F, O, CC, MM, and OO; see also Colton 1964:93; Roberts et al. 1995:36; Robinson and Towner 1993; Stokes and Smiley 1964). Previously recorded Diné oral histories do not give a reason for these unusual clusters of exceptionally well-preserved sites. We suggest that they were for trading, refuge, and defense, maybe a functional equivalent of the early to mid-1700s pueblitos in the upper San Juan drainage. A late 1600s Spanish document reports "Apachas" at war with the Havasupais (Tyler and Taylor 1958:301–302), and in 1776 Havasupais told Spanish explorer Fray Francisco Garcés that the "Guamua" (Navajos [Brugge 1983:498]) were hostile to them but allied with the "Oraibis" (Coues 1900:350–351, 457). Oral histories from Diné in far northwestern Navajoland attest to attacks on Diné of Gray Mountain and elsewhere by Utes and even Comanches and Mexicans (Roberts et al. 1995:29–31; Roessel and Johnson 1973:151–175).

In western Navajoland from the late 1700s until the Long Walk, then, Diné frontier landscapes formed along the ancient cross-regional routes that invaders also used. On and near these routes were lookouts, battle sites, and refuges. In the early years some refuges were pueblitos, perhaps because they served unusually large groups of families who also farmed and traded there. As raiding and warfare engulfed the land, though, families probably stopped settling in large groups. As Diné oral histories attest (Roessel and Johnson 1973), they took their livestock and scattered into the backcountry away from the trails, where they would be safest, and moved often. Lookout parties used smoke signals to warn others far away of intruders and perhaps to organize counterattacks or ambushes. It is not clear whether people signaled from their lookouts–probably not, lest they give their position away.

In eastern Navajoland, on an eastern extension of Mount Taylor called Łid Haagai (White Smoke Rising), an elder veteran explained techniques of smoke signaling. The signalers would dig an earth oven, fill it with chunks of lava, put pitchy wood on top, ceremonially kindle the fire, and leave it to smolder. The burnt lava cobbles are still there. Another signaling point was 15–20 miles northeast on the north end of Mesa Prieta (KFa, June 22, 1999). Both spots overlooked the Spanish and Mexican colonial Camino Real from Santa Fe around the north side of Mount Taylor to Zuni, as well as the mid-1700s pueblito of Big Bead and other 1700s to 1800s sites in the valley between them (Towner 2016). They surely served the Big Bead people as lookouts. According to a Casamero Lake elder, Diné traveling from "Arizona" came down a route past Casamero Lake and Mount Taylor to the Rio Grande, staying in the tree-covered mesas to avoid detection by the "many enemies" who were around (KFa, September 14, 23, 2015). The U.S. military called this route the "Great Navajo Trail," a well-beaten raiding route between the lower

Rio Grande valley and Navajoland that approximates present Interstate 40 (Correll 1976:307; see also U.S. General Land Office 1896; Wheeler ca. 1880). A local chanter named several landmarks in a 70-mile-long east–west row that make up a landscape of lookouts and smoke-signaling stations: Haystack Butte near present Grants, Hosta Butte, Ram Mesa, and Tsé Nizhóní (Pretty Rock) near present Gallup (KFa, September 23, 2015).

THE NAACHID AND THE LONG WALK

As warfare intensified in the mid-1800s, Diné leaders gathered more often for crises. These gatherings have been called "Naachid," reportedly referring to the gestures that warriors on a raid used instead of talking (Young 1978:23) or to gathering things up with the hand (Steven Begay, personal communication, January 19, 2017).

Diné elders have passed down many different stories about the Naachid, most unrecorded. Some say the Naachid was a gathering of chanters to diagnose a problem. The earliest Naachid in the recorded oral histories occurred when Diné were flourishing and forming clans in the upper San Juan drainage in the 1700s. People gathered for a Naachid for the leader God Tsoh (Big Knee), a curing ceremony that lasted all winter. It was at Tó Aheedlí (River Junction), a War God shrine and heavily traveled crossing between Navajo and Ute lands (Matthews 1994:146–147). Perhaps the Naachid during the 1700s ethnogenesis allowed leaders to negotiate the common cultural identity and sovereignty discussed in chapter 4. Perhaps "naachid" originally signified sign language, which leaders would have needed in the early stages of coming together.

AnCita Benally (2006:27–40), Robert W. Young (1978:17–24), and several scholars in the 1900s have described the Naachid based on talks with elders who had experienced it. Most described it as a winter-long event held in a huge, deeply excavated hogan with spruce boughs around it and a dance ground in front. People would come from all over to meet and take part in the ceremonies, the main purpose being for leaders to coordinate with each other, thereby centralizing decision making. Andrew Curley (2014:138ff.) has suggested that the 12 war chiefs and 12 peace chiefs attributed to the pre–Fort Sumner Naachid may be a post–Fort Sumner reinterpretation of oral tradition to assert continuity with the centralized political authority that developed under postconquest U.S. government pressure. Young (1978:23) has suggested that the Naachid was "a war organization concerned on the one hand with the planning and execution of raids, and on the other with a cooperative approach to the growing and storing of food" (also planning communal hunts, according to Benally [2006]) and that it required cooperation among many communities. We wonder if Jiłháál could have been the title of a Naachid leader in the late 1700s or perhaps a title for the runners who summoned people to the Naachid.

Historians have used the term "Naachid" for several gatherings of leaders, recorded in colonial documents, that concerned war and peace. The leaders seem to have favored the region around Canyon de Chelly for these gatherings, perhaps because of the crops stored there. In the late fall of 1840, headmen held such a gathering somewhere west of Canyon de Chelly, then sent an emissary to Mexican colonial authorities seeking peace (Brugge 1963; Correll 1976:146). Another may have been in 1846 at Red Lake (upper Black Creek Valley), where Diné leaders met with the U.S. Army as it was taking possession of Mexican territory during the Mexican War. A wife of paramount leader Narbona spoke forcefully for war until Narbona with his long fingernail gestured for others to take her out (McNitt 1970:108ff.; Harry Walters, personal communication, March 25, 2015; Young 1968:29ff.). The last recorded Naachid was held north of Canyon del Muerto in 1859. The issue was the aggression around Navajoland that the U.S. Army was unleashing from Fort Defiance, the first army outpost inside Navajoland, established in 1851 in the Black Creek Valley of south-central Navajoland. At the Naachid, Black Creek Valley leader Zarcillos Largos (Long Earrings) urged peace: the People might outnumber the army at Fort Defiance, but they were like only one hair on the back of a thousand fleeces. But Manuelito, successor to the late Narbona, in a breechcloth and body paint, argued for resistance and prevailed (see also Brugge 1970:31ff.; McNitt 1970:372ff.; Reichard 1928:109; Van Valkenburgh 1946).

Many Diné have told about Kit Carson's scorched-earth campaign to force them to surrender and go to Fort Sumner (see the introduction; see also Etsedi 1937; Luckert 1977; Roessel and Johnson 1977). Here we offer from our own experience a story of some who did not go (KFa, October 17, 23, 2013). In far northwestern Navajoland south of Lee's Ferry, Diné today say that their ancestors were herding by the time of the Long Walk and had hunted antelope there earlier (see also Henderson 1985). The antelope moved between the low desert south and east of the Colorado River and the higher grasslands of the Kaibito Plateau farther east using a trail called Jádí Habitiin (Antelope Trail) up the towering red backbone of Echo Cliffs. Forebears were part of a community led by Biigháanii (Backbone) of the Towering House clan, a local leader whom residents of the Kaibito Plateau recalled for Eric Henderson (1985:20–21); Alexa Roberts, Richard M. Begay, and Klara Kelley (1995:39); Navajo Land Claim archaeologists (NLC, archaeological site forms, site W-NM-NC-X); and us.

Backbone and his followers ranged around Black Mesa, Tuba City, Gray Mountain, the Bodaway Plateau, and Echo Cliffs, as well as taking refuge in the Grand Canyon with Havasupais at Indian Gardens. He had wives of Áshįįhí (Salt) and Tł'ízíłání (Manygoats) clans, as well as Nát'oh Dine'é Táchii'nii (Tobacco Red Forehead) clan. He evidently sometimes stayed with Hopis during the Long Walk. Indeed, according to some tellers, he was allied with the Hopis against the Diné and took Diné captives to sell as slaves (Roessel and Johnson 1973:151–155, 171–175). In 1858 the Mormons had started colonizing western Navajoland when they established a mission at Hopi and made a trail southward along the base of Echo Cliffs. By 1865 Backbone was harassing Mormons coming down that trail (Creer 1958:18–19). His followers included Utes and Paiutes, a hint that he took part in their 1860s Black Hawk war against encroaching Mormons (Peterson 1998:223; Roberts et al. 1995:29ff.). A rock hogan above Echo Cliffs northeast of Bitter Springs is identified with him; he had a cornfield near Bitter Springs; and Echo Cliffs offered hiding places. His descendants say that as a young warrior Backbone fought with the Spanish (maybe referring to traders along the Armijo Cutoff in the 1830s or so [Hafen 1947], though he would have been only a teenager then).

Descendants of Biigháanii and their neighbors told different stories about crude rock windbreaks among the boulders partway up Echo Cliffs, where in 2013 slumping earth cracked the highway up the cliff face and brought us there to try to protect historic sites before repair work was done. Some said the shelters could have been blinds or reconnaissance camps for antelope hunters waiting along Jádí Habitiin. Others said that they were among the many along Echo Cliffs where their ancestors had hidden to avoid the Long Walk, when Biigháanii and his family had used them. Perhaps the windbreaks could have served all these purposes, as well as hiding Biigháanii and his men while they watched the Mormons. These people never went to Fort Sumner, according to their descendants, though anthropologist Eric Henderson (1985) was told that Biigháanii went to Fort Sumner at the very end. Biigháanii was a very old man in 1899, living somewhere around the Dinnetbito Wash south of Black Mesa (Johnston 1972:91ff.).

FIGURE 26 Handwritten on back of photo: "Paul J. Randolph orderly for Gen. H. Scott commanding Texas New Mexico Border 1913—holding child. Next to him Bizoshe Navajo chief with three sons arrested by Gen. Scott near Beautiful Mountain New Mexico under orders from President Wilson in 1913—entrenched to fight the Agent. [Illegible] bloodshed—all four were taken for trial to Santa Fe before Fed judge Pope after surrender." Credit: National Anthropological Archives, Smithsonian Institution, Scott Collection, photo lot 4720, neg. 43,091.

PEACETIME

Diné landscapes of defense and resistance to colonial power did not end with the Fort Sumner experiment. The U.S. government, now an occupying power, bored deeper into Navajoland, triggering Diné resistance through civil disobedience. In the early 1900s, at Round Rock and Aneth, they confronted federal authorities who had come to take their children to boarding schools (McPherson 2012:100–132; Young and Morgan 1952, 1954:34–40, 108–113). At Beautiful Mountain in 1913, Chuska Valley men resisted being jailed for traditional polygamy by taking refuge on top of Beautiful Mountain, and federal troops confronted them (Bahr 2004:366–185; Evans 2005:93–97; Iverson and Roessel, eds. 2002:123ff.; McNitt 1962:347–358). Later on came the resistance to federal agents of stock reduction and to relocation from Black Mesa in the 1980s that the introduction describes. The struggle for sovereignty has persisted from earliest colonial times to the present.

This chapter tells how the People, now a self-conscious sovereign group, defended their land and sovereignty over it against colonizers and Indigenous raiders. In the 1860s they lost the last war but through smaller acts of resistance have continued to defend their hold on the land and their cultural sovereignty. The People have passed down the stories in this chapter to instill in their descendants a deep bond with the land and the specific places where their forebears defended it.

6

THE PEOPLE MEET "AMERICANS" ON
THE ARIZONA RAILROAD FRONTIER

W ITH THE Fort Sumner captivity, the Diné fight to stay free was over. When they returned home in 1868, the Diné were reduced to more limited resistance against the conquering and encroaching colonizers. Diné leaders signed the treaty wherein they agreed to keep only part of their homeland and cede the rest to Washindoon. The People nevertheless reoccupied as much of their original homeland as they could and pressured Washindoon agents directly or through their leaders to protect them against encroaching settlers. The unspoken arrangement was that leaders would keep their followers from violence against those settlers if Washindoon itself would keep the settlers in check. This was the bedrock of Diné political sovereignty after Fort Sumner. Then, bit by bit, the People regained more land and sovereignty, but not all they had lost.

This story has played out in all the borderlands of Navajoland, from the eastern Navajo Checkerboard southeast of Farmington (Bailey and Bailey 1982, 1999) south to the railroad (Kelley 1986) and on through the Zuni Mountains to Ramah (Son of Former Manybeads 1949); westward through the Lava Buttes country into the lower Little Colorado basin and north to Tuba City (Etsedi 1937; Johnston 1972; Roberts et al. 1995); and north of the San Juan River through Utah (Brugge 1966b; Correll 1971; King 1996) to Farmington (Bailey and Bailey 1982). Conquest has allowed colonizer records to swamp Diné oral

FIGURE 27 Diné gather at Fort Defiance in 1879 for rations, including beef that the army bought from contractors, soon to include ranchers in and near the Chambers Checker-board. Credit: National Anthropological Archives, Smithsonian Institution, gn_2459a.

histories in telling these stories, but those records are also full of ironies that Diné oral histories can expose. This chapter and the next tell how the People struggled to keep their lands in the southern Navajo borderlands, only to be removed by Washindoon three generations later. Little oral tradition about this time seems to have survived, testimony to how, when removal breaks the bond between the people and the land, the stories that reinforced the bond are lost.

In 1866, while the People were in captivity and the U.S. government claimed their land, Congress gave away a swath of it for a transcontinental railroad. The grant was south of the treaty reservation and consisted of a checkerboard of square-mile sections alternating with public domain (land claimed by Washin-doon) in a corridor soon expanded to 100 miles wide. The grant was supposed to generate funds to finance railroad construction, mainly from land sales to homesteaders (Corell and Dehiya 1978:3–7; Greever 1954:20; U.S. Commissioner of Indian Affairs 1868). But for generations before the Long Walk, many Diné from the Black Creek Valley around Fort Defiance to the Little Colorado basin had used these more southern lands. In 1960–61, 23 Diné elders from the Black Creek and Puerco Valleys told interviewers for the Navajo Land Claim that before the Long Walk their forebears ranged around the grasslands far southwest. They hunted and gathered there, moved their herds around to cope with unpredictable range and water, and sought refuge there from the constant warfare of the 1800s. They returned from Fort Sumner to the Black Creek Valley along with crowds of other families seeking rations. The crowding soon forced them to start living more permanently in the southern lands, outside the reservation, which were now a part of the railroad grant (NLC, Navajo oral history).[1]

There they collided with incoming self-styled "Americans"—colonizer cattle ranchers and settlers who hoped to profit from government contracts, as well as from sales in distant markets made accessible by the new railroad. Resistance to rancher encroachment would be tricky for the People here. Conquest had cut the power of their leaders down to an all-time low. Furthermore, soon after the return from captivity, several leaders who wanted to resist Washindoon were rumored to be witches and killed. Almost a century later, a descendant of one of the executioners remembered that the witches had taken leavings (hair, personal belongings, or such) of their victims, wrapped them in a copy of the 1868 treaty, and buried them in a graveyard. This burial was intended to bring poverty and death to the victims, including people who had made their marks on the treaty, as well as to make the treaty worthless (Hubbell Trading Post, oral history interview 679, quoted in Blue 1988:3ff.).

The treaty signers would not stand for this defiance. At Fort Sumner, about a month before the signing, Manuelito, Barboncito, and several other leaders had gone to Washington with U.S. Indian Agent Theodore Dodd to persuade President Andrew Johnson to let them return to their homeland. The president deferred the decision to the Peace Commission, which would make the treaty. At the treaty council, the Peace Commission tried to get the leaders to agree that the People would move to the Oklahoma Territory, but the Diné leaders staunchly refused and threatened to bolt from the Fort Sumner reservation. The Peace Commission gave in and made the treaty for part of the Diné homeland. The leaders had struggled mightily for this treaty, and several of the signers took part directly or indirectly in the executions. One was Tótsohnii Hastiin (Bigwater Clansman, Ganado Mucho), recognized by both the People and Washindoon

FIGURE 28 Tótsohnii Hastiin (Ganado Mucho), paramount western Diné leader, on a visit to Washington, D.C., in 1874 with nine other "chiefs" to help Fort Defiance agent W. F. Arny get part of the Navajo treaty reservation opened to mineral prospectors (McNitt 1962:151–153, 157). Credit: National Anthropological Archives, Smithsonian Institution, gn_02388.

after the Long Walk as the main leader southwest of the treaty reservation (Blue 1988; McNitt 1962:202–203; Thompson 1978). His role in executing the dissidents may have led U.S. government authorities at Fort Defiance to defer to his power to keep order.

VIOLENCE IN THE CHAMBERS CHECKERBOARD

The People southwest of the Black Creek Valley seem to have suffered more settler-colonist violence than most in the railroad grant. This afflicted land is what we call the Chambers Checkerboard, about 1,000 square miles around the early railroad stop of Chambers, Arizona. It lies within the much bigger area around which the forebears of Diné returnees from Fort Sumner had ranged. The main watercourse through the Chambers Checkerboard, the Rio Puerco of the West, heads on the Continental Divide in New Mexico and flows west 100 miles to the Little Colorado River in Arizona. From the New Mexico–Arizona state line, it flows west-southwest through the Chambers Checkerboard for 35 miles, with sparsely wooded dark red siltstone mesas on the north and rolling grasslands to the south.

In this dry country, light winter snow melts quickly and rain soon evaporates, probably even in the 1880s, when the climate was wetter and cooler. But water was and still is surprisingly plentiful in side drainages of the Puerco and in water holes, especially where water wells up. Several such water holes, now mostly silted up but flowing in the 1880s, are strung along a swale a few miles south of the Puerco Valley. There, an ancient trail passed from Zuni Pueblo through the swale northwest to the Hopi villages, Salt Woman's route mentioned in chapter 2 and the route described in chapter 5 by which Fray Escalante in 1775 returned to Zuni. From the farthest west water hole in the string, Navajo Springs near the railroad, the trail continued northwest from the Chambers Checkerboard through another big spring, Tanner Springs. Navajo Springs, Tanner Springs, and some others contained salt attractive to the antelope that used to abound there.

After the Fort Sumner captivity but before the railroad, the nearest colonizer settlements were at Fort Wingate in New Mexico and Fort Defiance and Saint Johns in Arizona, all 20–40 miles beyond the Chambers Checkerboard, plus a few outlying trading posts and ranches. Forts Wingate and Defiance were military posts meant to control the Diné. Saint Johns, on the upper Little Colorado

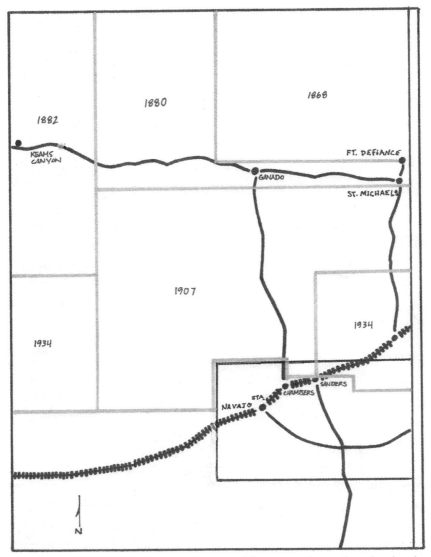

MAP 3 Map of the Chambers Checkerboard and the surrounding region, showing the reservation and additions, 1880s–1930s. The Chambers Checkerboard is the rectangle on the southeast outlined in black. Credit: Map by Garrett Francis.

River, was a center for farming, ranching, and trading. Hispanic families from western New Mexico first settled there in the 1860s, soon followed by Mormons (Granger 1960:9, 21; Kelley 1988a; Van Valkenburgh 1999:90).

Back then, the Chambers Checkerboard itself may have had only one colonizer settlement, that of James D. Houck from Cuba, New Mexico. In 1874 Houck was carrying mail between Fort Wingate and Fort Whipple in Arizona along the Overland Stage Road, a wagon road that had developed after military reconnaissances of a possible transcontinental railroad route in the 1850s and 1860s. The actual railroad would soon parallel the wagon road (Beale 1929; Kelly 1970:endpaper map; Whipple 1941). In the Chambers Checkerboard, the Overland Stage Road and the railroad paralleled the Rio Puerco of the West, forming a corridor that later accommodated U.S. Route 66, setting of many a twentieth-century song and story. Local Diné no doubt observed Houck setting himself up, possibly in a stage station, at or near Coyote Spring (soon called Houck's Tank) and at Navajo Springs. At both of Houck's places, the Overland Stage Road crossed the traditional trails between Zuni Pueblo and the Hopi villages. Houck traded and raised sheep (Hubbell Trading Post, oral history interview 51).

THE COMING OF THE RAILROAD, 1881–1883

In January 1881 Captain Frank Tracy Bennett, federal Indian agent for the Navajos at Fort Defiance, writes to the commissioner of Indian Affairs (CIA) in Washington, D.C., predicting trouble:

[A few days earlier] one of the Navajo captains [Diné appointed as police], Hosteen Dil-gnish-ey-Begah [Hastiin Dilwoshii Biye', Shouter's Son] and his father [a headman and war leader before the Long Walk] came in, and reported to me that they lived at a spring about 40 miles south west of here [probably Coyote Spring, Houck's Tank], in the vicinity of Puercho [sic] River, and that they had lived there for more than twenty (20) years past. That they farmed there, raised crops, and did not come to this Agency for rations, or supplies. That three (3) Americans had come there, was cutting logs, preparing to put up a house. And they supposed would soon attempt to drive them away from their home, and wanted me to protect them. . . . I would therefore respectfully request that I be instructed what advice to give these Indians, and how to decide other similar cases that may come up. I suppose that there will be quite a number of similar cases, as the Atlantic and Pacific Rail Road is now near here [Fort Defiance] and will be completed through the country twenty five (25) miles south of here, probably inside of six months. The question to be decided is, whether Navajo Indians—if they sever their tribal relations, cease to draw rations and supplies from the government, and settle on public lands, and comply with the requirements of the law regulating such cases—can hold the land the same as any settlers. (NLC, archive documents, letter of January 7, 1880 [1881])

Bennett's question about how off-reservation Diné can secure their land-use rights against colonizer-settlers will hang unanswered until the new century (see chapter 7). This legal vacuum will soon encourage a free-for-all over land.[2]

In May, military reports tell of a conflict between Diné and colonizers evidently somewhere near Navajo Springs. Captain Charles Parker has taken 49 troops from Fort Wingate and stayed at "Hauck's Ranch," probably Navajo Springs, where Diné have told him what happened. Some Diné had visited the place of Mr. Colgan, who had earlier swindled them in some way, and Mrs. Colgan mistakenly thought they "proposed to outrage her person." Parker thinks that the Rio Puerco Valley should be given to the Navajos because they grow a lot of corn there (NLC, archive documents, letters of May 17 and May 27, 1881).

In March 1882 F. W. Smith, superintendent of the Atlantic and Pacific (A&P) Railroad, telegraphs to ask Fort Defiance agent Galen Eastman to go to Navajo Springs and talk with Diné who demand $500 restitution for a Navajo man run over by a train "last week." Agent Eastman reports to the CIA that he went to Navajo Springs and announced that such restitution would not be available in the future and that "Indians" and their stock must learn to stay off the tracks. But he also asks the railroad to pay for items, including two plows, for the deceased's two sons, "who are farmers residing in the Puerco Valley of the west." In April Eastman writes to two settlers, Messrs. Bennett and Hardison, about delivering two steers to Navajo Charlie and his brother. The agency seems to have bought the steers from Bennett and Hardison for restitution (NLC, archive documents, letters of March 10, March 18, and April 7, 1882).

The railroad through the Chambers Checkerboard is finished in 1882. Between September 1882 and February 1883, mystified Diné would have watched land surveyors under contract with the U.S. General Land Office (GLO) survey and monument (or place markers where the lines surveyed intersect) the township, range, and section lines within the railroad land grant in the Chambers Checkerboard. The even-numbered sections within the townships are federally controlled public domain, open to homesteading, and the odd sections are part of the railroad grant. The GLO surveys, homesteading records, and other documents from 1882 and 1883 show what local Diné must see under construction: some colonizer settlement and the beginnings of a transportation and central place system that, little did they know, would connect the Chambers Checkerboard to national markets in which trading posts would enmesh them. Among the settlers are several who will figure in the violence of the next few years.

Infrastructure and central places on the GLO plats include the railroad and telegraph line, wagon roads and trails, and central places where the roads or trails cross the railroad. The two largest central places are Houck's Tank in the east and Navajo Springs in the west, the two places where branches of the Zuni–Hopi trail cross both the Overland Stage Road and the railroad. The segment of the Zuni–Hopi trail from Zuni to Navajo Springs is the road that military parties under Edwin F. Beale and A. W. Whipple reconnoitered in the 1850s as a possible railroad route (see Beale 1929; Whipple 1941). A few miles northwest of Navajo Springs, Navajo Station, according to GLO records, has a section house / eatery, engine house, water tank, two-story railroad depot and telegraph office, slaughterhouse, and corral. The GLO surveyors do not mention homesteader Lewis Lynch, who files a homestead claim at Navajo Station during this year. A single man of 26 years, he first lives in a tent while he builds a house (NARA, homestead proof file, patent 287). Diné descendants of Lewis Lynch's brother Hugh still live in the surrounding region today.

Between Navajo Station and Houck's Tank is a small station at Saunders (present-day Sanders) near Emigrant Springs where the Overland Stage Road meets another road north from Saint Johns and the Apache country farther south. At Houck's Tank, strung along the track for a couple of miles, are a well, pump, tank, railroad quarry, boardinghouse, Kinsella store, and James F. Bennett's store and dwelling, corral, and outbuildings (including saloon). In 1882 Bennett (not related to Captain Frank Tracy Bennett, as far as we can tell) is also trading about 15 miles northeast at Manuelito, the railroad shipping point for Fort Defiance 30-plus miles north. His partner is Stephen Aldrich, a veteran of the Apache wars and an army contractor (McNitt 1962:249). A few miles east of Houck's Tank is Allantown, which consists of another section house, telegraph house, and two tool houses.

Among the colonizer-settlers whom the GLO surveyors report are eight Hispanic men with houses and corrals; some also have sheep and gardens. One man's house is on a homestead patented in 1885 to a woman who evidently homesteaded in the Midwest and sold her husband's soldier's scrip—coupons that entitled Civil War veterans to 160 acres of public homesteading land. The

FIGURE 29 Lynch Brothers trading post along the railroad, Chambers Checkerboard, 1894, with a Diné youngster in front. Credit: National Anthropological Archives, Smithsonian Institution, photo lot 89, 2443-g.

scrip dealer who bought it then evidently sold the scrip to John A. Benson, a GLO land surveyor. In 1882 Benson uses the scrip to claim the spring near this house, as well as several springs in the Chambers Checkerboard and west.[3] The Hispanic men, all but one of whom have places in the eastern part of the Chambers Checkerboard, may be part of the wave of Hispanic families in the 1860s and 1870s who settled west-central New Mexico and the Saint Johns area. They may be the "Mexican" herders "working for whites" who, as a Diné woman will recall long afterward (NLC, Navajo oral history, statement 296), will eventually force her father, Cuthair, from his home (GLO surveyors recorded his home amid the scattered Hispanic dwellings).

The GLO surveyors also report houses and corrals of 20 other colonizer-settlers. One dwelling is at another spring that GLO surveyor Benson has "scripped." A third spring that Benson probably scripped, Jacob's Well, is near the dwelling of a Diné family. The settlers include several who figure in events to come. In addition to Palmer, north of Navajo Station (probably E. T. Palmer, who will figure in an 1887 incident), and James Houck at Navajo Springs, they include Commodore Perry Owen at Squaw Springs along the Overland Stage Road, a horse thief rather than a homesteader. As later documents will show, Perry Owen's exploits in the Chambers Checkerboard hardly predict the "colorful frontier sheriff" whom later generations will praise (Antram 1998:55; Tinsley 1993:63–64, 121). In a few years a photograph will capture Sheriff Owen and his flowing mane, kinked from being unbraided. Local Diné will later recall a "fierce white man with braids down his back" who camped at Navajo Springs around 1876 and then homesteaded there, stole Diné horses, and killed one of the People for trading horses too close to Owen's homestead (U.S. Senate, Subcommittee of the Committee on Indian Affairs 1937:17,967; see also Tinsley 1993:64). He will become Apache County sheriff in 1886 (Blue 2000:79).

The GLO surveyors also encounter Charles Hardison at Taylor Spring near the railroad. He had worked at Fort Sumner and returned to Fort Defiance with the People in 1868. He had been chief herder for the agency there until discharged on May 16, 1871, when he moved west of Fort Defiance to ranch on the lands of his Diné wife's family at Kin Lichee near Ganado and the treaty reservation's southwest corner. He had lived near Ganado as late as 1878, when one of the "witches" was killed in front of his house. Hardison applies for a homestead along the railroad (Brugge 1993a:15; McNitt 1962:246, 247n; NARA, homestead proof files P223 and P723, patents 311135 and 989477).

At Emigrant Springs along the Overland Stage Road, GLO surveyors find James Moore, probably John Walker, an Irishman with a Diné wife, Damasia, and children, one of whom, Frank, will become an interpreter at Saint Michaels Franciscan Mission south of Fort Defiance. After 1867 John Walker, under the name of John Garrett, had driven a stage between Fort Wingate and Fort Apache or had been a Pony Express rider between Santa Fe and Fort Huachuca. By the late 1880s, he will become a buddy of Commodore Perry Owen (Antram 1998:50–55; Franciscans, box 27, letter of May 19, 1909; Haile 1998:11). Farther east on a homestead at Graywater Spring was Freeman Hathorn, who had been a packer in the 1872–73 military campaign against the Apaches. In 1881 he was a cook and assistant to D. D. Graham, the first permanent trader at Zuni. Younger brothers will soon follow him to the Chambers Checkerboard and one will marry into a local Diné family (NARA, cash entry, patent CE-211). And at a spring about 15 miles northwest of Navajo Springs is Seth Tanner, who had moved there from the spring named after him farther northeast, where he had originally settled. Tanner had been part of the Mormon colonies near present

Winslow and at Tuba City in the 1870s. From him will come generations of Navajoland traders (Arrington 1979). Four unnamed settlers also have improvements in the Tanner Springs township.

Diné are probably aware that GLO surveyors also record several of their settlements. One of them is Tsii'agodii (Cuthair) near the Beale road, amid the scattered Hispanic homesites. Descendants will later recall that Cuthair went to Fort Sumner as a child and that he lived near where the GLO surveyors found him for a few more years until Mexican herders forced him to move near Coyote Spring (Houck's Tank). Cuthair's parents and their extended families ranged from south of Fort Defiance toward Saint Johns before the Long Walk (NLC, Navajo oral history, statements 296 and 416); descendants still live in the Chambers Checkerboard today. Another was Chee Dodge, whose "desert land claim" the surveyors locate near the railroad west of Navajo Station. Chee Dodge is the up-and-coming interpreter for the Navajo Agency at Fort Defiance, born before the Long Walk to a mother of the Navajo Jemez clan and a Bilagaana or Hispanic man attached to Fort Defiance (see chapter 8). South of Navajo Springs near the Beale road is the home of Many Horses, a large stockowner and the son of Ganado Mucho, who also uses land around Tanner Springs. Like his father, Many Horses is a mentor to the Ganado trader J. Lorenzo Hubbell (McNitt 1962:202).[4] Another large stockowner, Manuscito (Mancisco), lives along the Beale road near Jacob's Well, where decades later he will want to buy railroad land (Franciscans, box 26, letter of August 9, 1917; see chapter 7).

Near Graywater Spring are the homesites of unnamed Diné, perhaps including Hastiin Tółbaí (Mr. Graywater), named for the spring. He is later recalled by local Diné as a leader both before and after the Long Walk (NLC, Navajo oral history, statement 170). Diné raise all kinds of vegetables in fields along the Puerco and Overland Stage Road west of Houck (GLO, tract book 408). The farmers probably include Hastiin Ndaaz (Mr. Heavy), who will soon complain about a homesteader's stock in his field. Although the GLO surveyors do not report them, at least 12 other Diné and their families are in the Chambers Checkerboard, most of them probably relatives or in-laws of the Diné men named by the GLO surveyors, especially Many Horses and Cuthair. Besides nine Diné named in correspondence and cited in this chronicle, local Diné later will suggest the following heads of extended families in the Chambers Checkerboard in 1882–83: Hastiin Tsétah (Mr. Amid-Rocks) north of Jacob's Well (NLC, Navajo oral history, statement 354); Béégashii Neiłkaadí (Cowherder), born at Squaw Springs before the Long Walk and resident there afterward (NLC, Navajo oral history, statements 352 and 413); and Kinłichíínii Tsoh (Big Redhouse Clansman), a leader before and after the Long Walk who ranges throughout the Chambers Checkerboard (Franciscans, box 29, Simington letters, 1915; NLC, Navajo oral history, statement 232).

Altogether, then, at least 30 colonizer-settlers and 18 Diné men plus their families are in the Chambers Checkerboard. Most colonizer-settlers (at least the non-Hispanic ones) seem to be single men without dependents. The few with families have Diné wives and children. In contrast, most Diné residents named would have many dependents and relatives. Assuming eight people for each coresident family (Kelley and Whiteley 1989:230), Diné in the Chambers Checkerboard probably number 144-plus, compared with about 30-plus colonizers, not counting nonresident speculators, mobile railroad workers, and wandering cowboys. Yet even though the People probably outnumber colonizers by almost five to one, almost every reliable water source identified by the GLO surveys and other documents in the Chambers Checkerboard has some kind of colonizer presence at or near it, if only the scripped claim of an absentee speculator.[5]

TROUBLE SPOTS, 1883–1884: TANNER SPRINGS AND NAVAJO SPRINGS

Tanner Springs settler Barney Williams complains in June 1883 to Fort Defiance agent Denis Riordan that Navajos are threatening to kill him and other settlers if they do not let the Navajos water livestock at Tanner Springs. Only one Navajo, "To-yel-te" (probably Doo Yáłti'í, Silent One or Slow Talker), does have rights to the water, and Williams wants Riordan to come down and lay down the law (NLC, archive documents, letter of June 9, 1883). When Agent Riordan goes down, he tells the settlers to avoid violence and the Diné to leave the area except for Toh-yel-te, whom Riordan's predecessor Agent Eastman authorized by letter to use the spring. "I learned," Riordan writes the CIA, "that Tanner (after whom the spring is named) lived there for sometime but finally left it after a dispute with the Indians. . . . [T]he cause of his leaving was [Eastman's] letter." Riordan also pointedly repeats an early request to the CIA for useful guidance on how to handle such disputes (NLC, archive documents, letters of June 11 and 20, 1883).

Later in the summer, Williams and his neighbor John L. French complain again to Riordan that Navajos are stealing their horses and cattle (and those of trader Lewis Lynch of Navajo Springs [Station]) and vandalizing Williams's reservoir. One of the thieves is Ganado Mucho's son Many Horses of Navajo

Springs (NLC, archive documents, letter of August 9 and 14, 1883). Agent Riordan responds with a retinue of 20 troops from Fort Wingate and then crows to the CIA,

> The leader of the Indians, Toh-yel-te by name, declared his purpose to die right there sooner than give up the spring. I heard the story of each side fully. The Indians talked all night. After listening to everything bearing on the subject, I told Toh-yel-te he could begin getting ready to die just as soon as he pleased, that he must leave that place. . . . [T]he Indians came to me and accepted my terms.
>
> I then told them I was not disposed to be unnecessarily harsh with them, that they might stay there and gather the present crop of corn, after which they must move north of the southern line of the reservation.
>
> This matter has kept the settlers to the south and west of here thoroughly alarmed for some time past. It is now settled and, I trust, for all time. (NLC, archive documents, letter of August 24, 1883)

Riordan adds that on his June trip to Tanner Springs he also settled a dispute over two cows and four calves claimed by both a Navajo and a settler. He awarded the stock to the Navajo (NLC, archive documents, letter August 31, 1883).

Three weeks later all hell breaks loose. On September 15, 1883, rancher J. D. Houck telegraphs Riordan: "Indians fired on Ranche. Please assist us." A hysterical story in the *Albuquerque Globe Democrat* on the same day reports that 100 Navajos fired on the "Hancho ranch" a quarter mile (actually four miles) from Navajo Station. The Navajos had found a Navajo boy dead and believed a "Hancho" cowboy killed him (NLC, archive documents, letters of September 15 and 17, 1883; *Albuquerque Globe Democrat*, September 15, 1883). "Hancho" may be a misunderstanding of "Houck" or possibly of "Hashknife," the brand of the cattle company owned in part by railroad board members and nicknamed for its brand.[6]

Navajos reach Agent Riordan at Fort Wingate to report the killing. He follows them back to Navajo Springs with troops and learns that

> on Saturday early in the morning a Navajo boy, the son of a chief called Sin-ah-jin-ni-be-gay [Tsi'naajinii Biye', Son of Blackwood Streak Clansman] was shot twice by an American. The boy lingered until that night when he died. When he reached help, which he managed to do, he told his story which was, that a man named C. P. Owen [the future sheriff] had shot him, that he (the Indian) was unarmed and did not know the reason of his being shot.

Two other Navajos had started out with the one who was killed to herd up their horses, and who were a mile or so from him at the time of the shooting, immediately got on the trail of the murderer and followed him to his house, or rather, the house of J. D. Houck where he lived. I went over the ground with Lieut. Lockett of the 4th Cavalry and trailed the tracks right from the place where the Indian fell from his horse when he was shot to the door of Houck's house. I arrested Owen and charged him with the killing of the Indian boy. He is now in keeping of the military authorities at Fort Wingate.

These men Owen and Houck are men dangerous to the peace and good order of this region. I saw over twenty five Indians who have been shot at by them during the past year or two, including an Indian woman. I despair of securing a conviction of either of them; and realize that I am liable to be assassinated by them for undertaking to punish them for their crimes. [The letter then asks the CIA for a unit of scouts—Navajos who served with the military—or a platoon of cavalry to be based at Fort Defiance.] (NLC, archive documents, Riordan to CIA, September 21, 1883)

Two weeks after the incident, a judge in Albuquerque, New Mexico Territory, rules that Owen's crime comes under the jurisdiction of the civil authorities in Apache County, Arizona Territory. (The jurisdiction is not federal since Owen committed the crime off the reservation.) Owen is sent west. With more foresight than he showed about the Tanner Springs incident, Riordan writes the CIA:

My opinion is that no conviction will follow. In fact, I do not believe the man will even be tried.

Meanwhile, the other murderer I arrested [in another incident in northern Navajoland before September 15] lays in the guard house at Wingate, in irons. He too committed the crime off the reservation. But he is an Indian and habeas corpus acts don't reach such as he. (NLC, archive documents, letter of September 27, 1883)

Probably prompted by this incident, Riordan later notifies Tsi'naajinii, "chief of the Navajos living southwest of the reservation" along the railroad in Arizona Territory, that "he and his people" must move on the reservation the following spring and "never plant another crop in the valley of the Puerco." The reason is to prevent clashes with the settlers (NLC, archive documents, letter of December 22, 1883). But the next June, Barney Williams again complains to Riordan about Navajo encroachment and asks for troops (NLC, archive documents, letter of June 5, 1884).

The next month, John Bowman replaces Riordan as agent. Evidently in the first days of Agent Bowman's tenure, disputes have occurred at Emigrant Springs, Allantown, and Navajo Springs. "Old Man" Leonard seems to have replaced Houck at Navajo Springs (NLC, archive documents, Fort Defiance Agency letterbook notation of July 6, 1884). William Leonard is the licensed Fort Defiance post trader, and Barney Williams was working for him at Ganado in 1882 (see below). The Emigrant Springs dispute seems to be a complaint by an "old gray-headed man and sister" that John Walker sold land with a spring (Emigrant Springs) to Bennett (the trader at Houck's Tank), but they have occupied this land for years and have improvements on it. Bowman asks Bennett for his side of the story (NLC, archive documents, letter of July 16, 1884).

Agent Bowman writes to W. B. Leonard in August and September. Bowman first says he will send a scout to Leonard's place to investigate Leonard's complaint and tell the Navajos who are giving him trouble to stop or they will be punished. Whether Leonard's place is at Navajo Springs or Tanner Springs is unclear. Later, Bowman tells Leonard he is sending Chee Dodge, the interpreter, to fix things up for Leonard. Dodge will have a Navajo scout (agency policeman), Man the Dog Bit, arrest the offender. In November and December Bowman again is caught in the middle of complaints between Leonard and Navajos. Bowman deferentially sends Navajo scouts to Leonard twice to hear Leonard's complaints, and once sends Leonard a note with "Bearer," one "Little Man," who says he had some cows on Leonard's range and now cannot find them. Little Man wants Leonard to tell him where to find his cows.

ESCALATING VIOLENCE, 1885–1887

Early in 1885 Many Horses' protégé, Ganado trader J. Lorenzo Hubbell, becomes Apache County sheriff, based in Saint Johns. Later he will claim to have gone after Texans who had stolen Navajo horses, gotten the horses back, and jailed the Texans, but records of the time do not mention the incident (Blue 2000:72–73; a theft of horses from Ganado Mucho and others in 1887 may be this incident [see below], when Hubbell was no longer sheriff). In April trader-rancher William Leonard joins the Apache County Board of Supervisors, which oversees Sheriff Hubbell, and Hubbell visits Leonard at either Navajo Springs or Tanner Springs. A few weeks later, the supervisors start trying to remove

Hubbell from office, but their efforts fail. What has led to the split between Hubbell and the supervisors is not clear (Blue 2000:67, 72–80). The supervisors are cattle owners, while Hubbell's in-laws at Saint Johns raise sheep, so rivalries over rangeland may be at issue.

In May Agent Bowman writes to Leonard at Tanner Springs that an "old Indian" wants to plant at the wash near Leonard's place and that Ganado Mucho has endorsed the elder's request. Bowman has told the elder that he could plant only with Leonard's consent (NLC, archive documents, letter of May 11, 1885).

James Houck moves away to one of the new railroad towns to the west, Holbrook or Winslow.[7] Meanwhile, Peter-Joseph Hill applies for a homestead around the stage station west of Bennett's trading post at Houck's Tank, which may have been Houck's original trading post. Soon Hill's neighbor, Hastiin Ndaaz (Mr. Heavy), visits Fort Defiance to complain that Hill's cattle have eaten all his corn. Samuel E. Day, a clerk acting as agent, sends Hastiin Ndaaz to Hill with a note that Hill could pay him something. The field of Hastiin Ndaaz is probably the large Navajo field that GLO land surveyors reported in 1882 at a place just north of Hill's later homestead.[8]

Two years have passed since Owen killed the Diné youth near Navajo Springs. At the beginning of November, Andrew Cooper, a cowboy at Tanner Springs, shoots and kills the Navajo "To-yel-ti" in front of three Diné children and a man. The victim's kin, led by Ganado Mucho, threaten to massacre the other settlers at Tanner Springs, but acting agent Samuel Day Sr. intervenes. Cooper then holes up at Navajo Springs (NLC, archive documents, letters of November 3, 10, and 9, 1885; Fort Defiance Agency letterbook, November 10,1885). Agent Bowman asks the district attorney in Prescott, Arizona, to investigate and bring the killer to trial. Bowman offers some background:

> The place where this affair occurred is about thirty miles south of the Moquis [Hopi] reservation. Near this place there is a fine large spring, at which members of this tribe [Navajos] have lived for many generations although they have made no improvements of a substantial character. Some four years ago, two Americans took a small herd of cattle to this place, and made an agreement with the Indian who lived there (and the same one who was killed) to the effect that they would both live there and occupy, and own, the spring in common. [See the preceding subsection; the agreement probably refers to the agent's letter on behalf of Toh-yel-te that caused Seth Tanner to move away.] Everything went along smoothly for a while but finally the whites having erected a stone house, and made other

improvements, began to look on their Indian neighbor as a trespasser and to commence proceedings for getting rid of him. [This probably refers to efforts of Barney Williams.] The result was that by the means of coaxing, bribery, and intimidation, they induced the Indian to consent to move away and relinquish any claim to the spring. He moved away several miles and built his hogan at another small spring where he soon found himself in the way. The white men coaxed the Indian to sell his right to them and to leave the section. He did leave for a while but a few days ago moved back with his family and herds of sheep. The next day after his arrival, and while he was watering his sheep at a pool, a few miles west of this ranch, Cooper, a man who was employed as a herder by Mr. Smith, the present owner of the Tanner Springs ranch, rode down there and asked the Indian to take his sheep away. The white man could not talk Navajo and the Indian could not talk English. . . . N[o] one knows who fired first, but the white man shot the Indian's horse, which fell. In falling the Indian grasped the white man by the arm and both came to the ground together. The white man being by far the strongest shook off his opponent, and shot him twice killing him instantly, then started home on the run. (NLC, archive documents, Bowman to CIA, November 10, 1885)

The Diné take some of Smith's cattle. Bowman will soon send John N. Stuart, agency blacksmith and chief of scouts, among the Chambers Checkerboard Diné to buy them back (NLC, archive documents, letter of February 7, 1886).

Around 1970 a local Diné will recall that a "cow rancher" at Tanner Springs "didn't want sheep herders to herd sheep around his property. But there was this deaf mute [Doo Yáłti'í] that herded his sheep into that particular area and was shot to death. He was one of the leaders then." So trader J. L. Hubbell and a lot of Diné leaders went after "the long-haired rancher to kill him, but Long-hair was never found." The story went around that Longhair was killed. This happened when the railroad was being built (Hubbell Trading Post, oral history interview 26). We suggest that Longhair was Commodore Perry Owen and that this story compresses two similar killings by settlers.

Having quit in April 1886 as Fort Defiance agent, Bowman takes up a home-stead a mile and a half east of Navajo Station. Improvements are a stone house of four rooms, stable or barn, tool house or store house, two corrals, windmill, and tanks. He has an acre and a half in fruit trees and has tried without success to grow alfalfa. His cattle and horses range on the surrounding "public domain." These improvements could not have sprung up overnight. Records do not show whether Bowman built them while he was agent or whether they belonged to someone else (Leonard?) (NARA, cash entry CE-429). It turns out that Bowman also has land at Tanner Springs, which he sells at the end of January 1887 to the Defiance Cattle Company. When he acquired this holding is not clear, nor is the identity of Defiance Cattle Company (Franciscans, box 31, letter of February 25, 1915).

Later in the year, J. L. Hubbell loses his county sheriff seat to none other than Commodore Perry Owen, the candidate of Hubbell's opponents on the board of supervisors (Blue 2000:79).

A little more than a year after the murder of To-yel-ti comes the most violent incident yet (NLC, archive documents, letters of February 14, 15, and 18, 1887). It starts at Bennett's Houck's Tank store, when Hastiin Łichíí' (Mr. Red) brings in a stray horse for Bennett to find the owner. Bennett says that the horse belongs to Frank Palmer, who evidently works sometimes for Bennett, probably as a cowboy (Bennett later will say he was mentally unstable). Mr. Red leaves the horse with Bennett, who gives it back to Palmer. Palmer claims to find some damage to the horse and gets a warrant from the justice of the peace at Navajo Springs (Station?) to arrest Mr. Red for horse theft. A deputy, George Lockhart, Palmer, and one T. V. King then leave their home at Navajo Springs to go after Mr. Red.

The three men descend on a Diné hogan 15–20 miles south of Houck's Tank near Cuthair's home. Lockhart enters the hogan, shooting at the occupants, killing one "Ugly Gun," and wounding (perhaps mortally) José, a Spanish interpreter and sheep herder with Mr. Red's group. Others in the hogan shoot Lockhart down in the doorway. At least two Diné then run out, chasing Palmer and King. Four miles north of the hogan, the fugitives dismount because one horse is wounded and the terrain is too steep to descend on horseback. They may be trying to get back to Bennett's ranch at Emigrant Springs. There the Diné catch them and kill them.

Bowman's successor Agent Patterson discredits King and Palmer as army deserters. John Bowman himself helps search for the bodies and tells other settlers to be peaceful toward the Navajos. More than a century later, a local Diné woman will retell the story.

Trader Bennett was called Ntł'ahí [Lefty, Handicapped]. He had horses in a pen. A Navajo family—a man, his wife, and a young child—were living on the ridge south of the trading post. They came down in a two-wheeled wagon, bringing a rug to trade at the store. As they went home, a colt from the pen followed them, then turned around. The Bilagaanas at the trading post missed the colt, so two or three Bilagaanas chased after the Diné family the next day. The man was in the hogan, sewing moccasins. Another guy was there too. The Bilagaanas came into the hogan shooting. They asked where the colt was and shot the moccasin-maker. The other Navajo guy shot a Bilagaana going out the door, then shot the other when he was trying to get on the horse. The third Bilagaana got away. The hogan was about 8–10 miles south of Houck. After that, the Diné family fled to Navajo Mountain and never came back. (Kelley and Francis 1998b, November 12, 1998)

Cowboys steal 157 horses belonging to headman Ganado Mucho and others from near Navajo Springs and drive them 50–60 miles before Diné recover the horses. At Agent Patterson's request, General Miles stations troops from Wingate at Navajo Springs. Acting Fort Defiance agent Ford tells sheriff C. P. Owen that he cannot come on the reservation with a posse to arrest Navajos (NLC, archive documents, letters of March 21 and March 31, 1887; U.S. Commissioner of Indian Affairs 1887:175). Agent Riordan in 1883 rightly foresaw that Owen would remain free despite the Diné he had killed.

AFTER 1887

After the crescendo of conflict in 1887, silence falls. Financial panic grips the nation, and cattle prices nosedive (White 1991:225). Investors take their money out of ranches, and ranchers sell the cattle to pay off investors. The cattle disappear, and with them go the cowboys. The Bilagaanas who stay in the Chambers Checkerboard are those who have actually filed on homesteads and built trading posts: Lynch and Bowman at Navajo Station, Hardison nearby (until his death in a few years), Bennett at Emigrant Springs and Houck's Tank, along with his neighbor Hill (for a few more years) and the Hathorn brothers. Some of these people will have generations of descendants in the area, including Diné families.

Perhaps the most dramatic sign of economic reversal is that by 1891 two Diné have taken possession of Tanner Springs, the object of so much bloodshed. The new occupants are Arthur Chester and Chee Dodge. Dodge's desert land claim along the railroad west of Navajo Station was noted by GLO land surveyors in 1882. Since 1884 Dodge also has been a trader in partnership with S. E. Aldrich at Round Rock in the northern Navajo Reservation. Aldrich is the Apache wars veteran and army contractor who owns a store, earlier with James Bennett, later with Chee Dodge, at Manuelito (McNitt 1962:249, 279). Chee Dodge buys land from the Defiance Cattle Company (possibly W. B. Leonard) sometime after the Defiance Company got it in 1887 from John Bowman. Homesteader Freeman Hathorn may have brokered the sale (Franciscans, box 31, letter of February 25, 1915).

EARLIER, IN THE SEATS OF COLONIAL POWER . . .

The Chambers Checkerboard between 1882 and 1887 offers an oblique view of Fort Defiance, where the drama of early military and government agents and merchants set patterns for Diné history in the coming decades. The drama seems to flow from a conflict between civilian and military authorities. Civilian authority consisted of the hierarchy from agent up through commissioner of Indian Affairs to secretary of the interior. This hierarchy connected to philanthropists, like the Presbyterian Church, which Washindoon allowed to vet Indian Service appointments in the Southwest. It also connected to capitalists, like the mine speculators at whose behest Fort Defiance agent W. F. Arny tried to get part of the treaty reservation restored to the public domain between 1873 and 1875 (Graves 1998:69–91; McNitt 1962:142–165). Military authority consisted of the army west of the Missouri and its various outposts, most obviously Fort Wingate, which housed the garrison for Navajoland. Tied up with the military were merchants of the Santa Fe trade, whose coziness with the army went back to Fort Sumner and to Fort Union in northeastern New Mexico, the guardhouse of the Santa Fe Trail (Thompson 1978). These merchants contracted to supply the military posts and the traders licensed at those posts. These same merchants supplied trading posts at the civilian Indian agencies, including Fort Defiance. The Spiegelbergs seem to have been the main Santa Fe merchants involved with Fort Wingate and Fort Defiance in the 1860s and 1870s (McNitt 1962:107–115). The conflict seems to have pitted national elites that were aligned with civil authorities against territorial (mercantile) ones that were aligned with the military, though civilian agents and others might opportunistically shift between these larger alignments.

The conflict worked itself out at Fort Defiance between agents and certain traders, especially Thomas Keam, whose biographer, Laura Graves (1998:89–90), confirms that the Department of the Interior and the War Department "were locked in a bitter dispute over who should control Indian affairs." After the

Civil War, General William T. Sherman pressured the government to replace the civilian Indian agents with the military, the justification being that the army, with its fort system and quartermaster and commissary staffs in place, could most efficiently issue rations and annuity goods. When Keam applied in 1873 for a permanent position as Navajo agent at Fort Defiance, Sherman's support was enough for the interior secretary to disqualify him.

Backgrounds given above on Chambers Checkerboard residents of the early 1880s (Hardison, Chee Dodge, and William Leonard) show that, like Keam, they were 1870s alumni of the Fort Defiance Agency. By the late 1870s, Keam seems to have been a mentor of Leonard when Leonard was starting his ranch at Ganado. Though historians spotlight Keam as a pioneer trader to both Navajos and Hopis, his network of agency cronies who ranched in the Chambers Checkerboard during the 1880s suggests that his trading was actually a sideline to ranching, as it was for most early traders in northeastern Arizona (Graves 1998:118). The factional squabbles at the Fort Defiance Agency reveal the aims of these early ranchers. The story is as follows.

Keam was a soldier who mustered out at Fort Stanton (Apache country) in 1866 and was Spanish interpreter to agents James Carry French and then Frank Tracy Bennett at Fort Defiance by 1869 (French and Bennett were military). Keam soon became assistant agent (1871–72), then acting agent (1872–73). As agent, Keam got in good with Diné leaders, especially the precaptivity resisters Manuelito and Ganado Mucho, later appointed by agents as the main liaisons with local Diné leaders. Keam organized 13 headmen, each with 9 or 10 followers, into a short-lived Navajo police force, though it was disbanded when the agency could not pay the men or provide uniforms (Graves 1998:42; McNitt 1962:124–137).

In 1873, on the pretext that Keam and several other agency workers were living immorally with Diné women, the new civilian agent, W. F. Arny, fired the men. Arny's motive seems to have been to discredit Keam not only because Keam was a rival for Arny's position but also because he could (and did) expose Arny's corruption. Anson Damon (butcher), Jesus Arviso (interpreter), W. W. Owens (chief herder), William Clark, Charles Hardison (herder), and Perry Williams all went (Graves 1998:67–71; McNitt 1962:144–145). In Williams's case, the Diné woman in question seems to have been the one who raised Chee Dodge (Borgman 1948:85; one wonders whether Perry Williams and Barney Williams were related).

Arviso, Damon, Keam, and Hardison moved just across the reservation line, the first three just south of Fort Defiance, and Hardison to Kin Lichee. Perry

Williams got trading licenses at Fort Defiance and later north at Washington (Narbona) Pass. Keam promptly applied for a license to trade at Fort Defiance, with Santa Fe merchants Lehman Spiegelberg and Herman Ilfeld securing his bond. But Agent Arny refused to issue the license. (Maybe Keam's bad luck benefited Perry Williams.) Keam therefore traded from his place at Fair View, south of Fort Defiance outside the reservation, while he "plotted to get hired as the Navajos' agent" (Graves 1998:68, 70–71, 109, 258n1; see also McNitt 1962:114, 201n2). From then into the early 1880s, the army tried several times to get Keam to replace the existing agent, but the Presbyterians and the interior secretary would have none of it (Graves 1998:80–86, 89; McNitt 1962:166–175).

In 1875 Keam seems to have started to trade at the place later called Keams Canyon, east of the Hopi villages near both Hopi and Navajo communities. At this time there was no reservation for Hopis or for Navajos living west of the 1868 treaty reservation. Ganado, midway between Fort Defiance and Keams Canyon, was just outside the southwest corner of the 1868 reservation. The U.S. government had established an agency for the Hopis in 1869 at what was later called Keams Canyon, but no agent lived there until 1880. If there was a Hopi agent at all, he lived at Fort Defiance, though one agent in 1874 built a few structures at Keams Canyon. Keam's trading post was to be part of a cattle ranch, and the Spiegelbergs again secured the bond for Keam's license. (Though the place was not on any reservation, perhaps the license was necessary because the post was at an agent's headquarters.) The Fort Wingate commanding officer, Colonel J. Irwin Gregg, who presumably issued the license, had just replaced Arny as agent at Fort Defiance after a group of Diné leaders revealed that Arny had kept for himself annuity goods meant for Diné (Graves 1998:80, 173–174, 259n26; McNitt 1962:161, 181, 187).

The Hopi Agency was discontinued in 1876 for lack of funds. It reopened in 1878, but agents again lived at Fort Defiance. Keam continued with stores at both Keams Canyon and Fair View, with William Leonard working for Keam at Fair View in the late 1870s. In 1876 Leonard may have been a teacher at Fort Defiance, where the Presbyterians had been trying to run a boarding school since 1870. Between 1877 and 1879 he clerked for trader Romulo Martinez at Fort Defiance (Graves 1998:109; McNitt 1962:80n10, 138).

William Leonard was also in business with Barney Williams outside the reservation at Ganado, 40 miles west of Fort Defiance. Like Keam, Leonard and Williams were in the first wave of would-be rancher-traders to set up just outside the reservation so they could raise cattle and avoid running the gauntlet of federal licensing. Seemingly contradictory stories about early trading posts at Ganado tell of Williams or Leonard selling a store in 1876 or 1878 to future county sheriff J. Lorenzo Hubbell, starting Hubbell's career as a legendary trader (Blue 2000:37). Hubbell himself had clerked at stores in Fort Wingate and Fort Defiance sometime between 1874 and 1876. Hubbell's father was a former soldier and prominent merchant trader–military contractor in the Rio Grande valley, and his mother's family were wealthy Hispanic landowners south of Albuquerque. By 1880 Hubbell had a store in Saint Johns and was courting a daughter of Cebolleta, New Mexico, sheep ranchers who were among the first Saint Johns settlers (Blue 2000:8–54, 67–69; Brugge 1993:21–25). Were these the people whose Mexican herders in the Chambers Checkerboard mentioned above eventually displaced the Navajo Cuthair?

Why raise cattle as near the reservation as possible? What the 1870s agenda may have been shows up in 1881–83 correspondence of Fort Defiance agents with the military presented above. This correspondence always raises the issue of Navajos living outside the reservation. Agent Eastman, backed by the CIA and the secretary of the interior, says that Navajos can live outside the reservation. The military and Eastman's successor Riordan (1883), however, say the Navajos must stay within the reservation, where the agent must have authority to requisition rations for them because the reservation land base is too small to support them. Note that the Spiegelbergs, backers of Thomas Keam, in 1874 supplied almost $10,000 worth of cattle as rations to the Navajo Agency and 2,200 sheep for the Hopis (McNitt 1962:115).

The schools planned at the agency headquarters also would have been sources of beef contracts. These schools, however, amounted to little until 1887. In the meantime, to have access to other markets besides rations and an as-yet-insignificant school supply, one would want a ranch as near as possible to the proposed transcontinental railroad, which was to follow the Overland Stage Road, first marked out in 1858 and 1863. Ganado Mucho, whose range covered the area south of Keams Canyon and Ganado down to where the railroad was planned, found Keam and Hubbell cozying up to him. A few years later, Barney Williams tried to bully him. Marrying into Diné families, as Keam, Hardison, and the Lynches did, may have been a better choice for a trader-rancher to secure land use.

In January 1880 the Navajo Reservation boundary was extended, engulfing Keam's place at Fair View, as well as Ganado and Kinlichee (Correll and

Dehiya 1978:10–11). Keam closed the Fair View post and moved to the Keams Canyon post, which was still outside the reservation and which his brother had been running for him. Hubbell's "trading ranch," now just inside the reservation, had off-reservation public domain only a stone's throw across the boundary (Blue 2000:70–71; Graves 1998:110).

IN THE SEATS OF COLONIAL POWER DURING THE CHAMBERS CHECKERBOARD VIOLENCE

Now we are back to the beginning of the times of violence in the Chambers Checkerboard. Informal military fact-finder Captain J. G. Bourke, traveling to Hopi in April 1881, stays with Fort Defiance post trader Leonard, then at Ganado with Barney Williams. After moving on to Keam's place, Bourke is impressed by Keam's eagerness to accommodate him (Bourke 1984:71–80, 236; McNitt 1962:169–171). It almost seems like Keam built the compound to sell to the government for an agency headquarters and school.

In 1882, the year before he makes his presence all too well known at Tanner Springs, Barney Williams is complaining about the 1880 Navajo Reservation boundary extension. Dr. James Sutherland of Hopi reports to Fort Defiance agent Eastman that Williams is working for Leonard at the Ganado post while Leonard is still trading at Fort Defiance and also reportedly is in a "ring" with Thomas Keam. Williams has recently driven a herd of 500 cattle onto the reservation and is reportedly connected to Lambert M. Hopkins, post trader at Fort Wingate (NLC, archive documents, letter of March 20, 1882). The 1880 reservation extension is probably why Williams, presumably fronting for Leonard, sets up at Tanner Springs. The extension might also explain Hardison's move to the railroad, as well as Chee Dodge's desert land claim there, if Chee Dodge is in fact tied up with Leonard and his associates, who may be friends of Dodge's stepfather, Perry Williams (Perry Williams's name is not in the records cited here, however).

In December 1882 an executive order creates another reservation that encompasses the Hopi Mesas, the Lava Buttes to the south, and Black Mesa to the north, adjoining the 1880 Navajo Reservation extension to take in Keams Canyon. Rancher-traders who want to stay outside reservation land must move farther afield. The 1882 reservation results from a dispute between Hopi agent Fleming and Jeremiah Sullivan, son of former Hopi agent John Sullivan. Dr. Jeremiah Sullivan and another colonizer-settler named Merritt have been urging the Hopis to oppose the agent's efforts to send their children to boarding schools. Sullivan and Merritt challenge Fleming to evict them from Hopiland, since there is no reservation to evict them from, so Fleming asks for the 1882 executive order. The next step is a boarding school at Keams Canyon to get rid of one reason for Hopi opposition: the distance of schools from Hopiland (Correll and Dehiya 1978:12–14; Graves 1998:175; Indian Law Resource Center 1979; NLC, archive documents, letters of September 9, 15, December 4, 26, 1882; Redhouse 1985a). Keam does nothing to stop the 1882 executive order, even though a reservation seems likely to jeopardize his cattle ranch headquarters. Instead, he enlarges his compound in the canyon and takes out a desert land claim of 160 acres on the surrounding land. This claim will either protect his holdings or qualify him for federal compensation (Graves 1998:176).

By 1882–83 the same people connected with Ganado, Fort Wingate, and the pro-Keam faction at Fort Defiance also appear at Tanner Springs and Navajo Station: Charles Hardison, Barney Williams, and William Leonard. In 1882 trader Leonard leaves Fort Defiance for Navajo Springs and the stock business. One suspects that these intruders into the Chambers Checkerboard are still pursuing a plan to raise beef to supply the Navajo and Hopi Agencies and future schools with rations. The most advantageous range, between the new reservations and the railroad, is what they have already started using. By this time, Hubbell is filling large beef contracts (one for 60,000 pounds) with both Navajo and Hopi Agencies (Blue 2000:70–71; McNitt 1962:80n10). Hubbell's history of business ties with Leonard hints at a ring linking both Hubbell and Keam to Leonard and his Tanner Springs ranch.

Cattle prices are high, so as soon as the railroad comes in to give access to eastern markets, speculators back ranchers to move onto the land. GLO land surveyor Benson, who placed scrip on the springs, is clearly speculating on the cattle boom, as is the Hashknife Outfit (Aztec Land and Cattle Company) west of the Chambers Checkerboard (Meinig 1971:45). Early settlers like James Houck and Commodore Perry Owen may have ties to these interests. Hispanic sheepherders (possibly including herders for J. L. Hubbell's in-laws) probably gravitate toward the railroad from Saint Johns.

The Navajo and Hopi Agencies are also nudging school enrollments upward. The Fort Defiance school has a new building ready by 1884 to accommodate about 200 students, and Bowman is also pushing for a school for 250 Hopis. Sure enough, Bowman wants the government to use Keam's property, thereby enabling Keam to profit from both the sale and the cattle ranch. In 1887 the government finally agrees to rent the buildings, and the school opens with 40 students. This year of financial panic is also the year that schooling for Indian children becomes compulsory (Young 1961:8–10). Keam will deed his property to the U.S. government in 1889 for $10,000 (Graves 1998:121–124, 180–187, 269n19; NLC, archive documents, letter of December 27, 1884). Even though beef prices fall nationally, federal contracts for Indian agencies are paying above market value. In 1889 Keam will contract to supply 20,000 pounds of beef for $10 per 100 pounds and much more in later years. It is no surprise, therefore, that Keam will help the Hopi Agency and the U.S. Army take Hopi children from their homes for school, even at gunpoint (Graves 1998:189–190, 196–200, 291–292n70, 293n72).

As the schools will rescue Keam from the falling cattle market, trader-ranchers Chee Dodge and Arthur Chester at Tanner Springs (and Crystal on the Navajo Reservation north of Fort Defiance) will adapt in a different way. Chee Dodge is uniquely positioned because, unlike most of his fellow Diné on his mother's side, he has access to investment capital, and, unlike his fellow colonizers on his father's side, he can run livestock on the reservation without a license. This he reportedly starts to do in 1886 at Crystal, probably on range of his wife's family and in connection with his 1884 trading post partnership farther north at Round Rock (Borgman 1948; McNitt 1962:279; NLC, Navajo oral history, statement 465). Chester is from Mancos Creek, Colorado, and married into a Crystal family in the 1880s. He may have connected with Chee Dodge through the Round Rock Trading Post, which probably includes Mancos Creek in its trade area (Franciscans, box 28, genealogical card says that "Dodge's aunt" raised Chester). Chester will settle at Tanner Springs in 1890 or 1891, seemingly in partnership with Dodge. Chester's descendants later will recall that Chester's wife's mother was born near future Saint Johns around 1850 and that later her family moved up to Crystal because of raids by Zunis, Mexicans, and Western Apaches (Franciscans, box 28, Chester's letter to Navajo Tribal Council, 1951; NLC, Navajo oral history, statement 348).

IN HINDSIGHT

This chapter tells two tales. One recounts how "American" settlers tried to drive out the People they found outside the Navajo Reservation in the Chambers

Checkerboard as they introduced the first raw developments of frontier capitalism. The Diné adapted to newly limited political sovereignty and clung to their lands by trying to make their agent act on their behalf and, when their protests failed and settlers started killing them, by returning fire. With the help of a national depression, they prevailed for the moment.

The other story is about events in more distant seats of colonial power, mostly hidden from the People. Both Diné, wielding their newly limited political sovereignty, and settlers sought the power of the U.S. government agents to back their claims. (The agents, in turn, seem to have courted Ganado Mucho and Manuelito for their power to quell Diné dissidents.) But these agents were also locked in struggles to advance their own interests through the military, higher civilian government authorities, and merchants, who competed to control First Nations people, land, and resources. On the one hand, the military and merchants wanted to confine the People within the too-small reservation so that off-reservation areas would be free for "American" beef producers, who would then sell the beef to the agency to feed the People lacking enough land to feed themselves. On the other hand, civilian authorities supported the People's off-reservation land rights so as to undermine the military-mercantile "rings" that threatened their power and therefore perhaps also encouraged Ganado Mucho to keep control of dissidents. If Diné fought the colonizers, the military would take control from the civilian agents. These conflicts fueled violence in the Chambers Checkerboard. However, military, merchants, and civilian government agents all joined hands to support boarding schools. And when the national cattle market collapsed in the mid-1880s and Indian boarding schools not coincidentally became important as a possible market for beef, violence abated. Through resistance and persistence, the Diné had kept the land. Their struggles were not over, though. Chapter 7 continues the story.

7

INDIAN GIVING ON THE
RAILROAD FRONTIER

THIS CHAPTER continues the story begun in chapter 6 about how the railroad and colonizer-ranchers overran Diné south of the reservation in the 1880s and how the People then defended their land and their sovereignty.[1] This chapter tells how, after 1900, Franciscan father Anselm Weber, the railroad, and Washindoon helped the People secure their land rights. But the lands—trust-patented Indian allotments to individual Diné—were only temporary place-holders for a grander railroad scheme. Later, finding themselves in the way and threatened with dispossession, the People invoked their family histories to support their claims to the land, but to no avail. Only later, in an ironic turn of events, did the Navajo Nation government regain the land. But the families never did, and many details of their histories have probably been lost, as elders could not teach youngsters their family histories by visiting former family sites.

Most of us have struggled with endless government rules about land use and ownership. We don't realize that they were just as bad a century ago, as the documents for the Chambers Checkerboard show. Those documents also show the logistics of widely scattered, unschooled, non-English-speaking Diné making written applications for specific half-mile-square parcels of land, the allotments (with patents held in trust by Washindoon), and getting each square marked on the ground. Most of these families traded wool, livestock, and weaving at local trading posts for store credit but nevertheless managed to pay with hard currency for the surveys and leases on surrounding unallotted railroad lands. Much of the documentation used in this chapter is based on the paperwork that Diné had to file to hold onto their own lands. They had to make themselves "legible" (in Andrew Curley's term; see the introduction) to defend their land rights. In the 1930s Washindoon extended the Navajo Reservation boundary in Arizona southward to just north of the Chambers Checkerboard, canceled the trust-patented allotments ("trust" indeed!), and told the People to move onto the newly extended reservation (see Kelley 1979 about the allotting program).

THE PEOPLE TELL THEIR STORY

In two 1936 letters, the Chambers Checkerboard families protested to a subcommittee of the U.S. Senate Committee on Indian Affairs. In one, addressed to the president of the United States, they recounted their own history as follows.

> The Navajo Indians have lived on this land, including Sanders, Chambers, and Taylor Springs, Navajo, Squaw Springs, and Navajo Springs, before 1864, when our forefathers were moved to Fort Sumner as prisoners of war. Upon returning from there they came back to live in the same place. They lived here for a good many years and were happy [but not quite; see chapter 6].
>
> Then, over 30 years ago the government began to survey this land and gave it to the Indians in allotments. The Indians were urged to improve this land. They built homes, made corrals, and fenced in their fields, just as the Government had told them to do. Many of the Indians were granted "Pattens" [trust patents to Indian allotments] and land papers on their holdings. Then the first white man rancher [Charles Hardison; see chapter 6] settled on the Navajo Reservation [among the Navajo allotments] at Taylor Springs, he never gave the Indians any trouble, so the Indians left him in peace. Then a nephew of Burr Porter settled in Navajo, Ariz. Later Burr Porter, himself, took possession of this same place.
>
> Clifford Smith came to this country about 14 years ago. He lives at Squaw Springs. About 2 miles south of Squaw Springs another white rancher came to live. About 4 miles north of Chambers, Joe Mullan [Mullen] came to live. Later he sold his ranch to Burke McCarrow [Bert McCarrell]. Then old man Woods took his land near the Santa Fe Railroad, about 3½ miles east of Chambers. That was about 27 years ago, and his children live there yet. His ranch joins that of

Fran Davidson and Jene Eagles [Nelson]. Mr. and Mrs. Spencer Balcomb came to live in Chambers. Later they sold their land and trading store to Mrs. Cassidy. Tom Pelton has a ranch next to Frank Woods since a year ago. William Goodman lived in Sanders about 15 years, then he sold his store and land to Spencer Balcomb. He lived there about 9 years now. Most of the white ranchers took land near the Santa Fe Railroad in olden times. Those who came later settled on the Navajo Reservation [among the allotments] and took homesteads. On the St. Johns–Springerville Road, 1 mile from Sanders, Clifford [Carl?] Hill lived 28 years. Another white rancher has land next to his. We don't know his right name, but his nickname is "Cotton." With many of these white ranchers the Indians never had any trouble.

When Clifford Smith came to this country he homesteaded on the land belonging to an Indian named Jay Bauldin. The Indian had land papers and a good water hole, therefore Clifford Smith had no business taking his land. The Indian went several times to the Fort Defiance Agency about his land, but nothing was ever done to help him. At first his [Smith's] land was only 1 mile square. From there he has been moving his boundary line every year. Burke McCarrow and Burr Porter are also moving their boundary lines every year. They tell the Indians they own some of the land and they are leasing the rest. Where are they getting the authority to add so much land to their holdings? Clifford Smith has been buying cattle every year from the Navajos of Chin Lee and Black mountains. He brings these to his ranch to fatten them until late fall, when he sells them again for better prices. There are only about 20 head of cattle and several horses on his ranch of 12 square miles. . . . Just recently Clifford Smith moved his boundary line again, employing Indian labor at 60 cents a day.

About a year or two after the Government land allotments the Indians in these parts were forced to pay taxes on their lands, beginning with $5 to $40 each, according to the number of livestock they possessed. We are paying taxes on this land, and still we are always asked to move out. . . .

Burke McCarrow's fence is about 6 miles square. Outside of this land he is leasing more land about 4 miles long, 2 miles wide in some place[s], and one-fourth mile in others up to the foothills. Mr. McCarrow has 2,300 sheep, 10 horses, and 50 head of cattle. At first his homestead included 1 square mile. He is adding to it all the time. Burke McCarrow brings his sheep in the Navajo Reservation every year for sheep dipping and shearing. He leaves them there several days both times, using up all the range. He dips his sheep when the Indians dip theirs. His sheep get counted with the Indian sheep. We know that is not right, and we told [U.S. government agent] S. F. Stacher about this, but he won't do anything about it.

S. F. Stacher was up here about the last of February. He made some wonderful promises to us. He said he was from Crown Point [his agency headquarters in New Mexico] and he came to help the Indians. He said he settled all kinds of land problems for the Indians and he would be willing to extend the same service to us. He said he was letting us take other land for this land we are living on, so that the checkered land problems could be straightened out. . . . They are trying to fit us in where we overcrowd each other. He wanted us to take allotments near Dead River [northwestern Chambers Checkerboard]. It is all right for grazing, but no good at all for farming. Mr. Stacher said he was filing Government records and exchanging these lands for those in Dead River for us.

Well, he carried off all our land papers. . . . Jacob Lewis and several others gave up their papers of their land "pattens." . . . We want those papers back or copies of same land description. . . . The Indians do not want their land surveyed or exchanged. . . .

Little Silversmith, a Navajo, has a ranch at Jacobs Lake. His ranch was 12 miles and 6 miles wide until last year, when he lost half of it to a white man. They are also leasing some of the land adjoining theirs. He and his son-in-law [Ben Lynch] are paying taxes on their land. They are cattlemen and sheepmen, and they can afford it. If they are leasing land, then why do they herd their sheep inside the reservation? Now they come and tell us that they are leasing these lands we are living on. We do not believe this. . . .

By the time Clifford Smith, Burr Porter, and Burke McCarrow included so much land in their fences the Indians have a small district left south of the Gila [Puerco] River. There is only 1 mile of tableland, which is 4 miles long along the foothills [probably the Sanders farms]. There are about 15 families living here. They have permanent homes. This land is under cultivation and fenced. It is planted in corn at the present time. The land joining ours belongs to the Santa Fe Railroad. Clifford Smith fenced half of this land again recently. Where are the Indians going to graze their sheep and livestock? This district south of the Gila [Puerco] River has not enough range for big cattlemen with thousands of sheep and cattle. Little Silversmith and Ben Lynch want the Indians to pay them for grazing their sheep and horses here. Some of the Indians paid land taxes again August 11 this year. If we have to pay Ben Lynch, then we will be paying two times for the same land. . . .

In no way cowed by the high authority of the president of the United States, the letter writers concluded with the following forthright demand:

Just come right out here and see this district, the location of it, and all, to understand it good. Just sitting in the White House is a poor way to settle anything. . . .

Please see if this boundary can be fixed 12 miles south of Chambers at Navajo Springs. Have the Senate committee come out and investigate the matter thoroughly. . . . Please give this a good airing and we want no half job.[2]

THE STORY FROM DOCUMENTS

Documents give another slant on the People's chronicle above. Franciscan father Anselm Weber and the Santa Fe Railroad land commissioner, Howel Jones, together tried to get the best deals for both the Diné and the railroad within the limits of federal law, corporate profit maximization, and the vestiges of 1800s land-holding patterns. In 1898, with help from the wealthy Mother Katharine Drexel of Philadelphia, Anselm and other Franciscans from Cincinnati founded Saint Michaels Franciscan Mission 10 miles south of the Navajo Agency headquarters at Fort Defiance and about 30 miles north of the Chambers

FIGURE 30 Diné students at Saint Michaels Franciscan Mission school, ca. 1900. A few children from the Chambers Checkerboard went to this school. Credit: Courtesy of Sharlot Hall Museum Library & Archives / bus 5009p.

Checkerboard. The mission's relationship with the railroad literally came with the territory, since the mission had bought its land from the railroad (Wilkin 1955:25–48). Saint Michaels was Anselm's home base, a long day's horseback ride one way from the closest part of the Chambers Checkerboard.

THE RAILROAD REACHES OUT, 1904–1907

During the financial panic of 1893, the railroad had gone bankrupt (Myrick 1970:34; White 1991:225–262). In August 1904, now that the railroad company has come out of bankruptcy as the Atchison, Topeka and Santa Fe Railway (AT&SF), Howel Jones writes to Anselm that the railroad wants to lease all its lands to stockmen and wants to make land exchanges to consolidate its holdings into whole townships. The railroad grant consists of square-mile sections of railroad land checkerboarded with sections of public domain (government land) in several rows of 36-square-mile townships both north and south of the tracks. The railroad wants to exchange lands with Washindoon so that some townships will be entirely public domain and others will be entirely railroad land, which the railroad can lease to ranchers for more than if the townships remained checkerboarded. The railroad's strategy will be to get Diné to ask for railroad land, which the railroad will then offer Washindoon for Diné use in exchange for public domain in other townships nearby or larger tracts elsewhere.

Between 1904 and 1906, Anselm and Jones write to each other about two Diné land users: Chee Dodge, who wants to lease the railroad land in the Navajo Springs township in the western Chambers Checkerboard, and Dodge's partner, Arthur Chester, who wants to lease or buy railroad land around Tanner Springs northwest of the Chambers Checkerboard.[3] Wealthy and powerful Chee Dodge has had land in the Chambers Checkerboard since 1882 (see chapters 6 and 8). In 1904 Jones tells Anselm that the township the "half-breed" wants around Navajo Springs is already leased to colonizer-ranchers. A year later, these ranchers have failed to renew the lease, so Jones offers it to Dodge. Dodge stalls, however, because the ranchers, especially John McCarrell and Ed Howell, are still using the land.[4] Dodge offers to buy the land from the railroad, but the railroad wants to lease, not sell.[5] Meanwhile, the only other Diné attempt to get a land title in these years is by Charlie Yazhe, who in 1904 applies for an allotment on the public domain at Salt Seeps, an important spring along the "Emigrant" (Beale) Road, where an 1880s homestead entry has recently lapsed (see chapter 6). This is the first allotment application in the Chambers Checkerboard (NARA, Prescott Indian allotment patent file no. 61). Two years later, Silversmith, already a wealthy stockowner, applies for an allotment at the Crater, another important local spring along the Emigrant (Beale) Road near Navajo Springs (NARA, Phoenix Indian allotment no. 1).

Meanwhile, in 1905 Anselm writes to the U.S. General Land Office (GLO) in Prescott about getting a "topographical tracing" of the township south of Sanders, where Anselm in later years will push for allotments in the Diné farming area (Sanders farms hereafter) there (Franciscans, box 27, letter of August 6, 1905). A year and a half later, Anselm reminds Jones about five Diné in the Sanders farms who should get allotments in the railroad section (23, T21N, R28E), if the railroad will release ("relinquish") its title to Washindoon.[6]

Later in 1907 the railroad releases title to lands in several townships just north of the Chambers Checkerboard so that a presidential executive order can add most of these townships to the reservation, including the Tanner Springs township, with Arthur Chester's ranch (Franciscans, box 27, letter of September 5, 1907; NLC, archive documents, letters of September 14 and November 6, 1907). The Chambers Checkerboard is probably left out because the railroad wants to consolidate its holdings in most of those townships and lease them to Bilagaana ranchers. Anselm considers the allotments a step toward getting other whole townships added to the reservation, so the work is on to get the People there allotted.

THE FIRST OBSTACLES, 1908–1909

In the spring of 1908 Fort Defiance Agency superintendent William H. Harrison sends a policeman to locate the would-be allottees in the Sanders farms and bring them to Fort Defiance Agency headquarters. Many local Diné go to Fort Defiance to apply for allotments, and Harrison sends the paperwork to the GLO in Phoenix (NLC, archive documents, letters of May 7 and June 8, 1908). What probably pushes everyone into action is that the Southwestern (also referred to as Southwest) Development Company wants to buy this land from the railroad. Howel Jones makes clear why the railroad will help secure land rights for the Diné families:

> I think there are other sections in similar condition [to the Sanders farms], and I wish you would take such steps towards perfecting the rights of the Indians to these sections occupied by them, of railroad lands, in order that the Commissioner

[of the GLO] will request us to relinquish to the United States. . . . [W]e would like to help the Indians to get their homesteads, providing the commissioner of the General Land Office requested us to make relinquishment so we can get other lands in lieu thereof.[7]

The next year, though, the GLO refuses to make a land exchange with the railroad for giving up the Sanders farms until the Diné there apply for homesteads rather than allotments. This requirement is a roadblock, since Diné must apply at the federal land office in the faraway and racist railroad town of Holbrook. The Diné at Sanders farms also complain to Anselm that encroaching homesteader Carl Hill has thrown bones from a nearby Anaasází ruin into their wells, has threatened to throw the bones into their reservoir, and has waved guns and land papers at them. Anselm fires off "cease and desist" letters to Hill (Franciscans, box 27, letters of April 9, 17, May 4, and June 19, 1909; box 29, Peterson letter, September 28, 1909).

ALLOTTING AGENT AMONG THE DINÉ, 1909–1912

The allotting program gets a boost in the summer of 1909, when Washindoon sends a special allotting agent, W. M. Peterson, to speed it up. He goes among the Diné in and around the Chambers Checkerboard, taking applications, with an interpreter whom he pays $50 a month and a rodman (surveyor's assistant) at $2.50 a day. The rodman supplies his own horse and feed, and both pay for their own food, $12 to $15 a month each. Each family can apply for an allotment for one head of household (usually a man) and each juvenile child. The special agent fills out the allotment application and accompanying papers for signatures or thumbprints by applicant and witnesses. The cumbersome process continues, as the special allotting agent then must submit to the agency superintendent the following documents: a list of allotment applications taken; township plats for all allotment applications; and possibly a history and enumeration of each allottee family with age, sex, and number of adults and children. These kinds of documents found among the papers of Father Anselm (Franciscans, boxes 29 and 55) suggest that the agents also made copies for Anselm. The agency superintendent is to certify the accuracy of these records. Would-be allottees and their witnesses go to Fort Defiance, where the superintendent takes their applications directly. Peterson, rather than the agency superintendent, seems to be responsible for filing most of the applications directly with

Washindoon's land office in Prescott, Arizona. When the GLO approves them, Peterson sends the patents to the superintendent, who will summon the applicants to Fort Defiance for their patents.[8]

In the Chambers Checkerboard and elsewhere along the railroad, the special allotting agents also ask allotment applicants if they want to lease the railroad sections in the townships around their allotments. Ideally, groups of allottees will pool money to pay the annual lease fees for all railroad sections checkered amid the various allotments, for the railroad's policy is to make one lease covering all railroad sections in a township. Anselm alerts the allotting agents to report to Howel Jones which townships allottees want to lease. The special allotting agents are not allowed to arrange these leases, however. Jones must arrange them either with the allottees directly or with someone representing them, like the agency superintendent or Anselm (Franciscans, box 29, Peterson letters, July 12, 1908, and February 15, 1909; Kent file, letter of February 7, 1909).

In the summer of 1909, talk of the Black Creek irrigation project is also heating up. The Southwestern Development Company has applied to Fort Defiance superintendent Peter Paquette to make a reservoir north of the Chambers Checkerboard in the 1907 reservation extension. Fourteen Diné families are living and farming at the proposed reservoir site, with buildings, fences, and other improvements that would be razed. Also, Diné in the Sanders farms and more a few miles northeast at Houck now irrigate from Black Creek below the proposed dam, which would endanger their farms. Though the documents do not say so, surely these Diné not only oppose the project but also only grudgingly (if at all) accept the compensations proposed. The would-be developer, the Southwest Development Company, seems to consist of Gallup businessmen-speculators.[9]

From late summer of 1909 to January 1910, Peterson and his field team find the section corner markers of the original 1882 GLO survey of the railroad grant lands, then record would-be applications for quarter sections in the GLO lands between those markers from Diné scattered over the range and in the "crowded farming areas" south of Sanders and at Houck. These people then must take Peterson's paperwork to Fort Defiance, where the agency clerk will help them fill out application forms (Franciscans, box 29, Peterson correspondence file). Allotment applications in and near the Chambers Checkerboard are finished during 1910, and Washindoon (ignoring the earlier insistence on homestead applications) approves the allotment applications in the Sanders farms, which the railroad then relinquishes.[10]

Meanwhile, Bilagaana homestead entries in the Chambers Checkerboard this year shoot up to 14, more than twice the total for the past 20 years.[11] All but one new entry are around Chambers and Sanders, where the Southwest Development Company ditches are supposed to go. The land consists of two townships in the western Chambers Checkerboard around Navajo Springs and Chambers. The Navajo Springs township is the one that Chee Dodge wanted to lease between 1904 and 1906 but did not because John McCarrell and others were using it. McCarrell and maybe others probably kept using it all along but did not pay the railroad until they feared the new homesteaders might get leases.[12]

In 1912 the Black Creek irrigation project right-of-way is greatly enlarged to encompass the reservoir site on the Navajo Reservation north of the Chambers Checkerboard and ditches around Sanders and Chambers. Bilagaana homestead applications have been concentrated around the planned ditches since 1909 and will continue. But only a few homestead applications trickle in each year after 1909 (BLM, Historical Index and Homestead Entry microfiche). In the two townships around Chambers and Navajo Springs, where Washindoon has approved the irrigation project right-of-way, railroad land for grazing has gone unleased since mid-1911. Jones writes Anselm to invite Navajo leases, probably a gesture toward Chee Dodge. Dodge evidently does not bite, probably for the same reason as in 1906: because John McCarrell and other colonizer-ranchers are still using the land.[13]

CONGRESS AUTHORIZES LAND EXCHANGES WITH THE RAILROAD, 1913–1918

Early in 1913 Congress passes a law to let the railroad release its title to lands for Indian use and choose other lieu lands of equal value from the public domain, all to be done before the law expires in 1916. This trade will let more Diné apply for allotments in the Chambers Checkerboard (Franciscans, box 26, Peterson letter, April 26, 1913; Act of March 4, 1913). Having removed one obstacle, Washindoon replaces it with another in 1914, requiring Diné to pay for the surveys, submit the surveyor's description to Agent Paquette in Fort Defiance, fill out their own allotment applications, and send them to the nearest GLO branch. Not to be thwarted, the would-be allottees raise $1,545 to pay A. W. Simington, Peterson's successor, to do the surveys. Frank Walker, Saint Michaels Franciscan Mission interpreter (whose Irish father had homesteaded at Emigrant

Springs; see chapter 6), is his field assistant (Franciscans, box 27, letter of September 4, 1915; box 29, Simington letter, January 7, 1914).

But since 1913, a year after statehood, the state of Arizona has challenged the proposed railroad land exchanges that would make way for these would-be allottees to get titles to the land. Arizona objects that the railroad might choose substitute lands that the state itself might want as part of its statehood grant. In 1915 the GLO in Phoenix therefore holds up recent allotments on railroad lands in the Chambers Checkerboard and also essentially refuses to process the Diné applications for allotments on the public domain. The clock is ticking toward 1916, when the law allowing the exchanges expires. Meanwhile, special GLO agents start to inspect some allotments pending on railroad lands in the Chambers Checkerboard, presumably to see if applicants really use the land and have made improvements there.

Meanwhile, in 1914, as the war in Europe heats up U.S. livestock markets and colonizer-ranchers demand more land, Diné start leasing the railroad lands in certain townships of the Chambers Checkerboard to keep colonizers at bay. Simington (or Walker) works with Anselm to identify townships that certain groups of families want to lease. Walker also collects railroad lease money

FIGURE 31 Cattle at Squaw Springs, 1985, along the old Emigrant Road. The speckled longhorn is like those that ranchers of the late 1800s to early 1900s would have kept in the Chambers Checkerboard. Credit: Klara Kelley photo.

and turns it over to Anselm, who presumably will then pay the railroad. Railroad leases seem confined to the uplands southwest of Sanders and east of Navajo Springs, the domain of the extended family of Silversmith with his 1906 allotment at the Crater (Franciscans, box 27, Simington letters, January 7, 14, February 15, 1914; see also box 26, letters of June 19, 1915, March 8, 1916, February 28, 1919, and March 8, June 11, 1925).

In 1916 the railroad starts leasing lands in the Navajo Springs and Chambers townships to colonizer-rancher Burr Porter, who seems to share the range with John McCarrell. These lands seem to have gone unleased since 1911 (Franciscans, box 27, Weber to Paquette, undated letter; NARA, Indian allotment patent 743464, GLO inspector report, October 5, 1916). Meanwhile, the act of 1913 authorizing railroad land exchanges is extended through 1918 by Congress (Franciscans, box 27, letter of September 6, 1918; see also box 26, letters of October 26, 30, 1916).

Anselm tells Paquette how Diné find themselves squeezed between the Black Creek irrigation project and colonizer-ranchers:

> [The bearer of this letter] had a nice farm . . . on the reservoir site of the Black Creek Irrigation Project. On account of that project he abandoned that place, and he does not care to go back to it, since, if that project ever materializes, he would have to move again. It is true, land under that project has been reserved for those Indians who vacated the reservoir site; but that land is on the Navajo Springs township, and since Porter has leased the railroad lands, Charly Yazhe [in 1904, the first allottee in the Chambers Checkerboard, at Salt Seeps east of Navajo Springs] abandoned his place and no other Indian is willing to move there. (Franciscans, box 27, Weber to Paquette, undated but probably 1917 or 1918)

Nevertheless, despite the largest number of new homestead applications since 1909 (11, located mostly around Sanders [BLM, Historical Index and Homestead Entry microfiche]), in 1917 the Black Creek irrigation project is looking more and more like a dud to Howel Jones, who writes Anselm: "I have about concluded that the Black Creek Irrigation scheme was not commercially feasible. Do you know anything about it? If the Indians want to buy township 18 North, Range 28 East [the edge of the Silversmith extended family area], and they will make us an offer, we will be pleased to give it consideration" (Franciscans, box 26, Jones to Weber, July 28, 1917; see also Jones to Weber, August 9, 1917). The irrigation project will never

FIGURE 32 Salt Seeps, a natural well, in 1998, with descendants of Charlie Yazhe, who in 1904 applied for the first Diné allotment in the Chambers Checkerboard. Bilagaana ranchers 13 years later blocked him out of his allotment. Credit: Klara Kelley photo.

materialize, and investors will have relinquished the right-of-way by 1932 (BLM, Historical Index and Homestead Entry microfiche, rights-of-way 013948 and 01391).

In August 1917 Jones sends Anselm a list of townships that the railroad has avoided leasing and selling to colonizers, expecting them to be made a part of the reservation. These lands are all north and west of the Chambers Checkerboard (Franciscans, box 26, letter of August 30, 1917, box 26, letter of February 29, 1918, box 27, letter of February 7, 1918). The Chambers Checkerboard itself will never be part of a railroad land exchange, as Anselm predicts:

> Even if the reservation were extended over the [Lava] Buttes Country and the Pueblo Bonito Agency [New Mexico], there would still remain under the Fort Defiance Agency on the public domain 480 families, 2132 persons. . . .
>
> The vast majority of these Indians live south of the railroad track. I am quite certain no reservation will ever be made for them, but they, some of them I am afraid, will, eventually, be forced back on the reservation, though the reservation is over stocked and over-grazed. (Franciscans, box 27, Weber to Vaux, September 11, 1917)

RAILROAD LEASES TO DINÉ, 1918–1925

Many allotments are patented in 1919, and the railroad continues to renew the Silversmith extended family leases. To keep settler-ranchers at bay during the livestock boom of World War I, Diné have been leasing railroad land by the township since 1914.[14] But as Anselm tells a member of the Board of Indian Commissioners, the railroad has doubled or tripled the lease fees, and Navajos "who live off the Reservation have been living there all their lives, and would be only too glad to move on the Reservation to avoid paying taxes on their stock and other property, to avoid paying lease money, and to partake of the many other advantages." But other Navajo families on the reservation are already using all the land, of course. This letter seems to be a pitch to the U.S. Office of Indian Affairs to start paying for the railroad leases that Diné up to now have been paying for themselves (Franciscans, box 26, letters of February 28, May 31, 1919). In the next year, the Office of Indian Affairs seems to start paying the railroad to lease certain townships to Navajos, including not only townships north of the Chambers Checkerboard but also the two in the Chambers Checkerboard leased by the Silversmith extended family (Franciscans, box 27, letter of July 17, 1920).

In 1921 Father Anselm dies. His efforts to help Diné secure land will soon be thwarted.

In 1922 the brief federal subsidy of grazing leases on railroad land for the Silversmith extended family and other Diné outside the Chambers Checkerboard is in jeopardy. The People may have to go back to paying on the leases themselves. Things come to a head in 1925, when correspondence among Jones, the Franciscans, and the new Fort Defiance Agency superintendent, August Duclos, suggests that former Superintendent Paquette did not collect money from Diné for the 1925 railroad leases and that the agency might be able to pay something but not the full amount. So Father Emanuel Trockur and Frank Walker hold meetings in Sanders and Chambers, with Duclos present, to "spread the blanket"—take up a collection.

Washindoon's "Indian Office" (BIA) and Congress are also making Navajo tribal oil and natural gas royalties available for future leases of railroad land. Chee Dodge is chairman of the Navajo Tribal Council, newly formed to sign oil and gas leases but not always willing to rubber-stamp federal initiatives. The arrangement before 1925 seems to be that the agency and the council will each pay half.[15] But opposition comes from Tribal Council delegate Nelson Gorman at Chinle. "Why should Chinle people help" by letting their delegate vote to buy the land with oil money? Father Emanuel tells him, "To keep those people off the Reservation, so they won't crowd you." Then Frank Walker and Father Emanuel raise the whole amount (Hubbell Trading Post, oral history interview 51).

Perhaps for the first time (and perhaps reflecting lower demand from colonizer-ranchers because of the depressed livestock market), other Diné besides the Silversmith extended family are now leasing land from the railroad. Silversmith considers taking over the former Houck Trading Company lease on the southern edge of the Chambers Checkerboard but instead adds another township next to the ones his family has been leasing since 1914.[16] John Morgan is interested in two townships east of the Silversmith group but will take only one, because J. M. Williams, a trader at Zuni, already has the other (Franciscans, box 26, letters of March 8, July 30, August 31, 1925).

THE ARIZONA NAVAJO BOUNDARY OF 1934

Finally Congress ends this cumbersome, constantly shifting system of checkerboard landownership by passing the Arizona Navajo Boundary Act. That law is supposed to consolidate Navajo lands so that Washindoon can more effectively manage livestock reduction and thereby the soil erosion that threatens Hoover Dam and industrial development in Southern California. The act formalizes the boundary set by the 1900, 1901, and 1907 executive order extensions and adds two blocks of townships. One new block is northwest of the Chambers Checkerboard in the Lava Buttes region, south of the 1882 executive order reservation. The other is northeast of the Chambers Checkerboard in the lower Black Creek Valley. The railroad is to give up all its checkered sections in these areas and will get, in partial exchange, all of Washindoon's lands in townships south of the new boundary, including those of the Chambers Checkerboard. These lands include the Diné allotments, the ones that the allottees are defending in the letter at the beginning of this chapter (Corell and Dehiya 1978:45; NNLD, historic township plats). The act appropriates almost half a million dollars to buy privately owned lands and improvements (mostly railroad lands) within the reservation extension, for which the Navajo Tribal Council will use its royalties to reimburse the U.S. Treasury.

But for the allottees, compensation is less clear. The process for relinquishing an allotment seems to work as follows. Hoskie Cronemeyer, a bilingual local trader and child of a Diné mother and German father, visits the allottees, sometimes with Samuel Stacher, whose Eastern Navajo Agency in New Mexico is subject to the same type of land exchanges. Allottees go to Fort Defiance, where they must sign or thumbprint forms consenting to give up their allotments. In the end, Washindoon apparently will pay only about half of the allottees for the improvements they give up, with compensation ranging from $100 to $1,000. About half of the allottees who relinquish get lieu allotments. These people have relatives north of the Chambers Checkerboard amid the lands the railroad gives up to the Navajo Reservation. Of the 145 allotments in the Chambers Checkerboard townships, 56 are canceled or relinquished, but most allotments of the wealthy Silversmith extended family remain intact. Though many of the allottees were children when the allotment applications were first taken (mainly in 1909), those allotments are now adults. Therefore, the 56 relinquishments and cancellations represent about that many households, an estimated 250–300 people.[17]

For allottees, these miseries come on top of Washindoon's livestock reduction program. So at the very time when Washindoon is telling the People that the reservation lands can only support half the livestock that people own, it is forcing more families with whatever livestock they can salvage onto those same lands.

RELINQUISHMENT

In 1998 Diné former residents of the Chambers Checkerboard described the miseries of relinquishment (Kelley and Francis 1998b, condensed from the original Navajo).

CONSULTANT 1 (IN ENGLISH)

My mom was born in 1904. When she was about age six, she and her sister went to school at Saint Michaels. They were raised by their grandmother [father's mother]. And Father [Anselm] came down here, and my mom said a whole group of people were following him around, asking for allotments. So my great-grandmother [who received an allotment] asked for land for my mom and her sister. But the guy who was interpreting for Father [not Frank Walker] refused my great-grandmother's request because of the interpreter's relationship with a certain family. So I blame him for why my mom did not get an allotment. And also, I blame her father—he was working on the railroad at the time, he could have requested land. He had two wives, and he liked the other wife better than my mom's mother. So he pushed my mom and her sister aside.

Before our family was driven off, one man [Stacher] came around to collect the papers—those were the papers with the Teddy Roosevelt signature and the eagle. He said it was for copying, then they would be returned. But my grandma refused to give up the paper. One time at a chapter meeting [probably 1960s], Little Silversmith spoke there, something about getting land for himself. And my mom got up and accused him of not helping when we were all chased off. She said that white people were driving Little Silversmith out now [he seems to have been in debt and was selling to a Bilagaana rancher], but where was he when white people were driving us out?

My mom told me that we left our chickens, our wagons. She went back with my grandfather to our home to get our things, and saw them dumped like trash. Men formed a posse in Springerville, went through Saint Johns, camped some-place between Saint Johns and Sanders. Early in the morning they attacked Diné families around [the spring near the great-grandmother's allotment], drove them out at gunpoint.

Then, the site where we moved after we were driven out: my dad dug a hole, and we lived there through the winter. Then he built a hogan north of Sanders. First, we went across the [Puerco] river and tried to settle there, then were told to keep moving north, because that was allotted land, go farther north past where the allotments are. So we kept going and we went on land claimed by [certain relatives].

CONSULTANT 2 (IN NAVAJO)

We had many sheep, horses, and cattle. We'd plow the fields and plant a lot, too. We grew a lot of beans, put them in gunny sacks. Someone, I don't know if they were Bilagaanas, would buy them from us. We also used to live at another place over the hill with my maternal grandparents. There were several lakes where the livestock were watered. We lived in several places. . . .

We would hear people say that we pay for the land [taxes or railroad lease payments]. And one day we were told to move out toward the railroad [north]. They had been saying this to us for a few years now. There was a man named Big Schoolboy [Hoskie Cronemeyer], who went around with the Bilagaanas and told everyone to move out. He said that if we didn't move, they would take us back to Fort Sumner. They all carried guns. We were afraid that they might shoot us all.

This was two years after my mother died that they [Cronemeyer and the Bilagaanas] told us to move. My father had to take care of us children then. So we moved out. We put only a sewing machine and other little things in a wagon and left. We left with our sheep, many horses, the rams, and the cows. We just left with our clothes and went to a place called Graywater [about 10 miles away]. The horses were tired out by that time, but there was no grass, only a pond.

When we got the horses back [after the eviction], they were starved almost to death. There was sand sage, silvery sage, wormwood there. We got only 20 horses back—the others died—and never found the cattle. We took some cows with us when we left, but we left a lot there. The sheep we took, but we lost a lot of them too, some to thirst and starvation. We survived on the sheep but our horses died, even the one we used for the wagons. We barely got water. We had to use bottles. We had a very hard time. Then my maternal grandfather became ill. His kidneys wouldn't work, so they had to carry him around a lot. I don't know how many years it was, but he passed away too.

When we left our home, my little sister and I would go back to pick up some of our belongings now and then. We noticed that they [the Bilagaanas] had pushed our wagons off a cliff and they were all smashed up at the bottom. We had a small wagon, a big wagon, different types, also a well down there [windmill]. They shot it up, too. We don't know where they took our personal belongings and our clothes or what they did with them. They were all gone.

We barely bought this [current homesite] from a lady [a tract next to her father's lieu allotment, which consultant did not mention]. They used to live over there at the railroad. We got a wagon too that we used to get water with. She gave us some horses that we traded some sheep for. That's what we used to get water.

So we came out here. My grandmother was herding them at Graywater [about eight miles away]. We'd run out of water, our only water source was at [a spring away from the homesite]. We'd get water at night, fill the barrel and bring it back. Me, I'd cut logs at Graywater, and I'd bring them back here. That's how we built a house.

We had no water, but there used to be Bilagaanas who lived around here but they moved out. They used to have windmills here and there, so we asked one to take a windmill out for us. I traded some sheep for it, and they came here and installed a windmill. We settled here permanently after that. We had to herd rams for people, and they would give us a few sheep for it, and eventually we managed to fill our corral again.

AFTERMATH

Much has been written for several decades about the dispute between the Navajo and Hopi governments, misleadingly called the century-old Navajo-Hopi land dispute. The story of the resulting relocation of thousands of Diné from Black Mesa and the Lava Buttes, told in the introduction, is an international symbol of Washindoon's 1800s "Indian Removal" policy carried forward to the present (Redhouse 1985a, 1985b, 1986). That story from beginning to end is bound up with the story of the Chambers Checkerboard.

The roots of the Black Mesa / Lava Buttes relocation go back to 1882, when, as chapter 6 tells, Hopi agent J. H. Fleming asked President Chester A. Arthur to set aside land for an agency jurisdiction so that the agent could force Hopis to send their children to a boarding school. The president's resulting executive order set aside an arbitrarily drawn 55-by-70-mile rectangle, called the 1882 executive order reservation hereafter, for the Hopis "and other such Indians as the Secretary of Interior may see fit to settle thereon." The boundary cut across the interfingered, overlapping lands that Diné and Hopis used (Correll and Dehiya 1978:12–14; Graves 1998:175–200; Indian Law Resource Center 1979:12; NLC, archive documents, letters of September 9, 15, December 4, 26, 1882). By anchoring the Hopi boarding school, this new reservation encouraged trader-rancher Thomas Keam and his cronies to run cattle in and around the Chambers Checkerboard and usurp the land of Diné living there, who fought back.

In the 1920s and 1930s Washindoon induced Navajos and Hopis to centralize their governments. In the 1930s this tribal government reorganization became part of Washindoon's thrust to control use of land under its jurisdiction for the ultimate benefit of West Coast agri-industrial expansion (see chapter 11). From the middle of the 1882 reservation, Washindoon carved a grazing district for the Hopis alone. And just as Washindoon was expelling Diné from the Chambers Checkerboard in the name of "rational" grazing land use through land consolidation, so it expelled some Diné from Tallahogan Canyon, which was just inside the eastern boundary of the new Hopi grazing district (Indian Law Resource Center 1979:56–64; Iverson and Roessel, eds. 2002:33ff.).

Beginning in the 1950s, with federal encouragement, the Hopi Tribe sued the Navajo Tribe for more land (see chapter 11). Then in 1977, authorized by the 1974 federal Navajo-Hopi Land Settlement Act, a mediator partitioned the 1882 executive order reservation between the two groups. This law and its 1980 amendments also allowed the Navajo Nation government to get "new" lands for the 1882 reservation relocatees. For them the Navajo Nation bought a group of ranches south of the Navajo Reservation in Arizona along the New Mexico state line—the Chambers Checkerboard (Brugge 1994; Kammer 1980; Norstog 1988; Redhouse 1985a). Descendants of the People displaced from the Chambers Checkerboard in the 1930s remain outside. The federal agency in charge of administering these lands, the Office of Navajo and Hopi Relocation, ignorant of the history recounted in this chapter, with unintended irony named them the "New Lands."

These and other twentieth-century relocations (yes, there are more, from coal strip mines, from the Navajo Indian Irrigation Project) are worlds apart from Washindoon's attempted physical and cultural genocide of the Long Walk. Yet in all the relocations, the juggernaut of the corporate state has tried to force the People out of the way, no matter what the cost. In the Chambers Checkerboard, with their limited political sovereignty, the People had to find something in common with corporate interests, here the railroad, as a foundation for keeping their land and way of life. But that foundation soon crumbled as the corporate state strengthened its thrust to manage the land for national economic development. Most families then moved as close as they could to homelands they had left, crowding their relatives. The families and their way of life survived, but their relocation created rifts in the host communities that survive to this day, bonds to the land were weakened, and family histories were depleted (KFa, December 3, 2012).

The events recounted in this chapter, like those in chapter 6, manifest the partialness of Diné sovereignty nested within Washindoon's rule and the resulting disruption of the People's bonds to the land. Chapter 11 continues the story of Diné sovereignty under the corporate state's agri-industrial development thrust. But first, in the next three chapters, we look at what happened in the 1900s when some of the People, on their own land, took up the ways of the colonizers: mercantile trade and work in mines.

8

DINÉ TRADERS BEFORE THE 1950s

T HE LIFE histories of individual Diné are important parts of Diné oral history from the late 1800s to the present.[1] This chapter sketches the life histories of Diné who owned trading posts. Mainstream colonizer historical narratives declare Diné absent behind the counter, but these histories tell otherwise. We call these people Diné traders to distinguish them from the non-Navajos conventionally called Navajo traders. These stories incidentally show the variety of work for the colonizers in Navajoland in the first half of the twentieth century. But what do they tell about the land, the People, and sovereignty? The Diné traders seem to embody sovereignty as "just do it yourself." But is adopting a colonizer economic practice really doing it yourself or just enabling colonizer indirect rule? Does it disrupt traditional bonds to the land? This chapter presents the traders in order of when they started trading, then returns to this question at the end.

THE NAVAJOLAND TRADING POST SYSTEM: SOME BACKGROUND

After the Long Walk, back at home, the conquered People struggled to survive. They had lost livestock and the uplands around the edge of the traditional homeland, the best places for farming, hunting, and gathering. Now families would have to depend more on stockraising and on trading wool, weaving, and other products, later including livestock. As Diné life histories and documents attest, in the first 10 years after the return, Washindoon gave out sheep and goats, as well as food, clothing, and tools. In these distributions, the government agents often favored local leaders to redistribute the sheep and goods among their followers.

Trading posts sprang up to profit from marketing Diné products. These posts first appeared at Forts Defiance and Wingate in 1868, right after the Long Walk, where posts earlier had served the military. In the early 1870s came posts at Ganado and Keams Canyon (see chapter 6), as well as in far northwestern Navajoland, which Utah Mormons were colonizing. Posts multiplied throughout what was left of Navajoland after the railroad advanced along its southern edge in 1881–82. The railroad enabled the traders and their wholesale suppliers to get goods manufactured in the eastern United States, which the posts traded to the People for their products, and then to send those products to large firms in the East. The money they got from the Diné products was more than the cost of goods they traded to the Diné, and therein lay their profit (Berkholz 2007; Kelley and Francis 2018; M'Closkey 2002; McNitt 1962; Powers 2001).

By the early 1900s, most Diné families in all but far northwestern Navajoland were enmeshed to varying degrees in the trading post system. They got staple foods, cloth or clothing, basic tools, and other items now becoming necessities in exchange for wool in the spring and, in the fall, wool again (Bahr 2004:527) or (later) lambs. At first, most trade was direct barter, with pawn the main source of credit. This time was also the heyday of Diné weaving, when women cranked out huge quantities of rugs all year, giving the traders a source of profits more reliable than raw wool. Later, traders enlarged their trade with unsecured credit. Recollections of elderly Diné in recent decades show, however, that many Diné families were still getting most of their food from their herds, farms, and hunting and gathering even as late as World War II (see chapter 9; Frisbie 2018:7–31). Family histories were still rooted in the land, and elders used those histories to instill in youngsters a bond with the family land base.

The heyday of the trading post system was about 1900–1930. Colonizers operated most of the stores, but from earliest times some traders were Diné, and many more Diné worked inside the trading post system. The life histories in this chapter are limited to the best-documented stories of Diné who owned their own stores (see also Kelley and Francis 2018).

RETURN FROM FORT SUMNER CAPTIVITY
TO WORLD WAR I

Within a few years after the railroad arrived, Diné traders were part of the trading post system. All but the earliest were schooled, and many started in business with Bilagaana partners. Though most did not have a Bilagaana father to help them get started, most parents were at least entrepreneurs or property owners, and a few were Diné political leaders or had connections to the government or military. Late in the period, the colonizer Hubbell trading family helped a couple of them get started.

CHEE DODGE

Chee Dodge was born around 1860 to a woman of the Ma'ii Deeshgizhnii (Jemez) clan and a Hispanic or Bilagaana father. Chee Dodge's mother died in 1863, on the brink of the Long Walk, so his mother's sister raised him. She returned from Fort Sumner to Fort Defiance and married Perry Williams, a Bilagaana stock clerk (later trader). Between the mid-1880s and 1911, in partnership with Bilagaana Stephen Aldrich, Chee Dodge owned stores at Round Rock and Manuelito, the railroad point from which government supplies were freighted to Fort Defiance. The Round Rock store, 70 miles north of Fort Defiance, was one of the biggest wool buyers of the time. Chee Dodge got ranches at Tanner Springs and Crystal in the same period, with relatives and others to tend the herds. (Readers met Chee Dodge, who was also the Fort Defiance Agency interpreter, in chapters 6 and 7.) In later years he also had a ranch and homestead around Tsaya, west of Chaco Canyon. In 1913 Chee Dodge made the first of several loans to trader Lorenzo Hubbell Sr. of Ganado (see chapter 6 for Hubbell's earlier career) and held a mortgage on the entire Ganado property, its water rights, and accounts receivable. Chee Dodge was chairman of the first Navajo Tribal Council from 1923 to 1928 and served again as chairman from 1942 to 1946. He died in 1948 (Bahr 2004; Blue 2000; Borgman 1948; McNitt 1962; NAU, UITA, Joe Tanner and J. B. Tanner; Parman 1976; Young

FIGURE 33 Diné trader and leader Chee Dodge, early 1900s. Credit: Courtesy of Sharlot Hall Museum Library & Archives / DB 52, F3, 133.

1978:64–77, 89–92; a Schwemberger photo [Long 1992] shows Chee Dodge in his forties, around the time of his trading partnership with Aldrich).

JOE HATCH

Joe Hatch and his brother Ira Stearns Hatch were sons of Bilagaana Mormon missionary Ira Hatch and Maraboots (Sarah Maraboots Dyson). The parents of Maraboots were Ungka Poetes, a Paiute woman from Navajo Mountain, and the Diné leader of that region, whom the Mormons called Spaneshanks. Ungka Poetes died when Maraboots was a child, and Spaneshanks turned her over to Mormons in southern Utah, where she later married Ira Hatch. Son Ira Stearns Hatch, born in 1862, was the first of four children, and Joe, born in 1870, was the fourth. Sarah died in 1873, and her husband seems to have raised the children. For more on Ira Stearns Hatch, see the separate entry below in this section.

Joe Hatch traded early, far and wide. In the late 1880s he was at Fort Wingate, then married Lelia Kirk of a Bilagaana family from Arkansas by way of the Mormon colony south of Fort Wingate at Ramah. In 1889 the couple settled along the San Juan River in Mormon Fruitland near Joe Hatch's paternal cousins, where they started trading with the People. In 1895 Joe and Englishman Ed Thurland tried to establish a post in the northern Chuskas, possibly at Red Rock, but local leader Blackhorse ran them off. In 1898 they succeeded with a post near Hogback and the river. In these early years, Joe also seems to have hauled freight and to have worked for trader Dick Simpson at Gallegos Canyon south of Farmington.

By about 1900 until his death during World War II, Joe based himself at a ranch in Fruitland, where his youngest sons later established Hatch Brothers Trading Post. From 1902 to 1906 Joe managed the Meadows trading post west of Shiprock, then traded at a series of posts along or near the Togay Trail, an important freight route from Farmington south to the railroad. These posts included White Rock (1906–09), Ojo Alamo (1909), Bisti (1910–13), Brimhall Wash (1913–14), and Carson (1914). At the same time, the family ran cattle in the surrounding region, and at Bisti Joe had a blacksmith shop, where he fixed freight wagon wheels. Dick Simpson seems to have supplied merchandise. Around 1920 Joe or his son Ira or both may have managed the Gallegos Canyon post for Simpson. By the 1920s Joe Hatch also had silversmiths on his Fruitland ranch making jewelry, which he jobbed around Navajoland in a wagon. He traded the jewelry for livestock, which he held on the Fruitland ranch for sale to southern Colorado buyers. This enterprise may have been a response to the World War I easing of federal restrictions on buying Diné livestock.

In the mid-1920s Joe started trading along with his sons in southeastern Utah, first at Hatch Trading Post, near Montezuma Canyon, then on lower Montezuma Creek (around 1930), then farther north at Allen Canyon (in the 1930s and 1940s; see also "Children of Joe Hatch" below in this section). Joe and Lelia died during World War II (Bailey and Bailey 1982; Family Search n.d.; Forrest 1970; KFb, Stewart Hatch, July 7, 2005; McNitt 1962).

JOHN G. WALKER

John Walker's mother, Damasia, was Diné, and his father, also named John Walker, was a Bilagaana who drove a stage between Fort Wingate and Fort Apache and homesteaded in the Chambers Checkerboard (see chapter 6). Young John Walker was probably born in the early 1870s and went to school at Hampton Institute. His brother was Frank Walker, interpreter for the Franciscans (see chapter 7). In 1902 young John Walker established or bought a trading post at Saint Michaels in partnership with Bilagaana Thomas Osborne and became postmaster. In 1904 or 1905 John Walker moved west to Tolchaco on the Little Colorado River in the new Leupp reservation, where he built and ran the Navajo Trading Company. Babbitt Brothers, the Flagstaff wholesalers, owned the store later. In 1908 Walker moved upriver to the new government center at Leupp and started a store, which he sold to Hubert Richardson around 1920. This seems to have been his last trading post (AHS, Richard Van Valkenburgh Papers, MS 832, folder 107, manuscript "Frank Walker, interpreter to the Navaho"; Antram 1998:50–55; Bahr 2004:279; Bodo 1998:11; Hubbell Trading Post, oral history interview 51, Trockur; McNitt 1962:250; NAU, UITA, Babbitt; Richardson 1986:127–128; U.S. Commissioner of Indian Affairs 1904:145, 1905–1906:171).

NELSON GORMAN AND ALICE PESHLAKAI GORMAN

Nelson Gorman was born in 1874 near Chinle and was schooled at Fort Defiance and Santa Fe Indian Schools. Alice Peshlakai was born in 1885 to a woman of Dibé Łizhinii (Black Sheep, San Felipe) clan and Bééshłigai Atsidii Áłts'ósí (Slim Silversmith), Táchii'nii (Red Forehead) clan, a local leader around Crystal and an entrepreneur also—around 1900, he had a workshop with 10 silversmiths at Crystal. Alice attended Grand Junction Indian School, then married Nelson in 1903. During that same year, the Fort Defiance agency superintendent, Reuben Perry, had lined up money from an heir of the Doubleday publishing company and encouraged the couple to open their first store at the original government sawmill, northwest of Fort Defiance. After a few months, they closed the store and opened another in Beautiful Valley, a few miles south of Chinle.

In 1910 the Gormans moved their business to Chinle, hoping for trade from the new boarding school. They hired a Diné man to bake bread and also hired Diné teamsters. Alice ran the store while Nelson tended his cattle around

Black Mountain west of Chinle, where he had a line camp and commissary and employed 15 cowboys. In 1912, when local people came to the line camp for food, he started trading there, then sold it to J. L. Hubbell Sr. in 1914. Around 1918, deaths in the family and loss of savings when the McKinley County Bank in Gallup failed forced the Gormans to close their Chinle store. They gave the property to the local Presbyterian church, where they were members. Around 1925, Nelson Gorman reportedly served on the first Navajo Tribal Council, perhaps as an alternate (Clarence Gorman, conversation with Kelley and Francis, November 1, 2007; Greenberg and Greenberg 1984:5–23; Hubbell Trading Post, interview 51, Trockur; Mitchell 2001:423n10).

JACOB CASAMERA MORGAN

Born in 1878 northeast of Fort Wingate near Dalton Pass, Jacob Morgan was the son of Casamero, a Navajo scout in the Apache campaigns of 1886, launched from nearby Fort Wingate. His mother was a woman of the Áshįįhí (Salt) clan. Jacob Morgan was schooled at Fort Defiance and Grand Junction (1889) and at the Hampton Institute (1898). He graduated from Hampton in 1900 and returned as a teacher (1901–03). In 1901 he worked in the Phoenix Indian School and in 1905 helped establish the government agency on the new addition to the Navajo Reservation at Leupp. Between 1906 and 1908, with a brother and with some kind of help from Hans Neumann, a Bilagaana trader along the railroad east of Fort Wingate at Coolidge, Jacob Morgan operated a store north of Coolidge at Tóyee (Tuye Springs). The store was on the site of an earlier Bilagaana trading post, first in a building that belonged to the brothers' grandfather and later in a new store building. The brothers stocked food and dry goods, which they traded for wool, hides, and Diné weaving and silverwork. They did well until 1908, when a financial panic forced them to close.

Jacob Morgan then abandoned trading for teaching, missionary work with the Christian Reformed Church of Farmington, and politics. Between 1914 and 1925, he worked for the U.S. Indian Service (BIA) at the Crownpoint and Shiprock Agencies, then served on the Navajo Tribal Council from its beginning in 1923 until 1942. He served as chairman of the council from 1938 to 1942, having campaigned as an opponent of stock reduction and the other New Deal policies of CIA John Collier. Among Morgan's supporters were members of the Navajo Returned Students Association, including trader Robert Martin (see below) (AHS, Richard Van Valkenburgh Papers, folder 115, "Navajo

Biographies"; Gjeltema 2004; Parman 1976:18–19, 191, 284–285; Young 1978:64, 70–77, 89–93).

CLITSO DEDMAN (Łį́į́TSOH, BIG HORSE)

Clitso Dedman was born around 1879 near Chinle to a woman of the Táchii'nii (Red Forehead) clan and was schooled at Grand Junction Indian School. Then he worked as a carpenter and blacksmith, as a mechanic in Gallup, and as a stonemason on the Navajo Reservation. In 1897, by one account, he established the first post at Rough Rock, together with local leaders Tsi'naajinii Bilį́į' Łikizhii (Spotted Horse Blackwood Streak Clansman) and the latter's "uncle" (mother's brother?) Biwóógizhii (Gaptooth). There he traded first from a tent, where he offered coffee beans, flour, sugar, salt, and canned goods. Then in 1901 he built a small masonry store. Being from Chinle, he may have started at harvest time by bringing crops from Canyon de Chelly, where Rough Rock people had traditionally gone to trade meat for crops.

In 1909 he married a woman of Nazlini south of Chinle who was related to Chee Dodge. There the couple took over a trading post, with goods on credit from J. L. Hubbell Sr. of nearby Ganado. Dedman was one of the first Diné to have an automobile, in which he sometimes chauffeured Hubbell. In 1910 Clitso Dedman helped build the Franciscan Annunciation Mission in Chinle, and in 1915 the Dedmans sold the Nazlini store to Hubbell. Clitso Dedman then worked as a builder for the Bilagaana Chinle trader and dude rancher Cozy McSparron and ran a blacksmith shop nearby. He also seems to have worked around the Hubbell Black Mountain store around 1930, where he built a hogan for tourist-artist Laura Adams Armer (Armer 1962). From 1940 to his death in 1953, Clitso Dedman created noteworthy carved-wood figurines for collectors (Anderson 2000; Clifford 2017; Grein and Frisbie 2005:18; Valette and Valette 2000; Rebecca Valette, personal communication, November 23, 2017).

ZHEALY TSO AND DILLON PLATERO

Zhealy Tso was born in the 1880s, his mother being of the Tódích'íí'nii (Bitterwater) clan and his father being of the Tábąąhá (Edgewater) clan. He graduated from Riverside Indian School in 1904 and returned to the family home in Twin Lakes north of Gallup. Around 1905 or so, Zhealy's uncle Dillon Platero took him to a spring about 10 miles north of Chinle, where Dillon was setting up a store that Zhealy helped him build and run. Soon after that, Washindoon set up a sheep dip there. Zhealy married Asdzáán Tso of the Mashgálí (Mescalero) clan from near Canyon de Chelly. Later he bought his uncle's share in the store.

At first the store was in a tent, but later it expanded to a building with the store in the middle and living quarters on both ends. The post took wool and livestock in trade, extended credit, and took pawn. It offered general merchandise, including fresh and canned fruit that Zhealy's family grew nearby, as well as his wife's yeast bread and rolls. As late as the 1930s, Zhealy used several freight wagons to haul goods to and from Gallup. He still had the store around 1940 but had closed it by his 1946–50 term as vice chairman of the Navajo Tribal Council because of his demanding political duties. He also served as a Navajo Tribal Court judge in the 1950s. He had a fling with leasing land near the former store to a uranium prospector (apparently nothing was produced). He died on July 4, 1964 (Bahr 2004:51; Chenoweth 1990; KFb, March 17, October 25, 2005; Navajo Nation Museum, Milton Snow Collection, NO9-234; Paquette 1915, household 193; Tso 2012; Young 1958:398).

JACK NEZ AND BROTHERS

Jack Nez was of the Tsénjikiní (Cliffdwellers) clan and was born for Kii-yaa'áanii (Towering House) clan. His father was Hastiin Nééz (Mr. Tall), a chanter and local leader who helped lobby in Washington, D.C., to get the Navajo Reservation extended around Leupp in 1901. Hastiin Nééz was later a judge in the Keams Canyon Agency jurisdiction, which encompassed Hopis and Navajos. Meanwhile, Jack Nez attended school at Keams Canyon. When Hastiin Nééz broke his leg and came to Keams Canyon for a doctor, Lorenzo Hubbell Jr. (Naakai Tsoh) helped him get medical attention. Lorenzo Jr. had only recently taken over the Keams Canyon Trading Post and wanted to get to know the influential Hastiin Nééz, so Jack Nez interpreted for them. In 1910 Jack Nez was an axeman (a surveyor's assistant who cut brush and trees out of the way of the surveyor's line) for a U.S. General Land Office cadastral survey south of the Hopi mesas. He also hauled freight for Lorenzo Jr. between Gallup and Keams Canyon, mainly with the trucks that the Hubbell family had just started using.

Sometime after 1910, Jack Nez used the truck to haul lumber to his father's homesite at T'iists'óózi (Cottonwood Spring) in the Lava Buttes, southwest of

White Cone, where he built one of the three small stores that he ran between 1910 and 1918 on his parents' livestock range. The other two stores were at Shą́ą́' Tó (Sunnyside Spring), across the valley west of T'iists'óózi, and at the Navajo and Hopi farm settlement of Tallahogan to the north. The stores also served as commissaries for the family's herders. After Jack Nez died in the 1918 flu pandemic, his brothers continued to run the stores for a short while (GLO, cadastral survey plats and field notes, AZ T25N, R17-21E [1908–10]; Johnston 1972; KFa, August 28, 2002; NARA, agents' annual reports, Moqui Agency 1910–18; Navajo Nation Museum 2007; NLC, archaeological site forms, sites W-LLC-MB-E and W-LLC-MB-CCC).

IRA STEARNS HATCH AND DAUGHTER MARTHA HATCH HUNT

Ira Stearns Hatch, the older brother of Joe Hatch (see above), was born in 1862. Ira seems to have traded at Montezuma Creek from 1915 to 1917. His daughter Martha married John LaRay Hunt, who belonged to a Bluff Mormon family. The couple traded at Mexican Water from 1913 to 1918 in partnership with Martha's cousin Myrtle and her husband, Charles A. Ashcroft (see the next entry), and at Aneth from 1918 to 1921. (John also worked at the Meadows post, west of Shiprock, and at Teec Nos Pos, Tuba City, and Fruitland.) See the Joe Hatch entry above for sources.

CHILDREN OF JOE HATCH

Joe and Lelia Kirk Hatch had a daughter and five sons who traded with the People. Lelia Myrtle, born in 1893, married Bilagáana Charles A. Ashcroft. The couple traded at Mexican Water from 1913 to 1924, at first in partnership with Myrtle's cousin Martha and her husband, John Hunt (see Ira Hatch entry above). Later, they traded at Dinnehotso (1924–34) and Southside Trading Post in Fruitland (1937–39/1946). Their son Charles O. Ashcroft traded at Dinnehotso, Mariano Lake, and China Springs, and grandson Norman Ashcroft traded at Mariano Lake, Pine Springs, and Querino Canyon. Joe Jr., born in 1895, traded with his father, Joe, at Hatch Trading Post, Utah (upper Montezuma Canyon), in the mid-1920s and at Allen Canyon from the 1930s through the 1940s. Ira, born in 1898, also traded with his father, Joe, at Hatch Trading Post after 1927 and helped at Montezuma Creek around 1930. Ira also seems to have partnered with sister Myrtle and her husband at the Southside post in Fruitland, later trading at China Springs (1953–54) and Pine Springs (1956). Ira's son Sherman took over the Hatch Trading Post in 1949. See the Joe Hatch entry above for sources.

WORLD WAR I TO THE DEPRESSION AND STOCK REDUCTION

The traders in this group, like earlier ones, were schooled, and many had Bilagaana (or Hispanic) fathers. Others were children of Diné traders. The Hubbell family, as they had earlier, helped some traders get started. Money from cattle raising, perhaps from high World War I prices, was a new source of start-up funding.

BILLY GUY PETE (HASTIIN BÉÉSH BII' TÓ, MR. SPRING AMID THE FLINT)

Billy Guy Pete was born before the Long Walk and went to Fort Sumner with his family. His mother was of the Tó Tsohnii (Big Water) clan, and his father was of the Tsi'naajinii (Blackwood Streak) clan. His sister Asdzáán Łichíí' (Maggie Williams) married Diné trader Lewis Williams, whose post was farther east near Steamboat (see entry below in this section). Billy never went to school. In 1913 he worked at J. Lorenzo Hubbell Jr.'s Keams Canyon post and for the next two years worked for Lorenzo Sr. at Black Mountain Trading Post, recently bought from Diné trader Nelson Gorman (see entry above). Pete also had a small store at Pete's Spring (Béésh Bii' Tó), east of Keams Canyon. By this time he had three wives, sisters of a Diné judge (an advisor to the Keams Canyon agent). He also owned a lot of cattle, which is why he started the store. He carried mainly dry goods, got merchandise from the Hubbells, and used his own mule team to haul goods from Gallup, where the Hubbells had a warehouse. He also traveled as far as Saint Johns and Colorado to trade and sometimes worked as a bricklayer or stonemason. In 1930 he worked for Lorenzo Jr. at the Greasewood store, southwest of Ganado. He was a prominent leader in the Steamboat / Jeddito / Béésh Bii' Tó communities and between 1932 and 1938 served as a Navajo Tribal Council delegate (Colby 1972; KFb, August 12, 2004, July 12, 2005; NARA, agents' annual reports, Moqui Agency, 1914; Yazzie 2010; Young 1978:77).

FIGURE 34 Ruins of the post where Billy Guy Pete traded near Jeddito, Arizona, 1914–1915. Credit: Klara Kelley photo.

ROBERT MARTIN

Robert Martin was born in 1890 near Coyote Canyon. He attended Tohatchi, Santa Fe, Fort Defiance, and Hampton Indian schools. Between 1903 and 1916, he worked at the Shiprock Navajo Agency as an interpreter, then in 1916 and 1917 had a small store west of Shiprock near Sweetwater at the site of present Immanuel Mission. At that time, he also built a store a ways north at Red Mesa on a range that belonged to his wife's family. His brother Pete Martin hauled freight for him and later, in the 1940s and 1950s, operated a coal mine north of Gallup near Coyote Canyon to supply local schools. Bob Martin served on the Navajo Tribal Council from its beginning in 1923 to 1943. In 1933 he sold the Red Mesa post and opened another one on the south side of the San Juan River near present Nenahnezad School. After a few years, he sold the Nenahnezad store building to a son and son-in-law of longtime trader Joe Hatch (see Hatch entries above). Bob Martin died in 1955 (Bailey and Bailey 1982:416–417, 489; Girdner 2011:63; KFb, July 7, 2004, August 15, 2005, and May 11, 2011, 2005:102 [photo]).

NELLIE DAMON BLACK, BROTHERS CHARLES AND JAMES DAMON, AND NEPHEW NELSON DAMON

Nellie Damon's father, Bilagaana Anson Damon, was a soldier and butcher at Fort Sumner during the Navajo internment, where he married her mother, Tadeezbaa', of Hashtł'ishnii (Mud) clan. When the couple returned from Fort Sumner, Anson Damon worked at Fort Defiance as a butcher. He also had a homestead and store in partnership with Thomas Keam south of Fort Defiance near Natural Bridge (see chapter 6). Nellie attended Fort Defiance and Haskell Indian schools, then married Bilagaana Alexander Black, who had come to Fort Defiance in 1905 as a Presbyterian missionary. In 1917, with a $500 loan from Alexander's Kentucky cousins and probably other money from Nellie's family's livestock wealth, they started the Bonito Trading Store, on the south side of Fort Defiance. The Blacks traded merchandise from Gallup wholesalers directly for weaving, wool, livestock, hides, bone, hooves, and piñon nuts but offered little credit. After Nellie Black died in 1961, descendants kept the store going until about 1995 (AHS, Richard Van Valkenburgh Papers, folder 115, "Navajo Biographies"; KFb, August 25, 2005; M'Closkey 2003:141).

Older brother Charles Damon was schooled at Carlisle and translated oral traditions narrated by Navajo chanters for army surgeon and anthropologist Washington Matthews, who worked at Fort Wingate between the 1880s and mid-1890s. Charles may have had a small store at Sawmill in the mountains above Fort Defiance as early as 1915 or in the 1920s, or one of his sons may have done so. He had a ranch complex at Tóyee (Tuye Springs) near Jacob Morgan's former store (see entry in preceding section) and ran large herds there between the 1920s and World War II. In the 1930s he was one of Morgan's strong political supporters. When the war broke out, he moved his family from the Tóyee ranch headquarters west to the recently improved highway between Gallup and Shiprock (now U.S. Route 491), where they built a cinder-block trading post north of Twin Lakes. This store operated from the early 1940s to about 1948, when son Nelson Damon opened a store along the same highway a few miles north at Buffalo Springs (after 1952, Nelson leased this store to Bilagaanas) (KFb, July 9, 2004, August 9, 18, 25, 2005; M'Closkey 2003:141; McNitt 1962:246; Paquette 1915:10; Navajo Nation Museum, Milton Snow Collection, NE18-142 through 149 and NE18-187A, B [photos]; Van Valkenburgh 1938).

Nellie's younger brother James Damon, born in 1881, was schooled at Fort Lewis, Albuquerque Indian School, and Hampton Institute, then became a mason and carpenter. For two years in the 1920s, he had a small store at Divide, east of present Window Rock. He served on the Navajo Tribal Council from 1928 to 1932 (K, Smith, January 29, 1979; KFb, August 26, 2005; McNitt 1962:246; NMRCL, Frank McNitt Papers, box 10675, folder 15 [James Damon]).

LEE AND FRANK BRADLEY

The brothers Lee and Frank Bradley, close in age, were born around 1900. Their mother, Susie, was of the Tsénjikiní (Cliffdwellers) clan of Round Rock, where their Irish father, Arthur Bradley, hauled mail, presumably to the Chee Dodge post there. The Bradleys traded at Chilchinbeto beginning around 1915, with Lee and Frank helping their father in the summer. From their father's death in 1919 into the 1920s, the brothers ran the store.

In the 1920s and 1930s Lee Bradley ran horseback tours for trader John Wetherill from Wetherill's Kayenta Trading Post to Navajo Mountain and was a delegate to the Navajo Tribal Council from 1928 to 1936. He also hauled mail between Flagstaff and the Kayenta post office from 1930 to 1956 (the Wetherills had the U.S. government contract for the mail service). Lee's son, also named Frank, took over the route in 1956. In the 1930s Lee and his brother Frank scouted locations for water development for the New Deal Civilian Conservation Corps. Between the 1930s and World War II, Lee Bradley and sons mined coal on northern Black Mesa where the Peabody mines are now, supplying coal to schools at Kayenta, Dinnehotso, and even the Arizona State Teachers College (now Northern Arizona University) at Flagstaff. In 1950 young Frank Bradley, with help from his father, Lee, and his uncle, presumably the elder Frank Bradley, worked on the U.S. population census in northwestern Navajoland. They started as interpreters for Bilagaana enumerators, but when the logistics of enumerating Diné who moved around a large area with few automobile roads daunted the Bilagaana enumerators, the Bradleys took on the enumerating, too. In the 1950s brothers Frank and Lee interpreted with Diné extras and other employees for movie director John Ford during filming in Monument Valley (K, Townsends, June 27, 1974; KFb, April 27, 2009; Line 1991; Mike 2010; Moon 1992:108; Oshley 2000:71n63; Young 1978:70, 77, 90).

LEWIS WILLIAMS (HASTIIN NÁÁSHCH'IŁ, MR. SHUTEYE) AND SON
PAUL WILLIAMS (HASTIIN HÓK'ÁÁ', MR. HILLTOP)

Lewis Williams established Red Lake Trading Post, west of Steamboat, in the 1920s, financing it by trading cattle for merchandise. He seems to have been an in-law of Diné trader Billy Guy Pete (see entry in pre–World War I section), whose post was west of Red Lake. Son Paul Williams, schooled at Sherman Institute, came back to help his unschooled father run the store. The Williamses also raised livestock, including sheep and goats. They extended little credit but took wool and livestock in trade for general merchandise. They also sold a lot of hay out of big barns next to the store. They owned eight wagons pulled by four-horse teams, with which they hauled wool and general merchandise, picking up their wholesale merchandise, probably from Babbitt Brothers of Flagstaff, at the Babbitts' Indian Wells trading post farther south. The number of wagons suggests that they also did contract freighting. Around 1930 or 1935 the Williamses sold their store to the Lees, Bilagaana traders, who moved it a few miles east to present Steamboat.

In the 1950s Paul Williams and his wife, Lorena, were the plaintiffs in a lawsuit against Hugh Lee of Ganado Trading Company. Lee had come to their home when they were away and had taken 50 sheep for payment of a trading post debt. The case went to the U.S. Supreme Court, which ruled that non-Indians doing business on Indian lands must seek legal remedy in tribal courts rather than state courts, as Lee had done. The Williamses' persistence reinforced tribal political sovereignty (Austin 2009:27; KFb, July 12, 2005; Lee and Danoff 1982; *Navajo Times*, May 1, 2008, 2).

JOSÉ ANTONITO

José Antonito was born in the 1880s or early 1890s and was raised by a Hispanic family around the village of Blanco on the San Juan River east of Bloomfield. He married a woman of the Naashashii (Bear) clan, and they made their home in lower Blanco Canyon south of the river. In the late 1920s or so, José Antonito started a store about a mile west of Huerfano Mesa along the old road from Farmington and Bloomfield to Albuquerque. In later years, he ran the store in partnership with one or two of his daughters. The family traded merchandise for wool, lambs, and sheep pelts, which they then sold to dealers in Farmington. José Antonito, who spoke Navajo, Spanish, and English, also told anthropologists working for the Navajo Tribe on the Navajo Land Claim about Diné sacred places and in 1954 testified before the Indian Claims Commission. José Antonito died in 1958, and the family closed the store (KFb, September 27, 2016; NLC, Navajo oral history, statement 182; Van Valkenburgh 1974:29–31, 142–152).

THE DEPRESSION AND STOCK REDUCTION THROUGH THE AFTERMATH OF WORLD WAR II

A new development during this period was the involvement of the Navajo tribal government in operating trading posts and helping Diné get started as traders. With one possible exception, all were schooled. Cattle continued to be a source of start-up capital, along with a new source: wages from World War II military duty and from uranium mining.

ALBERT ARNOLD JR. AND ALICE ARNOLD; ETHEL ARNOLD HERRING

The mother of Albert Arnold Jr. was a daughter of Hastiin Béégashii Łání (Mr. Many Cows) of Coyote Canyon, and his father was Bilagáana trader Albert Arnold Sr. Between about 1915 and 1940, Albert Sr. owned stores at Tohatchi, Mexican Springs, Naschitti, and Gallup. Albert Jr. went to school at the Christian (Dutch) Reformed Rehoboth Mission in Gallup. Before 1934 Albert worked for his father at Tohatchi and may also have managed the store at Mexican Springs for his cousin (?) Walter Bitsie (see below). After Albert Sr. died around 1940, Albert Jr. and his wife, Alice, also from Coyote Canyon, ran the Tohatchi store until the family sold it in the early 1950s. Albert Jr. then went to work for his brother-in-law, Albert Herring, at a uranium mine on Mount Taylor, where he drove heavy equipment. Albert Jr. died around 1957. Albert Jr.'s sister Ethel Arnold, schooled at Rehoboth Christian Reformed Mission School in Gallup, married Bilagáana Albert Herring. Before her father died around 1940, the couple operated the Naschitti Trading Post, and she may have inherited her father's share in the post. The Herrings reportedly sold their interest to go into the uranium business near Grants (KFb, March 11, September 19, 2005; M'Closkey 2003:141).

WALTER BITSIE

Born to a woman of the Táchii'nii (Red Forehead) clan, Walter Bitsie was schooled at the Christian (Dutch) Reformed Tohatchi Mission and became a Christian Reformed preacher. He also owned a lot of cattle and sheep. As a leader in the Mexican Springs Cattle Growers Association, he organized and oversaw operation of the Mexican Springs store from the 1920s or 1930s until 1949. The store was one of several Navajo cooperatives of the period (see entry for Navajo Tribe below in this section). A business relationship with Albert Arnold Sr., who seems to have owned the store from the 1920s to around 1930 (see entry above), is unclear—Walter Bitsie may have been related to Albert Arnold Sr.'s wife. The Cattle Growers Association also had a summer trading post at Squirrel Springs in the Chuska Mountains west of Mexican Springs, where the clientele moved for summer range. Both stores were inside the area covered by a large U.S. Soil Conservation Service demonstration project in the late 1930s and 1940s. Diné ownership of the stores ended when the Cattle Growers Association dissolved in 1949 (KFb, September 6, 26, 2005).

JOHN WILLIAMS (JOHN SÁNÍ, OLD JOHN) AND SON BRUCE WILLIAMS

John Williams was born around 1890 and schooled at Blue Canyon southeast of Tuba City. He had a lot of cows, which he was forced to sell when livestock reduction started in the early 1930s. With the cash from selling his cattle, he started a small store along Dinnebito Wash southwest of Oraibi two to four miles above Sand Springs. He operated the store between 1933 and 1936, stocking mostly groceries and doing business mostly in cash. When local people with credit accounts at the larger, Hubbell-owned store nearby paid off those accounts seasonally with wool and lambs, some with a balance due would get cash, which they later spent at Williams's store. Williams had an old truck and hauled merchandise from Canyon Diablo on the railroad, where it had been sent by a wholesale house, the nearest being Babbitt Brothers in Flagstaff and J. L. Hubbell in Winslow. After serving in World War II, son Bruce Williams managed Hubbell stores at Na-ah-tee and Sand Springs, later becoming a school bus driver in Tuba City and earning a college diploma. John Williams died of a heart attack in 1944 while his son, Bruce, was still in the army (KFb, September 9, October 21, 2005).

BERT TSO, SONS OLIVER AND HERBERT, AND MANAGER PAUL BEGAY

Bert Tso was of Tódích'íí'nii (Bitterwater) clan. His mother's mother was a daughter of Hastiin Daaghaa' (Whiskers), leader of a group who escaped the Long Walk by hiding in the canyons west of Navajo Mountain. His mother's father, Sorefoot (Hastiin Ké Diniihí, or Keshgoli), traded with the Hopis after the Long Walk. Bert Tso's father, Gishii Bida' (Cane's Nephew), was a large livestock owner west of Navajo Mountain on the Kaibito Plateau in the early 1900s, reportedly having 1,500 sheep, 500 horses, and 200 cattle. He gave Bert and his other sons livestock to start their own flocks. Bert completed ninth grade at Phoenix Indian School, or completed 12 years total at Tuba City and Sherman Indian School. He started buying cattle from people around the Kaibito Plateau in the 1920s or 1930s and became the largest cattle owner there, with 405 head when he died. He visited people at their homes to buy their stock, which the people then drove to the post. From there the sheep were herded to the railroad at Winslow and Flagstaff and sold to (precontracted) buyers from Los Angeles or Albuquerque. He would send 8,000–9,000 head at a time with seven drovers on a 14-day trek.

Bert Tso had three stores: one at Kaibito; one at Thief Rock, about four miles south of Shonto; and one at Nazhoonskai (Na'ashshǫǫsh Tó or Adika'i Tó [?], Gambling Spring), about five miles north of Shonto. He may have started trading at Kaibito as early as the mid-1920s, closing the store there when he moved to Shonto to trade, but more likely he operated all three posts at the same time from 1934 to 1942. The manager at the Kaibito store was Paul Begay, who also checked on the other stores. Bert's sons, Oliver and Herbert, also helped in the stores, and all were paid a percentage of the receipts. All three stores were rock buildings that included a room for the manager's living quarters. The stores did not keep regular hours but were open on demand. They offered dry goods, coffee, sugar, flour, and other items, which Bert bought from Flagstaff (probably from Babbitt Brothers). Until 1939 he had workers haul wholesale merchandise from Tuba City by wagon (we presume that Babbitts relayed it from Flagstaff as far as their Tuba City post). In 1939 Bert Tso bought a two-ton Ford truck from the Babbitts dealership in Flagstaff and then had son Oliver truck the merchandise directly from there. He had gasoline trucked in large barrels from the Babbitts' Arizona Gas Station on the east side of Flagstaff, probably mainly for his own use, since most people were still using wagons. Bert Tso banked in both Flagstaff and Phoenix. He died in 1942.[2]

FIGURE 35 H. T. Donald's Tsegi Canyon Trading Post, west of Kayenta, 1954. Credit: Photographed by Milton Snow, courtesy of Navajo Nation Museum, Window Rock, Arizona, neg. no. NE18-UC.

H. T. DONALD (DONALD TSÉ ÁLTS'ÍÍSÍ, DONALD LITTLEROCK)

H. T. Donald was born around Shonto, his mother being of Tódích'íí'nii (Bitterwater) clan and his father of Tábąąhá (Edgewater) clan. He was schooled at Tuba City, then at Grand Junction or Colorado Springs. He then joined the police in the Tuba City Navajo Agency. In the 1930s and 1940s he worked at and managed Shonto Trading Post. In 1946, under newly revised Navajo tribal policies, he received a lease for a trading post, gas station, and tourist camp from the Navajo Tribal Council. By 1948, encouraged by Shonto traders Reuben and Mildred Heflin, he had started the Tsegi Trading Post, west of Kayenta, at first trading from a hogan. In 1951 he may have received a loan of $5,000 from the Navajo Tribe to build a well. He quit running the store in 1958 and leased it to others (the store closed around 1980). In the 1960s he served two terms as delegate from Shonto to the Navajo Tribal Council and also served as a Shonto chapter grazing official (Hegemann 1963:300–302; K, Porter, June 26, 1974; KFb, November 24, 2004; M'Closkey 2003:143n20; Nez 2009; Roberts 1987:119–120).

FIGURE 36 Trader John Foley at the grand opening of the Many Farms Navajo tribal store, 1942. Credit: Photographed by Milton Snow, courtesy of Navajo Nation Museum, Window Rock, Arizona, neg. no. NE18-30.

NAVAJO TRIBE, WITH SOME DINÉ MANAGERS

In 1939 the newly reorganized and enlarged Navajo Tribal Council passed a resolution that encouraged Diné to buy out non-Navajo traders. In the 1940s and early 1950s the Navajo government also briefly took over several stores and hired managers to run them or helped local communities to run stores as cooperatives (Bailey and Bailey 1999:256; KFb, July 28, September 6, 16, 30, 2005; M'Closkey 2003:129; NAU, UITA, Wagner; Parman 1976:81–84, 264–269; Young 1958:84). Included were stores at Sawmill (Navajo government store), ca. 1939–55; Mexican Springs (co-op), ca. 1939–49 (see entry above in this section for Walter Bitsie), with Hispanic manager Ernest Garcia; Many Farms (co-op), 1940s, with Diné manager John Foley; Pine Springs (Navajo government store), 1940s, managed by Bilagaanas Bill and Sally Lippincott; Tolani Lake (co-op), 1940s, with Diné manager Gene Potts; Pinon (co-op), ca. 1939–52 (see next entry for Clifford Beck; the Navajo government in the 1950s also took over the Hubbell family's Pinon Mercantile); Big Mountain, where the Pinon co-op got Tribal Council permission to have a branch in 1948 (see entries below for Alonzo Keshgoli and Kee Shelton, the store of one or the other presumably being this proposed branch); and Wide Ruins (tribal government store), bought from the Lippincotts in the early 1950s, managed by Ernest Garcia and later Diné Sam Day III.

CLIFFORD BECK

Clifford Beck was born north of Pinon near Forest Lake in 1905 to an Áshįįhí (Salt) clan mother and a Kiyaa'áanii (Towering House) father. His brother, Russell Tallsalt, was also a trader (see entry below). Clifford Beck attended schools at Tuba City, Kayenta, and Sherman Institute, then worked with U.S. government range riders during the 1930s stock reduction program. From about 1939 into the 1940s, he managed a Navajo co-op store in Pinon (see above). He served in World War II, then returned to the co-op. After 1950 he took over ownership of the former co-op store, which he named Round Valley Trading Post and kept into the 1990s, often hiring Bilagaana managers. He also served on the Navajo Tribal Council from 1950 to 1970 (Benally 2006; KFb, July 28, 2005; NAU, UITA, Jack Lee et al.; Roessel and Johnson 1974:203).

ALONZO KESHGOLI AND KEE SHELTON

Alonzo Keshgoli attended Albuquerque Indian School. He used his father's money to help J. L. Hubbell Jr. establish the Big Mountain store, north of Pinon, then managed the store for J. L. Jr. from 1939 to 1942. He served in World War II as a Navajo Code Talker. He was also connected with the Pinon co-op.

In 1940 Kee Shelton had a license to trade at Big Mountain in partnership with J. L. Hubbell Jr. Shelton ran the store with J. L. Jr. or the Hubbell family in 1939, 1942, and 1946 (J. L. Jr. died in 1942). The store was a log building about two miles north of the Hubbell Big Mountain store that was earlier managed by Alonzo Keshgoli. Kee Shelton died in 1946 (Colby 1972; KFb, July 28, August 11, 2005; Lapahie 1997; M'Closkey 2003:140).

BETTY ZANE WETHERILL RODGERS AND DAUGHTER WILMA SEELEY

Betty Zane's parents were a Diné couple of Lukachukai. Betty and her sister went to Tuba City boarding school, there to be discovered by Louisa and John Wetherill, the famous Bilagaana traders at Kayenta. The Wetherills adopted the sisters and put them to work at their Kayenta guest ranch. Betty Wetherill later went to school in Mesa, near Phoenix, where she lived with Wetherill daughter Ida. In 1937 Betty married Buck Rodgers, a Bilagaana freighter for the Wetherills, and between 1939 and 1975 Betty and Buck Rodgers owned Buck Rodgers Trading Post at Cameron. Eventually, they also owned Vermillion Cliffs Lodge, north of Lee's Ferry, and the tourist-oriented Antelope Hills Trading Post, south of Cameron, which they built. The Cameron store burned in 1975 but was rebuilt and taken over by daughter Wilma Seeley and her husband, Jack. The Seeleys also owned Bitter Springs Trading Post, south of Lee's Ferry, around this time (Comfort 1980:155–157; NAU, UITA, Betty Rodgers).

HARRY SHORTY (HASTIIN TSÉ ŁITSOÍ, MR. YELLOWROCK)

Harry Shorty was raised a few miles northeast of Kin Lichee and attended Fort Defiance Boarding School. Around 1940 he managed a store at Canyon Diablo, along the railroad west of Winslow, for Bilagaana rancher-trader Jot Stiles. Later in the 1940s he managed the Bidahochee post, north of Holbrook, for Bill McGee. From 1949 to 1957 he established and ran his own store east of Bidahochee at Twin Buttes, the home of his wife's family, and also raised sheep around nearby Yellow Rock. At the same time, he sold goods to summer logging crews from a hogan store on the Defiance Plateau, southwest of Sawmill, near the site of the original government sawmill (from the 1880s until 1907, where Nelson Gorman had his first store; see above). Shorty's hogan store sold mainly snack food, and the loggers ran small accounts, which they paid off on payday.

In 1957 Shorty built a store in Window Rock with some Navajo government funding. The store also had a gas station and café, where Mrs. Shorty baked bread and cooked hot lunches for Navajo government workers. The Shortys closed this store around 1970, possibly for their own health reasons (KFa, November 4, 2003; KFb, August 9, 11, 2005; United Indian Traders Association 1949).

YOUNGER SONS OF JOE HATCH

See various entries above for Joe Hatch and his older sons. Leonard, born in 1907, traded at Four Corners and Towaoc in the 1940s. Claude, born in 1914, and Stewart, born in 1916, both served in World War II. Claude had earlier helped brother Leonard at Four Corners, and after the war, both helped Leonard at Towaoc. In 1949 Claude and Stewart moved to their parents' Fruitland ranch, where they started Hatch Brothers Trading Post. Stewart's sons now operate the store (for sources, see entry for Joe Hatch above; see also Dalrymple 2013).

RUSSELL TALLSALT (ÁSHĮĮHÍ NÉÉZ) AND SONS CON JOE TALLSALT AND RAYMOND TALLSALT (RAYMOND KIIYAANII)

Russell Tallsalt was of the Áshįįhí (Salt) clan, born for Kiiyaa'áanii (Towering House), and brother of trader Clifford Beck of Pinon (see above). Russell got started freighting for the Hubbell family when they still used wagons. He started trading by planting corn and squash along Dinnebito Wash, east of Rocky Ridge, then taking wagonloads of crops on a circuit to schools at Leupp, Sand Springs, Hopi, and Winslow. In 1945 he used the money his daughter's husband received as a World War II veteran to establish a store west of Pinon at Hardrocks, just north of the mission and the present chapter house site. People traded wool, livestock, sheepskins, rugs, sheep, cattle, and horses, and the store also took pawn. The store sold food, dry goods, and hardware. Russell's son, Raymond Tallsalt, freighted merchandise from Gallup in the family's big truck.

In 1968 Russell retired from the store because of old age. The family moved the store about three miles west to the homesite of son Con Joe Tallsalt, Chíshii (Chiricahua) clan. It was a small cinder-block building with a gas pump. Con Joe Tallsalt quit trading there in 1980 because of competition from Bilagaana traders (KFb, July 28, August 26, October 12, 2005; Navajo Nation Museum 2007; Jolene Robertson, personal communication, November 28, 2011).

ELLA AND HELENA KESHGOLI AND ELLA'S DAUGHTER VIRGINIA BURNHAM

Ella Keshgoli was born in 1916, and her sister Helena was born a few years later. Their father was Hastiin Łįį' Bił Naagháí (Mr. Horse Rider), who owned a lot of livestock. They were related to Alonzo Keshgoli, who managed the Hubbell

Big Mountain Trading Post (see entry above in this section). The sisters were schooled at Fort Apache in the 1920s. Later, Ella worked for J. L. Hubbell Jr. and the Hubbell family at the Oraibi, Na-ah-tee, and Marble Canyon stores. During World War II both sisters worked at Camp Navajo, the munitions depot at Bellemont, west of Flagstaff, cleaning railroad engines. After the war, with their wartime earnings and backing from their father and the Hubbell family, they opened White Post Trading Post on the southeastern flanks of Big Mountain. They took wool, livestock, and hides in trade and offered some credit. They stocked staple foods and livestock salt blocks, which men of the family hauled from the Hubbell warehouse in Winslow in a truck, along with 55-gallon drums of gasoline to be dispensed by siphon. In the early 1950s, overwhelming demands of stockraising and child care forced them to close the store. Ella's daughter Virginia and her husband, Bruce Burnham, since the 1960s have operated several posts, most recently Burnham Trading Post in Sanders, Arizona (KFb, August 26, October 26, 2005).

WENDELL AND AMY REID

Wendell Reid was born in 1902 in the mountains west of Shiprock near Cove. His wife, Amy, was born into a Fruitland family. Both Amy and Wendell went to school at Riverside, California, where Amy was part of a group of girls who played mandolins and called themselves the Mosquito Band. But Wendell and Amy did not know each other until later, when they met in Durango, Colorado, where Amy was looking for work and Wendell, a railroad maintenance worker, was probably working on the narrow-gauge railroad. After uranium mining began around Cove in 1948, Wendell hauled for the uranium mines in the mountains south of Cove. He and Amy also served the miners with some sort of store near the mine.

Around 1948–49, at the request of Cove residents, Wendell and Amy established a store within a mile southwest of Cove Day School. The store was amid fields irrigated by a system that the U.S. government had built in the customary-use area of Wendell's family in the 1930s, not far west of the main road through Cove to the mines. A daughter, Mary Junes, worked in the store. The Reids had a peach orchard (a few trees remain) and a big field there but did not sell produce in the store, instead sharing it with neighbors and canning some for family use. The store had no refrigeration, but it did have a generator, housed in a dugout where the Reids stored potatoes and onions. They also raised chickens, sold eggs in the store, and kept a herd of sheep.

Around 1953, the Reids moved their store a short ways east along the main road through Cove, which went up to the mines. They did so because miners wanted to buy gas as they passed along that road, so the Reids installed a gas pump and hauled in the barrels of gasoline for it. Electricity came from the school nearby. Their daughter, other relatives, and local residents worked at the store, including the brothers George and Max Tsosie and a Mr. Light, who was in charge of cutting up meat. The store sold dry goods, food (meat and canned goods), yarn and dyes for local weavers, kerosene, lanterns, and basic tools such as hammers and nails. The nearby day school, built in the 1930s, again supplied electricity. Water came from a big tank up the hill nearby. During this time, the Reids also kept their sheep, which Wendell's sister Minnie took into her herd, grazing them up on the mountain in summer and between Red Valley and Cove the rest of the year. The Reids also had horses and cows.

Around 1955, the Reids sold the store, as well as their horses and cows, and moved to Shiprock. There they got a 10-acre farm assignment in the Shiprock irrigation project and grew hay, which Wendell hauled to Arizona to sell. In the winter, Amy worked as a dormitory attendant south of Shiprock in Toadlena and other government boarding schools. In summer, she worked every day along with Wendell on the farm. Though Wendell never worked in the mines, he was a contract trucker for them. Illnesses later in his life may have come from this exposure or from exposure to radioactive material that clung to the miners who came to the store. Wendell died in 1978 or 1979. Amy remained a lively and hard-working inspiration to her children and grandchildren for many more years (Darlene Tsinnie and Eva Hogue, personal communication, July 7, 2010, June 7, 2011).

THEMES IN THE LIFE HISTORIES

In the decades before 1950, schooling and knowledge of English were uncommon among the People. These lacks were some of the main obstacles for Diné to become traders, according to our Diné consultants. Diné who did own or manage stores overcame the English and schooling obstacles by having an English-speaking (usually Bilagaana) father, some schooling, or both. This statement may also apply to Diné wives of non- Diné traders (our list excludes Diné wives whose role in running the stores is unclear). However, the Diné wives more likely compensated for their husbands' language deficiencies rather than the reverse.

Lack of financing owing to institutional racism was an obstacle, one that persists today. Bilagaana traders could get started with backing from a general-merchandise wholesaler, but Diné rarely could. From the earliest times, many Diné traders belonged to families that included other entrepreneurs or property owners and themselves took on other kinds of businesses. Many Diné traders from World War I on had money from large family livestock holdings, especially cattle, for which non-Diné traders paid cash. Large stockowning families may also have put at least one son in school so he could help deal with Bilagaana traders and government workers on livestock matters (Henderson 1985). Other Diné traders got backing from trader-fathers, either Bilagaana or Diné. Though many Bilagaanas, especially Mormons, founded trading dynasties, among the Diné there was only the Hatch family, which also included many Bilagaana Mormons. Still other Diné started out as store workers or contract freighters for non-Diné traders who later helped them get started. The freighters' pay in cash, trade tokens, or merchandise might have stocked their stores (see also Old Mexican 1947:95). Starting in the 1930s, the Navajo tribal government also helped Diné get started by hiring them as managers in tribally owned posts or helping them finance their own posts, all to replace Bilagaana traders with Diné who could better serve local clienteles. Earnings from World War II and postwar uranium miners also bankrolled some.

The Hubbell family, especially J. Lorenzo Hubbell Jr., backed many Diné owners and managers (see Kelley and Francis 2018 for all of them). According to one Diné consultant who as a teenager worked at one of Lorenzo Jr.'s stores, Lorenzo Jr. did not trust Bilagaana store managers or partners and expected the Diné workers to keep an eye on them. Most of the Diné traders whom Lorenzo Jr. backed were in the Black Mesa country, the most undeveloped part of Navajoland and probably the least attractive to prospective Bilagaana traders. These Diné traders brought Hubbell into their remote homeland.

Also worth noting is the large proportion of Diné traders after World War I who held political office. For most, officeholding came after their stints as traders and probably depended on the same factors that had earlier helped them as traders: knowledge of English, schooling, and access to some kind of wealth. Whether having a trading post was itself a springboard to political leadership is not clear. Many Diné traders, according to some of our consultants, had trouble staying in business because it was hard to make a profit (or even pay bills to wholesale suppliers) while honoring obligations to extensive networks of kin. This problem thwarted the Navajo tribal government's efforts to replace

Bilagaanas with Diné traders. And indeed, while many Diné who managed stores had long careers, most who owned stores did not. Many went into politics instead.

Few women seem to have taken the lead in running trading posts before the 1950s. Most listed here seem to have worked alongside husbands who were in charge. According to Diné oral tradition, before the Long Walk, Diné men were mostly responsible for trading with non Diné, though some women also took part in trading expeditions (Hill 1948:382). The impression of Diné men controlling trading posts after the Long Walk, however, may come from biases in sources, especially documents, from a time when both Diné and Bilagaana expected men to lead in non-Diné matters like trading. Many Diné trader wives may well have been like Alice Peshlakai Gorman (not to mention Bilagaana trader wives), who ran the store every day while her husband was out freighting or ranching. Credit from wholesalers and banks, when available at all, would have favored men, as in the U.S. economy in general.

At least two Diné women were freighters in the early 1900s, one who freighted for the Hyde Exploring Expedition around Chaco Canyon (Pepper 1901) and another, Aɫnáánábaa' of Sawmill, who freighted from Fort Defiance to Chinle around 1920 for trader Cozy McSparron and camped near his post (Wilson Hunter, personal communication, May 17, 2011). These women, who did dangerous and strenuous work away from women's traditional sphere at home, suggest that Diné women may have had more authority in trading than the sketches here show. Here may be another false absence created by underdocumentation.

Returning to the question at the beginning of this chapter, have Diné traders simply enabled colonizer indirect rule, including disrupting Diné traditional bonds with the land, or have they also contributed to the bond of land and the People, their land-based ways of life, and the sense of shared identity that are part of sovereignty? We think that they have contributed in some ways, though they also deepened the inroads of the U.S. economy into Navajoland, with its ultimately disruptive effects on the bond with the land (see chapters 9 and 11). Many, especially before stock reduction, were large stock owners using their extended family lands, and their stores were a sideline to stockraising. Several traders knew traditional ceremonies. Most were doing entrepreneurially what other Diné had to do as wage workers in these times of too little land: supplement their land-based livelihood with jobs among the colonizers or with full-time weaving at home while their children herded. They knew that jobs would come and go, but the land was always there for them, and they tried to integrate jobs and businesses with Diné tradition. The next two chapters explore other examples of this new way to maintain some semblance of traditional life on the land and the resulting bond.

9

DINÉ TRADING AND SILVERSMITHING
AT BORREGO PASS TRADING POST

Back then, the land was beautiful with plenty of plants and grass. There were many sheep, cows, horses, donkeys and mules that belonged to our parents and grandparents. They also wove rugs and made silver jewelry. . . . We lived well until 1935, when Washindoon imposed other plans on us. . . . Washindoon said we must reduce [our livestock] to regenerate the land. Washindoon's range riders would ride into a herd and drive a bunch away to I don't know where. Then a man named Blue Eyes—Harold Prewitt [rancher]—wanted to swap lands [arranged by Washindoon without the family's consent]. All the good land in the flats where my family lived and herded he took. My father and his parents and his sister all lived there and used that land. In exchange, they [Washindoon] gave us this land here. (Original statement in Navajo, KFa, June 8, 2009)

T HE SPEAKER, Mabel Morgan, was born near the future Borrego Pass Trading Post and spent her first few years in her family's traditional land-use area before displacement. Even decades later, her attachment to the land and hurt at its loss are evident. She and her sister have tried to instill the same bond with the family land in their children, grandchildren, and great-grandchildren. Having grown up without access to the former family lands and with the long-term effects of stock reduction on the trading post system, the younger generations have been more and more entangled with wage work (starting with silversmithing) and store-bought goods. Though their bonds to the land may not be as strong, the bonds still exist.

This chapter offers a close look at one post, the Borrego Pass Trading Post, and its clientele from both Diné and trader recollections. Borrego Pass is in the eastern Navajo Checkerboard, which in the 1930s and earlier was much like the Chambers Checkerboard of chapters 6 and 7. This chapter shows how the People depended on the post to make a living from what remained of their lands and herds after the reductions of the 1930s, now supplemented by silversmithing. Recollections of local Diné present in concrete detail this world of transition away from the land. Through posts like Borrego Pass, the Diné became increasingly enmeshed in national and global markets. Eventually, after stock reduction, land loss, and the need for wage work had disrupted the bonds of many Diné with the land, the trading post system died. The traders' view shows the larger national and global forces that contributed to the system's failure.

The Borrego Pass Trading Post in its heyday was a fairly typical Navajoland post.[1] It is about 40 miles northeast of Gallup in the piñon-covered Continental Divide of the eastern Navajo Checkerboard area, which overlooks the grassy plains and barren mesas north toward Chaco. The post was established along a road that connected Chaco Canyon to the railroad at Thoreau (U.S. Bureau of Indian Affairs 1933). The forerunner of this road was a wagon freight road between Thoreau and Chaco Canyon that passed somewhat west of the post (Kelley and Francis 2005a:42; Shaler and Campbell 1907:Plate XXII). In 2003 widening and paving of this road threatened to disturb part of the trading post compound and brought us to the community to learn about the post's history (Kelley and Francis 2005a).

From 1925 to 1927 Ben and Anna Harvey had a small seasonal post about a mile east of the present one where Diné families came in the fall to pick and trade piñon nuts. The Harveys moved the store to its present site in 1927 and ran it until 1935. In 1933 they mortgaged the store to their cousins John J. and Ruth Kirk of the Gallup general-merchandise wholesale firm Kirk Brothers. The Kirks hired Bill and Jean Cousins to run the store when the Harveys left. In 1936 Vernon and Ruth Bloomfield took over the store but left in 1940 when a local resident shot at Vernon as he was gathering eggs. Vernon's sister Fern and her husband, Donald Smouse, then took it, and by the 1970s Vernon had returned to help. Local Diné told us that lots of Diné, having lost land and livestock in the 1930s, worked for the Smouses, constructing buildings, caring for the Smouses' livestock, making jewelry, and weaving. Silversmiths who worked for the Smouses (some of whom started with the Harveys and Kirks) had a workshop and living quarters at the post. Local Diné remember the Smouses as generous people who helped the community get many improvements, including the Borrego Pass school. The Smouses showed movies in the LDS chapel that they had built next to the store. Later, from 1991 to 1998, the aging Smouses got Merle and Rosella Moore to manage the store for them. Since then, Sonny and Josie Gonzales have leased the store from the Smouses' descendants.

PRODUCTS FROM THE LAND AND
GOODS FROM THE STORE

EARLY YEARS: 1930s AND EARLY 1940s

Like other Navajoland traders, now that Diné families lacked enough land to produce their own subsistence directly, the Harveys, Bloomfields, and Smouses took various Diné products, most from the land, in exchange for general merchandise. The details of this trade, recalled by local residents below, show that families were still strongly rooted in the land for their living. The traders bought all kinds of livestock (cattle, sheep, lambs, goats), as well as wool, rugs, silver jewelry, and piñon nuts. The Smouses also bought things that other traders would not buy, like hides. We did not learn how the traders marketed these items in the early years of the trading post. The jewelry making at the post is described later in this section. The Smouses also took weaving in trade. Among the local weavers were several men. The Smouses followed the earlier practice of Fern's parents, George and Lucy Bloomfield of Toadlena, who, with Ed Davies of the Two Grey Hills post, worked with local weavers there to develop rugs that would sell for higher prices. A lot of people came to the Borrego Pass post to buy the silver jewelry and rugs. The Smouses therefore did not depend on wholesalers to market these items and instead may have notified would-be craft buyers by mail. During World War II, the Smouses and other Crownpoint-area traders started working together toward better quality in local weaving. Eventually, the region's weavers, with help from these traders (and reportedly also from the Office of Navajo Economic Opportunity), organized the Crownpoint Rug Weavers Association and its famous auctions, which began in the 1960s.

Mabel Morgan, whose remembrances of the land begin this chapter, recalled that the traders would give store credit and tokens (tin "money" redeemable only at the store that issued it) for local products. For example, the Smouses might value a rug at six to eight dollars, and the customer would get tokens or credit for that amount. Don Smouse quit using tokens sometime between 1958 and 1963. Local families had accounts with Smouse, paying their balances with lambs in the fall and wool in the spring. If the value of the lambs or the wool was more than what the family owed on earlier merchandise purchased, the family would get the balance in cash, not credit. Others said that customers traded other things, like weaving, pelts and hides, and piñon nuts, in between the seasonal reckonings to eke out their credit or barter directly for merchandise.

With the credit or tokens, as Mrs. Morgan recalled, people would buy flour, sugar, coffee, salt, baking powder, lard, onions, eggs, potatoes, and soda pop. In early times, the store sold very little food in cans—even pop came in bottles. Prices were two dollars for 25 pounds of flour (four dollars for 50 pounds). Brands remembered were Red Rose flour and KC baking powder. These goods may have come from Cortez, Colorado (we note that Red Rose flour did; probably the other goods came from Gallup). The store also sold clothes, cloth, shoes (soles nailed on), and tools (axes, shovels, rakes), as well as wood-burning stoves (there was no butane back then) and kerosene for lamps. One could even order a wagon through Don Smouse—it cost $200, and for another $50 you would get the harness. The wagon came disassembled and was put together when it arrived. Smouse would also get other things on special order.

Sam Platero also described the trading post inventory in his earliest memories (ca. 1930). Mr. Platero enjoyed recalling the family purchases from his childhood, as have many other elders whom we have consulted around Navajoland. (Younger Diné readers might try asking their elders about the items on the list below.) Mr. Platero did not go to the store as a child but inferred what was available from what his parents brought home in those days. He remembered the following. (Our comments are enclosed in parentheses.)

Artifacts of production. See "house construction/maintenance" below.

Food. The store sold mainly staples: coffee, flour, salt, potatoes, sugar, apples, oranges (these fruits were treats). People also got fruit by bartering in surrounding communities (we note that Mormon farmers at Bluewater and Hispanic farmers at San Mateo had orchards). Local Diné back then produced most of their own foods—they still had a lot of sheep and butchered them when needed. Food brands are hard to identify when one does not read English. Flour sacks had a picture of a plant that looked like corn or wheat on them; the bluebird (trademark of the famously frybread-worthy Bluebird flour) came later. Sugar and salt were sold by the pound and came in cloth sacks like flour sacks. There was canned milk, but mainly Bilagaanas used it. Diné had goats for milk and only bought canned milk in lambing season, when some used it to feed orphaned lambs. Lard came in cans, not in the paper containers of today.

Indulgences. There were only a few types of sweets, not the shelf after shelf that you see today. Coffee was whole bean that you could grind yourself or else already ground, and it came in cloth sacks. Soda pop came in thick bottles, opened with a church key. There was a lot of Coke and a strawberry pop—Mr. Platero did not remember the names. Tobacco was a luxury, and parents didn't let children have any. Elders, too, were stingy with it. Flake tobacco was called "Bull" (presumably Bull Durham), and you rolled it in a cornhusk. There was also tobacco cut in thick plugs from a big cake.

Domestic small technology. Diné used sticks as utensils for such purposes as spearing dumplings out of the family pot. Some people had flatware, but Mr. Platero's family stuck with the traditional utensils. People moved around a lot, and too many possessions got in the way, so equipment needed to be multipurpose and lightweight. Cooking was done outside over an open fire, not on a stove. Food was basic—bread (homemade white-flour tortillas or fry bread) and potatoes—and there were no delicacies. Mr. Platero's family had a cast-iron stew pot with a lid—not a dutch oven—which they used to make both stew and fry bread. For tortillas, they used either a homemade grill of wire with looped-wire legs or a flat stone slab griddle. People did not use cast-iron griddles—those were for Bilagáanaas (see also Frisbie 2018). People washed clothes in playas after a rain, so they had washboards but no tubs. They spread the clothes on greasewood bushes to dry. The Platero family used a hard block of gray soap.

Household equipment. The Platero family made a kerosene lamp from a can. You put kerosene in it, which soaked up a wick made of a piece of cotton string or a strip of cloth. The can had a cover and holes punched in it around the top to draw. Glass lamps were not available until later, and the family did not know how to use manufactured metal lamps, which were small like a coffee pot (probably like an Aladdin lamp) with a wick and handle. People cooked outside on open hearths with rocks piled around them or made stoves out of sheet metal or oil barrels. People moved around a lot then, cooked outside or in shade houses, and moved to where firewood was at hand. Nonportable items like stoves had limited use for mobile people. Only Bilagáanas had water barrels, and they were made of wood. People moved to where water was and did not haul it over large distances. Mr. Platero did not remember when steel barrels appeared.

House construction/maintenance. From the store people got small tools: axes, shovels, rakes, and hoes for farming. It rained a lot then, and people farmed by planting with a digging stick. Plows came later. Crops were good. (Presumably the post also sold sheep shears.) People had hammers, screwdrivers, and pliers—things were put together with screws. Hogans were made of logs, not lumber. There was no need for windows, and no mass-produced items were used for house construction. Therefore, the store did not offer building materials.

Personal items. People did not use headache medicine or other patent medicines then. Instead, medicine men and women used herbs to cure people, even recently, until the drought made the plants disappear. Today people only use medicine from bottles. People made their own moccasins out of cowhide or deerhide, even for children. Mr. Platero did not remember when the store started carrying factory-made shoes. The store stocked some cloth and clothes, but long ago, when there was no cloth, people used flour sacks for clothes.

Entertainment. There were no toys except marbles. Children would make miniature cows and horses out of mud when it rained, and they made their own dolls from scraps of cloth. People got mad at you for playing with toys, saying not to play, you have to work. You played when you herded or elsewhere out of sight.

Transportation. The early wagons had big wheels. Those with smaller wheels came later. Wagons did not cost much then. People had lots of sheep and traded them to pay for the wagons. Leather harness for horses was available, but there was little horse equipment, just reins and shoulder straps. When things broke, people patched them with cowhide. Auto equipment came later.

By describing the things that local families used in their daily living, Mr. Platero delineated a whole way of life that seems unencumbered rather than impoverished (though stock reduction was beginning to change that). The People bought some things from the store, made others themselves, and did without things unsuited to their mobile herding way of life.

When Mr. Platero was young, the traders used many of the same kinds of consumer goods that local Diné did. They wore clothes from their own stores. The one memorable exception was the trader's auto, the first one in the area. It was high in the center, small-boxed, with a small engine, simple, and the People were amazed by it. Also, the traders (or other Bilagaanas) used canned milk more than did local Diné, as well as a greater variety of cast-iron cookware and wooden water barrels. The trading post hired a few Diné (see below), and they, too, used the same kinds of goods as everybody else.

Another local resident told us later about traditional foods before stock reduction, when his family had more than 1,000 sheep and goats (Kelley and Francis 2008). He was born in 1938, and the family was still feeding itself this way during his childhood. They would butcher four or five sheep at one time, cut them into equal-sized parts, and give some to their neighbors. They would save meat for winter by cutting it into strips and hanging them to dry, along

FIGURE 37 Women and children in a shade house with household goods common among Diné families of the 1920s to 1940s. The cooking area in front is a hearth with a coffee pot, cast-iron stew pot, frying pan, dutch oven, and small (lard?) pail. Credit: National Anthropological Archives, Smithsonian Institution, INV 02299700.

with corn and cut-up squash. They would pound the jerky, tear it up, add the vegetables and wild onions, and cook it. They also ate horses and donkeys in winter but not mules. They would keep mutton fat in buckets or take it with them in sacks to make gravy. They grew their own corn, watermelons, and squash and traded with people at Bluewater (a Mormon settlement south of Borrego Pass with a big irrigation system) for wagonloads of carrots, lettuce, and other vegetables, which they kept in a storehouse dug into a hillside. They also traded with the nearby Lagunas for corn, which was the main staple of life. The family of four used four barrels of fruit and vegetables over the winter. Bread and corn foods were staples—even the bread seems to have been of corn (probably tortillas). They made ta'naashgizh and táá'nil (types of corn mush) and k'ineeshbízhii (blue corn dumplings) and stored preroasted corn (presumably green-roasted, shelled, and dried—neeshjízhii).

Wild foods were important, too. The family ate jackrabbits and cottontails, prairie dogs, even porcupines, fresh or jerked. Plants included green amaranth (tł'oh deesk'idí), young beeweed (waa'), sumac berries (chiiłchin), yucca fruit (hashk'áán), wolfberry (haashch'ééhd33'), wild onions, and wild potatoes that they boiled with k'iish (sumac?). They gathered wild plums (didzé) and pounded them into a paste that they kneaded to make something like bread. Other wild plants that we cannot identify were noodǫǫzí (something striped) and haa'oogeed (something dug up): they would slice it, take out the pits, and lay the slices out to dry. They never went to hospitals and depended on traditional medicines from plants and animals.

This is what Diné food sovereignty was like back then. Elders' joyful recollections show that relishing the foods that the land provided encouraged youngsters to bond with the land.

SILVERSMITHING AT THE TRADING POST DURING THE 1930s AND 1940s

Local residents recalled that, soon after he started the trading post, Ben Harvey also hired silversmiths to make jewelry there. Silversmithing continued under the Bloomfields and the Smouses. Around 1930, Ben Harvey built a big workshop east of the trading post for the smiths.[2] Later he had three or four hogans built to house two to four smiths and their families, with another one or two hogans behind the store. Other smiths lived in their own homes a short distance away and walked to work at the post, where they worked in the biggest of the hogans, which also housed a smith and his family. Some of the wives wove on site while their husbands made jewelry. Later, during World War II, the silversmithing really got going. By that time, the smiths were no longer living east of the road but rather in clapboard huts behind the store. These and other smiths also worked at their homes. A few smiths were women.

Jewelry production at the trading post ended sometime after World War II. One resident said that silversmithing stopped when the smiths got old and younger ones did not know how to do the work. Possibly one reason that younger people did not learn the intricate and dangerous techniques of making jewelry was that other (though perhaps no less dangerous) work opened up around World War II, including railroad work, for which Smouse, like other traders, became a recruiting agent. We also suspect that changes in the regional organization of jewelry marketing after World War II had something to do with the end of the Borrego Pass Trading Post workshop. For decades after that, however, the Smouses still bought jewelry on consignment from smiths who worked at home. Kirk Brothers seems to have more or less gone out of business by around 1950, although one of the brothers, Mike, and his family continued to

FIGURE 38 Silversmith Alice Blackgoat in her workshop northwest of Gallup with tools typical of the 1930s and 1940s. Few women worked as silversmiths at that time. Credit: Photographed by Milton Snow, courtesy of Navajo Nation Museum, Window Rock, Arizona, neg. no. NC8-22.

run a wholesale jewelry business west of Gallup until about 1960 (Kelley and Francis 2018, Manuelito entry). The end of Kirk Brothers may have discouraged jewelry making at Borrego Pass.

Consultants whose fathers worked as silversmiths said that the smiths who worked for Ben Harvey included the brothers Juanito Platero and Herbert Platero (called "Crip" because he was crippled), Little Tom (?), Joe Bibo, John Barbone, and Tommy Yazzie. These men worked in the big hogan. Crip Platero and Little Tom started working before the others did. These smiths all lived nearby and walked to work every day. One silversmith, Tommy Begay, lived with his family in one of the hogans behind the store. Others who lived in the hogans east of the store were Joe Long (possibly a Platero in-law) and Little Tom, whose wives lived there with them and wove. Other, probably later, smiths were Barbone relative Dineh Tsoh, members of the Tolth family and their in-law Willie Jim, and Sam Platero. Daughters of John Barbone also made jewelry for Smouse at their home. John Barbone himself worked as a silversmith off and on from Ben Harvey's time all the way to the end of the silversmithing at the trading post site. The smiths made rings, bracelets, belts, and even bows and arrows, and they were paid by the piece in the form of store credit. The smith bought food and clothes on credit, and any wages left over were paid in tokens. The total value might have been $50 to $100 for a week's work (probably in the later 1940s).

The smiths and other families, even those with their own homesites near the trading post, did not keep livestock near the post because the trader controlled the surrounding range. For example, Crip Platero, who lived less than a mile from the store, had a place 10 miles or more east where his livestock ranged, and Tommy Begay kept his livestock farther west toward Smith Lake. The home of John Barbone was close enough to the store for him to walk to work but far enough that his wife and children herded sheep around the homesite and also had cornfields.

Smiths also did other kinds of work while their families herded and farmed. For example, John Barbone also at times in the 1940s worked for ranchers Harold Prewitt and Floyd Lee of San Mateo, fixing fences and herding livestock. Barbone's family had lost much of their land to Prewitt during Washindoon's land consolidation with the railroad. Barbone was also a government range rider (livestock permit enforcer) in the 1930s and 1940s. His family nevertheless lived mainly by herding, farming, gathering wild foods, and hunting. Thus silversmithing did not replace but rather supplemented the living that families drew from the land, as John Barbone's daughter attests at the beginning of this chapter.

Like the household technology of these cash-poor, mobile families, much silversmithing technology was improvised from common recycled items. The traders' minimal investment in tools enhanced the traders' profit margin while forcing the smiths to improvise their own dangerous equipment. Children of the smiths described their fathers' tools and techniques. John Adair (1944) tells more about this technology based on his work during the same period farther west at Pine Springs, Arizona. These tools and techniques are much like those of a generation or two earlier described by the Franciscan Fathers (1910:371ff.). John Barbone's daughters said that the smiths worked in sterling silver, copper, and brass. To smelt the metal, they built an open fire on the floor of the hogan, then put the hot coals in a five-gallon can (the forge). They used a bellows to blow the coals hotter. The bellows consisted of two round pieces of wood with leather in between, a handle on one side, and a metal tube with a hole in it on the opposite (blowing) end. It was pumped with a vertical motion. Details of the crucible are unclear. For solder they used baking soda mixed with metal scraps, which they mixed in a baking power can, heated, and applied with a tube. They poured the smelted metal into molds, let it cool, then shaped it on anvils made of sections of railroad track. Later they used propane torches to shape the metal.

Sam Platero provided more details. The trader supplied some tools, including hammers and pliers. There were small silver strips, which were cut and pounded to shape into bracelets. Smaller silver plates were used to draw wire. It was hard work. The smiths made their own solder then, too, out of copper and silver scraps. The smiths made their own stamps from hard metals. The anvil was a short length of railroad track, but Mr. Platero did not know how they got these pieces of track. The silver came in sheets and rounds. The forge was a metal container. The smith made a fire outside with piñon to get charcoal, which was brought inside and put in the container. The crucible was set on the coals, and the smith pumped up the heat with a bellows directed through a hole in the forge container. The bellows was pumped up and down (it was leather with wooden handles). The crucible was a can. The smiths put talc in the bottom to keep the melting silver from sticking. (The can was harder than the silver, so it would not melt when the silver did.) Then the smith put the silver in—this was scraps, clippings, which were melted down. When the scraps melted, the smith quickly poured the liquid into molds, which were commercially made blocks of steel with recesses for the shapes the smith wanted. When the silver cooled and hardened, the smith took it out and stamped designs on it. People didn't do sandcasting until later (but see Adair 1944). The smiths made the soldering tool (blowtorch) out of a can. It had a tube jutting upward from near the base of the can, which enclosed a wick. The smith put fuel in the can and lit the wick. A second tube extended across the top of the can to the tip of the tube, where the wick stuck out (the burning end). This second tube bent downward on the opposite side of the can from the wick. The solderer used this tube to direct the flame by blowing into the tube's lower end. It was very dangerous, but the smiths didn't realize that. Chanters say you burned your heart and lungs out. Your breath got burned.

Though their dependence on outside markets grew, people knew little about how the traders marketed the jewelry that the smiths made for the trading post. One thought that Gallup businesses supplied the traders with raw materials in exchange for the finished work. According to the Smouses' son Donald L. Smouse, there were two main contacts for silver supplies and marketing, both in Gallup: Woodwards, for independent smiths, and the Kirks (John and his son Dude), for larger-scale jewelry production operations like the one at Borrego Pass. Donald Smouse described the Kirks' business as wholesale grocery combined with bulk silversmithing supply and marketing.

THE SMOUSES AND VERNON BLOOMFIELD, 1974

By the 1970s, for local Diné as for those in general, making a significant part of one's living from land-based production, even for distant markets, had given way to the money income from wages and supplemental assistance, which drew people away from the land. In an interview on August 8, 1974, Vernon Bloomfield gave Kelley the following traders'-eye view of the store's inventory, both bought from the People and sold to them. Wool and livestock did not contribute much income to local families, as prices for these commodities were very low. Many trading posts were no longer handling them, but the Borrego Pass store still bought these products. (We add that Smouse probably took wool and livestock in exchange mainly for store credit, not cash. The Federal Trade Commission, spurred by Diné protests about trading posts, was investigating, however, so credit practices at the time were sensitive, and Kelley avoided asking about them.) Smouse in turn sold the wool to Roswell Wool and Mohair Company and hauled it to their Albuquerque warehouse, along with wool from trading posts farther west and northwest at Coyote Canyon and Tsaya. The previous spring, Smouse had handled 180,000 pounds. (This amount was much larger than most trading posts handled and may have included the Coyote Canyon and Tsaya wool.) Smouse hauled the cattle he had bought to Albuquerque to sell. Feedlot operators in Colorado, Kansas, and Nebraska sent trucks to haul the lambs away. Smouse did not use a broker to sell the lambs (a hint that the feeders had long-standing relationships with him). The previous fall, feeders had trucked away 1,200 head. Smouse did not buy crops, because local people grew them mainly for their own use.

Crafts were also still an important source of income for Borrego Pass families, jewelry being much more important than weaving. Local people made the jewelry at home and took it to trading posts all over the region, to Gallup and other border towns and even to Albuquerque, though the Borrego Pass post still had a little local jewelry taken on consignment. Smouse marketed these items directly to his personal network of buyers for "curio" stores in California, Colorado, and Sun Valley, Idaho. Smouse also got silver and turquoise from Gallup and supplied them to local smiths on consignment.

The store's customers were all local people, not tourists. The store carried a wider range of general merchandise than did most posts by that time: food, cloth and clothing, shoes, minor hardware and appliances, saddles and harness, major hardware and appliances (stoves, sewing machines), some auto parts, some lumber and building materials, and feed (hay and grain). Nevertheless, the store's clientele bought most of these things in Gallup. The store got its wholesale merchandise from Kimbell's in Gallup (most produce and groceries); Associated Grocers (AG) in Albuquerque (some groceries); Amarillo Hardware in Amarillo, Texas (hardware); and Isbel-Kent-Oakes (IKO) in Denver (dry goods). Don Smouse drove a truck to Gallup every Monday to haul food from Kimbell's and also hauled groceries from AG in Albuquerque. Amarillo and IKO sent merchandise to the trading post, but whether by their own delivery trucks, by UPS, or by parcel post was unclear.

Vernon Bloomfield estimated that local residents got 30–40 percent of their income from wages and 60–70 percent from public assistance, Social Security, and similar sources. Local people worked at local schools (Borrego Pass and Crownpoint) and on the railroad (Santa Fe, Union Pacific, Southern Pacific, and Denver and Rio Grande). The railroads used Smouse as a recruiting agent. (Agents also helped railroad workers apply for seasonal unemployment insurance, with both paychecks and unemployment checks mailed to the worker care of the trading post.) People applied at Crownpoint for school jobs.

MERLE AND ROSELLA MOORE, 1991–1998

By the 1990s products from the land not only provided little support for Diné families but also were even more enmeshed in national and international markets than before. In 2003 Rosella and Merle Moore described buying and selling during their time managing the store for the Smouses from 1991 to 1998. The Moores bought wool and mohair, lambs, and cattle, as well as crafts. They stopped buying these products at the end of their tenure, and that was the end of that. The Moores bought wool and mohair until 1997 and sold it to Roswell Wool and Mohair through a local agent, Dudley Byerley, at Cowtown in Gallup. In 1997 Roswell Wool and Mohair was taken over by other partners. Roswell Wool and Mohair used to ship wool to England, but the English buyers were substituting Australian wool, so the Navajo wool trade was no longer worthwhile to Roswell. Roswell bought most of the wool throughout Navajoland, so when they quit buying, the Navajoland wool market cratered. The Moores stopped buying wool and mohair when Roswell stopped sending trucks to the trading post for it. For a few years after that, local people took their wool to D. J. Elkins at Navajo Shopping Center (just north of Gallup) and Ellis Tanner in Gallup, but those stores stopped buying wool, too. Diné families then may have taken their wool directly to Dudley Byerley at Cowtown in Gallup.

In the 1990s the Moores had the cattle they bought trucked to sales yards at Los Lunas, Clovis, and Milan (near Grants) and also kept some for themselves. They sold the lambs through Roswell Wool and Mohair, which sent trucks to haul the lambs to feedlots. In 1997, when the new owners of Roswell Wool and Mohair quit sending trucks for wool, they also stopped sending trucks for lambs, so the Moores stopped buying. Also, the prices were terribly low, and the Moores could not pay producers much either. The federal price-supporting Wool Incentive Program stopped sending checks to producers in 1999, though around 2002 another price support program may have started.

In the late 1990s the Navajo Nation government tried to get people to sell livestock, especially horses, that were depleting the land because of the now 20-year drought. The Moores invited buyers from Albuquerque and Belen to the trading post, but local people did not want to sell. When the Navajo Nation had a horse vaccination program, the Moores had the rangers use the corrals at the trading post, and people brought in 500 horses, an indication of how many were out there, most of them not used for practical purposes but perhaps kept as wealth.

In the 1990s the Moores bought silver jewelry, rugs, and katsina figurines. Local residents were their best customers for the jewelry. Collectors bought more of the rugs and katsina figurines, especially people whom the Moores cultivated through various relationships, for example, an Indian Health Service doctor who collected katsina figurines and a contact at the University of New Mexico who brought eight long vans of visitors to buy rugs. Also, Merle Moore was active in western rodeo associations, and the Moores set up booths at rodeos in various western cities, where they sold arts and crafts and took special orders.

In the 1990s many local people still bought things on credit. But in the late 1990s, when Washindoon switched to direct (electronic) deposit of Social/Supplemental Security and other payments, "elderlies" were forced to open bank accounts. Many elderly Diné opened joint accounts with children or grandchildren, who would then get cash from the account or write checks and shop elsewhere. We note from personal experience that under the old system of mailed government checks, the check came directly to the elderly customer, often care of the trading post, and the customer would sign the check over to the trader to pay on their accounts. With direct deposit, the money goes into a bank account first before it can get to the trader, who therefore must demand cash or accept more risky personal checks as payment on accounts.

The Moores also quit taking pawn at Borrego Pass because complying with new government regulations was too hard. The Smouses used to hold pawn for customers "forever." They would not sell the pawn after it "went dead" (the redemption due date passed) because that would alienate customers. After the store quit taking pawn, local people were forced to pawn in Gallup, where they found transactions more impersonal. The pawnshops would not hold "dead pawn," and many people lost their valuables.

When the Moores took over the store, they inherited lots of different goods that the Smouses had held in storage for a long time. There were hundreds of coats and shoes in the warehouse, as well as lots of canned goods and frozen food (such as berries). Some of these items had been in storage too long and were discarded, but the Moores tried to sell as much as they could. After that, the store stopped offering such a varied inventory.

The Moores stocked the following items. This varied and heavily processed inventory (especially the meats!) shows how far Diné had moved from depending on the land since the 1930s. Foods and brands favored in the 1990s were Bluebird flour, Folgers and Hills Brothers coffee, and Bar S baloney (customers seemed to prefer products with red labels). Also Shur Fine and Shur Value products (Associated Grocers brands) sold all right. B&K and Libby's meats sold, but not Hormel. The Moores tried offering generic products because they were cheaper, but people preferred well-known brands. Fresh fruits and vegetables did not sell, because many customers lacked refrigeration, but canned produce did. The store also sold a lot of canned milk now that few people had milk goats. The inventory of dry goods inherited from the Smouses did not sell well, because even the wholesale prices were higher than those at Wal-Mart in Gallup. Therefore, the Moores quit offering dry goods at Borrego Pass. Minor hardware items—axes, nails, dishpans, and coffee pots—would sell.

Of the wholesalers, Kimbell's had stopped delivering around 1980. At Borrego Pass in the 1990s, it was possible to get goods delivered by Associated Grocers of Albuquerque. AG would deliver to Smith Lake a few miles west, with extra goods for Pinedale (same owner as Smith Lake) and Borrego Pass. The other traders picked up the goods at Smith Lake. (Pinedale and Borrego Pass were off the pavement at the time, while Smith Lake was along a paved road.) Hardware was from Amarillo Hardware but came through AG of Albuquerque. Bob Bolton, a former salesman for Henry Hillson Clothing (which went bankrupt in the 1980s and was bought by the Navajo Nation to supply its school clothing program), had a franchise for Pendleton blankets and supplied them. Some dry goods came from Rio Grande Sales in El Paso.

In general, both the Smouses and the Moores used the same kinds of goods that they stocked for their customers, although they had some different things for personal preference. Also, if an item didn't sell, the trader family would use it up. An example was the black-eyed peas that the Moores tried stocking— nobody bought them, so the Moores ate them themselves.

THE DECLINE IN A NUTSHELL

This chapter tells, from both Diné and trader viewpoints, about the relations between a Diné community and a mid- to late 1900s Navajoland trading post, relations that reflect (and contributed to) growing Diné detachment from the land: the exchange of goods, the larger marketing networks for Diné products, what the People bought from the store, the sources of supply for those goods, what goods the People made for themselves, what they did not want or need, and silver jewelry production based at the trading post.

In the 1930s and 1940s the People spent their daily lives producing the things they traded at the store for the small selection of goods they did not make for themselves, could afford, and could use as they moved around with their livestock. But after years of stock reduction and land consolidation, the People came to depend less on trading wool, weaving, and livestock at the trading post for supplies and more on wage jobs like railroad maintenance work, migrant agricultural work, and a little government work in Navajoland itself. After World War II, for the first time, most Diné children went to school as more and more of their parents came to depend more and more on different kinds of wage work. The U.S. and Navajo tribal governments paved roads and started developing public utilities to attract businesses and jobs to Navajoland. Schooling and jobs got in the way of adults traveling around the land with youngsters to teach them the stories.

Younger Diné instead took their knowledge of English and math, along with their paychecks, over the newly improved roads in the pickups and cars that they could now afford to shop in border towns around the edges of Navajoland, where goods were cheaper, more varied, and more entertaining. These towns had grown up in the late 1800s and early 1900s, most along the Santa Fe Railroad, partly because they were good places from which wholesalers could supply goods to Navajoland trading posts and also market the wool, weaving, and livestock they got back from the posts. In the 1950s and 1960s Borrego Pass, like most other trading posts, lost most of their business to border-town stores. Some families that had livestock and needed credit, however, still traded regularly at the post, where they wanted a greater variety of goods than in the old days. Now the traders were getting merchandise from a variety of specialized wholesalers and were marketing the wool, lambs, crafts, and other items through specialized dealers. Changes in the U.S. and international markets eventually forced most Navajoland posts to quit dealing in wool, livestock, and handicrafts and to become convenience stores.

Around 1970 Diné college students and the Federal Trade Commission reported abusive credit, pawn, and pricing practices widely in Navajoland (Federal Trade Commission 1973; Southwest Indian Development 1969). The Smouses were probably among the "honest and conscientious businessmen who contribute to the welfare of their communities," but even many such "good" traders engaged in "questionable" practices (Federal Trade Commission 1973:16; Southwest Indian Development 1969:9). One such practice was credit saturation, which virtually all traders practiced at a time when they were losing customers to border towns.

Subsisting on a meager and unpredictable income, the Navajo easily becomes indebted to the trader, who, through a policy known as "credit saturation," encourages his customers to buy goods on book credit up to the amount of known future income. However, once this limit is reached, the trader promptly refuses any further credit, regardless of need.

As it is common for many Navajos to receive their checks or other income in care of the local trading post, the trader has an accurate method of estimating an individual's income. By withholding the check upon arrival, he can force his clientele to charge at the store, thereby assuring himself of a large portion, if not all, of the check. (Southwest Indian Development 1969:5)

Thus traders, who had earlier monopolized marketing of Diné products from the land so as to offer goods to Diné on credit, now tried to control paychecks for the same purpose. The students declared their intent to advance political and cultural sovereignty:

The stranglehold of the trader on our communities must be diminished, and federal and tribal regulations to control the trading post system on the reservation must be systematically enforced. . . .

Anglos, billing themselves as Indian experts, for the past century got together and decided Indian Policy. Today, the young Indian is saying that this can no longer be, that Indians must decide Indian policy and exercise the right of self-determination and the responsibilities it entails. This action-research on traders and trading posts is written by Navajos for the Navajo people. It is hoped that this report will be seen as an effort of responsible self-determination on the part of Indian youth. (Southwest Indian Development 1969:iii)

The regulations mentioned in this passage were those that most traders felt they could not comply with and stay in business. Within little more than a decade, most traders had sold out to a chain of convenience stores. The new regulations by the Navajo Nation Council asserted Diné political sovereignty but could not keep the trading post system from failing. The ironic result has been that the People's wealth continues to enrich non-Diné outside Navajo government authority. Perhaps the harshness and impersonality of border-town shopping and predatory loan companies is one reason why so many Diné elders whom we have consulted about trading post histories enjoy recalling them. And of course, back then, in the heyday of trading posts, the elders were children, the world was new, and the People could and did still readily travel over the land with their children and grandchildren, teaching them the oral traditions and instilling bonds with the land.

10

DINÉ WORKERS IN UNDERGROUND
COAL MINES AROUND GALLUP

C OAL (ŁEEJIN, "dark earth") has a place in Diné ceremonialism. Chanters gather it from surface deposits and mix it with water to paint the
prayer sticks that they use as offerings to the deities. Some elders say
that the coal under Black Mesa is the liver of the female earth figure, whose
torso is the mesa. Others say that coal is the blood of Mother Earth. Many Diné
traditionalists today consider coal mining a desecration.

Yet from the early 1900s to the present, many Diné men and, more recently,
women have worked in coal mines both aboveground and below. Colonizer histories deny Diné presence in early coal mines outside the Navajo Reservation,
but again, Diné personal, family, and community histories tell otherwise. Some
Diné mine workers or their children have been chanters. Mindful of cultural
sovereignty, many miners have tried to reconcile tradition with working as miners for the wages that modern Navajo life requires. They have had ceremonies
done to protect themselves with offerings to atone for the desecration that they
take part in. Many other families have been forced to make way for coal mines
that appeared amid the lands where they and their forebears have lived, herded,
and farmed. This study, based mostly on interviews in 2015, concerns Diné
involvement with the underground coal mines around Gallup, New Mexico,
during their heyday of 1881 to the early 1960s. Most miners were also land users
whose families were there long before the first mines came in. Though, partly as

a result, they lost much land and all of their ability to support themselves from it, as well as opportunities to bond youngsters to the land through travels with stories, they have kept some kind of bond with the land to this day. Therefore, first we sketch the relations of the People and the mines through land use.[1]

COAL MINING AROUND GALLUP AND DINÉ LAND USE

The early Gallup mines were driven into the scrub-covered rocky cliffs that overlook the town of Gallup and the upper Puerco River valley. Two townships encompass most of the mines, the Gallup township and the Defiance township to the west. Most of the Gallup mines are in these two townships, while the rest, just north of the Gallup township, are the largest: Gibson, Heaton, Navajo, and Gamerco. The mines first supplied the railroad, then the Morenci copper smelter in southern Arizona.

From before coal mining to the present, Diné extended families have lived, herded, and farmed throughout the Gallup and Defiance townships and adjoining lands, including the area inside the intensive mining zone closest to Gallup.

FIGURE 39 Diné at the railroad with store-bought goods, Gallup, 1894, heading north. These people probably lived among the mining zones in the Gallup and Defiance townships. Credit: National Anthropological Archives, Smithsonian Institution, photo lot 89, neg. no. 2443-f.

The area is within the 1866 railroad grant discussed in chapters 6 and 7 and has a similar history (Gilpin et al. 2015; Redhouse 1984). The families lost the use of much acreage in these townships, as Washindoon and the railroad claimed the historically Diné lands and made them available to others. The expanding town of Gallup, which owed its existence to the coal mines, took land along the Rio Puerco, while the scattered sites of the mines and the townsites associated with many of them took more land in the surrounding hills. At one time or another, more than 100 mines operated around Gallup (Nickelson 1988).

Washindoon finally gave Diné families title to some of the lands they were already using in the form of allotments but tried not to give them such title in the coal-mining areas that had developed among them. (A few later mining claims were on allotments, since the allottees held only surface rights.) These allotments resulted from the same efforts of Franciscan father Anselm Weber as described in chapter 7, only here the families kept their lands. Around 1913–15 at least 23 Diné extended families, numbering about 230 people, plus 4,500 head of livestock were living in the Gallup and Defiance townships (Franciscans, box 28; Paquette 1915). They shared the land with the 2,200 people living in Gallup itself and nearly 800 miners and their families, most of whom probably lived outside Gallup in the mining camps (Gilpin et al. 2015:33). In the mid-twentieth century, at the end of the underground coal-mining period, land speculators took over much of the coal mine lands and eventually fenced them off, shutting out families who had been using them since before the mines first appeared.

When the coal mines closed, the shafts of many remained open for years, some even to this day. One consultant said that his father, a hataałii, taught him that coal mining was a desecration. Yet we did not hear stories of conflicts between Diné and the miners themselves. Many Navajo men worked in the mines. Some presumably died in mining accidents (though consultants identified only one), and many suffered and died of black lung afterward.

DINÉ MINE WORKERS

Since the late 1900s, just about all the miners in the enormous surface mines of Navajoland away from Gallup have been Diné men and women. Diné men also worked much earlier in small surface and underground mines, scattered around Navajoland away from Gallup. Washindoon opened many of these earlier mines to supply boarding schools and other government facilities, and most of the miners were Diné men. By the 1920s other Diné men worked their own small coal mines to supply their families and those of their neighbors, as well as people in border towns. In the 1940s the U.S. government contracted with Diné to operate many of the government mines. Several cultural resource management studies have documented these small surface and underground mines in Navajoland in connection with Navajo Nation Abandoned Mine Lands (AML) work (Gilpin 1985a, 1985b, 1985c, 1987; Kelley 1986a, 1987a, 1987b, 1988a; Kelley and Francis 1987; Kelley and James 1985, 1986; Maldonado 1981; Martin 1984, 1986; see also O'Neill 2005).

However, the documentation on underground coal mining outside Gallup has almost nothing to say about Diné working in the Gallup mines. We talked with many Diné living around Gallup, especially on and near the allotted lands, whose forebears had worked in various Gallup mines and who had seen mines in operation themselves. Their stories tell not only about mining in their parents' and grandparents' time but also (charmingly!) about what impressed them as children. The mines are discussed according to their direction from central Gallup.

SOUTH: CATALPA CANYON, SCHAUER, SOUTHWESTERN, AND BLACK STAR–MUTUAL MINES

CATALPA CANYON MINE

This mine operated from 1887 to 1902 (Nickelson 1988:27). Sometime between 1902 and 1905, Hataałii Tsoh (Big Chanter), an in-law of nearby allottee Siláo Yázhí (Little Scout), may have "worked around" the Catalpa Canyon Mine after it had shut down but was still being maintained and then salvaged (York 1981:189). This is the earliest date we have found for a Diné working at a coal mine near Gallup.

SCHAUER AND SOUTHWESTERN MINES

These two mines are just south of the original Gallup townsite (since expanded). Southwestern, a rather large mine, was open (at first under another name) between 1889 and 1963. The smaller Schauer Mine was open by 1919 and closed around 1963 (Nickelson 1988:21–28). By 1908 Diné men were doing "outside work" at Southwestern Mine, where the "Navajo boss" was paid $2.20 a day, and the other Diné outside laborers were paid $1.50 to $1.75 (OFP, VFMin,

"Schedule of Wages, Gallup Mines"; Stacher 1978:78). These were almost the lowest wages paid. Only slate pickers at the tipple and trappers underground got less than $1.50 a day, when most jobs paid more than $1.75. Herbert Stacher (son of the Crownpoint Agency superintendent who went to the Chambers Checkerboard in the 1930s, as described in chapter 7), who managed the mine beginning in 1922 and later owned it until 1947, incorrectly said that "Indians were superstitious and afraid to go into the darkness underground" and that only in the 1940s did a few Diné and Zunis work underground because there was no work for them above (OFP, VFMin).[2] A 1933 photo shows Diné workers among a tipple crew at this mine (Stacher 1978:112; see also Nickelson 1988:25).

One elder told us that her family used to herd around these mines, which were already running when she first became aware of them around age 11 (about 1938). Mules were kept in corrals aboveground to haul the ore cars in and out of the mine. Hispanics and Diné worked there, including men of her family—her mother's brother John Smith and his children, as well as her older brother. They worked underground and came home covered with coal dust. The mine site had an office where people were paid and a store where people had credit. There were also houses for miners, but only Hispanics lived in them.

Like all the other Diné miners, her uncle and her brother rode horseback to work, and lots of horses were always tied up outside the mine. Her family had a wagon, which her grandmother, mother, and maternal aunt used for their work while the men were in the mine. The women did many chores that men would ordinarily do in livestock care and farming. Even with the miners' wages, the women still wove to get goods from the trading post in between paychecks. They planted corn and squash, made food, and cared for children. One big chore was washing the miners' clothes, for which the women found that a washboard and tálá́wosh (yucca root) worked better than store-bought laundry soap. The family hauled water from wherever they could get it and did the laundry at the homesite.

Other workers were Hispanics and Doo Yáłti'í (nonspeakers [of local languages], "Foreigners" hereafter—Italians, Greeks, Austrians, French, and Slavs). The workers all got along together. The company store had merchandise that was different from what was in the local trading posts that served the People. Gallup did not have many buildings then, only a row of them in the middle of town. Near the lumber yards along the railroad was one big trading post where all the Diné around Gallup used to trade (Gross-Kelly, earlier C. N. Cotton).

BLACK STAR–MUTUAL MINE

The Black Star–Mutual Mine operated between 1928 and 1960, according to Howard Nickelson (1988:35–38), though a former mine worker said it continued into the 1960s and may have been the last to close. It is south of the Gallup Airport on the allotment of Tom Etcitty, whose descendants still live near the mine. A railroad spur ran along the hilltop west of the homesite, one mine shaft was west of the family's corral, and a windmill still stands nearby.

A grandson of Tom Etcitty told us that the mine was already in operation from his earliest memories (around 1950). His father, John Yazzie, a chanter from Defiance, worked there as a miner, as did other local Diné men, including Hoskie Pete and Jim Pete, along with the foreign miners. The mine owners were also Foreigners. The mine used no mules; instead, there was a hoist for the underground ore trains that was powered by electricity from the city of Gallup. The mine had blowers to suck out the methane and three buildings: two miners' houses and an office. The Foreigners rented the houses, whereas the Diné miners walked in from homes nearby. Railroad cars came up the spur from the main line and under the tipple with scales. Model T trucks also hauled coal to town for sale. The mine may have closed when local Diné forced the mine owners out (details were not forthcoming). The mine owners left all the facilities, equipment, ore cars, and so forth. Then Rico, a local automobile dealer, reopened the mine and ran it after about 1960 for two to four years using a dozer. The coal was broken into small chunks, hauled to the main rail line nearby, put in 50-pound sacks, and loaded in a boxcar to San Diego. The sacker at the time was Keith Yazzie, a member of the Etcitty family.

WEST: LEYBA, CHICHARELLO, DEFIANCE, AND CARBON CITY MINES

LEYBA MINE

This mine is on the footslopes of Twin Buttes, west of Gallup. According to inspectors' reports (Nickelson 1988:38), it was open between 1916 and 1920. However, a nearby allottee heard from her maternal grandmother that a mine on Twin Buttes, presumably the Leyba Mine, was still open perhaps as recently as 1940 and that an uncle, Jumbo Spencer, descendant of allottees near Defiance, worked in the mine. The discrepancy in dates suggests that the later mining was by Diné for truck sales and was off the inspectors' radar screen.

CHICHARELLO (TREE WELL) MINE

This mine is on an allotment west of Twin Buttes. Its first operators may have been the World War I period owners of the nearby Leyba Mine. In a 1987 interview (Kelley 1987:24–25), a granddaughter of the allottee said that in the early 1920s, the recently married Jim and Maria Chicharello moved there. Maria was a daughter of the allottee, and Jim Chicharello, of Italian ancestry, worked the mine. The Chicharellos first lived in a hogan at the site and later in a four-room rock house with their growing number of children. Sons eventually may have worked in the mine, along with others who lived at the site. The miners seem to have dug the coal from the sides of the canyon in untimbered dog holes, tunneling far enough into the coal beds to need ore cars on tracks to bring the ore out. Trucks hauled the coal from in front of each portal and were weighed on a scale next to the Chicharellos' house. Domestic water came from the Tree Well at the site, which Jim Chicharello dug. By the middle 1930s, the Chicharellos had abandoned the site and moved to another of Maria's family's allotments. A son, Dominic, worked at one of the Defiance mines in the 1940s (see below). During the 1950s, a daughter of the Chicharellos moved back to the homesite, but the mine remained unused.

DEFIANCE AND CARBON CITY MINES

The Defiance No. 1 (Mentmore) Mine was in operation from 1912 to 1952, and the other Defiance Mines were in operation from before 1948 to 1961. The Carbon City Mine was one of this group, all owned by the Defiance Coal Company (Nickelson 1988:77). Interviews in 1983 with two former miners and the son of an aboveground worker at these mines provide most of the information below (Kelley 1983:582–586).

David Tom, consulted in 1983, was born in 1933. His father, Fred Tom, was born around 1890 and raised around Rock Springs to the north. At age 16, Fred went to California to work, returned when he was about 20, and got a job at the Carbon City Mine, where he worked for the rest of his working life, his tenure coinciding with the life of the mine. At first he drove the mule train that hauled coal to the tipple at the main Santa Fe Railroad line near the mines. Later, when a railroad spur was extended to the Defiance Mine farther north, he drove a dump truck to carry waste rock from the mine mouth to a dump. At first Fred Tom rode a horse from Rock Springs to the mine every day, a 20-mile round trip. Then he married a daughter of Bilíí' Daałbahí Biye' (Son of Roanhorse), who had an allotment about three miles northwest of the mine and whose extended family had allotments around Defiance. Fred Tom and his household lived on his father-in-law's allotment until 1930, when they moved to the homesite near the Carbon City mine that descendants still occupied in 1983. They built a hogan there, planted a cornfield, and got water from a nearby well.

In 1933 coal miners all around Gallup went on strike (Rubenstein 1983). Fred Tom photographed National Guardsmen at the Defiance Mine. When the miners eventually won union recognition, Fred Tom joined the United Mine Workers of America (UMWA). His family proudly showed his union cards, which said that he paid dues of $1.00 a month in 1954 and $2.75 a month three years later. According to historian Colleen O'Neill (2005:113–114), during the 1933 strike, the Kaseman (Defiance No. 1) Mine hired many Diné, raising their number to 28 mine workers, 30 percent of the total workforce; the UMWA did not get collective bargaining agreements with Gallup coal producers until 1943.

Fred Tom's children went to school at a local mission with children of the other mine workers. At least one of Fred Tom's sons worked at the Carbon City Mine after finishing school. David Tom recalled from his childhood that the mine workers were Diné, Hispanics, and Bilagaanas, altogether perhaps 200–300 workers, and that Diné worked both aboveground and below. The company paid the workers partly in cash and partly in scrip redeemable at the company store. It also rented houses to employees, including miners, but, like Fred Tom, 10–15 other families—Diné, Hispanic, and Bilagaana—built their own houses on company land around the Carbon City Mine, for which the company did not charge them. Their children all went to school together at the mission. Other Diné commuted to work every day, including Jerry and Charley Spencer from Twin Buttes (probably relatives of Fred Tom's wife) and Dennison Kee from Defiance. When the mine closed, Fred Tom retired on Social Security and his UMWA pension. When the facilities were dismantled, the Tom family salvaged ties from the mine railroad to build a shed on the family allotment. Fred Tom died in 1969.

Dennison Kee and his younger relative Andrew Lee also worked for the Carbon City and Defiance Mines. Both lived a few miles west of the mines and had commuted to work there. Dennison Kee worked on the Defiance Mine probably in the late 1920s or early 1930s. The mine had a spur from the main Santa Fe Railroad line for a small coal-hauling train. Kee moved ore cars around the railroad yard as a helper to a Bilagaana. He started out earning a dollar a day, and his pay slowly rose.

Albert Lee was an underground miner first at Carbon City and then at Defiance Mine until he was laid off around 1946 or 1948. After 1948 he worked at another mine near Gallup (not named). He still had his earnings cards, which identified him as a "laborer" and showed total earnings for the month and deductions, including for blasting powder. The totals ranged from $51.69 in February to $201.00 in December, since work was not steady and was slowest in summer. Albert Lee was paid 50 cents per carload—each man had his own small ore car with its own number. Mules pulled the cars up steep grades in the tunnel, and a hoist pulled the cars out of the mine shaft. At the mine mouth, three men removed rocks from each car (often overzealously, the miners complained). Then the car was weighed. The miners were paid every 15 days, part in cash and part in scrip for the company store. Powder and blasting caps were deducted. Albert Lee belonged to the UMWA and paid fixed dues of six dollars every pay period. (The difference between his dues and those of Fred Tom presumably reflect their different jobs.) He considered the union of some benefit, since the workers would not have gotten raises without it. The union covered medical expenses for non–First Nations workers, but Diné probably went to the Indian Health Service. The coal company did not pay injured workers for medical leave. Neither Albert Lee nor Dennison Kee knew of cases of black lung.

Albert Lee recalled other local men who worked at the mines and commuted to work from homes on their traditional family lands. They included Charley Spencer, Homer Spencer (members of an allottee family near Defiance), and Dominic Chicharello, who weighed the ore cars and whose family had earlier operated the Chicharello Mine west of Twin Buttes. Other Diné mine workers lived near the mine, including Fred Tom at Carbon City and John Ross near the Defiance Mines. These men lived with their families in their own dwellings and used the miners' shower house. Other workers were Bilagaanas and Hispanics but no Slavs (who were prominent in other mines nearer Gallup). Each mine had two shifts with 30 men each underground for a total of 120 miners plus aboveground workers.

People consulted in 2015 recalled that most of the many Diné men who worked at these mines came from families around Gallup and Tsayatoh west of Defiance. One man, who grew up to work at the McKinley Mine, a large strip mine toward Window Rock, remembered the mines as a child in the 1950s. His maternal grandfather, Billy Notah, was from north of Tsayatoh and worked underground in one of the mines around 1950 along with Bilagaanas, blacks, and Hispanics. His family lived in company housing with Bilagaanas. Later, the family moved to their allotments north of Tsayatoh, and Billy Notah used to leave early in the morning to ride horseback to the mine, a trip of about 20 miles. Our consultant remembered the mules that used to bring the ore cars out of the pit. His grandfather said that the tunnels extended all the way to Gallup. The miners came out of the mine all black with coal dust, and the grandfather washed everything by hand in a washtub.

The coal company had a store, which is now a church and earlier served as the Mentmore post office. It sold groceries, hay, corn, clothing, cloth, rope, miners' lamps, and basically the same kind of merchandise as local trading posts with Navajo clienteles did. There was no fancy merchandise—miners' lamps might have been the one item not found in trading posts. When the mine closed, the store continued but quit carrying the miners' merchandise.

The school was in a big building that later became a church. Two children of Billy Notah went to school there, but our consultant himself went to school at Fort Defiance. In the 1950s another consultant, whose family had allotments near Twin Buttes, attended the school, which is now part of the Mentmore Mission. It was a one-room building a ways from what was then the store. The kids used to play around the mine works. A dairy farm farther east gave out single gallons of milk and was called Abe' Si'ání (Milk Place). This may have been the successor to Mulholland's Dairy of 1913, where Gallup businessman Gus Mulholland had an early mine claim (Franciscans, box 29, allotting agent's plat).

Unlike the 1983 interviewees, two people consulted in 2015 who recalled the school also recalled family members who died of black lung. One of the deceased was Billy Notah.

NORTH: ALLISON, GIBSON, NAVAJO, WEAVER, HEATON, "SKY CITY," BIAVA, AND GAMERCO MINES

ALLISON MINE

The Allison Mine is several miles east of Mentmore and was in operation between 1893 and 1939 (Nickelson 1988:73). We spoke with one man who grew up in Allison after the mine there closed, his father having worked for the mine as a blacksmith. He learned that when the mine was running, the Slavs formed an "enclave" in the housing that the company provided. This was also where his own, Anglo, family lived. Hispanic and Diné mine workers lived outside the company housing compound. The Hispanics lived south along the Rio Puerco in an area prone to flooding, while nearby, some of the many Diné mine workers bunked together in a boxcar. One of them seems to have been Tsihi Notah, a cousin of Billy Notah. These men rode their horses to work, stayed the week, and on weekends rode to their homes north of Tsayatoh.

GIBSON, NAVAJO, WEAVER, AND HEATON MINES

These large mines north of Gallup and west of the Gallup Hogback were open during the period 1881–1924 (Nickelson 1988:52–62). Gibson was the earliest and closed in 1904. Non-Navajo mine workers continued to live in and around the Gibson townsite while they worked at the other mines, and some workers at the Gamerco Mine (see below) lived there until the early 1940s, according to one local resident. Weaver was in operation from 1899 to 1924, Navajo from 1906 to 1924, and Heaton from 1904 to 1922 (Nickelson 1988:59). Facilities at Navajo and Gibson continued in use during the life of the Gamerco Mine. One elder recalled an expulsion of foreign miners from this area, who left in ox-drawn wagons. This memory may signify a strike in 1922 or perhaps the closing of the Weaver, Heaton, and Navajo Mines when chronic underground fires could not be controlled.

The 1915 Navajo census recorded one household living at the Gibson Mine, a middle-aged couple with four children, two of whom were young women (Paquette 1915, household 155). They had no livestock and were the only Diné family enumerated around the Gibson Mine. Therefore, we suspect that they worked in the Gibson town, the women perhaps as domestic workers for the bosses and the man perhaps also as a domestic worker if not a laborer connected with the nearby Navajo Mine. Our consultants, however, did not recall Diné doing domestic work at the mine settlements.

One Diné elder in 2015 said that her maternal grandmother, born around 1900 to a family living near the Heaton Mine, married a Greek man. The husband worked at the Heaton Mine, another mine in the same area (possibly Weaver), or both. He died of lung cancer in 1957. Another Diné elder recalled two mines near the Gallup Flea Market (probably Gibson and Navajo) where mules were used. These mines all closed when repeated efforts to put out a fire in their interconnected tunnels failed.

"SKY CITY" (CHIARAMONTE?) AND BIAVA MINES

The Chiaramonte Mine was a small family mine that operated from 1932 to 1961 in the Sky City neighborhood of Gallup's north side. The Biava Mine, another small family mine, was about a mile east and operated from 1933 to

1958 (Nickelson 1988:44, 47–48). One elder consulted in 2015 seems to have sometimes gone with his father to coal mines in the Sky City area, most likely Biava and Chiaramonte, as well as possibly to Mentmore, probably in the late 1940s and 1950s. His father, Navajo Jim, was from an allotment southeast of Gallup, where the small Navajo Jim Mine was named after him. These mines used hoists to bring the coal, miners, and mules up and down. The mules were kept underground. The coal was piled at the mine mouth, and truckers, including Navajo Jim, hauled it to Gallup businesses and homes. Earlier, mule-drawn wagons probably did the hauling. The mines were not served by railroad spurs.

GAMERCO MINE

This large mine, owned and operated by the Gallup American Coal Company, opened in 1921 and closed in 1951. It is within a mile west of the Gibson and Navajo Mines, was connected with their underground workings, and used some of their aboveground facilities. The company town of Gamerco was large and modern, with many amenities not found at other coal towns (Nickelson 1988:62–68). The townsite is now a sort of suburb of Gallup. Many of the original company buildings and mine facilities are still standing.

FIGURE 40 Men and mules at work in a Gallup mine, early 1900s. Elders today vividly recall the mules. Credit: Denver Public Library, Western History Collection, call no. 4076.

From the very beginning, Diné worked at the mine, when they made up 1–5 percent of the workers. They occupied their own hogans, while the large number of Hispanic miners had their own enclave outside the main "camp," and the "usual nationalities common to the average coal camp" occupied the housing provided by the company in the main part of the settlement (Allen 1966:102, citing Cooley 1923:28). About 400 people worked at the mine in 1923 (Nickelson 1988:68), so Diné workers there would have numbered between 4 and 20.

One Diné elder, who was born in 1919 and whose family ranged around Gallup and several miles north, recalled Gamerco as having many Hispanic residents and a big company store. The place was already known among local Diné for the smoke that came out of the ground there. The smoke may have been from the chronic fires in the nearby Navajo, Heaton, and Weaver Mines, whose main adits were closed to smother the flames and replaced by access from the new Gamerco Mine (to this day, Gamerco's tunnels extend several miles eastward). Diné started working at the Gamerco Mine fighting the fire, and soon many others were working there. The men and their families lived in tents around Gamerco amid enclaves of Hispanics and of Foreigners in the mine houses.

A wife and husband told us that both had relatives working at the Gamerco Mine by the 1940s and perhaps earlier. The husband's maternal uncle Mike Tso, maternal grandfather, and father all were coal miners. The father got up at three or four in the morning and rode horseback from Rock Springs several miles northwest to work. The wife's father, Harrison Yazzie, had an allotment about three miles northeast of Gamerco and also worked underground at the Gamerco Mine. Her father's elderly father, Hataałii Yázhí (Small Chanter), cared for the horses and mules used in the mine. Most of the workers were Hispanic, but other Diné men also worked there. Some of the Diné miners came from as far as Black Hat, about 10 miles northwest. Many Diné rode horses to work, even those from afar.

Mules pulled the ore cars and occupied a big corral. Sometimes they were kept underground for up to two weeks, then were brought up and others taken down. Many mules died underground. Most of the caretakers of the mules were Foreigners, both aboveground and below. There were mule corrals or stalls in both places. Both husband and wife as children saw the mules emerging from the mine portal pulling ore cars, but later the hoist seems to have brought the cars out and also took the mules up and down. (According to Diné activist-journalist Mervyn Tilden [2011], some say that the mules knew when it was quitting time on Friday, refused to pull the carts, and brayed.) After the mine closed, Diné quickly snapped up the mules because they were tame, strong, and hardworking.

The elders recalled that the miners had no protective gear, and the fumes got all over their bodies. There were also fumes where the coal was sold. The miners had to go to air shafts to breathe fresh air. Coal is like uranium (its particles get into one's lungs), and people got sick from the mines. The miners got paid $15 to $20 (time unit not specified) in brass tokens, which they took to the company store and other local trading posts such as China Springs, about a mile northeast of Gamerco. The husband went to school at Gamerco (probably in the late 1940s). He remembered buildings being moved to Gamerco from farther east (probably from Gibson and Navajo). All over Gamerco itself were buildings, including small houses 16 feet square for the Foreigners. Hispanic people did not live at Gamerco until later. He remembered a big store building (where the Tropics bar is now) owned by a Foreigner and selling all kinds of meats except mutton and goat.

GALLUP DINÉ COAL MINE WORKERS: AN OVERVIEW

Diné were working at underground mines around Gallup as early as 1905, at least in maintenance and salvaging at the Catalpa Canyon Mine. Many of these men were from local families who had lost grazing land to Gallup and the mines. As the families continued their traditional way of life in their reduced lands around the mines, these men worked to eke out the family livelihood. By 1908 the Southwestern Mine had several Diné men working aboveground under a "Navajo boss." Another Diné man started working aboveground at the Carbon City Mine around 1912, when it first opened. One or more members of a Diné family may have worked in some way at the Gibson Mine community in 1915, and as many as 20 Diné worked at the Gamerco Mine in 1923. Some of these men may have worked underground, but sources do not say so. By around 1930, however, Diné men were working underground, notwithstanding mine owner Herbert Stacher's opinion that "superstition" kept Diné from working there, though miners were mindful of cultural prohibitions against damaging Mother Earth. The upsurge in the 1930s surely was driven by stock reduction. Other men worked aboveground in mine maintenance and salvage, on tipple crews, driving and tending mules, moving ore cars, and driving trucks to deliver coal to local patrons.

The Gallup coal strike of 1933 brought more Diné into the mines, according to O'Neill (2005:111–117), because Diné were willing to cross the picket lines. Owing to the prevailing racism, Diné mine workers accepted low wages throughout their history in the Gallup mines. Many mine owners had separate pay scales for various ethnic groups, "Indians" being the lowest paid. According to O'Neill, the "Indian" jobs tended to be aboveground, including maintenance of company buildings. However, on O'Neill's evidence, it is hard to tell what jobs Diné were doing—on the company payrolls, they are lumped together (as they were at Southwestern in 1908, mentioned above), whereas other workers are divided by type of work. This type of recording lasted through World War II, at least at Gamerco. O'Neill guesses that Diné strike breaking in 1933 caused resentment among other miners, which in turn may have discouraged Diné from working in the mines later. After 1943 the UMWA won collective bargaining agreements with the biggest Gallup mines. Yet at that time, experienced Diné underground miners like Tsosie Blackgoat (who had worked in BIA mines in Navajoland and later ran one of his own near Window Rock) took only temporary jobs in Gallup mines, those not covered by union agreements (O'Neill 2005:115).

Recollections of local Diné consultants suggest that all mines around Gallup were using mules until about 1950, when most of the mines had closed. As children, our consultants seem to have been sensitive to the mules, perhaps because of helping to care for their own family livestock.

Wages in 1908 for aboveground Diné laborers were $1.50 to $1.75 a day, with $2.20 for the Navajo boss. Around 1930, starting pay at the Defiance Coal Company was even lower: a dollar a day for an aboveground "helper." By the 1940s wages may have risen to $15 to $20 a week or more. One man affirmed for us that Diné were paid less than others for the same work, whereas even Hispanics like himself got equal pay. The mine workers were paid partly in cash and partly in scrip or tokens redeemable at the company store. Gamerco tokens, at least, were negotiable at other local trading posts that served Diné. We suspect that smaller mines that did not have a company town or store may have paid partly in scrip redeemable at various Gallup general-merchandise stores, nearby Navajoland trading posts, or both.

Most of the wage increase between the 1920s and the 1940s probably resulted from the union recognition that followed the big 1933 Gallup coal strike and ensuing struggles. O'Neill (2005:113) thinks that the increase probably came about from the changing politics of World War II rather than the union strug-gles. In New Mexico, all workers in a group the majority of whom voted for union recognition were (and as of 2018 still are) required to join the union, so by 1943 Diné miners belonged to the UMWA. Dues for an aboveground worker were $1.00 a month in 1954 and $2.75 in 1957. For a miner they were apparently $6.00 or more.

Since most Diné mine workers lived within 10 miles of the mines, they com-muted by horseback. Those from 10 miles away or more either bunked near the mine (as in the boxcar near Allison) or built hogans for themselves and their wives and children on company land near the mine. This pattern seems to have been part of a larger housing segregation in which Anglo and foreign (Slavic, Italian, French, Austrian, and Greek) mine workers got most of the company housing, Hispanics built their own in a separate enclave nearby, and Diné had their own family homes and tent camps. Diné women took on the herding and farming chores that Diné men normally did, as well as heavy-duty washing of the men's clothes (some of the men also washed their own). By the 1940s many children of mine workers were going to school at the mining settlement with children of miners from other ethnic groups. Our consultants said that all the mine workers "got along" with each other.

We heard few stories about Diné miners who were hurt or killed in accidents, though several people named some who died of black lung or lung cancer. Drink-ing was not a problem among the Diné miners, according to one elder. Only after the mines closed, when Indian Prohibition was lifted in 1954, did the floodgates open. Then she saw children tending babies in cradleboards propped against the walls of the bars that lined Route 66 Avenue along the railroad in Gallup.

The miners knew that large-scale mining for profit went against Diné tradi-tions about respecting the natural world, with which humans must coexist. Our consultants said that many Diné mine workers had ceremonies done to protect themselves, as well as the mules and equipment that they used. The consultants did not know of specific ceremonies but suggested some forms of Blessingway, probably including offerings to Chahałheeł, the power of darkness.

AND AFTER . . .

When underground mining ended around Gallup, strip mining was poised to take its place. The new mines appeared on the outskirts of Gallup to the

FIGURE 41 Draglines at McKinley Mine northwest of Gallup. This surface mine opened after the underground mines around Gallup closed. A United Mine Workers of America (UMWA) strike in the summer of 2000 had idled the overhaul of the dragline. Credit: Klara Kelley photo.

southeast (Sundance, 1950–88), south (Carbon Coal No. 2 / Catalpa Canyon, 1981–88), and northwest (Carbon Coal No. 1 / Mentmore, 1976–88). Dwarfing these mines was the sprawling McKinley Mine, about 15 miles northwest on the edge of the Navajo Reservation (1962–2008) (Nickelson 1988:20–21, 29–30, 39–40, 79–80). As we have observed since the mid-1970s, many more Diné men and (eventually) women have worked for these mines than worked earlier in the underground mines. Most strip mine workers were paid better, since most were represented by the UMWA. We do not know whether the rates of injury, illness, and death among the Diné strip mine workers are comparable to those of their predecessors underground.

Yet, like the underground mines, the strip mines displaced many Diné extended families from much of their traditional use areas, according to one 2015 consultant (see also Kelley 1983; York 1981), even if one excludes the dozens displaced from the more distant McKinley Mine (see Kelley 1986b). Allotted families (at least at the McKinley Mine) eventually received part of the royalties on the coal taken from their allotments. Most payments were fairly small, however, because they were distributed among many heirs (see chapter 11).[3]

Underground mines have left patches of devastation amid open mine shafts, coal waste (slack) heaps, mining camp debris, and later domestic trash dumping that the mine wastes seem to invite. Even excluding the McKinley Mine, the smaller strip mines near town, though off-limits to dumping, have left comparable, if not larger, devastated lands. Even diligent, government-required reclamation at these smaller strip mines has not yet made them livable.

The Diné experience with coal mining around Gallup, including the history from the 1970s to the present, prompts the question, have Diné benefited from coal mining around Gallup? In terms of bonding with the land through stories and travel to storied places, at least, the answer is an emphatic no—generations without access, along with hundreds of square miles of destroyed land surface and obliterated remains of early family homesites, have disrupted this fundamental reinforcement of sovereignty. Still, families do what they can. Both authors have taken part in family visits to past homes before the families lost access, one before forced relocation to make way for Hopis, the other before strip mining destroyed family lands, later to revisit the few remaining sites and to recall the vanished land, now mine spoils covered with thorny plants.

One elder offered a more categorical answer. She had a prophetic dream about early Gallup coal mining based on memories that point to the future, which she recalled as follows (paraphrased from the original Navajo, KFa, December 29, 2014).

In the dream, there was nothing where Gallup and Gamerco are, just smoke coming out of the ground. Then it was clear why the towns had disappeared. It was because of the desecration from coal mining.

Long ago, when a fire happened at the Gamerco Mine, they put Diné to work fighting the fire. After that, many more went to work at that mine. They were put there because of the danger. A siren would sound in the morning, noon, and evening to signal start of work, lunch, and quitting time. There were tents all over, and a lot of Diné men moved around Gamerco with their families to work in the mines. The women stayed at their tents and fixed lunches, which they took to the mine at noon. There were a lot of other mines, too, and corrals with mules, which hauled the coal. Diné did a lot of the work. They didn't speak English, but some spoke Spanish and got along with the Hispanic workers. The Foreigners lived in the houses. Diné lived between the Foreigners and the Hispanics.

In one of the mines was a fire, and from Gamerco they dug into the shaft that had the fire. By digging that tunnel they put out the fire. Women stood around the pit and knew what was happening. There were disputes, and the Foreigners were chased out. They left in wagons pulled by oxen. Some moved into Gallup.

The ancestors of the People were big, ugly people, like the statue of Manuelito that used to be in the store [C. N. Cotton Company] in Gallup. They were like wild animals, at one with everything until the Bilagaanas came. They called the Bilagaanas "Doo Daatsaahii" [Those Who Don't Die] because no matter how many were killed, more came to take their places. The Wind told the People that the Bilagaanas would destroy them. But it was predicted that nature would take back the land. The People prayed with cornmeal and corn pollen morning, noon, and evening. The mountains spoke to the People and gave us rules for living. Mother Earth gave us everything to live by. The elders said, "Don't dig in the earth." The land is not ours to dig up, only to borrow for necessary use. We were told that we could use the coal and other minerals only when necessary, but all we do is fight over them for money. It was foretold that there would be fire in the earth and the mountains would burn. The whole traditional way of relating to the land is ignored. People just look at the land as property. Coal mining is part of a way of life that has undermined tradition, and now that tradition cannot cope with the desecration of coal mining.

11

DINÉ LAND USE AND CLIMATE CHANGE

When I was young [born 1924] it used to snow a lot, but not now. Our elders used to help each other, but now we don't do that. When I was a boy there was lots of grass. Our elders herded. We ate corn, corn cake. Then I started seeing store-bought food on the table, and from then everything went down. Everything is money, money, money. We don't offer prayers now, and maybe that's why the climate is drying out. (Original statement in Navajo, KFa, June 5, 2001)

BETWEEN 2001 AND 2015 we did 110 consultations with Diné elders, singly or in small groups, to talk about changes in land use and the weather that they had witnessed during their lifetimes (Kelley and Francis 2012, 2015; Redsteer and Wessells 2017; Redsteer et al. 2018). The work started in Tsézhin Bii', the Lava Buttes country of southwestern Navajoland, then continued farther southwest in the middle Little Colorado River basin (Leupp, Tolani Lake, and Bird Springs), and finally moved to around Canyon de Chelly (Chinle, Many Farms, and Tsaile). Many of the elders voiced the same ideas as the man quoted above. Taken together, the people said that the climate has gotten dryer, and especially there is less snow. People farm less. Water sources have been "improved," and some natural sources have disappeared. Government irrigation projects of the 1940s and 1950s have fallen into disuse. People raise less livestock. People no longer share work, land, or what they produce anymore. Instead of depending on producing things for themselves and helping one another, people work for wages, buy what they need, and do these things only for themselves and their immediate families. The result is haphazard land use, lack of sharing in the extended family, dependence on buying what you need, an epidemic of diabetes and other degenerative diseases, and an upsurge in land disputes.

FIGURE 42 Sheep coming down from summer range in the Chuska Mountains to Sano-stee in the fall of 1988. By that time, herds as big as this one were rare. Today, after more than 20 years of almost continuous megadrought, many more families have sold their cows, goats, and sheep. Credit: Klara Kelley photo.

And especially, too many people don't pray with offerings for rain and snow, because they don't depend on the land anymore. They have lost the sense of being caretakers of the land. No more dependence on land means no more prayers for rain and snow, and this is the cause of drought. If you don't use land and ask for moisture, you don't get it.

In this chapter, we first consider changes in grazing and the implications for a dispute within anthropology: whether First Nations people's traditions include deliberate natural resource conservation strategies. We then consider how Diné stockraising has become entangled with climate change and how Diné relate traditions to dealing with climate change today. We interpret the nuances of a Diné traditionalist theory of climate change to help non-Diné, as well as skeptical, formally educated Diné, to understand what we have in common and respect what we don't so that, working together, we can adapt to climate change in ways consistent with Diné sovereignty.

SHEPHERD KRECH AND TRADITIONAL
FIRST NATIONS HUNTERS

Anthropologist Shepherd Krech (1998) has stirred up the question of whether First Nations traditions include deliberate resource conservation strategies in connection with hunting. Krech claims that ethnohistorical records on many North American First Nations groups show no clear evidence of game conservation practices that are both "intentional" (deliberate) and "effective" (they work). Yes, there were intentional practices, like returning the remains of game animals to the earth so they could regenerate. But these, according to Krech, were not effective. There were also effective practices, namely, moving away from overhunted places, but these were not intentional, only an accident of low population density that allowed people to move into unoccupied areas (the absent Indian theme again!).

Our talks with elders in western Navajoland, together with interviews around 1960 for the Navajo Land Claim (NLC, Navajo oral history; see chapter 6, note 1), suggest that most Diné families there before the Long Walk depended heavily on hunting and gathering. They moved according to changing environmental conditions over dozens of miles—across most of the Little Colorado River drainage system and up into the San Francisco Peaks, or around the middle and lower San Juan River basin from the Chuska Mountains west. But they also had core home areas, often for farming. This Diné hunting-gathering-herding land-use pattern is comparable to the hunting that Krech talks about. The People also have conservation practices comparable to the offerings and moving that Krech found among hunters. Unlike Krech, though, we think that such practices form a conservation repertoire both intentional and, through its spirituality, effective.

Anthropologist Rosalie Fanale (1982) has described traditional Diné herding land use of the 1800s and early 1900s. Her findings are based partly on the life history of a man who ranged around western Navajoland, including Tsézhin Bii' after the Long Walk (Left-Handed 1967 [1938]), and partly on interviews in the San Juan basin of New Mexico. Each extended family had a customary seasonal round of moving among two or more herding areas. In some years they moved instead among relatives, often dozens of miles away. Drought in the home area or unusual bounty in the host area was the reason. People did not need empty areas to move into because they had clan and family ties with people in other places who let them move there temporarily, knowing that the guests would be their hosts when conditions were reversed. Some areas were iffy for everybody because they lacked surface water and could only be used in wet years. People also did ceremonial offerings for rain and vegetation. People were aware that moving and offerings together were necessary to conserve the range.

The ceremonies and moving formed an intentional and effective conservation repertoire. Under normal conditions, people kept to their usual land-use patterns and did ceremonies to maintain normal conditions. Under abnormal conditions, they moved and did ceremonies to restore normal conditions. Krech would probably argue that the ceremonies were an ineffective part of an otherwise effective practice. But in fact the ceremonies were effective: they gave participants a sense of responsibility for the land and the People's combined power to be good caretakers.

SOIL CONSERVATION SERVICE SCIENTISTS AND DINÉ ELDERS

Like the difference between First Nations traditionalists and Krech on whether prayer conserves game, Diné elders and academic scientists differ about whether prayer brings moisture. The elders find support for the idea that prayer brings moisture in the plentiful grass, rain, and snow that they remember before stock reduction. Indeed, the early twentieth century was unusually wet, according to geologist Margaret Hiza Redsteer's analysis (Redsteer et al. 2018). Was this the result of most Diné using certain prayers, or a reflection of a short-term weather cycle, or something more complex?

Depletion of grass through overgrazing in Navajoland became an issue after 1928. Engineering surveys revealed that silt in the Colorado River would endanger Hoover Dam, then under construction to supply hydroelectric power to Los Angeles (Roessel and Johnson 1974:73; U.S. Senate, Subcommittee of the Committee on Indian Affairs 1937:17,445). Washindoon blamed Diné overgrazing for much of the erosion, then demanded that Diné reduce their livestock by half and follow strict regulations about where they could herd their remaining stock. To the U.S. Soil Conservation Service, no amount of prayer and ceremony were going to fix the problem. Yet there are reasons to suspect that in the early 1900s much of Navajoland was not overgrazed but eroding from other causes. Navajo overstocking has been an article of faith among scholars for years, but consider the following.

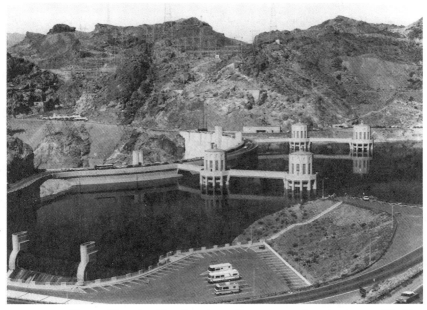

FIGURE 43 Hoover Dam in 1985, the trigger for 1930s stock reduction, as Washindoon frantically tried to curb soil erosion from the Colorado River watershed upstream. Credit: Klara Kelley photo.

Political ecologist Piers Blaikie (1994:8ff.) has noted that twentieth-century policies to control traditional grazing and farming elsewhere in the world have often followed investors' alarms about silting of hydroelectric dams. The policymakers have failed to recognize the complex causes of the erosion (including nonhuman causes), instead scapegoating small-scale farmers and herders. In the Diné case, we note that Navajoland is far from the only area drained by the Colorado. Other tribes and non–First Nations ranchers raised livestock in the rest of the area, which in any case is subject to a good deal of erosion even without livestock.

True, observers had sounded the alarm in Navajoland much earlier. In 1883 Agent Denis Riordan at Fort Defiance (see chapter 6) mentioned gullying and blamed it on Diné overgrazing (Parman 1976:10). Another observer was Father Anselm Weber in 1911 (U.S. Senate, Subcommittee of the Committee on Indian Affairs 1937:17,553–17,559), whose point was that the government must secure Diné lands from non–First Nations settler encroachment because already those lands were overgrazed (see chapter 7). The erosion that Riordan and Weber saw, though, was surely due at least in part to the onset of the most recent erosion episode in a series of 500-year cycles of channel downcutting and backfilling in the U.S. Southwest. By 1985 earth scientists and archaeologists had identified these cycles in the archaeological record going back at least 2,000 years, well before livestock came to the Southwest (Dean et al. 1985). Surely what Riordan saw, only 15 years after mostly herdless Diné had returned from Fort Sumner to rejoin their almost equally herdless relatives, could not have resulted from widespread overgrazing, unless the Fort Defiance Agency distributions of sheep were a lot more lavish than records show. However, for 10 years after the return, people flocked into the upper Black Creek Valley once a year to get their annuities, including sheep, camping in an area circumscribed by soldiers posted at the Haystacks, Saint Michaels, Sawmill, and Red Lake (Mitchell 2001:20). This annual event, along with the government livestock pastured around Fort Defiance, would have enhanced local downcutting in the early years of the latest erosion episode.[1]

In the Black Creek Valley by around 1900, large-scale Diné stock owners (ricos) like Chee Dodge (see chapters 6 and 8) seem to have been crowding families with much smaller herds into poorer-quality range beyond the edges of the valley—hilly country of mixed shrubs and grass amid rocky mesas. The ricos themselves dominated broad expanses of grassland in the valley where large herds could spread out (Henderson 1985:27ff.; Kelley 1986b:27–28). Kelley blamed this trend on the trading post system, which encouraged the ricos to market their considerable surplus livestock rather than distributing some of them to poorer relations and neighbors, as ricos had done before the Long Walk. Kelley suggested that, left on their own, the small stockraisers were limited in the number of livestock they could cut back to (14–20 mature sheep and goats per family member [see Kelley and Whiteley 1989:111–112]; compare 33–60 according to Navajo Tribal Council vice chairman Howard Gorman in 1941 [Iverson and Roessel, eds. 2002:190]). Overstocking ensued.

Yet overstocking was partly checked by the many Black Creek Valley families who seem to have been crowded off the range, lost their herds, and come to depend on relatives. A 1915 census of central and southern Navajoland (Kelley and Whiteley 1989:220–221; Paquette 1915) shows that the upper Black Creek Valley and southern Chuska Valley had more families without livestock than elsewhere in the census area—more than 40 percent. (About 5 percent of these were recorded as herdless but also were noted to have sheep in the herd of another household.) In the lower Black Creek Valley and toward Gallup,

22 percent of households had no herds. What's more, 70–75 percent of all families in these areas had fewer than 100 sheep and goats (including families with none). There were also more ricos with larger herds in the Black Creek Valley and southern Chuska Valley than elsewhere, including Diné traders Chee Dodge, Charles Damon, and the Arnold family (see chapter 8). Most herdless households were mature households—couples in their late twenties, thirties, and forties with children and other dependents. They were probably part of larger family clusters with at least one herd, from which the herdless got meat and milk (see Gilpin et al. 2015:Table 3.4; see also the introduction, final quote, for how one herdless family lived 15–20 years later). Ricos also hired people with few or no stock as herders, usually paying them with a share of the lamb and wool crop (Bingham and Bingham 1994:159–163).

The Black Creek Valley was the most populous and developed part of Navajoland in the late 1800s and early 1900s and may well have had more herdless households than the rest of Navajoland. After the Long Walk, some families did not return to their former homelands but stayed around Fort Defiance, including those whose descendants told Kelley that ricos had crowded them out of the valley. As the seat of Fort Defiance, the valley was also the oldest center of government activity, schools, and missions, including the Saint Michaels Franciscan Mission, from which Father Anselm Weber did much of his observing. Early wage workers could find alternatives to stockraising here. By comparison, in 1915 around Ganado, only 4 percent of families were herdless, and fewer than half had herds of 100 or less, a hint that there was enough grass for everyone. We suspect that most of the rest of Navajoland was like Ganado.[2]

The idea that much of Navajoland was like Ganado accords with range conditions that geologist Herbert Gregory saw as he rode around Navajoland between 1909 and 1913 (1916:22–49; Redhouse 1986:10). He noted overgrazing only in the Black Creek Valley, between the Black Creek Valley and Gallup (Manuelito Plateau), and on parts of Carrizo Mountain north of the Chuska Valley. He also made a point of noting gullying only on the Manuelito Plateau, winter range for Black Creek Valley and lower Chuska Valley herds (Kelley 1986b; Kelley et al. 2013). Elsewhere, grass ranged from "sufficient" for many sheep (Lobo Mesa east of Gallup), "fairly abundant" (Chuska Valley, Chinle Valley, Pueblo Colorado Wash Valley), and "fairly plentiful" (Shato [Shonto] Plateau northwest of Black Mesa) to "admirably adapted for stockraising" (Chaco Plateau), "very satisfactory" (west side of the Chuskas), "good grazing" ("Hopi" [Lava] Buttes), "luxuriant" (Rainbow Plateau), "excellent forage . . . to support thousands of sheep" (Tsegi Mesas), and "as a cattle country . . . has no superior within the limits of the Reservation" (Monument Valley).

We therefore suggest that in the late 1800s and early 1900s, erosion in Navajoland outside the Black Creek Valley / southern Chuska Valley and the neighboring Manuelito Plateau may have been due largely to the arroyo-cutting phase of the erosion cycle that began more than 2,000 years ago. The same may have been true elsewhere in the Colorado River watershed, perhaps along with overstocking by non–First Nations people, who did not necessarily practice range conservation. These perspectives support the elders who told us that there was plenty of grass before stock reduction, especially since the elders consulted were from Navajoland west of the Black Creek Valley. The correlation between abundance of both grass and prayers in the early 1900s and a lack of both later seems to support the elders' theory about the effectiveness of prayer.

Along with stock reduction, Washindoon and the Navajo tribal government imposed a grazing-permit system, still used today, that requires people to limit the numbers of livestock and restrict their stock to specific zones (grazing districts), regardless of local range conditions. As Diné have complained from stock reduction on (Iverson and Roessel, eds. 2002:25ff., 58, 187), the range-area restrictions undermine extended family cooperation and keep people from the effective traditional practice of changing the distribution of livestock on the range in response to changing local moisture and grass. And as Diné elders quoted above have also complained, after almost 80 years, three generations, the permit system (together with the dominant U.S. culture) has also, for many stockraisers, replaced collective extended family stewardship with a sense of individual property ownership. The range seems no better either, even though many families have switched to cattle (which do not need daily herding, as sheep do, thereby letting their owners hold jobs) and then have had to sell them off as the drought since the 1990s has worsened (Redsteer et al. 2018).

The overall drying of the climate since their childhoods, the elders now say, is the result of less dependence on the land and on one's relatives, which has followed stock reduction and grazing regulations. After stock reduction, people turned to wage work and consumerism, which now support most families and have undermined community cooperation, self-sufficiency, and collective bonds with the land. As a result, people have stopped making offerings to the Holy People who control moisture, and those Holy People therefore no longer provide moisture. Herding has become uncoordinated and chaotic. Land-use patterns have changed, then, not because of weather or climate change but

FIGURE 44 A Diné home having an Indian Health Service septic tank / drainfield system installed in 1985, decades after Diné coal and water were first used to generate electricity for southern Arizona, Nevada, and California. Credit: Klara Kelley photo.

because of the wage economy and how it has undermined group land-use practices and bonds focused with ceremonies. Climate change is the result of all this, they say, not the cause.

Probably most academic scientists would agree with the Diné elders that land-use changes are the result of changes in the Navajo economy. But to academic scientists, climate change is not the result of land-use changes caused by economic changes (though on a much larger scale of time and space, it is). The difference between the traditional Diné and academic scientists' ideas about what has caused the present drought hinges on different theories about how ceremonies work and on detachment.

DETACHMENT

We had a lot of livestock [in the 1930s] because of ceremonies, and we took care of them. We had a summer place and a winter place, so we never used up the plants in one place. There were three places. The summer place was in Táálahooghan Canyon, where the cornfields were. In the fall we moved [five or six miles] south to Be'ek'id Joobaa'í (Merciful Lake) on the east side of Star Mountain. In winter we moved still farther south to near our present homesite.

And with the animals, there was a certain person who took care of the sheep. Each family herded separately, but the various families got together and helped each other with special seasonal tasks like shearing, planting, harvesting.

The day after the Hopis started the land dispute [1937, by annexing Táálahooghan Canyon], the rain stopped and the land changed. For the last 11 years [since 1990] it has been really hot, plants don't grow, crops don't grow, everything comes up but then just dries up. Bugs and birds also have multiplied, eat the crops, so there's nothing left. This didn't happen earlier.

People ask why we don't have livestock anymore. It's because today people don't take care of them [ceremonially]. In the old days, we always had a lead sheep (billy, ram) for whom a no-sleep ceremony was done. Corn pollen was put in his mouth. Also we would have no-sleep ceremonies for the lambs. These were special Blessingway ceremonies with sheep songs. Sheep were a way of life and were treated with care and respect.

Sheep drinking water was on the ground in ponds. The stock were healthy because their water was part of the earth. All the older men knew sheep songs and did ceremonies over the sheep. They have taken that knowledge with them. Now no one does ceremonies, and livestock have declined. Today stock water comes from windmills and tanks. Minerals and rust are concentrated in the water, and the livestock don't fatten.

Plant life has also changed. We had mountain soil [Blessingway] bundles of two types, one the general type and another special kind for plants. They were used for ceremonies for livestock, weather, crops, and rain. The mirage stones [in these bundles] were used to bless the sheep before and after shearing.

Today livestock are ignored. People just let them out to wander around on their own, with only dogs to watch them. I compare the old ways and today. Today no one takes pleasure in their livestock. (Rose Francis, original statement in Navajo, KFa, August 16, 2001)

Ceremonies are part of careful stockraising and farming. They focus caring attention on the livestock, even on individual animals. Traditionally, the health of each animal was a concern of the whole family. Ceremonies also coordinate large groups of people. When you do ceremonies before the work, you get everybody in one place and put them in the right frame of mind. You teach the young through talk about the ceremonies and their purpose. Then everyone goes to work. This is a by-product of the ceremonies' main purpose, to enlist the help of the Holy People, personified powers of nature. The ceremony connects you and the other participants to each other and to the Holy People and through them to the landscapes they inhabit and the whole living cosmos. You have a sense of power and responsibility for the well-being of the whole, of which you are a part. The ethic of relatedness (k'é) and kinship terms of address extend to all of the cosmos, Our Mother Earth, Our Father Sky.

Academic scientists are taught not to think about the various forces of nature as beings with humanlike consciousness and humanlike or animallike forms (anthropomorphism)—like the Holy People, in other words. Avoiding this way of thinking lets one detach oneself from personal connections with the forces of nature that one is studying. A sense of personal connection is considered irrational and subjective. It will get in the way of the methods and procedures that the traditions of academic science have enshrined to advance knowledge about those forces. A sense of personal connection might prejudice one's research.

This detachment historically has contributed to both the fantastical understandings of the cosmos and technological achievements in the world that have taken off in the last few centuries. Detachment has a price: individual scientists may lose sight of their responsibility for the effects of their work. But many of these people probably lose their detachment when some force of nature strikes them with misfortune. Then, though they "know better," they may address these powers bigger than themselves as conscious "higher" beings—"Please don't flood my house, please don't let my child die." Thinking about the forces of nature as conscious beings and as our kin living among us on the land seems to be an important part of how we humans engage in ecologically responsible actions. This is the kernel of the differences between Krech and the First Nations hunters, and between SCS scientists and traditional Diné stockraisers.

Academic scientists, Diné and not, can respect that way of thinking (see Redsteer and Wessells 2017). Some academic scientists struggle with ways to communicate their models and theories to grassroots people. Instead, when introducing a new practice for, say, range conservation, why not engage a chanter to start the project with a prayer ceremony with project participants and community members before getting down to work? Get a chanter whose prayers and songs address the particular Holy People who control what you will be working on. Encourage the chanter to explain larger meanings of the songs and prayers, what they will accomplish, and how they will do it. This is espe-cially important for younger Diné participants. See for yourself if you have a sense of connectedness, personal responsibility, and power from relating to the forces of nature in this way. Give the chanter a chance to teach you something, and maybe then you can more effectively tell the people how it relates to what you have to teach.

FACING CLIMATE CHANGE TOGETHER

Grassroots First Nations people still bonded to the land and academic scientists need each other as we face the greatest challenge of our time. The world's cli-mate is changing much faster than academic scientists forecast even a few years ago. Production of oil, gas, and coal has replaced stockraising as a mainstay of the Navajo economy and contributes to global warming. Many Diné have actively opposed continued production in Navajoland of these fossil fuels, as well as uranium—the "clean alternative" that is anything but. Though Diné activists emphasize issues of environmental justice and disruption of traditional bonds to the land, they are also mindful of climate change. Here are some examples.

BLACK MESA COAL MINES AND THE NAVAJO GENERATING STATION

Diné activist scholar John Redhouse (1985a; see also Brugge 1994:250–252) tells how, in the 1950s and early 1960s, the juggernaut of industrialization in the west-ern United States triggered federal plans to develop Black Mesa resources, first oil and gas, then coal. As told above (in the introduction and chapters 6 and 7), Black Mesa and nearby parts of the 1882 executive order reservation were jointly held by Navajo and Hopi tribes until the 1930s, when Washindoon carved an exclusive Hopi grazing district from the center and forced some Diné to leave their homes there. Most of the 1882 reservation remained under joint tenure, however, until the Hopi Tribe's lawyer, John Boyden, got Washindoon and later aspirants interested in the bonanza of Black Mesa coal. Redhouse's analysis (especially pp. 30–33) suggests that Peabody and other Boyden clients saw Black Mesa as a big rock candy mountain of coal, which they wanted to control because it could be sent so cheaply to lucrative California power generating markets. All that was necessary was to mix it with Black Mesa water and pump it through pipelines as slurry. The coal would supply California for 100 years! These prospects, according to

Redhouse, led to the division of the 1882 reservation between Diné and Hopi and the relocation of thousands of Diné. The object was to remove Diné from over-burdening a century's worth of mines all over Black Mesa.

Peabody started mining coal on Black Mesa in 1970 to supply the Mohave power plant at Bullhead City, Nevada. Peabody pumped water from a deep aquifer and mixed it with the pulverized coal to make slurry, which it sent through a pipeline to the plant. That water was the only drinkable groundwater for much of western Navajoland and all of Hopi. In 1974 the Navajo Generating Station (NGS) near Page, Arizona, also started producing electricity with coal via railroad from another Peabody mine on Black Mesa, the Kayenta Mine. The two plants have sent power outside Navajoland to Nevada, California, and southern Arizona, while Diné on Black Mesa have lived without electricity and hauled water from springs and wells that the slurrying was sucking down. The NGS also has provided electricity to pump Colorado River water through the enormous canal system of the Central Arizona Project to Phoenix and Tucson (Kelley and Francis 1994:150–151; Reno 1981:108).

For decades, Diné living around the two mines and their supporters have protested the removal of residents from the leaseholds, air pollution from the power plants, waste of groundwater, desecration of sacred places, and desecration of Mother Earth as a whole. In the 1990s Black Mesa elder Roberta Blackgoat said,

> The coal they strip-mine is the Earth's liver. The earth's internal organs are dug up. Mother Earth must sit down. The uranium they dug up for energy was her lungs. Her heart and her organs are dug up because of greed.
>
> It is smog on the horizons. Her breath, her warmth, is polluted now and she is angry when Navajos talk of their sickness. . . .
>
> No compassion is left for the motherland. We've become her enemy. Money does this. This is what I say. Our prayers lose their meanings when the land becomes an industry. (Benally 2011:31–32)

At the same time, workers at the Peabody mines voiced conflicting feelings about their work. In 1996 miner Eugene Badonie told a public meeting, "Right now, I can't afford to let go of my job. I don't always agree with Peabody, but when it comes to my bread and butter, I'll stand up for it" (Wicoff 1996).

Mr. Badonie's statement was a response to grassroots Diné and Hopi activists and others who were starting to protest the waste of drinking water for slurry. That waste was even more outrageous at the onset of what has now been two decades of almost continuous drought and record temperatures that go with global warming (Redsteer et al. 2018). In 2005 the Navajo Nation government finally canceled Peabody's pumping permit. Diné activists also spoke against proposed multiparty Navajo water-rights settlements in 2010 and 2012, never ratified, which they see as warnings of future raids on a Diné resource becoming all the more precious as global warming speeds up. Advocates of the settlements, which limit Diné claims on river and groundwater in exchange for water pipeline funding, say that only thus can Diné communities get the water they need (Hansen 2014).

At the same time, Southern California Edison closed its aging, megapolluting Mohave plant rather than invest in air pollution control technology. The activists then formed the Just Transition Coalition and in 2013 got Southern California Edison to use money received for cutting sulfur dioxide emissions (by closing the plant) to fund renewable energy projects that benefit Diné, Hopi, and California ratepayers. Now, a decade plus after Mohave closed, the owners of NGS have voted to close their plant, since natural gas can generate power

FIGURE 45 Navajo Generating Station near Page, Arizona, 1997. Credit: Klara Kelley photo.

more cheaply (Black Mesa Water Coalition 2016; Harrelson 2017; Powell and Long 2010:234–235).

When the Mohave plant closed, Peabody closed the Black Mesa Mine that supplied it and laid off hundreds of local workers, who had been getting good wages under union contracts. Now, Peabody's Kayenta Mine, which supplies the NGS, must also close unless Peabody can find another buyer for the coal. In 2015 Peabody declared bankruptcy (the company has since emerged from bankruptcy protection [Komal 2017]) but continues to operate the mine. Whether Peabody can pay for full reclamation of both Black Mesa and Kayenta Mines is a big concern (Indigenous Environmental Network 2016).

The Navajo Nation government and Peabody looked in vain for investors to keep the mine and power plant going. In 2018 the Navajo Transitional Energy Company (NTEC), a Navajo tribal enterprise created in 2016 to operate another large coal mine near Shiprock (see below), announced its interest in buying both the power plant and the mine (Navajo Transitional Energy Company 2019). But Black Mesa resident Percy Deal, former council delegate and chapter president, said,

> "No tribal officials have been to the communities to hear from them, to listen to them about the 50 years of impact; they are just focused on the jobs and revenues. . . ."
>
> Deal said they [elders] remember the herbs and plants that [they] once used as medicine for themselves and their families and the livestock they no longer have to feed themselves and their families and to have for religious ceremonies.
>
> They've also witnessed the disappearance of wildlife and the destruction of sacred sites, he said.
>
> Deal added that hundreds of families, including himself, who live in and around Black Mesa, are without running water, but the Navajo Nation provides 34,100 acre-feet of water from the Colorado River to Navajo Generating Station and 6,100 acre-feet of water from the Navajo Aquifer to Peabody at a very cheap rate.
>
> "If there is any extension for any period to continue the power plant and mining, all the above will worsen," he said. "We will not see and enjoy our water for many more years. It's already been 50 years." (Shebala 2017)

As of December 2017, the present owners, the Navajo Nation, and federal agencies have agreed to close the plant in 2019, followed by five years of site reclamation. Peabody's Kayenta Mine is also likely to close. The reclamation period offers time to find alternative uses for the site (power generation with renewable energy being a possibility) and retrain workers, but workers and Navajo Nation government officials hope to keep the plant going with Peabody coal.

EASTERN NAVAJOLAND CHECKERBOARD AREA: OIL AND GAS

In the 1950s oil and gas boomed in far northeastern Navajoland, a checkerboard of Indian allotments and federal, state, and private lands (see chapters 6 and 7).[3] Many of these parcels have different owners of surface and mineral rights. Most oil and minerals are administered by the U.S. Bureau of Land Management (BLM). Production has roller-coastered between boom and bust since 1950. Between about 1980 and 2008, when the market became glutted and prices fell, the industry enjoyed a boom in coal-bed methane, much of which seems to have gone to California to replace coal in generating electricity (Engler et al. 2001; Fassett 2013; Thompson 2016).

In 2008 oil prices were still high, however, and producers wanted to get at deep deposits in shale, where oil must be recovered by fracking. That technology injects a witches' brew of chemicals through wells into the rock, using enough pressure to crack the rock and let the oil flow from tiny pockets into the bigger fracked spaces, where it can be pumped out. Low oil prices since 2014 have interfered with the fast track that Washindoon at first planned for oil development in eastern Navajoland (Matlock 2014), but more leases are now on offer.

Meanwhile, residents and activists have complained of companies tearing up the land for well pads, access roads, and pipelines; polluting the ground with oil and chemical spills; polluting the air with dust from truck traffic and from fumes of leaked or flared gas; desecrating sacred places and graves; threatening Chacoan Anaasází archaeological landscapes; polluting surface and groundwater (with fracking fluids of special concern); and vandalism, disrespect, and violence from Bilagaana field crew workers. In 2014 scientists discovered the world's highest concentration of methane, a potent contributor to climate change, hovering over this area. They attribute it to leaks from all the wells (Robinson-Avila 2016). Many Diné and other activists are calling for a moratorium on oil and gas production in the area until these issues can be worked out.

The allotments and royalty payments are also a source of discord among Diné. Few, if any, original allottees are still alive, and most did not leave wills. The BIA probate court identifies heirs from census records and through

hearings where members of the deceased's family give genealogical information. The court then determines each heir's share in the jointly held allotment and apportions shares according to state probate law, not Diné custom.
For example, the spouse of a deceased allottee gets a quarter share, and the
remaining three-quarters are divided equally among the children. If the spouse
remarries and later dies, his or her quarter share is divided the same way,
among the deceased's new spouse and their children. The new spouse and
children may have no connection to the original allottee's family, and Diné
custom does not recognize claims from such people. Yet they get oil and gas
royalties from the allotment, which other heirs may resent. Another example
is the great difference in size of individual shares and therefore payments. In
contrast, Diné custom would probably divide shares somewhat evenly among
all descendants. Older people and those with the fewest siblings are likely to
have the largest shares and may be more willing to lease an allotment than
those with only small shares. Similarly, heirs living elsewhere may be more
willing to lease an allotment than those who live on it and who bear the brunt
of the disturbance and pollution.

As the generations pass, each allotment becomes more and more fractured
into smaller and smaller shares, so determining payments is an accounting
nightmare. More complications include that a given heir may have shares in
several allotments, on each of which more than one operator may be pumping
from more than one pool. The complexity historically has been a smokescreen
for deals between the companies and government workers, for example, to
underreport production and let the company pocket the unpaid royalties. So
in 1984, at the beginning of the most recent boom, eastern Navajo allottees
organized as the Shii Shi Keyah Association to hold the U.S. government to
account (U.S. Senate, Select Committee on Indian Affairs 1992:46–49). The
same thing was happening elsewhere. The protests peaked with Montana allottee and banker Elouise Cobell's lawsuit against the U.S. government for 100-
plus years of mismanaging individual Indian trust assets, most of which are
allotments; the suit was settled in 2010 (Hevesi 2011).

In 1992, at a hearing on Indian Trust Fund Management before the U.S. Senate Select Committee on Indian Affairs (1992:46–49), Shii Shi Keyah's lawyer
Alan Tarradash bore witness to the suffering of allottees in the eastern Navajo
oil and gas fields.

> Typical of many members of Shii-Shi-Keyah Association, Navajo allottees, are
> people like Dorothy Blackee. . . .

Dorothy Blackee is a woman who is in her early sixties, lives in northwestern New Mexico with her daughter and two grandchildren who are below the age of 6. Her royalty income in a good month is about $85 a month. She, her daughter, and the two grandchildren survive on that $85 a month, in addition to commodity foods.

Because they are recipients of royalties, they are not eligible for any other kind of welfare that might be available to someone in such circumstances.

She lives in a house that she built out of boards that she retrieved from wooden boxes and corrugated cardboard covered with mud.

Last October I took the Deputy Director of the Minerals Management Service and his associate director . . . out to visit her in her home so they could understand why it is that accurate accounting of her funds is important. . . .

By way of background, I should explain that we have been in litigation with the Secretary of the Interior since 1984 over his failure to comply with the Federal Oil and Gas Royalty Management Act. (U.S. Senate, Select Committee on Indian Affairs 1992:47)

Even in the early days, though, some families got a lot of money, enough to buy new vehicles and mobile homes. Many of these Diné oppose activists and other allottees who advocate a moratorium on oil and gas production (Bitsoi 2015).

THE NAVAJO MINE, FOUR CORNERS POWER PLANT, AND THE NAVAJO GOVERNMENT

Besides the individual Diné who get wages, royalties, and lease payments, the Navajo Nation government itself gets revenues on fossil fuels produced on its lands (treaty, deeded to the Navajo Tribe, and executive order reservation). To shore up both Diné jobs and its own income, the Navajo Nation government in 2013 bought the Navajo Mine on the reservation near Shiprock in a situation somewhat like that of Peabody's Kayenta Mine. Since about 1960, that mine has supplied the nearby Four Corners Power Plant, which generates power for western cities outside Navajoland. That plant discharges more nitrous oxide into the air than any other in the United States, as well as greenhouse gases and other pollutants (Wild Earth Guardians 2016).

As at the Mohave, owners of three units of the plant chose to shut them down rather than retrofit them with pollution control equipment that new federal air quality standards require. Lacking other customers for its coal and forecasting shrinking profits, mine owner BHP Billiton threatened to close the mine.

The Navajo government stepped up to the plate and bought the mine in the name of saving Navajo jobs. The Navajo Nation operates the mine through the tribal enterprise NTEC, which then gave BHP Billiton a contract to operate the mine temporarily until another contracted operator took over. The Navajo Nation is also paying BHP Billiton in installments for the mine itself while also considering buying the NGS and Kayenta mine (Navajo Transitional Energy Company 2019). To activists, this is a big step backward in coping with global warming. They advocate for the Navajo Nation government and Four Corners Power Plant to replace the complex with a solar or wind generating plant on the reclaimed coal land staffed with retrained plant and mine workers (Black Mesa Water Coalition 2013; Horseherder 2017; Powell and Long 2010:247).

A WAY FORWARD?

The Navajo Tribal Utility Authority has built a 27.5-megawatt utility-scale solar generating plant near Kayenta that could provide power to as many as 13,000 homes in the surrounding region. Along with tax credits and federal loans, Salt River Project, a partner in the NGS, has provided some funding. In New Mexico, the Navajo Nation government is considering a much larger, 2,100-megawatt solar plant on the Paragon Ranch south of the Navajo Mine (Bowman 2017; U.S. Department of Energy 2015, 2016). In the late 1970s the ranch was to accommodate the coal-fired power plant of a New Mexico utility until activists revealed the speculative nature of the plant and its federal coal supply and recession soured the market. In the early 1980s the Navajo Nation government bought the ranch with money from the Navajo-Hopi Land Settlement Act, which is to benefit relocatees from Black Mesa and from other lands partitioned to the Hopis (Kelley and Francis 1994:154–155; Radford 1986:149–161; see also chapter 7). The proposed Navajo Nation utility-scale solar generating station at Paragon would produce that benefit. Effects on Diné living near this proposed facility are unclear.

Some Diné have misgivings about large-scale power projects, even based on renewable energy sources, especially those that would imitate the coal-fired plants by serving people outside Navajoland. Activist Tom Goldtooth has said,

> I am concerned we will have wind and solar systems built on the same capitalist model that is depleting the abilities of Mother Earth to meet the needs of an industrialized world. I am an advocate for our Native Nations to develop wind

and solar, but most of our tribes have traditional belief systems that must guide us in these forms of development. *When we, as Native Nations, create massive wind-power projects, we must have ceremonies to obtain permission to utilize the sacred elements to harness and process wind and sun into electricity* that will be exported off our Native lands into these colonial systems that don't directly benefit our people. So how do we, as Diné, or Dakota, or any other tribes, reconcile the approach and model of energy development we engage in? We've only begun to ask these questions. (Quoted in Powell and Long 2010:254; emphasis added)

AND . . .

There was a time, according to the elders, when Diné grazing-based land use and the climate were in balance. Though pressed by colonizer encroachment and Diné ranchers with large commercial herds, families tried to keep that balance by ceremonies that kept people working together and mindful of their caretaker responsibilities, the ultimate expression of the bonds to the land. Stock reduction forced people to support themselves with wage work and consumerism and thereby destroyed the balance. The Holy People turned their backs. Climate change followed. Dependence on the money economy has disrupted Diné bonds with the land and opened the way to coal, oil, and gas production. It is also the price that the People pay to run the very government that enhances their political sovereignty.

Diné activists are looking to restore the lost balance, but there's no going back to the old stockraising way of life. In 1930 there were more than 1,000,000 head of livestock, mostly sheep and goats, for 40,000 Diné (Kelley and Whiteley 1989:207–209). Today there are more than four times as many people living in Navajoland (170,000 in the 2010 census [Y. Begay 2014:112]) and about two-thirds the number of livestock in sheep-goat equivalents (in 2007 200,000 sheep and goats; 80,000 cattle, equal to 320,000 sheep and goats; and 38,000 horses, equal to 190,000 sheep and goats [U.S. Department of Agriculture 2009:43–45]). Yet as the foregoing chapters show, the land, the People, the bond between them, and the stories that make the bond are still there. Using Diné sovereignty—"do it yourself, do it the Diné way"—to revive the traditional Diné caretaking ethic and the ceremonies that frame it seems like a starting point toward rebalance, but enhanced political sovereignty must go with it.

AFTERWORD

B Y TELLING the people "how we came to be who and where we are," oral traditions make a bond between the people and the land that strengthens sovereignty, which in turn protects that bond. "The people" are the Diné (literally translated, "the People") and the land is, as Diné oral tradition delineates it, the area amid the Four Sacred mountains—Blanca Peak, Colorado; Mount Taylor, New Mexico; the San Francisco Peaks, Arizona; and La Plata Mountain, Colorado. The bond is really many bonds: between the Diné as a whole and the land amid the Four Sacred Mountains; between chanters and the landscapes delineated in the histories of their ceremonies; between extended families and the land where they have lived, herded, and farmed; between a person and the place where the family buried her or his umbilical cord at birth. These bonds are instilled by elders telling youngsters the ceremonial, clan, and family histories and taking them to the places in the stories.

The oral histories are many, too—large empowering stories that everyone knows and, beneath those big trees, a dense understory of smaller stories about particular events, places, and people. In the introduction, we sketched the empowering stories best known among the People, most of which include victories that empower the People. In the 11 chapters that follow, we have offered some smaller, more particular oral histories. These we have supplemented with information from archaeology and documents, most done by colonizers. Colonizer archaeology and documentation may try to undermine the bond that particular Diné oral histories create between the People and the land. However, the documents and even the archaeology exist because colonizers, too, have taken part in these stories (in the case of archaeology, retroactively). Their stories, presented critically within a framework of Diné oral history, may illuminate the struggles of the People to assert and defend their bonds to the land and their sovereignty, defined here as self-determination: "Just do it yourself, do it the Diné way."

As these stories and the supplementation show, Diné sovereignty has been damaged by colonizer hegemony. Yet the many bonds between the Diné and the land are still pretty strong. So how does sovereignty do this work? A threat to the land, the People, and the bond (not to mention Diné ways of life) is a threat to sovereignty as well. Therefore, the People, singly and in groups, have struggled for sovereignty, not just to "do it ourselves" (political sovereignty) but to "do it our way" (cultural sovereignty), to keep access to the landscapes in the stories and to pass knowledge of both land and stories to youngsters. These struggles, however limited their successes, have been enough to keep the bond between the People and the land. We leave to others theorizing about what makes a struggle successful or not. Other scholars are also better suited than we are to theorize about the general relationship between traditional history and sovereignty, both cultural and political. Nevertheless, here we offer a few thoughts on how oral history is involved in the creation of and struggles for sovereignty. We are concerned mainly with the struggles of colonized peoples who have kept at least some of their lands. We leave to others the important question, what can self-determination be like for peoples who have lost their lands? Also, struggles among colonizers themselves have their own, different, complexities, as recently resurgent white supremacist movements around the world are showing.

According to scholar Gerald Vizenor (2009:1), colonizer stories diminish "Natives" by portraying them, through "nihility" and "literary tragedy," as victims ("victimry") or by not portraying them at all (absence). By portraying colonized peoples as passive and voiceless about their own history, victimry creates a kind of absence: the colonized people as active experiencers and confronters-resisters are absent from colonizer stories. A people's accounts of their own history both critique and refute the self-serving stories of absence, "victimry," and voicelessness that colonizers use to take Indigenous land and resources.

Moving colonized people to assert their sovereignty requires that the people know their own traditional history and how it relates to their land. Taken together, their stories form the people's own cultural encyclopedia. Those stories also are the only sources of both certain facts and a view of their forebears' own experience of their world, including but not limited to encounters with the colonizers. Oral tradition tells about past struggles for sovereignty. It advances the struggle both by teaching lessons from the past and by critiquing and refuting outsider claims to the people's own land and resources.

At the same time, though, colonizers' accounts offer valuable insights into their own experiences with the colonized people and must be included in any careful study of that people's history. A colonized people's own traditional history alone will not always provide rich insights into the past or effectively address the struggle for sovereignty because that struggle involves both colonized and colonizers. Colonizer sources (including their oral traditions) are often rich in factual detail, as well as views inside the colonizers' experiences with each other, which have affected how they have dealt with the colonized. Colonizers also sometimes succeed in cutting people off from their land, and without the land the stories lose their meaning and are forgotten.

We avoid addressing here the nature of "facts" and "truth." Reports of someone's direct observations (a partial, working definition of fact) also include the reporter's biases. Sources from both colonizer and colonized have their own biases. Therefore, one must interpret all sources critically, ironically, even use them to critique each other. In addition, both colonized and colonizer stories usually have diverse versions, which one can use to critique each other. Oral histories offer special challenges because of their tendency to compress information as it passes from one generation to another.

The struggle for sovereignty itself, of course, is actually many struggles. Here we have brought out Diné oral histories to push back against politically dominant others, colonizers. Other struggles not portrayed here occur within Diné society itself. Examples include struggles between various grassroots people and the Navajo Nation government, between traditionalists and Native American Church believers, and, surely, among various groups when they have come together through ethnogenesis. Many such struggles are about different ideas of political and cultural sovereignty itself (Powell 2018; Sherry 2002).

As aspects of sovereignty, political and cultural sovereignty go together, but not in lockstep. Political sovereignty, "doing it ourselves," does not necessarily support cultural sovereignty, "doing it our way," as activist critics of the Navajo Nation government's energy policies attest (see chapter 11). Like other Indigenous peoples, those of the United States possess limited sovereignty "nested" within that of the colonizer state as "dependent sovereign nations" under U.S. law (Powell 2018:113–138; Simpson 2014). The colonizer state reorganizes Indigenous political forms the better to rule, forces Indigenous governments to gain sovereignty in some spheres by sacrificing sovereignty in others, and swamps Indigenous culture with colonizer culture. But Indigenous peoples and their governments can and do push back. In practice, colonizer sovereignty is also limited, even for the most powerful nation-states, whose sovereignty is now nested in globalized corporate networks.

Even limited political sovereignty can support cultural sovereignty: witness the continuing survival of much Diné tradition and the land-People bond. Other insights might come from studying the process of ethnogenesis to learn how polities and cultures of commingling groups reinforce or subvert each other during the transition. According to Diné oral tradition, during the most recent period of intense ethnogenesis (the 1300s to 1700s), leaders of equal status literally negotiated a common cultural framework. Though the oral tradition does not give specifics, this framework likely included what Diné scholars consider the foundations of Diné culture today: extension of the clan system (k'éí), kinship norms (k'é), and the Blessingway ceremony (hózhǫ́) to cover all the people coming together. Within this framework, the diversity of stories, ceremonies, and other cultural practices that the different peoples brought with them into the emerging People could survive and evolve. This diversity persists today, including traces of where the different stories and other cultural elements came from, scattered among ceremonialists, communities, families, and individuals. It takes the stories of all these people combined, and the big beautiful land they cover, to make a complete oral history of the People.

The process of ethnogenesis makes the people aware of a common identity and thereby creates a foundation for their sovereignty. The sharing and merging of oral traditions among the people who come together through ethnogenesis help create this common identity and the sovereignty that emerges from it. Oral tradition, ethnogenesis, and sovereignty reinforce each other, as Dine oral traditions presented in this book show.

Political and cultural sovereignty are tied together through the land base of a people. The chapters in this book portray the bond between the Diné and land created by stories—first, as it developed in precolumbian times (chapters 1–4), then as Diné have struggled to preserve the land and their lifeways upon it under colonization (chapters 5–11). As oral tradition protects the People's hold on the land, the hold on the land protects oral tradition. For without the land, the stories attached to it, the creation stories, oral maps, and all the rest lose their meaning and are forgotten.

The struggles for political and cultural sovereignty by Diné and other modern Indigenous groups are directed at colonizers, who often pit one group against another to promote colonizer control of land, water, and other resources. This process of dividing and ruling enhances nationalism within Indigenous groups and hinders them in relating to each other through shared or overlapping oral traditions and cultural practices. By focusing on Diné sovereignty, we too have ignored this matter. We hope that other scholars will pursue it.

So we have made this book first and foremost for Diné youngsters. Learn Diné traditional stories and other traditions about the places on the land. Most of you do not understand or speak the Diné language very well, but so what? You can learn enough at least to get the gist of what your Diné-only-speaking elders tell and to recognize reliable English translations of traditional stories recorded long ago. And your progress in learning Diné, however far you get, could make the boarding school story into an empowering story with a victory in the Diné language revived.

NOTES

CHAPTER 1

An earlier version of this chapter was published as "Anthropological Traditions versus Navajo Traditions in Early Navajo History," by Klara Kelley and Harris Francis, in *Diné Bikéyah: Papers in Honor of David M. Brugge*, edited by Meliha S. Duran and David T. Kirkpatrick (Albuquerque: ASNM, 1998), pp. 143–155.

1. Tree-ring dating (dendrochronology) is based on the growth rings that a tree adds under its bark every year of its life and patterns of thick and thin rings that have been linked to events dated by other methods. The date tells when the piece of wood died, not necessarily when people used it (Stokes and Smiley 1996). Radiocarbon dating (carbon-14 or ^{14}C dating) tells when an organism died. All living plants take in ^{14}C from the air, water, and soil, while animals get it from eating plants. After the organism dies, the ^{14}C gradually changes to ^{12}C, and the amount of ^{12}C compared to ^{14}C shows how long ago (Bowman 1990). Different pottery types consistently appear on sites with other dated items within certain limited time ranges. A newer dating method for pottery, not yet widely used, is thermoluminescence, a laboratory technique that can date the time when the pottery was actually fired (Aitken 1985).

2. After World War II, the U.S. government appointed the Indian Claims Commission to adjudicate claims by federally recognized tribes to lands taken from them by the federal government and award monetary compensation for lands that the commission agreed were taken (inevitably far less than each tribe claimed). The U.S. government then planned to abrogate all treaties and "terminate" recognition of tribal sovereignty and treaty obligations. Fortunately, only three tribes suffered the injustice of termination. Research to show the Navajo presence in the tradi-

tional Navajo homeland included locating archaeological sites all over the vast area, oral history interviews with more than 400 Diné elders, and review of masses of colonizer documents.

3.   A study by archaeologists Chip Colwell and T. J. Ferguson (2017) unintentionally shows what a skewed picture of the past can result from ignoring the cultural and archaeological contexts of ambiguous dates. They originally did the study for the Hopi Tribe in a water rights claim against the Navajo Nation, which asserts that the Hopis were in Arizona first (Kelley was an expert for the Navajo Nation in this matter). Oblivious of both Diné wood-use customs and the scholarly consensus (if not always practice) that considers all dates equally worth analyzing in their contexts (Towner 2003:30), Ferguson and Colwell ignored sites that lack clusters or cutting or near-cutting dates. These sites, the smallest and worst preserved, also tend to be earliest. Then they concluded that no good evidence of Navajos in the Little Colorado basin dates before 1760. In contrast, analyzing a larger data set that includes the same sites and considering all dates in their contexts, Kemrer (1974; see also Gilpin 1996; Robinson and Towner 1993) concluded that some sites could date as early as the 1600s to early 1700s.

CHAPTER 2

An earlier version of this chapter originally appeared as Klara Kelley and Harris Francis, "Abalone Shell Buffalo People: Navajo Narrated Routes and Pre-Columbian Archaeological Sites," *New Mexico Historical Review* 78(1) (January 2003): 29–58, © 2003 by the University of New Mexico Board of Regents, all rights reserved. Reprinted by permission (with modifications). We did field research under various Navajo Nation Historic Preservation Department permits, including B99293, C9813E, and C0109E. Lists of the sites on the trail routes are in a confidential manuscript (Kelley and Francis 2000b).

1.   For buffalo (three narratives), see Wheelwright (1958:23); Reichard (1977b:68–71); and Haile (1943:178–217). Antelope (one narrative): Van Valkenburgh (1974:97). Deer (one narrative): Luckert (1975:32–72, 1978). Plant medicine (two narratives): Kelley and Francis (2000a:section 0000, 2001c:section 9701); also buffalo stories cited above. Shell beads (15 narratives): Kelley and Francis (2000a:section kf9701); Wyman (1970:447–459) (cf. Mitchell 1978:180ff.); Wyman (1970:327–333); Clinton (1990:16–17); Luckert and Cooke (1979:para. 2–6, 16–17) (cf. Wheelwright 1956); Richard (1977:26); Haile (1981:162–175); Fishler (1953:91–102); Klah (1942:114–122); Luckert (1977:58–60); O'Bryan (1993:166–175) (cf. Goddard 1933:168–179); Matthews (1897:135–159); Preston (1954:23–27, 98–102). Bighorn sheep (two bead-people narratives): O'Bryan (1993:166–175); Luckert (1977:38–60) (other narratives that do not cross mid-Navajoland place bighorn in the Grand Canyon to the west and along the Continental Divide to the east). Turquoise and miscellaneous items exchanged for it (three narratives): Kluckhohn (1967:158–160, 165–167); O'Bryan

(1993:144, 155–157); Haile (1978:para. 4–10, 127–158); O'Bryan (1993:47–48) (cf. Goddard 1933:127–128).

2.   The routes we discuss in this chapter are specifically for beings who embody shell, big game, plant medicine, turquoise, and related items. Other Diné ceremonial stories delineate other routes for other types of beings outside the routes traced here. For example, Salt Woman, an immortal who controls salt, traveled from the mouth of the Little Colorado River southeast, eventually to Zuni Salt Lake, or from the Emergence Place in southwestern Colorado south down the Black Creek Valley to Zuni and Zuni Salt Lake (Fishler 1953:85–91; Hill 1940a:7–8; Stephen 1930:104; Wheelwright 1993:53–54). Parts of her routes are inside mid-Navajoland but south of the trail zone discussed here. The greater part of Salt Woman's routes lie outside mid-Navajoland. Another story (Haile 1978; O'Bryan 1993:52, 143ff.) traces the travels of Downy Home man, who may embody the macaw. His routes are confined to the region around Chaco, but before he took the name Downy Home Man he originated at Waving Willow, which may be the Mimbres. Precolumbian sites with monumental architecture are at most of the stopping places of both Salt Woman and Downy Home Man.

3.   Other archaeological sites are also on the routes, but the story versions consulted here leave those locations unnamed. The stories also name many more landmarks without known big precolumbian architecture nearby.

4.   Archaeological and ethnohistorical work in western Mexico (Adams 1991:322–326; Anawalt 1997; Vargas 1995) suggests precolumbian trade along the Gulf of California in boats. The trade network may have extended as far south as coastal Ecuador. Traders from there may have sailed as far north as the Gulf of California for *Spondylus* shell to trade to the highland Peruvians for ceremonial offerings. To Anawalt (1997), shaft tombs, pottery, metallurgy, and clothes suggest that certain western Mexican groups, including Tarascans, may have been enclaves of these Ecuadorians. The clothing, incidentally, includes a shell penis cover that can hardly fail to remind one of the humpbacked fluteplayer in precolumbian (trailside?) petroglyphs all over the Colorado Plateau, including the routes described in this chapter. The Tarascans of Michoacán, western Mexico, florescent politically and metallurgically from 1000 to 1500, may have spoken a language related to the Zuni language and the South American Macro-Chibcha family (Adams 1991:324–325). They seem to have been the main source of copper bells in the southwestern United States after 1200 (Vargas 1995). The Allantown site is near the heart of the traditional Zuni land base. The storeroom with the *Spondylus* at Allantown probably dates to 600–900 (before the Tarascan florescence), as do other occurrences of *Spondylus* in the Anasazi region such as Chaco and also the Artificial Leg Site in the Rio Grande valley (Mathien 1997:1153, 1155, 1162). Allantown is in the zone that Salt Woman traveled through on her way to Zuni Salt Lake (see note 2).

5.   The routes may even have delineated hunting territories. For comparison, see post-columbian Chemehuevis (Laird 1976:119).

6. In Navajo and Western Apache clan histories, Deeshchíí'nii and linked clans Tł'ááshchí'í, Tsi'naajinii, and Kinłichíí'nii originated or traveled along the corridor identified with antelope in the Chinle / Pueblo Colorado Wash zone. The Western Apache Deeshchíí'nii clan, perhaps the largest Western Apache clan, as well as Kinłichíí'nii and Kiyaa'áanii, migrated south from Antelope Mesa because of warfare (Fishler 1953:101; Goodwin 1942:614–616; see chapters 4 and 5).

7. Note also high-status individuals at both Chaco (the old part of Pueblo Bonito [Frisbie 1978, 1998]) and the San Francisco Peaks area (Ridge Ruin, Eldon Pueblo [Pilles 1987]), which have similar assemblages of "exotic" items. These goods include labrets, ceremonial wands or canes, and conch shell trumpets, which Frisbie (1998) identifies with specialist long-distance traders from Mesoamerica. Wiegand (2001) reports that Cerrillos turquoise, the most common identified type at Chaco, is also in sites from the same time period on the Mexican west coast and in Yucatán (Chichen Itza).

8. See Gilpin (1994:207); Mathien (1997:1139–1147); Robins and Hays-Gilpin (2000:233–239); Damp and Kotyk (2000:102, 112); Reed et al. (2000:212); Gilpin and Benallie (2000:161–162); Altschul and Huber (2000:146–147); and Lekson (2009:31–70).

CHAPTER 3

This chapter is reprinted, with modifications, from the original article, "Traditional Navajo Maps and Wayfinding," *American Indian Culture and Research Journal* 29(2), by permission of the American Indian Studies Center, UCLA. © 2016 Regents of the University of California. See the original article for a discussion of traditional Diné visual maps and other North American First Nations peoples' traditional maps. We did field research under various permits from the Navajo Nation Historic Preservation Department, including C9813E and C0109E.

1. For examples of verbal maps that describe physiographic zones, especially by presenting them metaphorically as human or animal bodies, see Matthews (1994:113–116) and Williams (2000). For examples of studies of Navajo traditional geography, see Jett (1970, 1997).

2. For examples of larger stories that include the monster-slaying stories, see O'Bryan (1993); Fishler (1953); Matthews (1994); Newcomb and Reichard (1975); Wheelwright (1958); and Wyman (1970a).

3. According to Lyon (1987:27, 40n82), early in 1930 (the year Haile and Slim Curley recorded the story), Sapir's protégé, Harry Hoijer, sent Haile "Herzog's machine," presumably the wax-cylinder phonograph that folklorist George Herzog recommended for field use as late as 1936 with cylinders that could be shaved and reused (Brady 1999:25, 52–88, 122, 212).

4. West of the westernmost cairn, the line meets the zone where the Little Colorado and Colorado Rivers join, a zone with emergence iconography and stories for Navajos, Hopis, Zunis, and Western Apaches (Courlander 1971:14, 30, 58; Ferguson

and Hart 1986:20–21, 126; Fishler 1953:85–88; Forbes 1966:343; Goodwin 1942:607, 628; Kelley and Francis 1993; Klah 1942:69–72). The cairns themselves evoke Mountains One, Two, Three, and Four, which surround the Emergence Place or extend from it in Diné origin stories (Matthews 1994:135; Wyman 1970a:109–138, 169–198, 321–326, 447–459).

5. A grinding slick is a spot or streak of a few inches to more than a foot in length or diameter that has been rubbed smooth on a rock surface. Archaeologists think that these marks result from grinding plants or minerals.

6. See, for example, Colton (1964:93); Gregory (1916:end map); Haile (1981:169–174); Kelly (1970:endmap); Klah (1942:101–106); Kluckhohn (1967:Appendix 4); Newcomb (1940:40–77); and Wyman (1970a:456–457, 630–634).

7. This great-grandfather was Mr. Crawler; Wyman (1975:63) mentions a Mountaintopway ceremony at Black Mountain, Arizona, performed by Mr. Crawler during which a sand painting was recorded.

8. Cairns are common along First Nations trails, both precolumbian and postcolumbian, throughout the southwestern United States, western North America, Mexico, and Peru (Gulliford 2000:72–75; Jett 1994:129–145; Kincaid 1988:Chapter 2).

CHAPTER 4

An earlier version of this chapter was an uncopyrighted technical report entitled "Diné-Anasazi Relations around Ndeelk'id (Long House Valley) and Tséyi' (Tsegi Canyon)," submitted on March 25, 2016, to EcoPlan Associates Inc., Mesa, Arizona. In 2016 we did all fieldwork under a permit from the Navajo Nation Historic Preservation Department (NNHPD), Window Rock, Arizona. Funding for the technical report came from the Federal Highway Administration in connection with construction of a passing lane in the Long House Valley by the Arizona Department of Transportation (ADOT).

1. More details about these and other clans are in the following sources: Begay (2003); Forbes (1966); Franciscan Fathers (1910:424–435); Goddard (1933:165–179); Goodwin (1942: 63–67, 600–628); Haile (1981:169–174); Matthews (1994:135–158); Mitchell (2003, see index under "clans"); Preston (1954:23–27); Reichard (1928); Sapir (1942:81–97); Van Valkenburgh (1974:38, 150–151; 1999:3, 35, 40, 43, 57, 63, 78, 83–84, 103); and Wyman (1970:325–340, 447–459, 634).

2. Anonymous (1938); connections based on Matthews (1994:135–159); Reichard (1928); Goddard (1933); Goodwin (1942); Preston (1954); Sapir (1942); Franciscan Fathers (1910:424–433); Klah (1942); Wyman (1970); Fransted (1979); and Winnie (1982). See also Begay (2003); R. Begay and S. Begay (2003); and O'Hara (2004) for recent corroboration.

3. Bierhorst (1985:17, 1990); Boas (1897); Parmentier (1979:615); Brugge (1968, 1981, 1996a); Towner (2003:13–14); Hill (1937); Reed and Reed (1996:107–108); Torrez-Nez (2003); Kearns (1996); LeBlanc (1999:102, 297–298); Riley (2005:97); Griffith (1983); Baldwin (1997); Carter (2009: 36–37); Matthews (1994:41).

4.   Hopis (Patterson 1994:27–28) and Zunis (Tedlock 1978:226–227) have similar sto-
      ries about pottery and the threat of annihilation.

CHAPTER 5

The fieldwork on which this chapter is based was conducted under several
Navajo Nation Historic Preservation Department permits, including A0904 and
B99293.

1.   The information on Jıłháál and his sites above and below is based on Hubbell
      Trading Post oral histories collected in 1971–72, interviews 4, 21, 36, 44, 45, and
      Brugge (1993b); 1960 records for the Navajo Land Claim (NLC, Navajo oral his-
      tory statements 289, 460, 527, and archaeological site forms for S-MLC-LP-O,
      S-ULC-UP-L, W-CH-UC-I, and W-LLC-MJ-E); Jett (2001:100); and our own
      interviews. Dates for precolumbian sites are from Adler and Johnson (1996).

2.   For more on the Awatobi massacre, see Brugge (1966a, 1985, 1994); Yava (1978:88–
      97); Courlander (1971:175–184, 1982: 55–60); Lomatu'wayma et al. (1993:275–410);
      Whiteley (1996); Kelley and Francis (1998b); Brooks (2016); and Montgomery et
      al. (1949).

3.   Navajo oral histories tell of other attacks at nearby places that have been confused
      with this ambush. One took place at the Big Bend of the Chaco to the east in the
      summer (Newcomb 1964:14). Another took place a few miles south of Narbona
      Pass near Whiskey Lake in the summer of 1860 (Van Valkenburgh 1943).

CHAPTER 6

This chapter is reprinted, with modifications, from *American Indian Culture
and Research Journal* 25(3), by permission of the American Indian Studies Center,
UCLA. © 2016 Regents of the University of California. See the original article
for more details. We did field research under permits C9528E and C98240E from
the Navajo Nation Historic Preservation Department.

1.   The main document source for the material in this chapter is the NLC, archive doc-
      uments. All land records are for AZ T18-22N, R25-31E. We have also relied on inter-
      views with Diné residents of the area around Lupton, Houck, Chambers, Sanders,
      and Navajo, Arizona, that we and Navajo Nation Historic Preservation Department
      staff members conducted between 1994 and 1998 (Kelley and Francis 1998b).

2.   We use the present tense here to signal that we are tracking the story through on-
      the-spot documents and to contrast this material with a section later in the chapter
      that is earlier in time.

3.   NARA, homestead certificate 86, which also covers a spring about 40 miles north-
      east in the Lava (Moqui) Buttes country. According to Father Anselm Weber, "In
      1882 and 1883, Mr. John A. Benson made the official survey of that tract [Lava
      Buttes country], secured title to six springs by placing soldiers' scrip on them. Con-
      victed of land frauds in California, Mr. Benson went into bankruptcy and these

springs were bought, under forced sale, by Chas. L. Day and Daniel Mitchell, partners in business, in 1907 or 1908" (Franciscans, box 27, letter to James McLoughlin, July 20, 1913). Anselm lists six springs in the Lava Buttes country, including the spring covered by homestead certificate 86. Other correspondence in the Franciscan files shows that Day had the spring near the Gabaldon house (Goodluck Spring), and a list unattached to explanatory documentation lists the six Lava Buttes springs plus Goodluck Spring and Cottonwood Seeps in the western Chambers Checkerboard, suggesting that Goodluck and Cottonwood were part of the holdings that Day got from Benson. The Cottonwood Seeps patent also covered Jacob's Well (NARA, homestead file patent 79).

4.   In 1915 Many Horses, age 90, was still living near Navajo Springs, according to the 1915 Navajo Agency census (Paquette 1915:household 8042). Descendants still live near the Chambers Checkerboard (NLC, Navajo oral history, statement 414).

5.   Only three known dependable springs in the Chambers Checkerboard had no houses next to them: Crater (BLM, Historical Index and Homestead Entry microfiche, desert land entry P-252, 1884, lapsed 1895), where the entry person was a speculator in railroad land; Salt Seeps (BLM, Historical Index and Homestead Entry microfiche, homestead entry TC-Prescott-71, 1885, lapsed 1902); and Kiits'iil Spring (NARA, homestead file patents 357896 and 930752), where Kurt Cronemeyer may have had a trading post as early as 1882, though not recorded in the GLO survey. Salt Seeps and Crater were covered by Indian trust patents to individual Navajos after the homestead entries lapsed; Navajo use in the 1880s perhaps prevented houses at these two springs.

6.   Meinig (1971:45); Tinsley (1993:40) says that not until 1885 was the brand registered in Apache County to the Aztec Land and Cattle Company (a railroad subsidiary formed in 1884).

7.   Barnes (1935:213); Granger (1960:13); Hubbell Trading Post, oral history interview 51. Houck left in 1885 and later ran sheep around Winslow (Kelley and Francis fieldnotes 1980, August 7, 1980) or the Mogollon Mountains (Richardson 1986:3–20). Houck committed suicide at Cave Creek, Arizona, on March 21, 1921 (Franciscans, box 19, Houck Mission file).

8.   In 1909 Hastiin Ndaaz was 77 years old and applied for an allotment just northeast of Hill's former homestead, right next to the 1882 field location (Franciscans, box 55, May 1914 allotment map and notebook listing allottees, allotment 54).

CHAPTER 7

This chapter is reprinted, with modifications, from "Indian Giving: Allotments on the Arizona-Navajo Railroad Frontier, 1904–1937," *American Indian Culture and Research Journal* 25(2), by permission of the American Indian Studies Center, UCLA. © 2016 Regents of the University of California. See the original article for more details. We did field research under permits C9528E and C98240E from the Navajo Nation Historic Preservation Department (NNHPD).

1. The main document source for the material in this chapter is the Saint Michaels Franciscan Mission Collection at the University of Arizona. All land records pertain to Arizona T18-21N, R26-31E. We have also relied on interviews with 75 local Navajo and non-Navajo residents of the area around Lupton, Houck, Chambers, Sanders, and Navajo, Arizona, that we and Navajo Nation Historic Preservation Department staff members conducted between 1994 and 1998 (Kelley and Francis 1998b).

2. Sanders Navajos to J. C. Morgan, Navajo Tribal Council delegate, August 13, 1936. See also Navajos of Chambers and Sanders to Senate Committee on Indian Affairs, September 7, 1936. Both letters appear in U.S. Senate, Subcommittee of Committee on Indian Affairs (1937:17,965–17,969).

3. Franciscans, box 26, 1904–07 correspondence, especially Jones to Weber, September 23, 1904. Arthur Chester filed for a homestead at Tanner Springs on March 5, 1907 (BLM, Historical Index and Homestead Entry microfiche, homestead application record 03632). He relinquished it in 1915, probably because the land was part of several hundred square miles that had been placed in trust for the Navajo Tribe by the executive order of August 9, 1907.

4. BLM, Historical Index and Homestead Entry microfiche, and NARA, homestead application records 03753 and 042816, patents 322235 and 989477; applications P-223 and P-723 (McCarrell homesteads), and homestead application record 019906, patent 209505 (Howell); see also homestead application record 013602, patent 539160; and NARA, homestead file patent 539160, for Charles Clark.

5. Franciscans, box 26, letters of August 23, September 19, 1904, October 9, 23, November 1, 21, December 6, 21, 1905, January 10, 15, 23, 29, 1906.

6. Franciscans, box 26, letter of January 6, 1907; see also NLC, archive documents, letters of January 30 and December 21, 1907. One of the would-be allottees, Man the Dog Bit, had served as a "scout" (agency policeman) during the local troubles of the 1880s (see chapter 6).

7. Franciscans, box 26, Jones to Weber, May 13, 1908. This letter mentions earlier correspondence about the irrigation project, a hint that Father Anselm could have heard something about it as early as 1905, when he first asked the U.S. GLO in Phoenix for a map of the township south of Sanders.

8. Franciscans, box 29, Kent letter, November 9, 1908; NLC, archive documents, Harrison to CIA, February 15, 1908, and Stacher to CIA, September 7, 1909; Paquette to Register and Receiver, Santa Fe, January 2, 1909; Paquette to Peterson, February 10, 1909; Paquette to CIA, April 11, 1910; Stacher to U.S. Land Office, Santa Fe, June 26, 1911.

9. NLC, archive documents, Paquette to CIA, July 1 and September 7, 1909; Franciscans, box 29, Peterson letter, August 13, 1909. The irrigation project will apply for right-of-way under the Act of March 3, 1892 (26 Stat. L. 1095). The secretary of the Southwest Development Company around this time was C. M. Sabin of Gallup (Franciscans, box 16, Jones to Weber, July 28, 1917).

10. Franciscans, box 27, letters of December 27, 1909, and January 10, 1910; box 29, Peterson letters, December 23, 1909, January 8, 30, and July 7, 1910; box 26, letters of November 11, 1910, January 14, 1911, and September 19, 1912; box 27, letters of November 22, and December 19, 1910.

11. BLM, Historical Index and Homestead Entry microfiche, entries 1888–1908, total six: one in 1891, two in 1906, and three in 1908; in 1882–87 there were nine (counts include additional homesteads of earlier homesteaders but not refilings because of initial filing error or refilings by heirs of entrypersons who failed to prove up). All figures are for T18-21N, R26-31E.

12. Franciscans, box 26, Jones to Weber, April 16, 1909. Leaseholder is R. R. Pollack for one year starting March 20, 1909. The 1936 letters by Chambers and Sanders Navajos quoted at the beginning of this chapter and our own 1998 interviews point to John McCarrell as the most likely user. Pollack is unidentified, possibly a lawyer or other professional advisor to McCarrell.

13. Franciscans, box 26, letters of May 16, 1911 and April 25, June 17, November 25, 1912; NLC, archive documents, Paquette to CIA, June 22, 1912. The most recent leaseholder was Julius Wetzler, a local Holbrook rancher who had owned the Bidahochee trading post in the Lava Buttes country northwest of the Chambers Checkerboard from 1888 to 1892 (Granger 1960:235). He could have sublet the land to John McCarrell.

14. Franciscans, box 27, Tallman to Secretary of the Interior, August 27, 1915, endorsed September 17, 1915 by CIA; Weber to Hauke, September 4, 1915; box 26, Weber to Jones, August 3, 1916; NARA, Indian allotment patent 743464, GLO inspector report, October 5, 1916.

15. Franciscans, box 29, Simington letters, February 28, May 31, 1919; box 27, letter of March 18, 1919; box 26, letter of February 28, 1919; see also Delgado letter to GLO Commissioner, July 16, 1919; BLM, Historical Index and Homestead Entry microfiche, T18-21N, R26-31E. See also Franciscans, box 27, Paquette to CIA, July 17, 1920; Paquette recommends leasing railroad lands, mostly in New Mexico, and also T22-23N, R29-31E, and T19-20N R28E. These (except T19-20N R28E) are among the railroad lands added to the Navajo Reservation in 1934. Franciscans, box 27, Paquette to Troester, March 21, 1922, indicates that the Indian Office actually did pay for such leases.

16. Franciscans, box 27, Paquette to Troester, March 21, 1922; box 26, Jones to Haile, January 23, February 26, 1925, Trockur to Jones, March 8, 1925, and Duclos to Jones, June 10, 1925. In 1924 railroad lands in the Silversmith family townships were leased in the name of Peter Paquette for about $280 each (Franciscans, box 26, Jones to CIA, June 11, 1925).

17. BLM, Historical Index and Homestead Entry microfiche, T18-21N, R26-31E; NARA, Indian allotment files. A sample of 16 allottees chosen from all parts of the Chambers Checkerboard and representing the main groups of extended families suggests that about half the allottees were to receive lieu allotments. See

especially list of October 26, 1935, CIA to Secretary of the Interior, in NARA, Indian allotment patent 743464.

CHAPTER 8

An earlier version of this chapter was published under the same title in *Southwestern Interludes: Papers in Honor of Charlotte J. and Theodore R. Frisbie*, edited by Regge N. Wiseman, Thomas C. O'Laughlin, and Cordelia T. Snow (Archaeological Society of New Mexico Papers 32, 2006), pp. 87–102. We did field research under permit C0420E from the Navajo Nation Historic Preservation Department (NNHPD). A list of Diné traders that includes those after 1950 is in an appendix to our Navajoland trading post encyclopedia (Kelley and Francis 2018). Both the 2006 article and the encyclopedia are based on an online precursor of the encyclopedia (Kelley and Francis 2006–2017).

1. See Frisbie (2001) for a discussion and bibliography; other life histories published later include Holiday and McPherson (2005); Lamphere (2007); McCloskey (2007); Holiday and McPherson (2012); McPherson et al. (2012); Nez (2012); and Tohe (2012). Martin (2002) and Denetdale (2007) offer family biographies.
2. This information is taken from Eric Henderson's field notes of 1975–76. Personal communications to Klara Kelley, August 8 and 18, 2013. These notes are in the authors' possession. See also Henderson (1985).

CHAPTER 9

We did most of the fieldwork for this chapter for a project of Zuni Cultural Resources Enterprise (ZCRE) and the Navajo Nation Historic Preservation Department Roads Planning Section (permit no. NABR 89-188.18). Our original work was reported in Kelley and Francis (2005a).

1. The trading post is listed on the National Register. Sources for most information in this chapter are our original report (Kelley and Francis 2005a) and the National Register nomination form (Makeda and Kelley 2010).
2. The archaeological traces of the silversmithing structures were part of archaeological site NM-Q-25-52, which also includes precolumbian remains. ZCRE conducted archaeological testing and excavations at this site (Dongoske and Quam 2005; Ruppé et al. 1999).

CHAPTER 10

This chapter is based on an uncopyrighted report for PaleoWest Archaeology, Phoenix, which became a chapter in a larger report for the U.S. Bureau of Reclamation's Navajo-Gallup Water Supply Project (Gilpin et al. 2017). The report includes a more detailed analysis of land and census data. We did field research under a permit from the Navajo Nation Historic Preservation Department issued to PaleoWest.

1. In 2015 we consulted 41 people in and near Gallup, most of them Diné, as well as readily available local and regional archives.

2. The source consists of typed responses to an interviewer's prepared questions, which are presumed (based on internal evidence) to be by Herbert Stacher.

3. When it granted the allotments, the U.S. government reserved the coal rights for itself, so it collected the royalties, and the allottees got nothing (NARA, Indian allotment patent files, T15-16N, R19-21W). However, in the 1980s, as Kelley has witnessed, Diné sued Washindoon for improperly reserving the coal rights (*Etcitty v. United States*). The settlement of this suit in the 1990s gave the allottees a share of the royalties.

CHAPTER 11

This chapter is based partly on interviews between 2001 and 2014 for an interdisciplinary project of the U.S. Geological Survey, Flagstaff, Arizona, directed by Margaret Hiza Redsteer. We did fieldwork under permits C0108E and C0204E from the Navajo Nation Historic Preservation Department.

1. In 1880 Fort Defiance agent F. T. Bennett estimated that Navajos produced 900,000 pounds of wool (McNitt 1962:80), which suggests 225,000 or more sheep and goats, assuming two pounds per animal for each of two shearings a year (shears were inefficient, some being tin can lids). That would be more than three times as many pounds as the (fragmentary) records show the agency had distributed by 1872 (Brugge 1980:52–72, 118–121; Young 1961:146). Many Diné got more sheep by trading their annuity goods, presumably with Zunis, other Puebloans, and Hispanos (Brugge 1980:56, 60).

2. Besides the two Black Creek Valley districts (Agency and Saint Michaels / Railroad / Zuni) and Ganado, the 1915 census had a fourth district, Chinle. The Chinle district had about the same percentage of herdless households as the lower Black Creek Valley (Saint Michaels district), and, as in the Black Creek Valley, most were mature households. But in the Chinle district, more than two-thirds of these households had farms of two or more acres, whereas in the Black Creek Valley, only one-quarter had farms. The Ganado district was probably more typical of Navajoland beyond the Black Creek Valley / Manuelito Plateau (Gallup) area; see Gregory (1916:22–49).

3. This area is north of the railroad grant in New Mexico but has a similar patchwork of small parcels with different types of ownership, including allotted, federal, state, and deeded.

BIBLIOGRAPHY

BOOKS, ARTICLES, AND MANUSCRIPTS

Aberle, David M. 1982. *The Peyote Religion among the Navajo*. 2nd enlarged ed. Chicago: Aldine.

Adair, John. 1944. *The Navajo and Pueblo Silversmiths*. Norman: University of Oklahoma Press.

Adams, E. Charles. 1991. *The Origin and Development of the Pueblo Katsina Cult*. Tucson: University of Arizona Press.

Adams, Eleanor B., ed. 1963. Fray Silvestre and the Obstinate Hopi. *New Mexico Historical Review* 38(2):98–138.

Adams, Richard E. W. 1991. *Prehistoric Mesoamerica*. Rev. ed. Norman: University of Oklahoma Press.

Adler, Michael, and Amber Johnson. 1996. Mapping the Puebloan Southwest. In *The Prehistoric Pueblo World, A.D. 1150–1350*, edited by Michael A. Adler, pp.255–266 Tucson: University of Arizona Press.

Aitken, M. J. 1985. *Thermoluminescence Dating*. Orlando, FL: Academic Press.

Allen, James B. 1966. *The Company Town in the American West*. Norman: University of Oklahoma Press.

Allen, Kristen. 2017. I Won This Battle. *Navajo Times*. April 6:A-1.

Altschul, Jeffrey H., and Edgar K. Huber. 2000. Economics, Site Structure, and Social Organization during the Basketmaker III Period: A View from Lukachukai Valley. In *Foundations of Anasazi Culture*, edited by Paul F. Reed, pp.145–160 Salt Lake City: University of Utah Press.

Amsden, Charles Avery. 1949. *Prehistoric Southwesterners from Basketmaker to Pueblo*. Los Angeles: Southwest Museum.

Anawalt, Patricia Rieff. 1997. Traders of the Ecuadorian Littoral. *Archaeology* 50(6):48–52.

Anderson, Gary Clayton. 1999. *The American Southwest, 1580–1820: Ethnogenesis and Reinvention*. Norman: University of Oklahoma Press.

Anderson, Lorena. 2018. Táchii'nii Clan Story. *Leading the Way* 16(9):10.

Anderson, Michael F. 2000. National Register of Historic Places Nomination Form for Rough Rock Trading Post (draft). Manuscript on file, Cultural Resources Compliance Section, Navajo Nation Historic Preservation Department, Window Rock, AZ.

Anonymous. 1938. Clan Membership—Navajo Reservation. Def. Ex. 2634, *Masayesva v. Zah*. Manuscript on file, Navajo Nation Justice Department, Window Rock, AZ.

Antram, Cormac. 1998. *Laborers of the Harvest*. Saint Michaels, AZ: Franciscan Fathers.

Archaeology Southwest. 2017. What We Do: Investigations; Social Networks in the Late Precontact Southwest. www.archaeologysouthwest.org/what-we-do/investigations/ networks (accessed March 16, 2017).

Arrington, Leonard. 1979. The John Tanner Family. *Ensign*. March 1979.

Ashley, George H. 1918. *Cannel Coal in the United States*. Bulletin 659, U.S. Geological Survey, https://pubs.usgs.gov/Bul/0659/report.pdf (accessed December 16, 2016).

Austin, Raymond D. 2009. *Navajo Courts and Navajo Common Law: A Tradition of Tribal Self-Governance*. Minneapolis: University of Minnesota Press.

Bahr, Howard M., ed. 2004. *The Navajo as Seen by the Franciscans, 1898–1921: A Source Book*. Lanham, MD: Scarecrow Press.

Bailey, Garrick, and Roberta Glenn Bailey. 1982. *Historic Navajo Occupation of the Northern Chaco Plateau*. Tulsa, OK: Faculty of Anthropology, University of Tulsa.

———. 1999. *A History of the Navajos: The Reservation Years*. Rev. ed. Santa Fe, NM: School of American Research Press.

Bailey, Lynn. 1964. *The Long Walk: A History of the Navajo Wars, 1846–1868*. Los Angeles: Westernlore Press.

———. 1973. *Indian Slave Trade in the Southwest*. Los Angeles: Westernlore Press.

Baldwin, Stuart J. 1997. Apacheans Bearing Gifts: Prehispanic Influence on the Pueblo Indians. *Arizona Archaeologist* 29. Arizona Archaeological Society.

Barbujani, Guido. 1997. Invited Editorial: DNA Variation and Language Affinities. *American Journal of Human Genetics* 61:1011–1014.

Barnes, Will C. 1935. *Arizona Place Names*. Tucson: University of Arizona Press.

Barth, Frederik. 1998. *Ethnic Groups and Boundaries*. Reprint. Prospect Heights, IL: Waveland Press.

Bartlett, Katharine. 1940. How Don Pedro de Tovar Discovered the Hopi and Don Garcia Lopez de Cardenas Saw the Grand Canyon, with Notes upon Their Probable Route. *Plateau* 12(January):37–45.

———. 1942. Notes upon the Route of Espejo and Farfan to the Mines in the Sixteenth Century. *New Mexico Historical Review* 17(1):21–36.

Beale, Edwin F. 1929. Surveys for a Wagon Road from Fort Defiance to the Colorado River. 35th Cong., 1st sess., House Ex. Doc. 124, 1858. In *Uncle Sam's Camels: The Journal of May Humphreys Stacey, Supplemented by the Report of Edward Fitzgerald Beale (1857–1858)*, edited by Lewis Burt Lesley. Cambridge, MA: Harvard University Press.

Begay, Richard M., and Steven Begay. 2003. *Nihikék'eh Nahazʼą́: Our Place in This Land.* Window Rock, AZ: Navajo Nation Historic Preservation Department.

Begay, Richard M., and Alexa Roberts. 2003. Hane' Nazt'i: Webs of Meaning across the Grand Canyon Landscape. Paper presented at the 53rd Annual Meeting of the Society for American Archaeology, Phoenix, AZ.

Begay, Robert M. 2003. Exploring Navajo-Anaasází Relationships Using Traditional (Oral) Histories. MA thesis, Northern Arizona University, Flagstaff.

Begay, Yolanda. 2014. Historic Demographic Changes That Impact the Future of the Diné and the Development of Community-Based Policy. In *Diné Perspectives: Revitalizing and Reclaiming Navajo Thought,* edited by Lloyd L. Lee, pp. 105–128. Tucson: University of Arizona Press.

Benally, AnCita. 2006. Diné Binahatʼáʼ, Navajo Government. PhD diss., Arizona State University, Phoenix.

Benally, Clyde, Andrew O. Wiget, John R. Alley, and Garry Blake. 1982. *Dinéjí Nákéé' Nááhane': A Utah Navajo History.* Monticello, UT: San Juan School District.

Benally, Malcolm. 2011. *Bitter Water: Diné Oral Histories of the Navajo-Hopi Land Dispute.* Tucson: University of Arizona Press.

Benedek, Emily. 1992. *The Wind Won't Know Me: A History of the Navajo-Hopi Land Dispute.* New York: Vintage Books.

———. 1995. *Beyond the Four Corners of the World: A Navajo Woman's Journey.* New York: Alfred A. Knopf.

Benedict, Ruth. 1981 [1931]. *Tales of the Cochiti Indians.* Reprint. Albuquerque: University of New Mexico Press.

Bennett, Edna Mae. 1966. *Turquoise and the Indian.* Denver, CO: Sage Books.

Bennett, Kay. 1964. *Kaibah: Recollections of a Navajo Girlhood.* Los Angeles: Westernlore Press.

Berkholz, Richard. 2007. *Old Trading Posts of the Four Corners: A Guide to Early-Day Trading Posts Established on or around the Navajo, Hopi, and Ute Mountain Ute Reservations.* Lake City, CO: Western Reflections.

Berlant, Tony, Evan Maurer, Cristine Van Pool, and Thomas Wynn. 2017. Decoding Mimbres Painting. https://cognitivearchaeologyblog.wordpress.com/tag/datura (accessed March 14, 2017).

Bierhorst, John. 1985. *The Mythology of North America.* New York: William Morrow.

———. 1990. *The Mythology of Mexico and Central America.* New York: William Morrow.

Bingham, Sam, and Janet Bingham. 1987. *Navajo Chapters.* Rev. ed. Tsaile, AZ: Navajo Community College Press.

———. 1994. *Between Sacred Mountains: Navajo Stories and Lessons from the Land.* Tucson: Sun Tracks and University of Arizona Press.

Bitsoi, Alastair Lee. 2015. Allottees in Oil-Rich Land Oppose Grassroots Interference. *Navajo Times.* June 4:A-3.

Black Mesa Water Coalition. 2016. Solar potential on the Navajo Nation, www.blackmesawatercoalition.org (accessed December 16, 2016).

Blaikie, Piers. 1994. *The Political Economy of Soil Erosion in Developing Countries*. Reprint. Essex, UK: Longman Scientific & Technical; New York: John Wiley and Sons.

Blakeslee, Donald J., Douglas K. Boyd, Richard Flint, Judith Habicht-Mauche, Nancy P. Hickerson, Jack T. Hughes, and Carrol L. Riley. 2003. Bison Hunters of the Llano in 1541: A Panel Discussion. In *The Coronado Expedition, from the Distance of 460 Years*, edited by Richard Flint and Shirley Cushing Flint, pp. 164–186. Albuquerque: University of New Mexico Press.

Blue, Martha. 1988. *Witch Purge of 1878*. Tsaile, AZ: Navajo Community College Press.

———. 2000. *Indian Trader: The Life and Times of J. L. Hubbell*. Walnut, CA: Kiva Press.

Boas, Franz. 1897. Northern Elements in the Mythology of the Navaho. *American Anthropologist* 10 (old series):371–376.

Borgman, Francis. 1948. Henry Chee Dodge, the Last Chief of the Navaho Indians. *New Mexico Historical Review* 23(2):81–93.

Bourke, John G. 1984. *Snake Dance of the Moqui*. Reprint. Tucson: University of Arizona Press.

Bowman, Sheridan. 1990. *Radiocarbon Dating*. Berkeley: University of California Press; London: British Museum.

Bowman, Terry. 2017. Tribal Utility Launches Renewable Energy Program. *Navajo Times*. August 3:A-7.

Brady, Erika. 1999. *A Spiral Way: How the Phonograph Changed Ethnography*. Jackson: University of Mississippi Press.

Bradley, Ronna Jean Earthman. 1996. The Role of Casas Grandes in Prehistoric Shell Exchange Networks within the Southwest. PhD diss., Arizona State University, Tempe.

———. 2000. Networks of Shell Ornament Exchange: A Critical Assessment of Prestige Economies in the North American Southwest. In *The Archaeology of Regional Interaction: Religion, Warfare, and Exchange across the American Southwest and Beyond*, edited by Michelle Hegmon, pp.167–188. Boulder: University Press of Colorado.

Brooks, James F. 2002. *Captives and Cousins: Slavery, Kinship, and Community in the Southwest Borderlands*. Chapel Hill: University of North Carolina Press.

———. 2016. *Mesa of Sorrows: A History of the Awat'ovi Massacre*. New York: W. W. Norton.

Brotherston, Gordon. 1992. *Book of the Fourth World: Reading the Native Americas through the Literature*. New York: Cambridge University Press.

Brown, Gary M. 1996. The Protohistoric Transition in the Northern San Juan Region. In *The Archaeology of Navajo Origins*, edited by Ronald H. Towner, pp. 47–69. Salt Lake City: University of Utah Press.

Brugge, David M. 1963. Documentary Reference to a Navajo Naach'id in 1840. *Ethnohistory* 10(2):146.

———. 1964. Vizcarra's Navajo Campaign of 1823. *Arizona and the West* 6(3):223–244.

———. 1966a. Events in Navajo History: Origin of the Ma'iidesgizhnii Clan. *Navajo Times* 7(23):9.

———. 1966b. Navajo Use and Occupation of Lands North of the San Juan River in Present-Day Utah to 1935. MS on file, NLC Collection, cabinet 7, drawer 2 from top, Navajo Nation Library, Window Rock, AZ.

———. 1968. Pueblo Influence on Navajo Architecture. *El Palacio* 75(Autumn):14–20.

———. 1969. Pueblo Factionalism and External Relations. *Ethnohistory* 16(2):191–200.

———. 1970. *Zarcillos Largos, Courageous Advocate of Peace.* Navajo Historical Publications 2, Research Section, Navajo Parks and Recreation. Window Rock, AZ: Navajo Tribe.

———. 1980. *A History of the Chaco Navajos.* Santa Fe, NM: National Park Service.

———. 1981. *Navajo Pottery and Ethnohistory.* Navajo Nation Papers in Anthropology 4. Rev. ed. Window Rock, AZ: Navajo Nation Cultural Resource Management Program.

———. 1983. Navajo History to 1850. In *Southwest*, edited by Alfonso Ortiz, pp. 489–501. Handbook of North American Indians, Vol. 10, William C. Sturtevant, general editor. Washington, D.C.: Smithsonian Institution Press.

———. 1989. Who Were They and When Were They Where? Paper presented at New Mexico Archaeological Council conference, Albuquerque, NM.

———. 1992. Thoughts on the Significance of Navajo Traditions in View of Newly Discovered Early Athabaskan Archaeology North of the San Juan River. In *Why Museums Collect: Papers in Honor of Joe Ben Wheat*, edited by Meliha S. Duran and David T. Kirkpatrick, pp. 31–38. Archaeological Society of New Mexico No. 19. Albuquerque: Archaeological Society of New Mexico.

———. 1993a. *Hubbell Trading Post National Historic Site.* Tucson: Southwest Parks and Monuments Association.

———. 1993b. Traditional History of Wide Reed. Appendix 1 in *Wide Reed Ruin*, by James E. Mount, Stanley J. Olsen, John W. Olsen, George A. Teague, and B. Dean Treadwell. Professional Paper No. 51. Santa Fe, NM: Southwest Cultural Resources Center, National Park Service.

———. 1994. *The Navajo-Hopi Land Dispute.* Albuquerque: University of New Mexico Press.

———. 1995. El derrotero del Padre Tomas Ignacio Lizasoain: Desde Janos a Moque en 1761. *Colonial Latin American Historical Review* 4(4) Fall:465–475.

———. 1996a. Navajo Caches of the Dinetah. In *La Jornada: Papers in Honor of William F. Turney*, edited by Meliha S. Duran and David T. Kirkpatrick, pp. 33–45. Archaeological Society of New Mexico No. 22. Albuquerque: Archaeological Society of New Mexico.

———. 1996b. The Twin Figurines of Frances Canyon. Manuscript on file, U.S. Bureau of Reclamation, Upper Colorado Regional Office, Salt Lake City, and Museum of Indian Arts and Culture / Laboratory of Anthropology, Museum of New Mexico, Santa Fe.

———. 2006. When Were the Navajos? In *Southwestern Interludes: Papers in Honor of Charlotte J. and Theodore R. Frisbie*, edited by Regge N. Wiseman, Thomas C.

O'Laughlin, and Cordelia T. Snow, pp. 45–52. Archaeological Society of New Mexico Papers 32. Albuquerque: Archaeological Society of New Mexico.

———. 2012. Emergence of the Navajo People. In *From the Land of Ever Winter to the American Southwest: Athapaskan Migrations, Mobility, and Ethnogenesis*, edited by Deni J. Seymour, pp. 124–149. Salt Lake City: University of Utah Press.

Brugge, David M., and Raymond Wilson. 1976. *Administrative History of Canyon de Chelly National Monument*. NPS Report 577. Washington, D.C.: National Park Service.

Brugge, David M., Ives Goddard, and Willem de Reuse. 1983. Synonymy. Appendix to "Navajo Prehistory and History to 1850" by David M. Brugge. In *Southwest*, edited by Alfonso Ortiz, pp. 496–500. Handbook of North American Indians, Vol. 10, William C. Sturtevant, general editor. Washington, D.C.: Smithsonian Institution Press.

Brugge, Doug, Timothy Benally, and Esther Yazzie-Lewis. 2006. *The Navajo People and Uranium Mining*. Albuquerque: University of New Mexico Press.

Byrkit, James W. 1988. The Palatkwapi Trail. *Plateau* 59(4).

Campbell, Lyle. 1997. *American Indian Languages: The Historical Linguistics of Native America*. New York: Oxford University Press.

Carlyle, Shawn W., Ryan L. Parr, M. Geoffrey Hayes, and Dennis H. O'Rourke. 2000. Context of Maternal Lineages in the Greater Southwest. *American Journal of Physical Anthropology* 113(1):85–102.

Carter, William B. 2009. *Indian Alliances and the Spanish in the Southwest, 750–1750*. Norman: University of Oklahoma Press.

Castaneda, Pedro de. 1990. *The Journey of Coronado*. Translated by George Parker Winship. Reprint. New York: Dover.

Chenoweth, William J. 1990. *Uranium Occurrences on the Zhealy Tso Mining Permit near Chinle, Apache County, Arizona*. Contributed Report 90-B, Arizona Geological Survey. http://repository.azgs.az/gov/sites/default/files/dlio/files/2010/u15/CR-90-B.pdf (accessed May 20, 2016).

Clifford, Casey Jones, Sr. 2017. Carrying Our History Forward. *Leading the Way* 15(1):14–18.

Clinton, Alvin. 1990. Interview. In "I Am a Child of This Sacred Land," by the Teesto Navajos Affected by the Relocation Efforts. Manuscript on file, Navajo Hopi Land Commission, Window Rock, AZ.

Colby, Clint. 1972. Persons at Hubbell Trading Posts. Manuscript on file, Hubbell Papers, Special Collection AZ 2375, University of Arizona Library, Tucson.

Collman, Robert Christie. 1975. Navajo Scouts, 1873–1895: An Integration of Various Cultural Interpretations of Events. Senior paper, Franconia College, Franconia, NH.

Colton, Harold S. 1964. Principal Hopi Trails. *Plateau* 36:91–94.

Colwell, Chip, and T. J. Ferguson. 2017. Tree-Ring Dates and Navajo Settlement Patterns in Arizona. *American Antiquity* 82(1):25–49.

Comfort, Mary Apolline. 1980. *Rainbow to Yesterday: The John and Louisa Wetherill Story*. New York: Vantage Press.

Condie, Carol, and Ruthann Knudson, eds. 1982. *The Cultural Resources of the Proposed New Mexico Generating Station Study Area, San Juan Basin, New Mexico.* Publication 39. Albuquerque, NM: Quivira Research Center.

Cooley, H. B. 1923. *Story of a Complete Modern Coal Mine.* Reprint in booklet form of a series of articles in *Coal Age.* August–September.

Cordell, Linda S. 1979. Prehistory: Eastern Anasazi. In *Southwest*, edited by Alfonso Ortiz, pp. 131–151. Handbook of North American Indians, Vol. 9, William C. Sturtevant, general editor. Washington, D.C.: Smithsonian Institution Press.

———. 1984. *Prehistory of the Southwest.* Orlando, FL: Academic Press.

Cordell, Linda S., and Maxine E. McBrinn. 2012. *Archaeology of the Southwest.* 3rd ed. Walnut Creek, CA: Left Coast Press.

Correll, J. Lee. 1971. Navajo Frontiers in Utah and Troublous Times in Monument Valley. *Utah Historical Quarterly* 39(2):145–161.

———. 1976. *Through White Men's Eyes, Vol. 1.* Window Rock, AZ: Navajo Nation Museum.

Correll, J. Lee, and Alfred Dehiya. 1978. *Anatomy of the Navajo Indian Reservation: How It Grew.* Rev. ed. Window Rock, AZ: Navajo Times.

Coues, Eliott, trans., ed., and annotator. 1900. *On the Trail of a Spanish Pioneer: The Diary and Itinerary of Francisco Garcés, in His Travels through Sonora, Arizona, and California, 1775–1776.* 2 vols. New York: Francis P. Harper.

Courlander, Harold, ed. 1971. *The Fourth World of the Hopis.* New York: Thomas Crown.

———. 1982. *Hopi Voices.* Albuquerque: University of New Mexico Press.

Creer, Leland Hargrave. 1958. *Mormon Towns in the Region of the Colorado.* Anthropological Paper 32. Salt Lake City: Department of Anthropology, University of Utah.

Cronk, Lynn. 1989. *Excavations at a Twentieth-Century Trading Post (LA 20237), San Juan County, NM.* Note 498. Santa Fe: Laboratory of Anthropology, Museum of New Mexico.

Cummings, Byron. 1915. Kivas of the San Juan Drainage. *American Anthropologist* 17:272–282.

Curley, Andrew. 2014. The Origin of Legibility: Rethinking Colonialism and Resistance among the Navajo People, 1868–1937. In *Diné Perspectives: Revitalizing and Reclaiming Navajo Thought*, edited by Lloyd L. Lee, pp. 129–150. Tucson: University of Arizona Press.

Cushing, Frank Hamilton, and Barton Wright. 1988. *The Mythic World of the Zuni.* Albuquerque: University of New Mexico Press.

Dalrymple, Larry. 2013. Stewart Hatch: A Lifetime Trading with the Navajo and Ute. *Journal of the Southwest* 55(4):495–505.

Damp, Jonathan E., and Edward M. Kotyk. 2000. Socioeconomic Organization of a Late Basketmaker III Community in the Mexican Springs Area, Southern Chuska Mountains, New Mexico. In *Foundations of Anasazi Culture*, edited by Paul F. Reed, pp.95–114. Salt Lake City: University of Utah Press.

Davis, Anselm G., Jr. 2017. Education as if Being Diné Mattered. *Leading the Way* 15(3):16–18.

d'Azevedo, Warren L., ed. 1986. *Great Basin*. Handbook of North American Indians, Vol. 11, William C. Sturtevant, general editor. Washington, D.C.: Smithsonian Institution Press.

Dean, Jeffrey S., Robert C. Euler, George J. Gumerman, Fred Plog, Richard H. Hevly, and Thor N. V. Karlstrom. 1985. Human Behavior, Demography, and Paleoenvironment on the Colorado Plateau. *American Antiquity* 50(3):537–554.

Denetclaw, Pauly. 2017. Tribe May Be Ready to Allow Genetic Research. *Navajo Times*. September 14.

Denetdale, Jennifer Nez. 2007. *Reclaiming Diné History: The Legacies of Navajo Chief Manuelito and Juanita*. Tucson: University of Arizona Press.

———. 2014. The Role of Oral History on the Path to Diné/Navajo Sovereignty. In *Diné Perspectives: Revitalizing and Reclaiming Navajo Thought*, edited by Lloyd L. Lee, pp.68–82. Tucson: University of Arizona Press.

———. 2017. Introduction. In *Navajo Sovereignty: Understandings and Visions of the Dine People*, edited by Lloyd Lee, pp. 3–16. Tucson: University of Arizona Press.

de Reuse, Willem. 1983. Synonymy. Appendix to "The Apachean Culture Pattern and Its Origins," by Morris E. Opler. In *Southwest*, edited by Alfonso Ortiz, pp. 385–392. Handbook of North American Indians, Vol. 10, William C. Sturtevant, general editor. Washington, D.C.: Smithsonian Institution Press.

Dick, Herbert. 1965. *Bat Cave*. Monograph 27. Santa Fe, NM: School of American Research Press.

Dietrich, R. V. 2015. GEMROCKS Index. www.stoneplus.cst.emich.edu/jct/htm (accessed March 9, 2017).

Diné of the Eastern Region of the Navajo Reservation. 1991. *Oral History Stories of the Long Walk = Hweeldi Baá Hane*. Collected and recorded by Patty Chee, Milanda Yazzie, Judy Benally, Marie Etsitty, and Bessie C. Henderson, Lake Valley Navajo School, White Rock, NM, 1991. Reprint. Ann Arbor: University of Michigan Library.

Dongoske, Kurt E., and Donovan K. Quam. 2005. *Phase II Data Recovery at Sites NM-Q-25-51 and NM-Q-25-52 along County Road 19, Borrego Pass, McKinley County, New Mexico*. Report No. 834. Zuni, NM: Zuni Cultural Resource Enterprise.

Douglas, John E. 2000. Exchanges, Assumptions, and Mortuary Goods in Pre-Paquime Chihuahua, Mexico. In *The Archaeology of Regional Interaction: Religion, Warfare, and Exchange across the American Southwest and Beyond*, edited by Michelle Hegmon, pp.189–200. Boulder: University Press of Colorado.

Downer, Alan S., Richard Begay, Harris Francis, Klara B. Kelley, and Alexandra Roberts. 1988. *Navajo Nation Historic Preservation Plan Pilot Study: Identification of Cultural and Historic Properties in Seven Arizona Chapters of the Navajo Nation*. Window Rock, AZ: Navajo Nation Historic Preservation Department.

Downum, Christian E., ed. 2012. *Hisat'sinom: Ancient People in a Land without Water*. Santa Fe, NM: School for Advanced Research Press.

Doyel, David E. 1991. Hohokam Exchange and Interaction. In *Chaco and Hohokam: Prehistoric Regional Systems in the American Southwest*, edited by Patricia L. Crown and W. James Judge, pp.225–252. Santa Fe, NM: School of American Research Press.

Duff, Andrew I. 2002. *Western Pueblo Identities: Regional Interaction, Migration, and Transformation.* Tucson: University of Arizona Press.

Dunbar-Ortiz, Roxanne. 2014. *An Indigenous Peoples' History of the United States.* Boston: Beacon Press.

Echo-Hawk, Walter R. 1993. Native American Religious Liberty: Five Hundred Years after Columbus. *American Indian Culture and Research Journal* 17(3):33–52.

Eichstaedt, Peter H. 1994. *If You Poison Us: Native Americans and Uranium.* Santa Fe, NM: Red Crane Books.

Elson, Mark D., and Michael H. Ort. 2012. Fire in the Sky: The Eruption of Sunset Crater Volcano. In *Hisat'sinom: Ancient Peoples in a Land without Water,* edited by Christian E. Downum, pp. 27–34. Santa Fe, NM: School for Advanced Research Press.

Emerson, Larry. 2014. Dine Culture, Decolonization, and the Politics of Hózhǫ́. In *Diné Perspectives: Revitalizing and Reclaiming Navajo Thought,* edited by Lloyd L. Lee, pp. 68–82. Tucson: University of Arizona Press.

Engler, Thomas W., Brian S. Brister, Her-Yuan Chen, and Lawrence W. Teufel. 2001. *Oil and Gas Resource Development for the San Juan Basin, New Mexico.* Albuquerque, NM: U.S. Bureau of Land Management, Albuquerque Field Office. www.blm.gov (accessed December 16, 2016).

Espinosa, Jose Manuel. 1934. The Legend of Sierra Azul. *New Mexico Historical Review* 9(2):113–158, 228.

Etsedi, Peshlakai. 1937. The "Long Walk" to Bosque Redondo. Recorded by Sallie Brewer. *Museum Notes* 9(11). Flagstaff: Museum of Northern Arizona.

Evans, Will. 2005. *Along Navajo Trails.* Edited by Susan E. Woods and Robert S. McPherson. Logan: Utah State University Press.

Fall, Patricia L., James A. McDonald, and Pamela C. Magers. 1981. *The Canyon del Muerto Survey Project: Anasazi and Navajo Archaeology in Northeastern Arizona.* Western Archaeological Center Publication in Anthropology 15. Tucson: National Park Service.

Family Search. n.d. Maraboots Life Summary. https://familysearch.org/photos/stories/937712 (accessed April 21, 2015).

Fanale, Rosalie. 1982. Navajoland and Land Management: A Century of Change. PhD diss., Catholic University, Washington, D.C.

Farella, John R. 1984. *The Main Stalk: A Synthesis of Navajo Philosophy.* Tucson: University of Arizona Press.

Faris, James C. 1990. *The Nightway: A History and a History of Documentation of a Navajo Ceremonial.* Albuquerque: University of New Mexico Press.

Fassett, James E. 2013. *The San Juan Basin, a Complex Giant Gas Field, New Mexico and Colorado.* www.searchanddiscovery.com (accessed April 21, 2015).

Federal Trade Commission. 1973. *The Trading Post System on the Navajo Reservation: Staff Report to the Federal Trade Commission.* Washington, D.C.: U.S. Government Printing Office.

Ferguson, T. J., and Richard Hart. 1986. *Zuni Atlas.* Norman: University of Oklahoma Press.

Fewkes, Jesse Walter. 1898. Archaeological Expedition to Arizona in 1895. In *Seventeenth Annual Report of the Bureau of American Ethnology, 1895–1896, Part 2*. Washington, D.C.: Smithsonian Institution Press.

———. 1900. Tusayan Migration Traditions. *Nineteenth Annual Report of the Bureau of American Ethnology, 1897–1898, Part 2*, pp. 573–634. Washington, D.C.: Smithsonian Institution Press.

———. 1919. Designs on Prehistoric Hopi Pottery. In *33rd Annual Report of the Bureau of American Ethnology*, pp. 207–284. Washington, D.C.: U.S. Government Printing Office.

Fishler, Stanley A. 1953. *In the Beginning: A Navaho Creation*. Anthropological Paper 13. Salt Lake City: University of Utah Press.

Foley, John Miles. 1988. *The Theory of Oral Composition*. Bloomington: Indiana University Press.

———. 1995. *The Singer of Tales in Performance*. Bloomington: Indiana University Press.

Forbes, Jack D. 1966. The Early Western Apache, 1300–1700. *Journal of the West* 5(3):336–354.

Ford, Dabney. 1979. *Testing and Excavation of an Early Aceramic Navajo Site in Carrizo Canyon*. Report No. 78-SJC-080. Farmington: New Mexico State University Cultural Resource Management Program.

Ford, Richard I. 1983. Inter-Indian Exchange in the Southwest. In *Southwest*, edited by Alfonso Ortiz, pp. 711–722. Handbook of North American Indians, Vol. 10, William C. Sturtevant, general editor. Washington, D.C.: Smithsonian Institution Press.

Forrest, Earle R. 1970. *With a Camera in Old Navaholand*. Norman: University of Oklahoma Press.

Fowler, Andrew, and John Stein. 1991. The Anasazi Great House in Space, Time, and Paradigm. Manuscript in authors' possession.

———. 2001 [1992]. The Anasazi Great House in Space, Time, and Paradigm. In *Anasazi Regional Organization and the Chaco System*, edited by David E. Doyel, pp. 101–122. Reprint. Albuquerque, NM: Maxwell Museum of Anthropology.

Franciscan Fathers. 1910. *An Ethnologic Dictionary of the Navaho Language*. Reprint. Saint Michaels, AZ: Franciscan Fathers.

Francisconi, Michael. 1995. Economic Trends and Everyday Life on the Navajo Nation 1868 to 1995: The History of the External Economy of the Diné. PhD diss., University of Oregon, Eugene.

Fransted, Dennis. 1979. *An Introduction to the Navajo Oral History of Anasazi Sites in the San Juan Basin Area*. Fort Defiance, AZ: Navajo Aging Services.

Friedman, Jonathan. 1999 [1979]. *System, Structure, and Contradiction*. Reprint. Walnut Creek, CA: Altamira Press.

Frisbie, Charlotte J. 1987. *Navajo Medicine Bundles or Jish: Acquisition, Transmission, and Disposition in the Past and Present*. Albuquerque: University of New Mexico Press.

———. 1996. Gender Issues in Navajo Boarding School Experiences. In *The Construction of Gender and the Experience of Women in American Indian Societies*, edited by Harvey

Markowitz, pp. 138–179. D'Arcy McNickle Center for the History of the American Indian, Occasional Papers in Curriculum Series 20. Chicago: Newberry Library.

———. 2001. Introduction to *Tall Woman: The Life Story of Rose Mitchell, a Navajo Woman, c. 1874–1977*. Albuquerque: University of New Mexico Press.

———, ed. 2018. *Food Sovereignty the Navajo Way: Cooking with Tall Woman*. Albuquerque: University of New Mexico Press.

Frisbie, Theodore. 1971. An Archaeo-ethnological Interpretation of Maize Deity Symbolism in the Greater Southwest. PhD diss., Southern Illinois University, Carbondale.

———. 1978. High Status Burials in the Greater Southwest: An Interpretive Synthesis. In *Across the Chichimec Sea*, edited by Carroll L. Riley and Basil C. Hedrickk, pp. 202–227. Carbondale: Southern Illinois University Press.

———. 1998. New Light on the Pochteca Concept and the Chaco Phenomenon. In *Diné Bikéyah: Papers in Honor of David M. Brugge*, edited by Meliha S. Duran and David T. Kirkpatrick. Archaeological Society of New Mexico Papers 24. Albuquerque: Archaeological Society of New Mexico.

Galinat, Walton C., and James H. Gunnerson. 1969. Appendix I: Fremont Maize. In *The Fremont Culture*, edited by James H. Gunnerson. Paper of the Peabody Museum 59, No. 2. Cambridge, MA: Harvard University Press.

Gilpin, Dennis. 1985a. Archaeological and Ethnohistoric Investigations at the Chilchinbito Mining District, Navajo County, Arizona, NNCRMP 85-383. Manuscript on file, Navajo Nation Cultural Resource Management Program, Window Rock, AZ.

———. 1985b. Archaeological and Ethnohistoric Investigations at the Cow Springs Coal Mining District, Black Mesa, Navajo County, Arizona, NNCRMP 85-384. Manuscript on file, Navajo Nation Cultural Resource Management Program, Window Rock, AZ.

———. 1985c. Archaeological and Ethnohistoric Investigations at the Jack Johnson Mine Area, Coyote Canyon, McKinley County, New Mexico, NNCRMP 85-375. Manuscript on file, Navajo Nation Cultural Resource Management Program, Window Rock, AZ.

———. 1987. The Navajo Coal Mines: Industrial Archaeology on the Navajo Indian Reservation. Paper presented at the Navajo Studies Conference, Northern Arizona University, Flagstaff, February 19–21.

———. 1989. Great Houses and Pueblos in Northeastern Arizona. Paper presented at the Pecos Conference, Bandelier National Monument, Los Alamos, NM, August 17–20.

———. 1994. Lukachukai and Salina Springs: Late Archaic / Early Basketmaker Habitation Sites in the Chinle Valley, Northeastern Arizona. *Kiva* 60(2):203–218.

———. 1996. Early Navajo Occupation West of the Chuska Mountains. In *The Archaeology of Navajo Origins*, edited by Ronald H. Towner, pp. 171–196. Salt Lake City: University of Utah Press.

———. n.d. Boundaries of Tsegi Phase Architecture in Northeastern Arizona. Manuscript on file, SWCA Environmental Consultants, Flagstaff, AZ.

Gilpin, Dennis, and Larry Benallie Jr. 2000. Juniper Cove and Early Anasazi Community Structure West of the Chuska Mountains. In *Foundations of Anasazi Culture*, edited by Paul F. Reed, pp. 161–174. Salt Lake City: University of Utah Press.

Gilpin, Dennis, Klara Kelley, and Harris Francis. 2017. *Historic Rural Landscapes of the Gallup New Mexico Area: A Historic Context for 1881–Present Cultural Resources, Navajo-Gallup Water Supply Project Reach 27, Technical Report 15-39.* Technical Report 15-39. Phoenix, AZ: PaleoWest Archaeology.

Gilpin, Laura. 1968. *The Enduring Navaho*. Austin: University of Texas Press.

Girdner, Alwin J. 2011. *Dinétah: My Reservation Days, 1923–1939.* Tucson, AZ: Rio Nuevo Publishers.

Gjeltema, Bruce. 2004. Jacob Casimera Morgan and the Development of Navajo Nationalism. PhD diss., University of New Mexico, Albuquerque.

Glowacki, Donna M. 2015. *Living and Leaving: A Social History of Regional Depopulation in Thirteenth-Century Mesa Verde.* Tucson: University of Arizona Press.

Goddard, Pliny Earle. 1933. *Navajo Texts.* Anthropological Papers of the American Museum of Natural History 34(1).

Goodwin, Grenville. 1942. *Social Organization of the Western Apache.* Chicago: University of Chicago Press.

Granger, Byrd H. 1960. *Will C. Barnes' Arizona Place Names.* Tucson: University of Arizona Press.

Grant, Campbell. 1987. *Canyon de Chelly: Its People and Rock Art.* Tucson: University of Arizona Press.

Graves, Laura. 1998. *Thomas Varker Keam, Indian Trader.* Norman: University of Oklahoma Press.

Greenberg, Henry, and Georgia Greenberg. 1984. *Carl Gorman's World.* Albuquerque: University of New Mexico Press.

Greever, William S. 1954. *Arid Domain: The Santa Fe Railway and Its Western Land Grant.* Stanford, CA: Stanford University Press.

Gregory, Herbert. 1916. *The Navajo Country: A Geographic and Hydrographic Reconnaissance of Parts of New Mexico, Arizona, and Utah.* U.S. Geological Survey Water Supply Paper 380. Washington, D.C.: U.S. Government Printing Office.

Grein, B., and C. J. Frisbie. 2005. *Blessings Brought, Blessings Found: Annunciation Mission, 1905–2005, Our Lady of Fatima Parish, Celebrating 100 Years of Franciscan and Church Presence in Chinle, Arizona.* Chinle, AZ: Our Lady of Fatima Parish.

Griffith, James Seavy. 1983. Kachinas and Masking. In *Southwest*, edited by Alfonso Ortiz, pp. 764–777. Handbook of North American Indians, Vol. 10, William C. Sturtevant, general editor. Washington, D.C.: Smithsonian Institution Press.

Guernsey, Samuel James. 1931. *Explorations in Northeastern Arizona: Report on the Archaeological Fieldwork of 1920–1923.* Papers of the Peabody Museum of Archaeology and Ethnology 12, no. 1. Cambridge, MA: Harvard University Press.

Gulliford, Andrew. 2000. *Sacred Objects and Sacred Places.* Boulder: University Press of Colorado.

Gumerman, George J., and Jeffrey S. Dean. 1989. Cooperation and Competition in the Western Anasazi Area. In *Dynamics of Southwest Prehistory*, edited by Linda S. Cordell and George J. Gumerman. , pp. 99–148 Washington, D.C.: Smithsonian Institution Press.

Gumerman, George J., and Emil W. Haury. 1979. Prehistory: Hohokam. In *Southwest*, edited by Alfonso Ortiz, pp. 75–90. Handbook of North American Indians, Vol. 9, William C. Sturtevant, general editor. Washington, D.C.: Smithsonian Institution Press.

Hafen, LeRoy R. 1947. Armijo's Journal. *Huntington Library Quarterly* 11(1):87–101.

Hafen, LeRoy R., and Ann W. Hafen. 1954. *The Old Spanish Trail*. Spokane, WA: Arthur H. Clark Press.

Haile, Berard. 1938. *Origin Legend of the Navaho Enemy Way: Text and Translation*. Yale University Publications in Anthropology 17.

———. 1943. *Origin Legend of the Navaho Flintway*. University of Chicago Publications in Anthropology, Linguistic Series.

———. 1947. The Legend of Ałkéé' Naa'aashii. In *Head and Face Masks of Navajo Ceremonialism*, by Berard Haile, pp. 95–101. Saint Michaels, AZ: Saint Michaels Press.

———. 1978. *Love Magic and Butterfly People: The Slim Curly Version of the Ajiłee and Mothway Myths*. Flagstaff: Museum of Northern Arizona.

———. 1981. *The Upward Moving and Emergence Way: The Gishin Biye' Version*. Lincoln: University of Nebraska Press.

———. 1998. The Story of the Ethnologic Dictionary. Appendix 2 in *Tales of an Endishodi*, edited by Father Murray Bodo, OFM. Albuquerque: University of New Mexico Press.

Haines, Francis. 1995. *The Buffalo: The Story of American Bison and Their Hunters from Prehistoric Times to the Present*. Reprint. Norman: University of Oklahoma Press.

Hammond, George P., and Agapito Rey, eds. and trans. 1953. *Don Juan de Oñate, Colonizer of New Mexico, 1595–1628*. Albuquerque: University of New Mexico Press.

———. 1966. *The Rediscovery of New Mexico*. Albuquerque: University of New Mexico Press.

Hansen, Mary. 2014. Beating Climate Change by Retooling the Economy: The Story Begins in Navajo Country. *YES! Magazine*. October 16. www.yesmagazine.org (accessed December 8, 2016).

Harrelson, Scott. 2017. Navajo Generating Station Will Operate through December 2019. Press release, November 29. www.srpnet.com/newsroom/releases/112917.aspx (accessed February 9, 2019).

Havelock, Eric A. 1986. *The Muse Learns to Write: Reflections on Orality and Literacy from Antiquity to the Present*. New Haven, CT: Yale University Press.

Hayden, David J., Lloyd A. Miola, and Yvonne R. Oakes. 1998. *The Datil Mountain Project: Archaic, Puebloan, and Athabascan Campsites along U.S. 60, near Datil, Catron County, New Mexico*. Archaeology Note 177. Santa Fe: Office of Archaeological Studies, Museum of New Mexico.

Hegmon, Michelle, ed. 2000. *The Archaeology of Regional Interaction: Religion, Warfare, and Exchange across the American Southwest and Beyond.* Boulder: University Press of Colorado.

Helm, June, ed. 1981. *Subarctic.* Handbook of North American Indians, Vol. 6, William C. Sturtevant, general editor. Washington, D.C.: Smithsonian Institution Press.

Henderson, Eric. 1985. Wealth, Status, and Change among the Kaibito Plateau Navajo. PhD diss., University of Arizona, Tucson.

Hevesi, Dennie. 2011. Elouise Cobell, 65, Dies; Sued U.S. over Indian Trust Funds. *New York Times.* October 17. www.nytimes.com/2011/10/18 (accessed December 18, 2016).

Hickerson, Nancy Parrott. 1994. *The Jumanos: Hunters and Traders of the South Plains.* Austin: University of Texas Press.

Hill, W. W. 1937. *Navajo Pottery Manufacture.* Anthropological Series 2(3). University of New Mexico Bulletin.

———. 1940a. *Navaho Salt Gathering.* Anthropological Series 3. University of New Mexico Bulletin.

———. 1940b. Some Aspects of Navajo Political Structure. *Plateau* 13:23–28.

———. 1940c. *Some Navajo Culture Changes during Two Centuries (with a Translation of the Rabal Manuscript).* Smithsonian Miscellaneous Collections, Essays in Historical Anthropology of North America 100. Washington, D.C.: Smithsonian Institution Press.

———. 1948. Navaho Trading and Trading Ritual: A Study in Cultural Dynamics. *Southwest Journal of Anthropology* 4:371–395.

Hodge, Frederick W., George P. Hammond, and Agapito Rey. 1945. *Fray Alonso de Benevides' Revised Memorial of 1634: Reflections on Orality and Literacy from Antiquity to the Present.* Albuquerque: University of New Mexico Press.

Hodge, William. 1969. *The Albuquerque Navajos.* Anthropological Paper 11. Tucson: University of Arizona.

Holiday, John, and Robert S. McPherson. 2005. *A Navajo Legacy: The Life and Teachings of John Holiday.* Norman: University of Oklahoma Press.

Holiday, Sam, and Robert S. McPherson. 2013. *Under the Eagle: Samuel Holiday, Code Talker.* Norman: University of Oklahoma Press.

Horseherder, Nicole. 2017. Now's the Time for a Bold Vision. *Navajo Times.* April 16:A-6.

Hudson, Luanne B. 1978. A Quantitative Analysis of Prehistoric Exchange in the Southwest United States. PhD diss., University of California, Los Angeles.

Hughes, Richard E., and James A. Bennyhoff. 1986. Early Trade. In *Great Basin*, edited by Warren L. D'Azevedo, pp.238–255. Handbook of North American Indians, Vol. 11, William C. Sturtevant, general editor. Washington, D.C.: Smithsonian Institution Press.

Hull, Sharon, Mostafa Fayak, F. Joan Mathien, and Heidi Roberts. 2014. Turquoise Trade of the Ancestral Puebloans: Chaco and Beyond. *Journal of Archaeological Science* 45:187–195. http://dx.doi.org/10.1016/j.jas.2014.02.016 (accessed March 14, 2017).

Hymes, Dell. 1957. A Note on Athapaskan Glottochronology. *International Journal of American Linguistics* 23(4):291–297.

Indian Law Resource Center. 1979. *Report to the Hopi Kikmongwis and Other Traditional Hopi Leaders on Docket 196 and the Continuing Threat to Hopi Land and Sovereignty.* Washington, D.C.: Indian Law Resource Center.

Indigenous Environmental Network. 2016. Peabody's Declaration of Bankruptcy Is "No Surprise." www.ienearth.org (accessed December 16, 2016).

Iverson, Peter, and Monty Roessel. 2002. *A History of the Navajos.* Albuquerque: University of New Mexico Press.

———, eds. 2002. *For Our Navajo People: Diné Letters, Speeches, and Petitions, 1900–1960.* Albuquerque: University of New Mexico Press.

Jennings, Jesse D. 1966. *Glen Canyon: A Summary.* Anthropological Paper 6. Salt Lake City: University of Utah.

———. 1978. *Prehistory of Utah and the Eastern Great Basin.* Anthropological Paper 98. Salt Lake City: University of Utah.

Jett, Stephen C. 1970. An Analysis of Navajo Place-Names. *Names* 18(3):175–184.

———. 1994. Cairn Trail Shrines of the Navajo, the Apache, and Puebloans, and of the Far North. In *Artifacts, Shrines, and Pueblos: Papers in Honor of Gordon Page,* edited by David Kirkpatrick and Meliha Duran, pp. 129–145. Archaeological Society of New Mexico Papers 20. Albuquerque: Archaeological Society of New Mexico.

———. 1997. Place-Naming, Environment, and Perception among the Canyon de Chelly Navajo of Arizona. *Professional Geographer* 49:481–493.

———. 2001. *Navajo Trails and Placenames in the Canyon de Chelly System, Arizona.* New York: Peter Lang Publishing.

Jett, Stephen C., and Editha Watson. 1997. Sacred Places of the Navajo. Manuscript on file, Navajo Nation Historic Preservation Department, Window Rock, AZ.

Johnson, Broderick, ed. 1977. *Navajos and World War II.* Tsaile, AZ: Navajo Community College Press.

Johnston, Bernice Eastman. 1972. *Two Ways in the Desert: A Study of Modern Navajo-Anglo Relations.* Pasadena, CA: Socio-Technical Publications.

Judge, W. James. 1989. Chaco Canyon, San Juan Basin. In *Dynamics of Southwest Prehistory,* edited by Linda S. Cordell and George J. Gumerman, pp. 209–262. Washington, D.C.: Smithsonian Institution Press.

Kaestle, Frederika, and David Glenn Smith. 2001. Ancient Mitochondrial DNA Evidence for Prehistoric Population Movement: The Numic Expansion. *American Journal of Physical Anthropology* 115:1–12.

Kammer, Jerry. 1980. *The Second Long Walk: The Navajo-Hopi Land Dispute.* Albuquerque: University of New Mexico Press.

Kearns, Timothy. 1996. Protohistoric and Early Historic Navajo Lithic Technology in Northwest New Mexico. In *The Archaeology of Navajo Origins,* edited by Ronald Towner, pp. 109–145. Salt Lake City: University of Utah Press.

Kelley, J. Charles. 1986. The Mobile Merchants of Molino. In *Ripples in the Chichimec Sea,* edited by Frances Joan Mathien and Randall H. McGuire, pp. 81–104. Carbondale: Southern Illinois University Press.

———. 2000. The Atatlán Mercantile System and the Northwestward Expansion of Mesoamerican Civilization. In *Greater Mesoamerica: The Archaeology of West and Northwest Mexico*, edited by Michael S. Foster and Shirley Gorenstein, pp. 137–154. Salt Lake City: University of Utah Press.

Kelley, Klara. 1979. Federal Indian Land Policy and Economic Development in the U.S. In *Economic Development in American Indian Reservations*, edited by Roxanne Dunbar-Ortiz. Albuquerque: Native American Studies Program, University of New Mexico.

———. 1982. *The Chaco Canyon Ranch: Ethnohistory and Ethnoarchaeology.* Navajo Nation Papers in Anthropology 8. Window Rock, AZ: Navajo Nation Cultural Resource Management Program.

———. 1983. Ethnohistory: Navajos and the Coal Mines around Gallup. In *The Gamerco Project: Flexibility as an Adaptive Response*, compiled by Cherie Scheick, pp. 562–604. Archaeology Division Report 71. Santa Fe, NM: School of American Research Press.

———. 1986a. An Archaeological Survey for the Balakai Mine Reclamation Project, Tselani, AZ, Report 86-300. Manuscript on file, Navajo Nation Cultural Resource Management Program, Window Rock, AZ.

———. 1986b. *Navajo Land Use: An Ethnoarchaeological Study.* Orlando, FL: Academic Press.

———. 1987a. An Archaeological Survey for the Chinle Mine No. 1 Reclamation Project near Blue Gap, Arizona, NNCRMP 86-301. Manuscript on file, Navajo Nation Cultural Resource Management Program, Window Rock, AZ.

———. 1987b. An Archaeological Survey for the Tree Well and John Joe Mine Reclamation Project near Mentmore, New Mexico, NNCRMP 86-302. Manuscript on file, Navajo Nation Cultural Resource Management Program, Window Rock, AZ.

———. 1988a. *Archeological Investigations in West-Central New Mexico, Vol. 2: Historic Cultural Resources.* Cultural Resources Series No. 4. Santa Fe, NM: U.S. Bureau of Land Management.

———. 1988b. Archaeological Surveys for the Blackgoat and Window Rock AML Areas, McKinley County, New Mexico, NNAD 86-304 and 86-315. Manuscripts on file, Navajo Nation Cultural Resource Management Program, Window Rock, AZ.

Kelley, Klara, and Harris Francis. 1987. An Archaeological Survey for the Big Rock Hill Coal Mine Reclamation Project near Coyote Canyon, New Mexico, NNCRMP 86-303. Manuscript on file, Navajo Nation Cultural Resource Management Program, Window Rock, AZ.

———. 1993. Navajo Sacred Landscape in the Lower Little Colorado: Its Significance to Navajos and Their Concerns about Its Future. Manuscript on file, Navajo-Hopi Land Commission, Window Rock, AZ.

———. 1994. *Navajo Sacred Places.* Bloomington: Indiana University Press.

———. 1998a. Anthropological Traditions versus Navajo Traditions in Early Navajo History. In *Diné Bikéyah: Papers in Honor of David M. Brugge*, edited by Meliha S. Duran and David T. Kirkpatrick, pp. 143–155. Archaeological Society of New Mexico Papers 24. Albuquerque: Archaeological Society of New Mexico.

————. 1998b. Nahat'á Dziil (Chambers-Sanders Trust Lands) field and research notes. Manuscripts in authors' possession.

————. 1998c. Navajo (Diné) Ethnography. In *Ethnohistorical Interpretation and Archaeological Data Recovery along Navajo Route 9101, Jeddito Road, Navajo County, Arizona*, prepared by David C. Eck, pp. 681–716. Pueblo of Zuni, NM: Zuni Cultural Resource Enterprise.

————. 2000a. Navajo Nation Historic Preservation Plan: Background Study for Diné (Navajo) Traditional Cultural Places, Phase 2: Confidential Stories and Story Geographies. Manuscript on file, Navajo Nation Historic Preservation Department, Window Rock, AZ.

————. 2000b. Pearlshell Buffalo People. Paper presented at the Sixth Occasional Anasazi Symposium, San Juan College, Farmington, NM, October 25–28.

————. 2001a. Indian Giving: Allotments on the Arizona Navajo-Railroad Frontier, 1904–1937. *American Indian Culture and Research Journal* 25(2):63–92.

————. 2001b. Many Generations, Few Improvements: "Americans" Challenge Navajos on the Transcontinental Railroad Grant, Arizona, 1881–1887. *American Indian Culture and Research Journal* 25(3):73–101.

————. 2001c. Navajo Nation Historic Preservation Plan: Background Study for Diné (Navajo) Traditional Cultural Places, Phase 3: Confidential Stories and Story Geographies. Manuscript on file, Navajo Nation Historic Preservation Department, Window Rock, AZ.

————. 2003. Abalone Shell Buffalo People: Navajo Narrated Routes and Pre-Columbian Archaeological Sites. *New Mexico Historical Review* 78(1):29–58.

————. 2005a. *Navajo Ethnohistorical Account of the Borrego Pass Region, and Ethnographic Investigations at Site NM-Q-25-52. In Phase II Data Recovery at Sites NM-Q-25-51 and NM-Q-25-52 along County Road 19, Borrego Pass, McKinley County, New Mexico*, prepared by Kurt E. Dongoske and Donovan K. Quam, pp. 32–50, 193–225. Report 834. Pueblo of Zuni, NM: Zuni Cultural Resource Enterprise.

————. 2005b. Traditional Navajo Maps and Wayfinding. *American Indian Culture and Research Journal* 29(2):85–111.

————. 2006a. Diné Traders before 1950: Report of Work in Progress. In *Southwestern Interludes: Papers in Honor of Charlotte J. and Theodore R. Frisbie*, edited by Regge N. Wiseman, Thomas C. O'Laughlin, and Cordelia T. Snow, pp. 87–102. Archaeological Society of New Mexico Papers 32. Albuquerque: Archaeological Society of New Mexico.

————. 2006b. An Ethnographic Study of Navajo Cultural Resources around the Four Corners Generating Station, Navajo Nation, San Juan County, New Mexico. Appendix A in *Cultural Resources Reconnaissance and Ethnographic Assessment of the Four Corners Generating Station, San Juan County, New Mexico*, by Donald W. Jolly and Thomas E. Jones. Project No. 04-135-02. Tempe, AZ: Archaeological Consulting Services Ltd.

————. 2006–2015. Navajoland Trading Post Encyclopedia (in progress). Published online at www.navajolandtradingposts.info.

———. 2008. Field notes for *Sharing the Sheepherding Landscape of El Segundo Mine*, 2011. Video produced by Southwest Archaeological Consultants, Santa Fe, and Lee Ranch Coal Co., Grants, NM.

———. 2012. Climate Change in the Middle Little Colorado River Basin, Navajo Nation: A Navajo Oral History (Phases 1 and 2). Manuscript on file, U.S. Geological Survey, Flagstaff, AZ.

———. 2013. Navajo Ethnographic Study for the U.S. 191 Wide Ruins Archaeological Project. In *Archaeological Investigations along U.S. 191 near Wide Ruins, Apache County, AZ*, edited by Sarah A. Herr, pp. 293–320. Technical Report No. 2007-06. Tucson, AZ: Desert Archaeology.

———. 2015. Diné Oral History of Land Use and Weather: Changes around the Chinle, Tsaile, and Many Farms Area of the Navajo Nation. Manuscript on file, U.S. Geological Survey, Flagstaff, AZ.

———. 2017. Navajos and Coal Mines around Gallup and the Navajo-Gallup Water Supply Project Reach 27. In *Historic Rural Landscapes of the Gallup New Mexico Area: A Historic Context for 1881–Present Cultural Resources, Navajo-Gallup Water Supply Project Reach 27*, by Dennis Gilpin, Klara Kelley, and Harris Francis, pp. 58–99. Technical Report 15-39. Phoenix, AZ: PaleoWest Archaeology.

———. 2018. *Navajoland Trading Post Encyclopedia*. Window Rock, AZ: Navajo Nation Museum.

Kelley, Klara, and Teddy James. 1985. An Archaeological Survey for the Montezuma's Chair and Round Top Mine Reclamation Projects near Teesto, Arizona, NNCRMP 85-432. Manuscript on file, Navajo Nation Cultural Resource Management Program, Window Rock, AZ.

———. 1986. Navajo Ethnohistory and Archaeology of the Window Rock Lease, NNCRMP 85-508. Manuscript on file, Navajo Nation Cultural Resource Management Program, Window Rock, AZ.

Kelley, Klara, Rena Martin, Clarina Clark, Tonia Clark, Harris Francis, and Clifford Werito. 2013. Navajo-Gallup Water Supply Project Traditional Cultural Resources Inventory and Assessment, Reach 12.1. Manuscript on file, PaleoWest Archaeology, Phoenix, AZ, and U.S. Bureau of Reclamation, Durango, CO.

Kelley, Klara, Peggy F. Scott, and Harris Francis. 1991. Navajo and Hopi Relations. Manuscript on file, Navajo-Hopi Land Commission, Window Rock, AZ.

Kelley, Klara, and Peter Whiteley. 1989. *Navajoland: Family Settlement and Land Use*. Tsaile, AZ: Navajo Community College Press.

Kelly, Laurence C. 1968. *The Navajo Indians and Federal Indian Policy, 1900–1935*. Tucson: University of Arizona Press.

———. 1970. *Navajo Roundup: Selected Correspondence of Kit Carson's Expedition against the Navajo, 1863–1865*. Boulder, CO: Pruett.

Kelly, Roger E., Richard W. Lang, and Harry Walters. 1972. *Navajo Figurines Called Dolls*. Santa Fe, NM: Museum of Navajo Ceremonial Art.

Kemrer, Meade Francis. 1974. The Dynamics of Western Navajo Settlement, A.D. 1750–1900. PhD diss., University of Arizona, Tucson.

Kincaid, Chris, ed. 1988. *Chaco Roads Project, Phase I: A Reappraisal of Prehistoric Roads in the San Juan Basin, 1983.* Albuquerque, NM: U.S. Bureau of Land Management.

King, Beth. 1996. *Life along the San Juan River.* Bluff, UT : Canyon Echo and San Juan County Historical Commission.

Kipp, David F. 1983. *Tse'laa': The Incredible True Story of Navajo Fortress Rock.* Privately published.

Klah, Hosteen. 1942. *Navajo Creation Myth.* Santa Fe, NM: Museum of Navajo Ceremonial Art.

Kluckhohn, Clyde. 1967. *Navaho Witchcraft.* Reprint. Boston: Beacon Press.

Kluckhohn, Clyde, W. W. Hill, and Lucy Wales Kluckhohn. 1970. *Navaho Material Culture.* Cambridge, MA: Belknap Press of Harvard University.

Komal, Khettry. 2017. Peabody Energy Emerges from Bankruptcy Protection. April 3. www.reuters.com/article/US-peabody-energy-bankruptcy (accessed February 9, 2019).

Krech, Shepherd. 1998. *The Ecological Indian: Myth and History.* New York: W. W. Norton.

Kuznar, Lawrence A. 2001. Ecological Mutualism in Navajo Corrals: Implications for Navajo Environmental Perceptions and Human/Plant Coevolution. *Journal of Anthropological Research* 57:17–39.

Laird, Carobeth. 1976. *The Chemehuevis.* Banning, CA: Malki Museum Press, Morongo Indian Reservation.

Lambert, Ruth. 2012. Home and Garden: Learning about Small Structures through Excavation. In *Hisat'sinom: Ancient Peoples in a Land without Water,* edited by Christian Downum, pp. 113–117. Santa Fe, NM: School for Advanced Research Press.

Lamphere, Louise, and Eva Price. 2007. *Weaving Women's Lives: Three Generations in a Navajo Family.* Albuquerque: University of New Mexico Press.

Lapahie, Harrison, Jr. 1997. Portal to the Navajo Intranet: Code Talkers. http://www. lapahie.com (accessed December 16, 2016).

Leading the Way: The Wisdom of the Navajo People. 2002–2017. Various articles.

LeBlanc, Steven A. 1999. *Prehistoric Warfare in the American Southwest.* Salt Lake City: University of Utah Press.

Lee, Albert Hugh, and Ella Ruth Lee Danoff. 1982. *Gaamaliitsoh, Indian Trader: An Autobiography of Albert Hugh Lee (1897–1976).* Privately published.

Lee, Lloyd. 2006. Navajo Cultural Identity: What Can the Navajo Nation Bring to the American Indian Identity Discussion Table? *Wicazo Sa Review* 2(6):79–104.

———. 2013. *Diné Masculinities: Conceptualizations and Reflections.* North Charleston, SC: Createspace Independent Publishing Platform.

———, ed. 2014. *Diné Perspectives: Revitalizing and Reclaiming Navajo Thought,* Tucson: University of Arizona Press.

———, ed. 2017. *Navajo Sovereignty: Understandings and Visions of the Dine People.* Tucson: University of Arizona Press.

Left-Handed. 1967 [1938]. *Son of Old Man Hat: A Navaho Autobiography.* Recorded by Walter Dyk. Lincoln: University of Nebraska Press.

———. 1980. *Left-Handed: A Navajo Autobiography.* Edited by Walter Dyk and Ruth Dyk. New York: Columbia University Press.

Lekson, Stephen H. 2009. *A History of the Ancient Southwest*. Santa Fe, NM: School of Advanced Research Press.

———. 2015. *The Chaco Meridian*. 2nd ed. Lanham, MD: Rowman and Littlefield.

Levy, Jerrold E., Raymond Neutra, and Dennis Parker. 1995. *Hand Trembling, Frenzy Witchcraft, and Moth Madness: A Study of Navajo Seizure Disorders*. Tucson: University of Arizona Press.

Lewis, G. Malcolm, ed. 1998. *Cartographic Encounters: Perspectives on Native American Mapmaking and Map Use*. Chicago: University of Chicago Press.

Liebmann, Matthew, and Robert W. Preucel. 2007. The Archaeology of the Pueblo Revolt and the Formation of the Modern Pueblo World. *Kiva* 73(2):195–218.

Line, Francis Raymond. 1991. The Kayenta Mail Run. *Arizona Highways*. January:29–31.

Loebig, Douglas. 1996. *An Ethnographic/Ethnohistoric Study, Ensenada Mesa, Rio Arriba County, New Mexico, 95-SASI-014E*. Durango, CO: Southwest Archaeological Services.

Lomatuway'ma, Michael, Lorena Lomatuway'ma, Stanley Namingha Jr., and Ekkehart Malotki. 1993. *Hopi Ruin Legends*. Lincoln: University of Nebraska Press for Northern Arizona University.

Long, Paul V. 1992. *Big Eyes: The Southwestern Photographs of Simeon Schwemberger*. Albuquerque: University of New Mexico Press.

Lorenz, Joseph G., and David Glenn Smith. 1996. Distribution of Four Founding mtDNA Haplogroups among Native North Americans. *American Journal of Physical Anthropology* 101:307–323.

Luckert, Karl W. 1975. *The Navajo Hunter Tradition*. Tucson: University of Arizona Press.

———. 1977. *Navajo Mountain and Rainbow Bridge Religion*. Flagstaff: Museum of Northern Arizona Press.

———. 1978. *A Navajo Bringing-Home Ceremony: The Claus Chee Sonny Version of Deerway Ajilee*. Flagstaff: Museum of Northern Arizona.

Luckert, Karl W., and Johnny C. Cooke. 1979. *Coyoteway: A Navajo Holyway Healing Ceremonial*. Tucson: University of Arizona Press.

Lyon, William H. 1987. Ednishodi Yashe: The Little Priest and the Understanding of Navajo Culture. *American Indian Culture and Research Journal* 11(1):1–41..

Makeda, Lillian, and Klara Kelley. 2010. National Register of Historic Places Registration Form: Borrego Pass Trading Post Historic District. Manuscript on file, National Park Service, Washington, D.C..

Maldonado, Ronald P. 1981. Window Rock Coal Mine Archaeological Survey, NNCRMP 81-014. Manuscript on file, Navajo Nation Cultural Resource Management Program, Window Rock, AZ.

Malhi, Ripan. 2012. DNA Evidence of a Prehistoric Athabaskan Migration from the Subarctic to the Southwest of North America. In *From the Land of Ever Winter to the American Southwest: Athapaskan Migrations, Mobility, and Ethnogenesis*, edited by Deni J. Seymour, pp. 241–248. Salt Lake City: University of Utah Press.

Malotki, Ekkehart, and Michael Lomatuway'ma. 1987. *Maasaw: Profile of a Hopi God*. Lincoln: University of Nebraska Press.

Manville, Richard H. 1980. The Origin and Relationships of American Wild Sheep. In *The Desert Bighorn: Its Life History, Ecology, and Management*, edited by Gale Monson and Lowell Sumner, pp. 1–6. Tucson: University of Arizona Press.

Marek-Martinez, Ora. 2016. Archaeology for, by, and with the Navajo People: The *Nihokáá' Dine'é Bíla Ashdla'í* Way. PhD diss., University of California, Berkeley.

Marshall, Michael P. 1997. The Chacoan Roads: A Cosmological Interpretation. In *Anasazi Architecture and American Design*, edited by Baker H. Morrow and V. B. Price, pp. 62–74. Albuquerque: University of New Mexico Press.

Martin, Rena. 1984. An Archaeological Survey of the Nenahnezad Abandoned Mine for the Navajo Reclamation Division, NNCRMP 84-77. Manuscript on file, Navajo Nation Cultural Resource Management Program.

———. 1986. Archaeological and Ethnographic Investigations at Four Coal Mine Areas South of Shiprock, San Juan County, New Mexico. Manuscript on file, Navajo Nation Cultural Resource Management Department, Window Rock, AZ.

———. 2002. Two Navajo Clan Traditions: Our Mothers, Our Fathers, Our Connections. MA thesis, University of New Mexico, Albuquerque.

Martin, Rena, Klara Kelley, Clarina Clark, Tonia Clark, and Clifford Werito. 2014. Navajo-Gallup Water Supply Project: Traditional Cultural Resources Inventory and Assessment, Reach 6. Manuscript on file, PaleoWest Archaeology, Phoenix, AZ, and U.S. Bureau of Reclamation, Durango, CO.

Mathien, F. Joan. 1996. Trials and Troubles with Turquoise Tests. Paper presented at Bead Expo, San Antonio, TX, March 9.

———. 1997. Ornaments of the Chaco Anasazi. In *Ceramics, Lithics, and Ornaments of Chaco Canyon*, edited by Frances Joan Mathien, pp. 1119–1220. Chaco Canyon Studies, Publications in Archeology 18G. Santa Fe, NM: National Park Service.

Matlock, Staci. 2014. New Oil Boom Coming to San Juan Basin. *New Mexican*. March 3. www.santafenewmexican.com (accessed December 16, 2016).

Matthews, Washington. 1907. *Navaho Myths, Prayers, and Songs*, edited by Pliny Earl Goddard. Publications in Anthropology and Archaeology, Vol. 2. Berkeley: University of California.

———. 1970. *The Mountain Chant: A Navaho Ceremony*. Reprint. Glorieta, NM: Rio Grande Press.

———. 1978. *The Night Chant: A Navaho Ceremony*. Reprint. New York: AMS Press.

———. 1994. *Navaho Legends*. Reprint. Salt Lake City: University of Utah Press.

McClain, Sally. 2001. *Navajo Weapon: The Navajo Code Talkers*. Tucson, AZ: Rio Nuevo Publishers.

McCloskey, Joanne. 2007. *Living through the Generations: Continuity and Change in Navajo Women's Lives*. Tucson: University of Arizona Press.

McKenna, Peter J. 1987. Evaluation of Ceramics at the Sand Dune Site, Hubbell Trading Post, NHS. Manuscript on file, Southwest Cultural Resources Center, National Park Service, Santa Fe, NM.

M'Closkey, Kathy. 2002. *Swept under the Rug: A Hidden History of Navajo Weaving*. Albuquerque: University of New Mexico Press.

————. 2003. Trading Accounts: Sam Teller of Two Gray Hills. *New Mexico Historical Review* 78(2):128–146.

McNitt, Frank. 1962. *The Indian Traders*. Norman: University of Oklahoma Press.

————. 1970. *Navajo Wars*. Albuquerque: University of New Mexico Press.

McPherson, Robert S. 1992. *Sacred Land, Sacred View: Navajo Perceptions of the Four Corners Region*. Provo, UT: Brigham Young University.

————. 2001. *The Northern Navajo Frontier, 1860–1900: Expansion through Adversity*. Reprint. Logan: Utah State University Press.

————. 2012. *Dinéjí Na'nitin: Navajo Traditional Teachings and History*. Boulder: University Press of Colorado.

————. 2014. *Viewing the Ancestors: Perceptions of the Anaasází, Mokwič, and Hisatsinom*. Norman: University of Oklahoma Press.

McPherson, Robert S., Jim Dandy, and Sarah E. Burak. 2012. *Navajo Tradition, Mormon Life: The Autobiography and Teachings of Jim Dandy*. Salt Lake City: University of Utah Press.

Meinig, D. W. 1971. *Southwest: Three Peoples in Geographical Change, 1600–1970*. Oxford: Oxford University Press.

Miera y Pacheco, Bernardo. 1970. Plano geográfico de los descubrimientos hechos por don Bernardo Miera y Pacheco y los reverendos padres Fray Francisco Atanasio Domínguez y Fray Silvestre Vélez, 1778. A facsimile of the original in the Western Americana Collection of the Beinecke Rare Book and Manuscript Library, Yale University. Meriden, CN: Meriden Gravure Company.

Mike, Richard. 2010. Arthur Bradley, U.S. Cavalry, Company C, 6th Regiment. *Kayenta Township Today*. Spring:3 ff.

Mills, Barbara. 2002. Acts of Resistance: Zuni Ceramics, Social Identity, and the Pueblo Revolt. In *Archaeologies of the Pueblo Revolt: Identity, Meaning, and Renewal in the Pueblo World*, edited by Robert Preucel, pp. 85–98. Albuquerque: University of New Mexico Press.

Mitchell, Frank. 2003. *Navajo Blessingway Singer: The Autobiography of Frank Mitchell, 1882–1968*. Edited by Charlotte J. Frisbie and David P. McAllister. Reprint. Tucson: University of Arizona Press.

Mitchell, Rose. 2001. *The Life Story of Rose Mitchell, a Navajo Woman, c. 1874–1977*. Edited by Charlotte J. Frisbie. Albuquerque: University of New Mexico Press.

Montgomery, Ross Gordon, Watson Smith, and John Otis Brew. 1949. *Franciscan Awatobi: The Excavation and Conjectural Reconstruction of a 17th-Century Spanish Mission Establishment at a Hopi Indian Town in Northeastern Arizona*. Papers of the Peabody Museum of American Archaeology and Ethnology, Vol. 34. Cambridge, MA: Harvard University Press.

Moon, Samuel. 1992. *Tall Sheep: Harry Goulding, Monument Valley Trader*. Norman: University of Oklahoma Press.

Morris, Elizabeth Ann. 1980. *Basketmaker Caves in the Prayer Roc District, Northeastern Arizona*. Anthropological Papers 35. Tucson: University of Arizona Press.

Mount, James E., Stanley J. Olsen, John W. Olsen, George A. Teague, and B. Dean Treadwell. 1991. *Wide Reed Ruin*. Professional Paper No. 51. Santa Fe, NM: Southwest Cultural Resources Center, National Park Service.

Munro, Kimberly. 2011. Prehistoric Macaws of the American Southwest. *Popular Archaeology*. April 1. www.popular-archaeology.com/issue/April-2011/article/prehistoric-macaws-of-the-american-southwest (accessed March 12, 2017).

Myrick, David F. 1970. *New Mexico's Railroads, an Historical Survey*. Golden: Colorado Railroad Museum.

Nát'oh Diné'é Táchii'nii Clan People. 1981. Transcript of meeting on August 23, 1981. Manuscript in authors' possession.

Navajo Nation Human Rights Commission. 2012. The Impact of the Navajo-Hopi Land Settlement Act of 1974, P.L. 93-531 et al. Public Hearing Report. Navajo Nation Human Rights Commission, Window Rock, AZ.

Navajo Nation Museum. 2007. *1950s dóó yowohdą́ą́' Diné naalyéhé yá naazdáago bił ndahashzhiizhgo baa hane': Legacy of Diné Traders before the 1950s*. Video and exhibit. Window Rock, AZ: Navajo Nation Museum.

Navajo Times. 2008. Sovereignty Matriarch Honored. May 2:2.

Navajo Transitional Energy Company. 2019. Navajo Transitional Energy Company: Resources Benefitting the Navajo People. www.navajo.tec.com/history and www.navajo.tec.com/media (accessed February 9, 2019).

Navajo Tribe. 1967. Proposed Findings of Fact in Behalf of the Navajo Tribe of Indians in Area of the Overall Navajo Claim, Docket 229 before the Indian Claims Commission. 6 Vols. Window Rock, AZ: Navajo Nation Department of Justice.

Navajo Uranium Miner Oral History and Photography Project. 1997. *Memories Come to Us in the Rain and the Wind: Oral Histories and Photographs of Navajo Uranium Miners & Their Families*. Boston, MA: Department of Family Medicine and Community Health, Tufts School of Medicine.

Nelson, Ben A. 2000. Aggregation, Warfare, and the Spread of the Mesoamerican Tradition. In *The Archaeology of Regional Interaction: Religion, Warfare, and Exchange across the American Southwest and Beyond*, edited by Michelle Hegmon, pp. 317–340. Boulder: University Press of Colorado.

Nequatewa, Edmund. 1967. *Truth of a Hopi*. Reprint. Flagstaff, AZ: Northland Press.

Newcomb, Franc J. 1940. Origin Legend of the Navajo Eagle Chant. *Journal of American Folklore* 53:50–77.

Newcomb, Franc J., and Gladys Reichard. 1975. *Sandpaintings of the Navajo Shooting Chant*. Reprint. New York: Dover.

Nez, Chester, and Judith Schleiss Avila. 2012. *Code Talker: The First and Only Memoir by One of the Original Code Talkers of World War II*. Berkeley: University of California Press.

Nez, Frank. 2008. Some Clan Musings. *Leading the Way* 6(10):9.

Nez, Mabel. 2009. My Dad, H. T. Donald—Todich'iinni, Ta'baahi. Presentation at Navajoland Traders Gathering, Navajo Nation Museum, Window Rock, AZ, October 10.

Nichols, Johanna. 1997. Modelling Ancient Population Structures and Movement in Linguistics. *Annual Review of Anthropology* 26:359–384.

Nickelson, Howard B. 1988. *One Hundred Years of Coal Mining in the San Juan Basin, New Mexico.* New Mexico Bureau of Mines and Mineral Resources Bulletin 111. Socorro: New Mexico Institute of Mining and Technology.

Nies, Judith. 2014. *Unreal City: Las Vegas, Black Mesa, and the Fate of the West.* New York: Nation Books.

Norstog, John. 1988. Nahat'a Dziil and the Retaking of Dine Bikeya: Two Planning Paradigms and the Recovery of Lost Indian Land. Paper presented at the 30th Annual Conference of the Western Social Sciences Association, Denver, CO, April 27–30.

Oakes, Yvonne R. 1996. Expanding Athabaskan Chronometric Boundaries in West-Central New Mexico. In *La Jornada: Papers in Honor of William F. Turney,* edited by Meliha S. Duran and David T. Kirkpatrick, pp. 139–149. Archaeological Society of New Mexico No. 22. Albuquerque: Archaeological Society of New Mexico.

Oakes, Yvonne R., and Dorothy A. Zamora, eds. 1999. *Archaeology of the Mogollon Highlands: Settlement Systems and Adaptations.* Office of Archaeological Studies Archaeology Notes 232. Santa Fe: Museum of New Mexico.

O'Bryan, Aileen. 1993. *The Dine: Origin Myths of the Navaho Indians.* New York: Dover, 1993.

O'Hara, Michael. 2004. Navajo Archaeology and Ethnohistory of the Beautiful Valley, Arizona. Paper presented at the 15th Navajo Studies Conference, Durango, CO, October 22.

———. 2012. Hohokam and Chaco in the Sierra Sin Agua. In *Hisat'sinom: Ancient Peoples in a Land without Water,* edited by Christian E. Downum, pp. 59–68. Santa Fe, NM: School for Advanced Research Press.

Old Mexican. 1947. *A Navaho Autobiography.* Edited by Walter Dyk. Viking Fund Publications in Anthropology No. 8. New York: Wenner-Gren Foundation for Anthropological Research.

O'Neill, Colleen. 2005. *Working the Navajo Way: Labor and Culture in the Twentieth Century.* Manhattan: University Press of Kansas.

Opler, Morris E. 1983. The Apachean Culture Pattern and Its Origins. In *Southwest,* edited by Alfonso Ortiz, pp. 368–391. Handbook of North American Indians, Vol. 10, William C. Sturtevant, general editor. Washington, D.C.: Smithsonian Institution Press.

Ortiz, Alfonso, ed. 1979. *Southwest.* Handbook of North American Indians, Vol. 9, William C. Sturtevant, general editor. Washington, D.C.: Smithsonian Institution Press.

———, ed. 1983. *Southwest.* Handbook of North American Indians, Vol. 10, William C. Sturtevant, general editor. Washington, D.C.: Smithsonian Institution Press.

Oshley, Navajo. 2000. *The Journey of Navajo Oshley: An Autobiography and Life History.* Edited by Robert S. McPherson. Logan: Utah State University Press.

Paquette, Peter. 1915. Census of the Navajo Reservation, Year 1915. Manuscript on file, Record Group 75, file no. 64386-034, National Archives and Records Administration, Washington, D.C..

Parman, Donald S. 1976. *The Navajos and the New Deal*. New Haven, CT: Yale University Press.

Parmentier, Richard J. 1979. The Mythological Triangle: Poseyemu, Montezuma, and Jesus in the Pueblos. In *Southwest*, edited by Alfonso Ortiz, pp. 609–622. Handbook of North American Indians, Vol. 9, William C. Sturtevant, general editor. Washington, D.C.: Smithsonian Institution Press.

Pasternak, Judy. 2010. *Yellow Dirt: An American Story of a Poisoned Land and a People Betrayed*. New York: Simon and Schuster.

Patterson, Alex. 1994. *Hopi Pottery Symbols*. Boulder, CO: Johnson Books.

Pearce, Margaret Wickens, and Renee Pualani Louis. 2008. Mapping Indigenous Depth of Place. *American Indian Culture and Research Journal* 32(3):107–126.

Pepper, George. 1901. Notes on Chaco Canyon 1901. George Pepper Archives, reel 3, microfilm (box 2[11]), Tulane University, New Orleans.

Peterson, John Alton. 1998. *Utah's Black Hawk War*. Salt Lake City: University of Utah Press.

Pilles, Peter J. 1987. The Sinagua: Ancient People of the Flagstaff Region. In *Wupatki and Walnut Canyon: New Perspectives on History, Prehistory, Rock Art*, edited by David Grant Noble. pp. 2–11. Santa Fe, NM: School of American Research Press.

———. 1996. The Pueblo Period along the Mogollon Rim: The Honanki, Elden, and Turkey Hill Phases of the Sinagua. In *The Prehistoric Pueblo World A.D. 1150–1350*, edited by Michael J. Adler. Tucson: University of Arizona Press.

Piper, June-el, comp. 2001. Native Voices: An Informal Collection of Papers Presented at the AAA Meeting, November 2000. *American Indian Quarterly* 25(1).

Powell, Dana. 2015. The Rainbow Is Our Sovereignty: Rethinking the Politics on the Navajo Nation. *Journal of Political Ecology* 22:53–78.

———. 2018. *Landscapes of Power: Politics of Energy in the Navajo Nation*. Durham, NC: Duke University Press.

Powell, Dana, and Dáilan Long. 2010. Landscapes of Power: Renewable Energy Activism in Diné Bikéyah. In *Indians & Energy: Exploitation and Opportunity in the American Southwest*, edited by Sherry L. Smith and Brian Frehner, pp. 231–262. Santa Fe, NM: School for Advanced Research Press.

Powers, Willow Roberts. 2002. *Navajo Trading: The End of an Era*. Albuquerque: University of New Mexico Press.

Preston, Scott. 1954. The Clans. In *Navajo Historical Selections*, edited by Robert Young and William Morgan, pp. 23–27 and 98–101. Phoenix, AZ: U.S. Bureau of Indian Affairs.

Preucel, Robert, ed. 2002. *Archaeologies of the Pueblo Revolt: Identity, Meaning, and Renewal in the Pueblo World*. Albuquerque: University of New Mexico Press.

Radford, Jeff. 1986. *The Chaco Coal Scandal: The People's Victory over James Watt*. Corrales, NM: Rhombus.

Redhouse, John. 1984. *The Leasing of Dinetah: An Eastern Navajo Odyssey*. Albuquerque, NM: Redhouse / Wright Productions.

———. 1985a. *Geopolitics of the Navajo Hopi Land Dispute*. Albuquerque, NM: Redhouse / Wright Productions.

———. 1985b. *Holy Land: A Navajo Pilgrimage Back to Dinetah.* Albuquerque, NM: Redhouse / Wright Productions.

———. 1986. *The Forgotten Long Walk: When the Navajos Had Too Many People.* Albuquerque, NM: Redhouse / Wright Productions.

Redsteer, Margaret H., Klara B. Kelley, Harris Francis, and Debra Block. 2018. Increasing Vulnerability of the Navajo People to Drought and Climate Change in the Southwestern United States: Accounts from Tribal Elders. In *Indigenous Knowledge for Climate Change Assessment and Adaptation*, edited by Douglas Nakashima, Jennifer Rubis, and Igor Krupnik, pp. 59–72. Cambridge: Cambridge University Press.

Redsteer, Margaret H., and Stephen M. Wessells. 2017. *A Record of Change: Science and Elder Observations on the Navajo Nation.* General Information Product 181. . Flagstaff, AZ: U.S. Geological Survey, Flagstaff, AZ.

Reed, Lori Stephens, C. Dean Wilson, and Kelley A. Hays–Gilpin. 2000. From Brown to Gray: The Origins of Ceramic Technology in the Northern Southwest. In *Foundations of Anasazi Culture*, edited by Paul F. Reed, pp. 203–230. Salt Lake City: University of Utah Press.

Reed, Paul F., and Lori Stephens Reed. 1996. Reexamining Gobernador Polychrome: Toward a New Understanding of the Early Navajo Chronological Sequence in Northwestern New Mexico. In *The Archaeology of Navajo Origins*, edited by Ronald S. Towner, pp. 83–108. Salt Lake City: University of Utah Press.

Reichard, Gladys. 1928. *Social Life of the Navajo Indians.* Contributions to Anthropology 8. New York: Columbia University.

———. 1944. *The Story of the Navajo Hail Chant.* New York: J. J. Augustin.

———. 1977a. *Navaho Religion: A Study in Symbolism.* Reprint. Princeton, NJ: Princeton University Press.

———. 1977b. *Navajo Medicine Man: Sandpaintings and Legends of Miguelito.* Reprint. New York: Dover.

Reno, Phil. 1981. *Mother Earth, Father Sky, and Economic Development.* Albuquerque: University of New Mexico Press.

Reyman, Jonathan. 1978. Pochteca Burials at Anasazi Sites? In *Across the Chichimec Sea: Papers in Honor of J. Charles Kelley*, edited by Carroll L. Riley and Paul G. Hedrick, pp. 242–259. Carbondale: Southern Illinois University Press.

Rice, Karen. 2012. Linguistic Evidence Regarding the Apachean Migration. In *From the Land of Ever Winter to the American Southwest: Athapaskan Migrations, Mobility, and Ethnogenesis*, edited by Deni J. Seymour, pp. 249–270. Salt Lake City: University of Utah Press.

Richardson, Gladwell. 1986. *Indian Trader.* Tucson: University of Arizona Press.

Riley, Carroll. 1995. *Rio del Norte: People of the Upper Rio Grande from Earliest Times to the Pueblo Revolt.* Salt Lake City: University of Utah Press.

———. 2005. *Becoming Aztlan: Mesoamerican Influence in the Greater Southwest, AD 1200–1500.* Salt Lake City: University of Utah Press.

Roberts, Alexa, Richard M. Begay, and Klara Kelley. 1995. *Bits'íís Nínééz
 í (The River of Neverending Life): Navajo History and Cultural Resources of the Grand Canyon*

and the Colorado River. Window Rock, AZ: Navajo Nation Historic Preservation Department.

Roberts, Willow. 1987. *Stokes Carson: Twentieth-Century Trading on the Navajo Reservation.* Albuquerque: University of New Mexico Press.

Robins, Michael R., and Kelley A. Hays-Gilpin. 2000. The Bird in the Basket: Gender and Social Change in Basketmaker Iconography. In *Foundations of Anasazi Culture,* edited by Paul F. Reed, pp. 231–250. Salt Lake City: University of Utah Press.

Robinson, William F., and Ronald H. Towner. 1993. A Directory of Tree-Ring-Dated Native American Sites in the American Southwest. Manuscript on file, Laboratory of Tree-Ring Research, University of Arizona, Tucson.

Robinson-Avila, Kevin. 2016. NASA: Four Corners' Methane "Hotspot" Tied Largely to Natural Gas. *Albuquerque Journal.* August 15. www.abqjournal.com (accessed December 18, 2016).

Rodgers, Larry, Vera J. Tso, and Jasper Rodgers. 2004. *Chapter Images 2004: Profiles of 110 Navajo Nation Chapters.* Window Rock, AZ: Navajo Nation Division of Community Development.

Roessel, Ruth, and Broderick Johnson, eds. 1973. *Navajo Stories of the Long Walk Period.* Tsaile, AZ: Navajo Community College Press.

———. 1974. *Navajo Livestock Reduction: A National Disgrace.* Tsaile, AZ: Navajo Community College Press.

Roney, John R. 2001. Prehistoric Roads and Regional Integration in the Chacoan System. In *Anasazi Regional Organization and the Chaco System,* edited by David E. Doyel. Reprint. Albuquerque, NM: Maxwell Museum of Anthropology.

Rubenstein, Harry. 1983. Political Repression in New Mexico: The Destruction of the National Miners' Union in Gallup. In *Labor in New Mexico: Strikes, Unions, and Social History since 1881,* edited by Robert Kern, pp. 91–140. Albuquerque: University of New Mexico Press.

Rubin, David C. 1995. *Memory in Oral Traditions: The Cognitive Psychology of Epic, Ballads, and Counting-Out Rhymes.* New York: Oxford University Press.

Rundstrom, Robert A. 1995. GIS, Indigenous Peoples, and Epistemological Diversity. *Cartography and Geographic Information Systems* 22(1):45–57.

Rundstrom, Robert, Douglas Duer, Keith Berry, and Rick Winchell. 2003. American Indian Geography. In *Geography in America at the Dawn of the 21st Century,* edited by Gary L. Gaile and Cort J. Willmott, pp. 600–616. Oxford: Oxford University Press.

Ruppé, Patricia, Janet Hagopian, Jeffery R. Waseta, Donovan K. Quam, James W. Kendrick, and Jonathan E. Damp. 1999. Phase I Data Recovery at Sites LA 81671 and LA 81672 along County Road 19, Borrego Pass, McKinley County, New Mexico, Report 607. Pueblo of Zuni, NM: Zuni Cultural Resource Enterprise.

Sapir, Edward. 1942. *Navaho Texts.* Iowa City: Linguistic Society of America, University of Iowa.

Scudder, Thayer. 1982. *No Place to Go: The Effects of Compulsory Relocation on Navajos.* Philadelphia, PA: Institute for the Study of Human Issues.

Seymour, Deni J. 2012. "Big Trips" and Historic Apache Movement and Interaction: Models for Early Athapaskan Migrations. In *From the Land of Ever Winter to the American Southwest: Athapaskan Migrations, Mobility, and Ethnogenesis*, edited by Deni J. Seymour, pp. 377–409. Salt Lake City: University of Utah Press.

———, ed. 2012. *From the Land of Ever Winter to the American Southwest: Athapaskan Migrations, Mobility, and Ethnogenesis*. Salt Lake City: University of Utah Press.

Shaler, K., and M. R. Campbell. 1907. *Investigations of the Coal Fields of New Mexico and California in 1906*. Contributions to Economic Geology, U.S. Geological Survey Bulletin 316, Part II. Washington, D.C.: U.S. Government Printing Office.

Shebala, Marley. 2017. Black Mesa Residents Seek Talks with Leaders. *Gallup Independent*. March 31:1.

Shepardson, Mary, and Blodwen Hammond. 1970. *The Navajo Mountain Community*. Berkeley: University of California Press.

Sherry, John. 2002. *Land, Wind, and Hard Words: A Story of Navajo Activism*. Albuquerque: University of New Mexico Press.

Simpson, Audra. 2014. *Mohawk Interruptus*. Durham, NC: Duke University Press.

Smith, David, Joseph Lorenz, Becky K. Rolfs, Robert L. Bettinger, Brian Green, Jason Eshleman, Beth Schultz, and Ripan Malhi. 2000. Implications of the Distribution of Albumin Naskapi and Albumin Mexico for New World Prehistory. *American Journal of Physical Anthropology* 111:557–572.

Smith, David Glenn, Ripan S. Malhi, Jason Eshleman, Joseph G. Lorenz, and Frederika A. Kaestle. 1999. Distribution of mtDNA Haplogroup X among Native North Americans. *American Journal of Physical Anthropology* 110:271–284.

Snow, David H. 1973. Prehistoric Southwestern Turquoise Industry. *El Palacio* 79(1):33–51.

———. 2006. Diné Bikéyah Redux. In *Southwestern Interludes: Papers in Honor of Charlotte J. and Theodore R. Frisbie*, edited by Regge N. Wiseman, Thomas C. O'Laughlin, and Cordelia T. Snow, pp. 167–180. Archaeological Society of New Mexico Papers 32. Albuquerque: Archaeological Society of New Mexico.

Son of Former Many Beads (Hastiin Biyo' Łání Yéę Biye'). 1949. *The Ramah Navahos*. Translated by Robert W. Young and William Morgan. Phoenix, AZ: U.S. Bureau of Indian Affairs, Phoenix Indian School Printing Department.

Southwest Indian Development. 1969. *Traders on the Navajo Reservation: A Report on the Economic Bondage of the Navajo People*. Window Rock, AZ: Southwestern Indian Development.

Spurr, Kimberly, Richard M. Begay, and Alfred Livingston. 1996. A Cultural Resources Survey of Proposed Indian Health Service Waterline Extensions and Well Tank Sites in the Hopi Buttes District, Navajo County, Arizona. Manuscript on file, U.S. Indian Health Service, Navajo Area Office, Window Rock, AZ.

Stacher, Herbert. 1978. A Factual History of the Gallup Southwest Coal Company. Manuscript on file, Octavia Fellin Public Library, Gallup, NM.

Stein, John R. 1995. Untitled List of Anasazi Ceremonial Sites in Present Navajoland. Manuscript in authors' possession.

Stein, John R., and Andrew P. Fowler. 1996. Looking beyond Chaco in the San Juan Basin and Its Peripheries. In *The Prehistoric Pueblo World, A.D. 1150–1350*, edited by Michael A. Adler, pp. 114–130. Tucson: University of Arizona Press.

Stephen, Alexander M. 1930. Navajo Origin Legend. *Journal of American Folk-Lore* 43:88–104.

———. 1936. *Hopi Journal of Alexander M. Stephen*. Edited by Elsie Clews Parsons. Contributions to Anthropology 36. New York: Columbia University.

Stewart, Irene. 1980. *A Voice in Her Tribe: A Navajo Woman's Own Story*. Anthropological Papers No. 17. Socorro, NM: Ballena Press.

Stokes, Marvin A., and Terah L. Smiley. 1964. Tree-Ring Dates from the Navajo Land Claim: II. The Western Sector. *Tree-Ring Bulletin* 26(1–4):13–27.

Sutton, Mark Q. 2000. Prehistoric Movements of Northern Uto-Aztecan Peoples along the Northwestern Edge of the Southwest: Impact on Southwestern Populations. In *The Archaeology of Regional Interaction: Religion, Warfare, and Exchange across the American Southwest and Beyond*, edited by Michelle Hegmon, pp. 295-316. Boulder: University Press of Colorado.

Swidler, Nina, Kurt E. Dongoske, Roger Anyon, and Alan S. Downer, eds. 1997. *Native Americans and Archaeologists: Stepping Stones to Common Ground*. Walnut Creek, CA: Altamira Press.

Talbot, Richard. 2000. Fremont Farmers: The Search for Context. In *The Archaeology of Regional Interaction: Religion, Warfare, and Exchange across the American Southwest and Beyond*, edited by Michelle Hegmon, pp.275–294. Boulder: University Press of Colorado.

TallBear, Kim. 2013. *Native American DNA: Tribal Belonging and the False Promise of Genetic Science*. Minneapolis: University of Minnesota Press.

Tedlock, Dennis. 1978. *Finding the Center*. Rev. ed. Lincoln: University of Nebraska Press.

Thompson, Gerald. 1976. *The Army and the Navajo: The Bosque Redondo Reservation Experiment 1863–1868*. Tucson: University of Arizona Press.

Thompson, Jonathan. 2016. "New Mexico's DAPL" Is Dead. *High Country News*. February 26. www.hcn.org/article/new-mexicos-dapl-is-dead (accessed December 28, 2016).

Thompson, Kerry F. 2009. Ałk'idaa Da Hooghanée (They Used to Live Here): An Archaeological Study of Late Nineteenth and Early Twentieth Century Navajo Hogan Households and Federal Indian Policy. PhD diss., University of Arizona, Tucson.

Thompson, Kerry F., and Ronald H. Towner. 2017. Navajo Archaeology and a Century of Alternative Navajo History. In *Oxford Handbook of the Archaeology of the American Southwest*. Oxford: Oxford University Press.

Thompson, Stith. 1966. *Tales of the North American Indians*. Reprint. Bloomington: Indiana University Press.

Tilden, Mervyn. 2011. A Brief History of Lost Mining Towns near Gallup. *Gallup Journey*. December 2. http://gallupjourney.com/a-brief-hitsory-of-lost-mining-towns-near-gallup/ (accessed April 16, 2017).

Tinsley, Jim Bob. 1993. *The Hash Knife Brand*. Gainesville: University Press of Florida.

Titiev, Mischa. 1937. A Hopi Salt Expedition. *American Anthropologist* 39(2):244–258.

Tohe, Laura. 2012. *Code Talker Stories*. Tucson, AZ: Rio Nuevo Publishers.

Toll, H. Wolcott. 1991. Material Distributions and Exchange in the Chaco System. In *Chaco and Hohokam*, edited by Patricia L. Crown and W. James Judge, pp. 77–107. Santa Fe, NM: School of American Research Press.

Torres[-Nez], John. 2003. Early Navajo Lithic Technology of Dinetah. In *The Morris 1 Site Early Navajo Land Use Study: Gobernador Phase Community Development in Northwest New Mexico*, edited by Douglas D. Dykeman, pp. 191–231. Navajo Nation Papers in Anthropology 39. Window Rock, AZ: Navajo Nation Archaeology Department.

Torroni, Theodore G. Schurr, Chi-Chuan Yan, Emoke J. E. Szthmary, Robert C. Williams, Moses S. Schanfield, Gary A. Troup, William C. Knowler, Dale N. Lawrence, Kenneth M. Weiss, and Douglas C. Wallace. 1992. Native American Mitochondrial DNA Analysis Indicates That the Amerind and the Nadene Populations Were Founded by Two Independent Migrations. *Genetics* 130(1):153–162.

Towner, Ronald H., ed. 1996. *The Archaeology of Navajo Origins*. Salt Lake City: University of Utah Press.

———. 2002. Archaeological Dendrochronology in the Southwestern United States. *Evolutionary Anthropology* 11:68–84.

———. 2003. *Defending the Dinetah*. Salt Lake City: University of Utah Press.

———. 2016. Early Navajo Land Use in Northwest New Mexico: Big Bead Mesa in Regional Perspective. *Journal of Field Archaeology* 41(1):118–129.

Tso, Eddie. 2012. Grandpa Zhealy and Grandma Zoncho Tso, Shii Na'lee. Manuscript in authors' possession.

Turner, Christy G., II. 1971. *Petrographs of the Glen Canyon Region*. Glen Canyon Series 4, Museum of Northern Arizona Bulletin 38. Reprint. Flagstaff: Northern Arizona Society of Science and Art.

Twenty-Two Navajo Men and Women. 1977. *Stories of Traditional Navajo Life and Culture*. Tsaile, AZ: Navajo Community College Press.

Tyler, S. Lyman, and H. Darrel Taylor. 1958. The Report of Fray Alonso de Posada in Relation to Quivira and Teguayo. *New Mexico Historical Review* 33(4):285–314.

United Indian Traders' Association. 1949. Membership list. Manuscript on file, box 7, folder 125b, United Indian Traders Association Collection (Special Collection 299), Cline Library, Northern Arizona University.

Upham, Steadman. 2000. Scale, Innovation, and Change in the Desert West: A Macroregional Approach. In *The Archaeology of Regional Interaction: Religion, Warfare, and Exchange across the American Southwest and Beyond*, edited by Michelle Hegmon, pp. 235–256. Boulder: University Press of Colorado.

U.S. Bureau of Indian Affairs. 1933. Map of the Navajo Country. MS 831, box 2, folder 53a, "Irrigation Report," Van Valkenburgh Papers, Arizona Historical Society.

U.S. Commissioner of Indian Affairs (CIA). 1869–1911. *Annual Reports*. Washington, D.C.: U.S. Government Printing Office.

U.S. Department of Agriculture. 2009. *Census of Agriculture 2007: American Indian Reservations, Vol. 2*. Washington, D.C.: U.S. Department of Agriculture.

U.S. Department of Energy, Office of Indian Energy Policy and Programs. 2015. Winning the Future: Navajo-Hopi Land Commission Leverages DOE Grant to Advance Solar Ranch Project, February 22, 2015, https://energy.gov (accessed December 16, 2016).

———. 2016. Navajo Tribal Utility Authority Moves Forward with First Utility-Scale Solar Plant. January 14. https://energy.gov (accessed December 16, 2016).

U.S. General Land Office. 1896. Territory of New Mexico. Manuscript (map) on file, Museum of New Mexico History Library, Santa Fe.

———. 1903–1936. Land Patent Records (Homestead Patents). www.glorecords.blm.gov (accessed repeatedly, 2012–2017).

U.S. Senate, Select Committee on Indian Affairs. 1992. Indian Trust Fund Management. Hearing before the Select Committee on Indian Affairs, United States Senate, 102nd Cong., 1st sess., August 12. Washington, D.C.: U.S. Government Printing Office.

U.S. Senate, Subcommittee of the Committee on Indian Affairs. 1937. *Survey of Conditions of Indians in the United States, Part 34*. Washington, D.C.: U.S. Government Printing Office.

Valette, Rebecca M., and Jean-Paul Valette. 2000. The Life and Work of Clitso Dedman, Navajo Woodcarver (1879–1953). *American Indian Art* 26(1):54–67.

Vansina, Jan. 1985. *Oral Tradition as History*. Madison: University of Wisconsin Press.

Van Valkenburgh, Richard F. 1938. Guidebook for a Historical and Geographical Map of the Navajo Country. MS 831, box 4, folder 110, Van Valkenburgh Papers, Arizona Historical Society.

———. 1940a. Sacred Places and Shrines of the Navajos, Part II: Navajo Rock and Twig Piles, Called Tsenadjihih. *Plateau* 13(2):6–9.

———. 1940b. We Found the Tower of Hashk'eh Likizhii. *Desert Magazine* 3(8)23–25:.

———. 1943. Massacre in the Mountains. *Desert Magazine* 6(2):18–23.

———. 1946. Last Powwow of the Navajo. *Desert Magazine* 10(1):4–7.

———. 1956. Report of Archaeological Survey of the Navajo-Hopi Contact Area, Final Draft. Manuscript on file, Laboratory of Tree Ring Research, University of Arizona, Tucson.

———. 1974. Navajo Sacred Places. In *Navajo Indians III*, edited by David A. Horr, pp. 9–199. New York: Garland.

———. 1999. *Diné Bikéyah*. Reprint. Mancos, CO: Time Traveler Maps.

Vargas, Victoria D. 1995. *Copper Bell Trade Patterns in the Prehispanic U.S. Southwest and Northwest Mexico*. Archaeological Series No. 187. Tucson: Arizona State Museum.

Vizenor, Gerald. 2009. *Native Liberty: Natural Reason and Cultural Survivance*. Lincoln: University of Nebraska Press.

Voyles, Traci Brynne. 2015. *Wastelanding: Legacies of Uranium Mining in Navajo Country*. Minneapolis: University of Minnesota Press.

Walters, Harry. 1991. A New Perspective on Navajo Prehistory. BA thesis, Goddard College, VT.

Walters, Harry, and Hugh C. Rodgers. 2001. Anasazi and "Anaasází": Two Words, Two Cultures. *Kiva* 66(3):317–326.

Warburton, Miranda, and Richard M. Begay. 2005. An Exploration of Navajo-Anasazi Relationships. *Ethnohistory* 52(3):533–562.

Ward, Elizabeth. 1951. *No Dudes, Few Women.* Albuquerque: University of New Mexico Press.

Warhus, Mark. 1997. *Another America: Native American Maps and the History of Our Land.* New York: St. Martin's Griffin.

Warner, Ted J., ed. 1976. *The Domínguez-Escalante Journal: Their Expedition through Colorado, Utah, Arizona, and New Mexico in 1776.* Translated by Fray Angelico Chavez. Provo, UT: Brigham Young University Press.

Watson, Adam S., Stephen Plog, Brendan J. Culleton, Patricia A. Gilman, Steven A. LeBlanc, Peter M. Whiteley, Santiago Claramunt, and Douglas J. Kennett. 2015. Early Procurement of Scarlet Macaws and the Emergence of Social Complexity in Chaco Canyon, NM. *Proceedings of the National Academy of Sciences* 112(27):8238–8243. www.doi.10.1073/pnas.1509825112 (accessed March 12, 2016).

Weber, David J. 1992. *The Spanish Frontier in North America.* New Haven, CT: Yale University Press.

———, ed. 1999. *What Caused the Pueblo Revolt of 1680?* Boston: Bedford / St. Martin's.

Weiner, Robert S. 2018. Sociopolitical, Ceremonial, and Economic Aspects of Gambling in Ancient North America: A Case Study of Chaco Canyon. *American Antiquity* 83(1):34–43.

Weisiger, Marsha. 2011. *Dreaming of Sheep in Navajo Country.* Seattle: University of Washington Press.

Wetherill, Louisa Wade, and Harvey Leake. 2007. *Wolfkiller: Wisdom from a Nineteenth Century Navajo Shepherd.* Salt Lake City, UT: Gibbs Smith.

Wheeler, George M. ca. 1880. Part of Central New Mexico, Atlas Sheet No. 77 (based on surveys of 1873–1878). Manuscript map on file, New Mexico State Archives, Santa Fe.

Wheelwright, Mary Cabot. 1946. *Hail Chant and Water Chant.* Navajo Religion Series 2. Santa Fe, NM: Museum of Navajo Ceremonial Art.

———. 1951. *Myth of Mountain Chant and Myth of Beauty Chant.* Bulletin 5. Santa Fe, NM: Museum of Navajo Ceremonial Art.

———. 1956. *The Myth and Prayers of the Great Star Chant and the Myth of the Coyote Chant.* Navajo Religion Series 4. Santa Fe, NM: Museum of Navajo Ceremonial Art.

———. 1958. *Red Ant Myth and Shooting Chant.* Santa Fe, NM: Museum of Navajo Ceremonial Art.

Whipple, A. W. 1941. Report of the Explorations for a Railway Route near the Thirty-Fifth Parallel of Latitude, from the Mississippi River to the Pacific Ocean. 37th Cong., 2nd sess., H. Doc. 129, 1854. In *A Pathfinder in the Southwest: The Itinerary of Lieutenant A. W. Whipple during His Explorations for a Railway Route from Fort Smith to Los Angeles in the Years 1853 and 1854,* edited by Grant Foreman, pp. 25–273. Norman: University of Oklahoma Press.

White, Richard. 1983. *The Roots of Dependency.* Lincoln: University of Nebraska Press.

———. 1991. *"It's Your Misfortune and None of My Own": A New History of the American West.* Norman: University of Oklahoma Press.

Whiteley, Peter. 1996. Re-imagining Awat'ovi. In *Archaeologies of the Pueblo Revolt: Identity, Meaning, and Renewal in the Pueblo World*, edited by Robert Preucel, pp. 147–166. Albuquerque: University of New Mexico Press.

Wicoff, Mary. 1996. Black Mesa Mine Faces Shutdown. *Gallup Independent*, April 22:1.

Wiegand, Phil C. 2001. The Macroeconomic Role of Turquoise within the Chaco Canyon System. In *Anasazi Regional Organization and the Chaco System*, edited by David E. Doyel, pp. 169–176. Reprint. Albuquerque, NM: Maxwell Museum of Anthropology.

Wilcox, David R. 1981. The Entry of Athabaskans in the American Southwest. In *Protohistoric Period in the North American Southwest, A.D. 1450–1700*, edited by David R. Wilcox and W. Bruce Masse, pp. 213–256. Anthropological Research Papers No. 24. Tempe: Arizona State University.

———. 1986. The Tepiman Connection: A Model of Mesoamerican-Southwest Interaction. In *Ripples in the Chichimec Sea: New Considerations of Southwest-Mesoamerican Interactions*, edited by Frances Joan Mathien and Randall H. McGuire, pp. 135–153. Carbondale: Southern Illinois University Press.

———. 2006. The Changing Contexts of Warfare in the North American Southwest, A.D. 1200–1700. In *Southwestern Interludes: Papers in Honor of Charlotte J. and Theodore R. Frisbie*, edited by Regge N. Wiseman, Thomas C. O'Laughlin, and Cordelia T. Snow, pp. 203–232. Archaeological Society of New Mexico Papers 32. Albuquerque: Archaeological Society of New Mexico.

Wild Earth Guardians. 2016. Four Corners Fact Sheet. www.wildearthguardians.org/site/DocServer/four_corners_fact_sheet.pdf (accessed December 16, 2016).

Wilkin, Robert L. 1955. *Anselm Weber, O.F.M.: Missionary to the Navaho, 1898–1921*. Milwaukee, WI: Bruce.

Wilkins, David E. 2003 [1999]. *Navajo Political Experience*. Lanham, MD: Rowman and Littlefield.

Williams, Aubrey. 1970. *Navajo Political Process*. Washington, D.C.: Smithsonian Institution Press.

Williams, Jay Scott. A Use of Navajo Metaphor and Metonymy in Conjunction with the Landscape: Oral Cartography. MA thesis, University of New Mexico, Albuquerque.

Wills, W. H. 1988. *Early Prehistoric Agriculture in the American Southwest*. Santa Fe, NM: School of American Research Press.

Wilshusen, Richard H. 2010. The Diné at the Edge of History: Navajo Ethnogenesis in the Northern Southwest, 1500–1750. In *Across the Great Divide: Continuity and Change in Native North American Societies, 1400–1900*, edited by Laura L. Scheiber and Mark D. Mitchell, pp. 192–211. Tucson: University of Arizona Press.

Wilson, Joseph. 2016. The Union of Two Worlds: Reconstructing Elements of Proto-Athabaskan Folklore and Religion. *Folklore* 127(1):26–50.

Winnie, Ray. 1982. Origin of Clan. Manuscript on file, Cultural Research Program, Navajo Community College, Tsaile, AZ.

Winter, Joseph C., Karen Ritts-Benally, and Orit Tamir. 1993. *Across the Colorado Plateau: Studies for the Transwestern Pipeline Expansion Project, Volume VIII*. Albuquerque: Office of Contract Archeology; Maxwell Museum of Anthropology, University of New Mexico.

Winter, Mark. 2011. *The Master Weavers*. Newcomb, NM: Historic Toadlena Trading Post.

Woodbury, Richard B., and Ezra B. W. Zubrow. 1979. Agricultural Beginnings, 2000 B.C.–A.D. 500. In *Southwest*, edited by Alfonso Ortiz, pp. 43–60. Handbook of North American Indians, Vol. 9, William C. Sturtevant, general editor. Washington, D.C.: Smithsonian Institution Press.

Woodward, David, and G. Malcolm Lewis, eds. 1998. *Cartography in the Traditional African, American, Arctic, Australian, and Pacific Societies, Vol. 2, Bk. 3, The History of Cartography*. Chicago: University of Chicago Press.

Wyman, Leland C. 1952. *The Sandpaintings of the Kayenta Navajo*. Publications in Anthropology No. 7. Albuquerque: University of New Mexico.

———. 1957. *Beautyway: A Navaho Ceremonial*. Princeton, NJ: Princeton University Press.

———. 1962. *The Windways of the Navaho*. Colorado Springs, CO: Taylor Museum.

———. 1965. *The Red Ant Way of the Navaho*. Santa Fe, NM: Museum of Navajo Ceremonial Art.

———. 1970a. *Blessingway*. Tucson: University of Arizona Press.

———. 1970b. *Sandpaintings of the Navaho Shootingway and the Walcott Collection*. Smithsonian Contributions to Anthropology 13. Washington, D.C.: Smithsonian Institution Press.

———. 1975. *The Mountainway of the Navajo*. Tucson: University of Arizona Press.

Yava, Albert. 1978. *Big Falling Snow: A Tewa-Hopi Indian's Life and Times and the History and Traditions of His People*. Edited by Harold Courlander. Albuquerque: University of New Mexico Press.

Yazzie, Peter. 2010. Recording Family History. *Leading the Way* 8(7):2–5.

York, Fred. 1981. An Ethnohistory of the Catalpa Canyon Navajo Indians. In *An Archaeological Survey of the Catalpa Mine, and an Ethnographic Profile of the Catalpa Canyon Navajo*, edited by James Moore, pp. 178–208. Albuquerque, NM: Office of Contract Archaeology, University of New Mexico.

———. 1990. Capitalist Development and Land in Northeastern Navajo Country, 1880s to 1980s. PhD diss., State University of New York, Binghamton.

Young, Robert W. 1958. *The Navajo Yearbook*. Window Rock, AZ: Navajo Agency.

———. 1961. *The Navajo Yearbook*. Window Rock, AZ: Navajo Agency.

———. 1968. *The Role of the Navajo in the Southwestern Drama*. Gallup, NM: Gallup Independent.

———. 1978. *A Political History of the Navajo Tribe*. Tsaile, AZ: Navajo Community College Press.

———. 1983. Apachean Languages. In *Southwest*, edited by Alfonso Ortiz, pp. 393–400. Handbook of North American Indians, Vol. 10, William C. Sturtevant, general editor. Washington, D.C.: Smithsonian Institution Press.

Young, Robert W., and William Morgan. 1952. *The Trouble at Round Rock, by Left-Handed Mexican Clansman and Others*. Phoenix, AZ: U.S. Indian Service.

———. 1954. *Navajo Historical Selections*. Phoenix, AZ: U.S. Indian Service.

———. 1987. *The Navajo Language: A Grammar and Colloquial Dictionary*. 2nd ed. Albuquerque: University of New Mexico Press.

Younging, Gregory. 2018. *Elements of Indigenous Style: A Guide for Writing by and about Indigenous Peoples*. Edmonton, AB Brush Education.

Yurth, Cindy. 2017. *Exploring the Navajo Nation Chapter by Chapter*. Flagstaff, AZ: Salina Bookshelf.

Zah, Peterson, and Peter Iverson. 2012. *We Will Secure Our Future: Empowering the Navajo Nation*. Tucson: University of Arizona Press.

ARCHIVES, ONLINE ARCHIVES, AND PHOTOGRAPH COLLECTIONS, WITH ABBREVIATIONS USED IN THE TEXT

AHS. Arizona Historical Society, Tucson, AZ
  Richard Van Valkenburgh Papers, MS 831
Apache County Clerk's Office, Saint Johns, AZ
  Plat book, ca. 1918–1930
BLM. U.S. Bureau of Land Management, Phoenix, AZ
  Historical Index and Homestead Entry microfiche
CIA. U.S. Commissioner of Indian Affairs
Denver Public Library, Western History Collection
  Photographic collections
Franciscans. See University of Arizona Library below
GLO. U.S. General Land Office
  Cadastral survey plats and field notes (see also www.glorecords.blm.gov)
  Tract book
Hubbell Trading Post National Historic Site, Ganado, AZ
  Oral history interviews, manuscripts
  Photograph collection
K. Miscellaneous field notes by Klara Kelley, 1973–1984. Manuscripts in author's possession.
KFa. Miscellaneous field notes by Klara Kelley and Harris Francis, 1987–2017. Manuscripts in authors' possession.
KFb. Field notes by Klara Kelley and Harris Francis for Navajoland trading post encyclopedia, 2004–2017. Manuscripts in authors' possession.
NAA. National Anthropological Archives, Washington, D.C.
  Photograph collection
NARA. National Archives and Records Administration, Washington, D.C.
  Agents' annual reports, 1910–1935, Record Group 75, microfilm series M1011, microfilm rolls 33–34 (Eastern Navajo), 65–66 (Hopi), 68 (Kayenta Sanitorium), 79 (Leupp), 88 (Moqui), 89–90 (Navajo), 93 (Northern Navajo), 110 (Pueblo Bonito), 126–127 (San Juan School), 141 (Southern Navajo), 166–167 (Western Navajo)

Homestead proof files (including cash entries and GLO inspector reports), Record Group 49

Indian allotment patent files (including GLO inspector reports), Record Group 75

NAU. Northern Arizona University, Cline Library, Special Collections, Flagstaff

Photograph collections, http://archive.library.nau.edu/search/collection/cpa.

UITA. United Indian Traders Collection, Collection 299

Navajo Nation Museum, Window Rock, AZ

Photograph collections

NLC. Navajo Land Claim Collection, Navajo Nation Library, Window Rock, AZ

Archaeological site forms

Archive documents

Fort Defiance Agency letterbook

Navajo oral history statements

NMAI. National Museum of the American Indian

Photograph collections

NMRCL. New Mexico Records Center and Library, Santa Fe

Frank McNitt Papers

NNLD. Navajo Nation Land Department, Window Rock, AZ

Historic township plats

OFP. Octavia Fellin Public Library, Gallup, NM

Photograph collection

Vertical files, call number VFMin

Sharlot Hall Museum, Prescott, AZ

Photograph collection

University of Arizona Library, Special Collections

Saint Michaels Franciscan Mission Collection, AZ500 (Franciscans)

University of New Mexico, Center for Southwest Research

Doris Duke Oral History Collection, audiotapes

INDEX

Page numbers in *italics* refer to illustrative matter.

ABOUT THE AUTHORS

Klara Kelley, a Bilagaana (Euro-American), has lived and worked in Navajoland since 1977. She is an independent cultural resources consultant for various Navajo Nation government programs and enterprises and federal programs. Before this work she taught anthropology and economics at Navajo Community College (now Diné College); and she worked as an archaeologist for the Navajo Nation Archaeology Department, as an ethnohistorian for the Navajo Nation Historic Preservation Department, and as a self-employed cultural resources consultant in between. She is the author of *Navajo Land Use: An Ethnoarchaeological Study* (Academic Press, 1986) and coauthor of *Navajoland: Family Settlement and Land Use* (Navajo Community College Press, 1989). Kelley earned a PhD in anthropology from the University of New Mexico in 1977.

Harris Francis was born and raised in Navajoland in a traditional family speaking the Navajo language. He is Nát'oh Diné'é Táchii'nii clan, born for Tábąąhá clan, from Teesto, Arizona. He served in the U.S. Army from 1973 to 1976, and he attended Central Texas College and the College of Ganado, Arizona (total two semesters). He graduated from the Navajo Paralegal School Program, in Flagstaff, in 1979. Between 1976 and 1986 he worked in Navajoland as a social worker and as a paralegal with the Navajo Tribal Legal Department (Navajo Nation court system), then as an archaeological technician / cultural specialist for the Navajo Nation Archaeology Department, and as a Navajo cultural specialist for the Navajo Nation Historic Preservation Department. Since then he has been an independent Navajo cultural rights consultant.

Francis and Kelley have worked together as independent cultural resource consultants for various Navajo Nation government programs and enterprises, federal programs, and more since 1993. Most of their projects are consultations with historically knowledgeable Navajo people, including many prominent hataałiis (traditional ceremonialists) and presentations at local community meetings. They are the coauthors of *Navajo Sacred Places* (Indiana University Press, 1994); *Navajoland Trading Post Encyclopedia* (Navajo Nation Heritage and Historic Preservation Department, 2018); "Places Important to Navajo People," in *American Indian Quarterly* (1993); and many more journal articles. They have also contributed to several museum exhibitions and educational films.